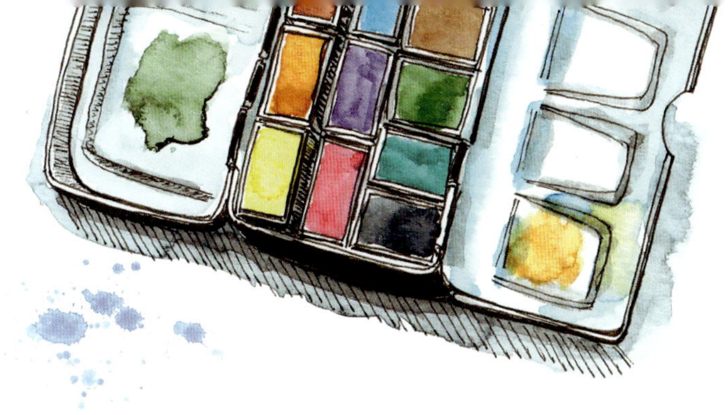

THE BEGINNER'S GUIDE TO

URBAN SKETCHING

EVERYTHING YOU NEED TO KNOW TO CAPTURE YOUR FAVORITE PLACES IN INK AND WATERCOLOR

TARIA DAWSON
CREATOR OF URBAN SKETCHING WORLD

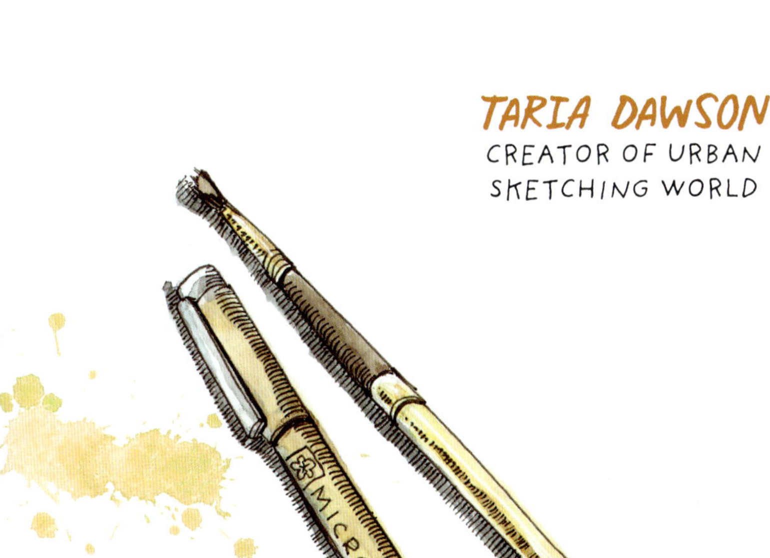

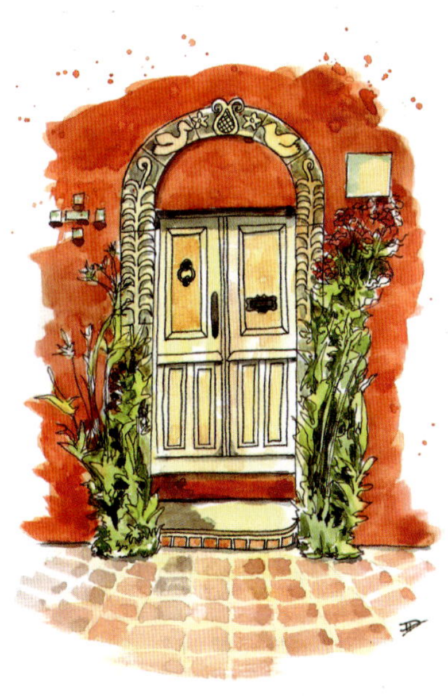

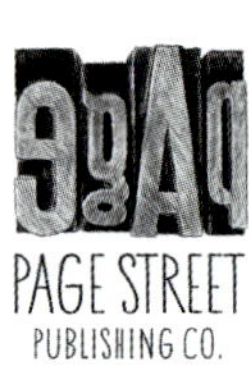

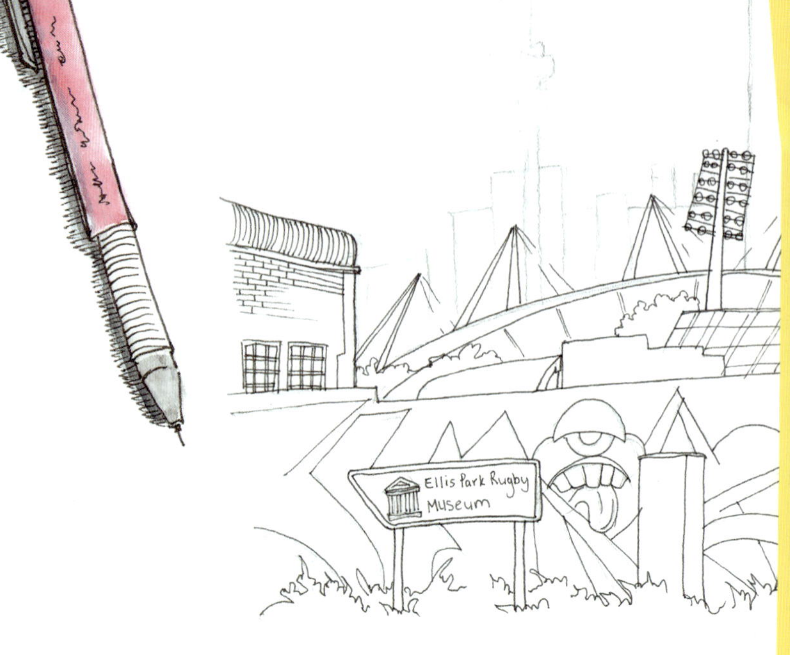

First published in 2023 by
Page Street Publishing Co.
27 Congress Street, Suite 1511
Salem, MA 01970
www.pagestreetpublishing.com

Distributed by Macmillan, sales in Canada by The Canadian Manda Group.

29 28 27 26 3 4 5 6

ISBN-13: 978-1-64567-928-8
ISBN-10: 1-64567-928-4

Library of Congress Control Number: 2022952256

Cover and book design by Molly Kate Young for Page Street Publishing Co.
Photography and illustrations by Taria Dawson

Printed and bound in China

Page Street Publishing protects our planet by donating to nonprofits like The Trustees, which focuses on local land conservation.

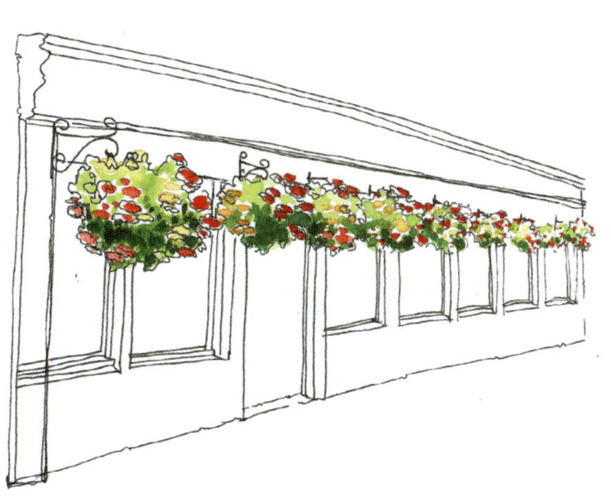

FOR MY FAMILY AND FRIENDS WHO HAVE SUPPORTED MY TRAVELS AND MY SKETCHING HABIT OVER THE YEARS. TO SARAH FOR OUR LONG CHATS THAT ALWAYS MAKE ME FEEL LIKE I CAN CONQUER THE WORLD AGAIN. AND, FINALLY, TO MY HUSBAND DUNCAN, WHO NEVER LETS ME GIVE UP AND MAKES ME LAUGH EVERY SINGLE DAY.

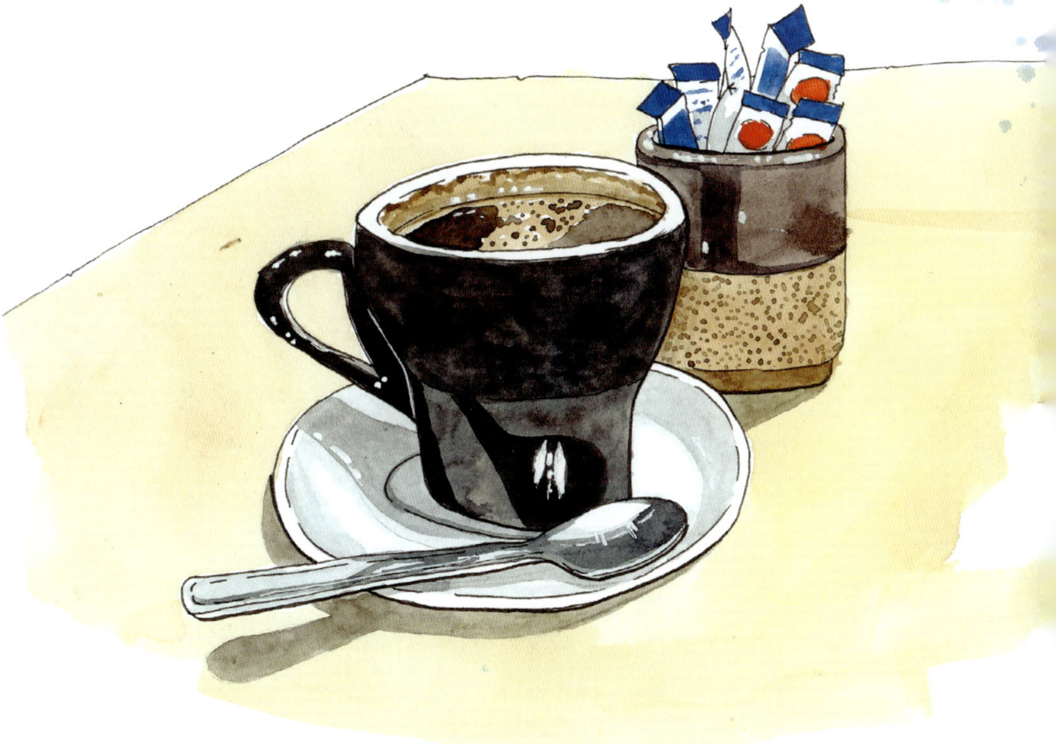

CONTENTS

INTRODUCTION

It would not be an exaggeration to say that urban sketching changed my life. The call to travel hit me square in the face at 30 years old. I couldn't stand my desk job any longer. I just wanted to grab my backpack and hit the road. The other call I had was to sketch while doing it.

I think the first person I came across who was sketching their life and sharing it was Danny Gregory. His book *Everyday Matters* blew my mind. I bought some of his other books and *An Illustrated Journey: Inspiration from the Private Art Journals of Traveling Artists, Illustrators and Designers* really set something in motion within me. I thought: *I want to do that.*

My first solo backpacking trip ended up only being three months long, but I sketched every day I could. My old life called, and I returned home (for a while). But I knew something special had started. I took a job with an adventure travel company and this paved the way for me to visit countries such as Iran, South Sudan and Somalia. I knew I wanted to work remotely while living in different countries. South Africa called, then Mexico and onward. I think I spent most of 2019 traveling, and I did my best to sketch as much as possible.

We all know what happened in 2020.

All of a sudden there wasn't much work in the travel industry. I decided to pivot. After listening to a particularly inspiring podcast episode while sitting in quarantine in March 2020, I decided to start my own blog about urban sketching. Several months later, I decided to share a few little process videos on YouTube of some different sketching techniques I was playing with. Who knew sharing my ideas on sketching would connect me with so many people all over the planet? And, so I am told, have such a positive impact on people learning or rekindling their passion for drawing.

This book is everything I would have loved to share with my past self as a beginner. I have no formal art education. I am just a person who has figured out some stuff, so now I am passing on to you how to do that stuff, step by step. I want you to know that anyone can sketch their world. If you love doing it and you do it lots, you will get better and better. That's the journey I'm on. And I want to help you get better a little faster than if you hadn't read and practiced the skills in this book.

I believe the art of urban sketching is a unique pastime in which we get to combine our love of creating art with being out in the world: experiencing and observing it and then recording it. I can't wait for you to get started along your own sketchy adventure.

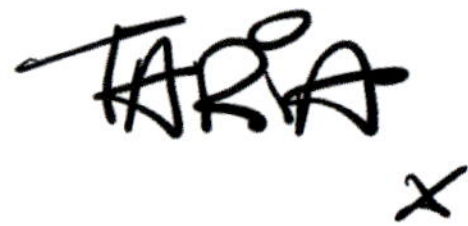

PRINCIPLES OF URBAN SKETCHING

The term "urban sketching" was coined by Seattle journalist and illustrator Gabriel Campanario. Gabi sketches what's around him on location in Seattle as part of his work but also for his own satisfaction. In the earlier days of the internet, he discovered other like-minded artists around the world who also sketched their surroundings, no matter where they lived and how mundane the subject matter. Sketchers connected via a photo-sharing and storage website called Flickr. In 2007, Gabi formalized the group under the label of "urban sketchers" and later created a blog, urbansketchers.org. He invited sketchers from different parts of the world to become "correspondents" and report what was going on around them through their sketches. And so, urban sketching was born. This led to the very first International Urban Sketching Symposium held in Portland, Oregon. Interest in urban sketching has grown exponentially since then with Urban Sketchers chapters (page 181) in a substantial number of cities around the world.

Did you know that urban sketching has its own nonprofit organization with its own manifesto? At this stage, the most important thing to focus on is the first statement of the manifesto:

We draw on location . . . capturing what we see from direct observation.

URBAN SKETCHERS MANIFESTO

The "rules" of urban sketching are set out in the Urban Sketchers Manifesto (as found on urbansketchers.org), otherwise known as the organization's vision and values:

1. We draw on location, indoors or out, capturing what we see from direct observation.
2. Our drawings tell the story of our surroundings, the places we live and where we travel.
3. Our drawings are a record of time and place.
4. We are truthful to the scenes we witness.
5. We use any kind of media and cherish our individual styles.
6. We support each other and draw together.
7. We share our drawings online.
8. We show the world, one drawing at a time.

This is the crux of urban sketching. This doesn't mean you can never sketch from a photo! It just means it's not regarded as urban sketching. Drawing from photos is great for learning how to use your supplies and practicing fundamental concepts, such as perspective, which we will cover in the next chapter.

As a beginner, the best thing to do is to keep things simple and clear. This will give you the best chance of success in the early stages of developing your urban sketching habit. You don't want to put yourself off by being unable to draw how you would like and, as a result, never open your sketchbook again. That would be a disaster.

WHAT IF I DON'T LIVE IN A CITY?

Notice the manifesto doesn't mention that you have to draw in a city or even in an urban setting. Don't let the word *urban* in the name "urban sketching" deter you. Even if you don't live in a city (which I haven't for several years), you can still draw on location and capture what you see from direct observation. Read through each point of the manifesto. Can you achieve all those things in the area where you live? The answer is probably yes.

Don't let anything put you off. There's always something to draw and something new to discover, even in your immediate neighborhood.

FINDING TIME FOR URBAN SKETCHING

Learning to draw is a skill just like learning a musical instrument, another language, to cook or to code. Therefore, it requires time investment to learn. However, urban sketching can fit into daily life without too much fuss if you let it.

We do not need to put time aside to urban sketch. The point of urban sketching is to record life—what's going on around us—right there and then. Therefore, in some regard, you don't really need to schedule time to do it. Urban sketchers draw wherever they are and whenever they choose. Sketching on location allows you to capture special moments especially while on holiday or in your travels, as well as in your neighborhood.

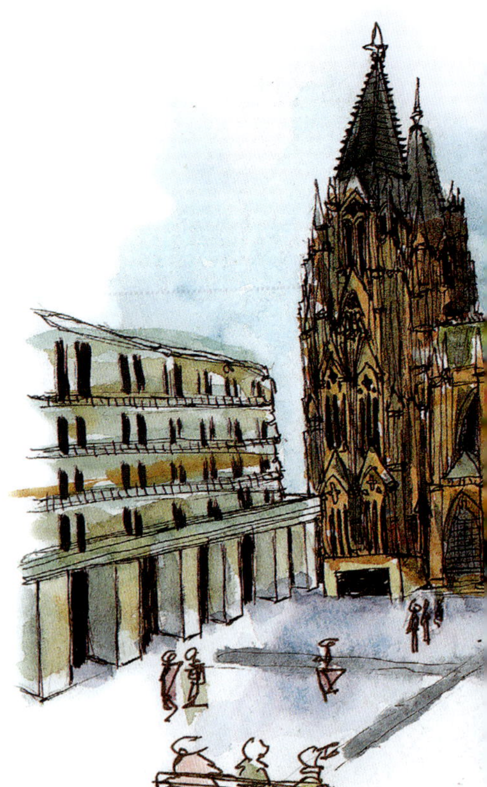

Nonetheless, I have some tips to help you fit urban sketching into your undoubtedly busy schedule:

1. **Carry your sketching supplies with you at all times,** even if it's just a passport-sized sketchbook and pencil.

2. **Get used to drawing when you are with other people,** whether it's your family or friends. You'll find over time you can multitask and both socialize as well as draw.

3. **Draw while you wait.** Perhaps you have kids and you have to wait for them to finish their after-school activities. Perhaps you have to wait for that friend who is ALWAYS late (we all have them).

4. **Get used to drawing mundane things.** I am guilty of seeking out pretty buildings or scenes to draw when actually urban sketching means sketching the world around us, warts and all!

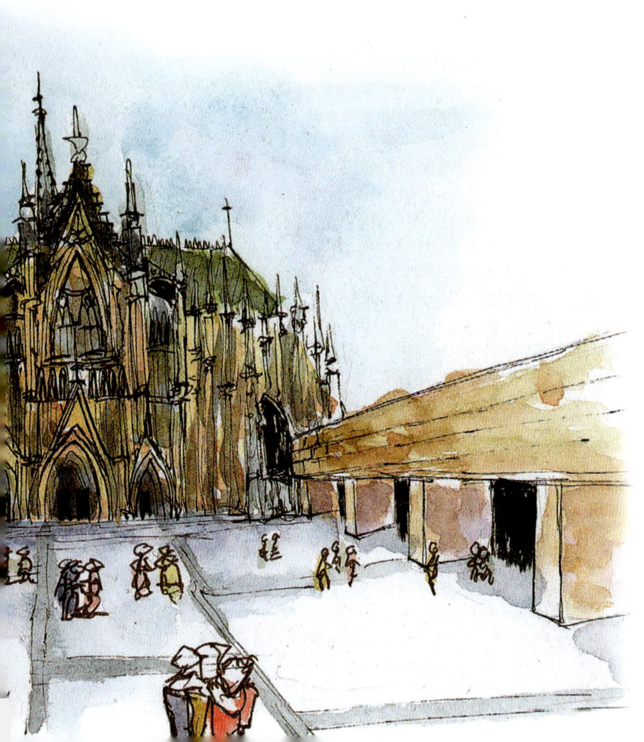

5. **You don't have to finish a sketch.** There are plenty of examples of unfinished sketches in many an urban sketcher's sketchbook. There's that old saying that it's about the journey, not the destination. This is true of urban sketching. While a lovely finished sketch is always pleasing to look at, it's more about the process, especially when you are trying to work urban sketching into your life as a habit.

6. **Size matters.** If you have limited time and you would prefer to have a finished sketch, then don't start a double-page epic. Keep it small and focus on certain details or a singular item that catches your attention.

7. **You don't have to draw everything.** This ties in to the point above. What's the focus of your sketch? What's the story? What's most interesting to you? White space in a sketch is always super interesting to look at. Don't be afraid to let your sketch trail off.

8. **Keep it loose.** If you would like to do a bigger sketch and you want to fit in a few more elements than perhaps you will have time for, don't get lost in the details. Instead, keep your sketch loose. By this, I mean inferring details rather than rigidly trying to draw every detail. We will delve further into this throughout the book.

ART SUPPLIES

You don't need endless supplies in order to get started with urban sketching. At the very least, you need a sketchbook and a pencil, although a vast majority of urban sketchers use ink and watercolor to sketch with, myself included. In which case, you will need a pen with waterproof ink in it, as well. Here is what I recommend to get started:

PENS

Fineliners come in a variety of line widths from 0.05 mm (being extremely fine) to 0.8 mm (which is very thick). Often you can buy them in sets of varying line widths, and they are relatively inexpensive and last a long time. They usually state on the body of the pen if they contain waterproof ink. Popular brands are Pigma Micron®, Uni Pin, Staedtler®, Copic® and Faber-Castell®.

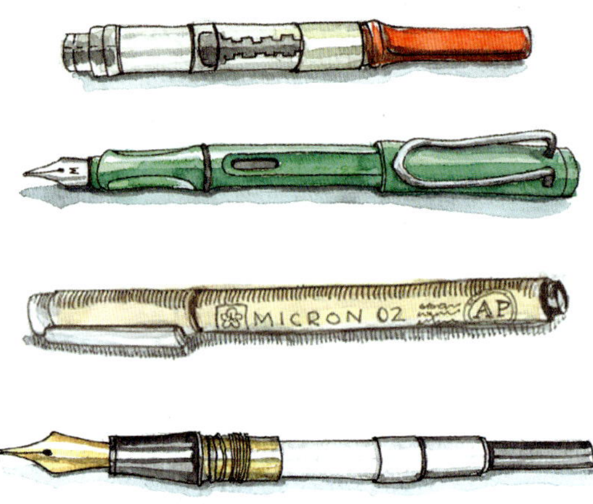

You could also use a fountain pen and fill it with waterproof ink. There's a vast array of pens available and sketchers enjoy trying out and indeed collecting various brands and models. It's a bit of a rabbit hole, so if you would like to find out more, I recommend doing some research on YouTube, as well as visiting urban sketcher Liz Steel's blog (lizsteel.com); she has written a lot about fountain pens and tested many different ones.

Some other pens I like to carry are a black brush pen and a white gel pen, as well as a white paint marker (like a Posca®). These are certainly not essential, but I find they are great to add finishing touches and they are popular tools for many urban sketchers.

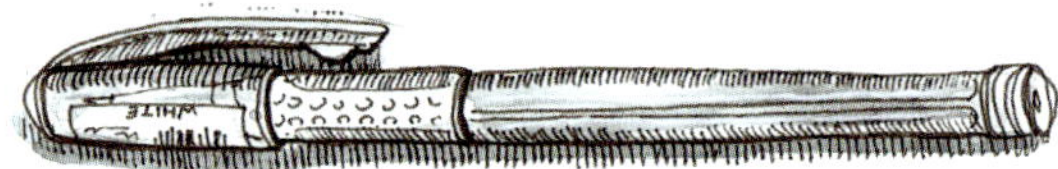

WATERCOLORS

If you're interested in watercolors, I recommend a set of twelve colors. If you can, I recommend skipping student-grade paint and going straight to artist grade. You can find reasonably priced sets in your local art store or online. Most premade sets have a great selection of colors to get started with. Some beginner sets come with white and black in them. These colors are unnecessary and often aren't included in artist-grade sets. For more information on watercolor sets, you can take a look at some of the videos on my YouTube channel or visit my blog, urbansketchingworld.com.

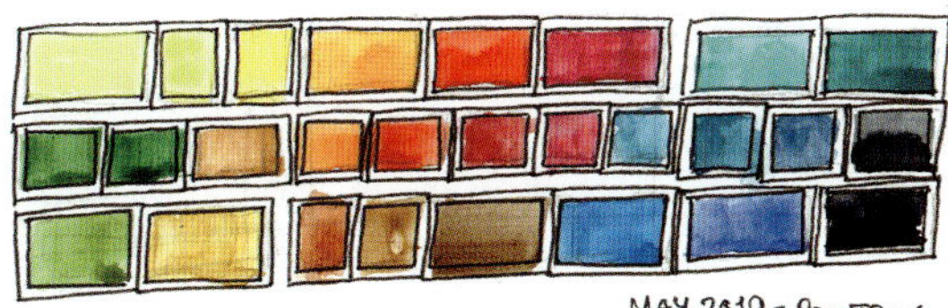

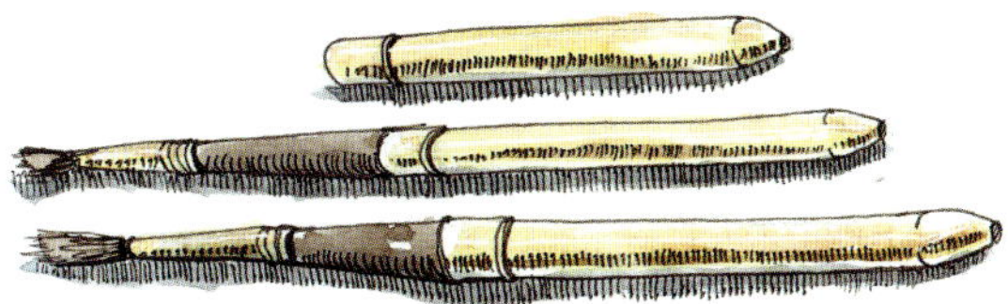

BRUSHES

You will need some watercolor brushes. As with many of the art supplies in this section, things can get fancy and expensive. However, for urban sketching, you don't need to go wild. Brushes are usually made with synthetic hair, animal hair or a mixture of both. Synthetic hair brushes tend to be cheaper. Animal hair brushes tend to hold a lot more water and the difference can be quite noticeable, especially when you are using very cheap synthetic brushes. However, some brands, such as Princeton, have developed their synthetic brushes to carry an astonishing amount of water. The technology of brush making is evolving, so I shall avoid sweeping statements of which types of brush are "better." If you are vegan or prefer to avoid buying animal products, then stick to synthetic brushes.

Brushes have different shapes of bristles that make them more suited to certain subjects or techniques. Round brushes are suited for all types of painting, and flat brushes are particularly useful for painting straight lines or around objects with straight edges, like architecture.

The numbers indicate the size of the brush; a small number indicates a smaller brush and a large number indicates a larger brush. However, not all manufacturers stick to the same sizing scale, so a #10 may not be the same size across all brands.

Flat brushes are measured in inches and the size refers to how wide the brush is.

I would recommend buying three brushes to start with: a #6 round brush, a #10 or #12 round brush and a ½-inch flat brush.

Another type of brush that is handy to have is a water brush. These brushes are plastic and carry water inside the handle. If you gently squeeze the handle as you paint, it will release water. It takes a little getting used to and they are not the best brushes; however, if you want to add a bit of paint to your sketch, they are super convenient, as you don't need a separate pot of water. Some urban sketchers, such as Inma Serrano and Lapin, almost exclusively use water brushes, meaning they can keep their sketching kits very minimal. These brushes are widely available, are inexpensive and come in a few different sizes.

SKETCHBOOK

You will also need a sketchbook with watercolor paper. I recommend sketchbooks by Hahnemühle®, Stillman & Birn® and Etchr®. Ensure that you read the product description properly as brands usually have a range of sketchbooks for different types of media. The paper should be at least 200 gsm up to 300 gsm, and it should say explicitly that the paper can handle water-based media.

Some brands also offer an option of different types of watercolor paper inside the sketchbook. For example, Etchr offers sketchbooks with either cold press or hot press paper inside. Cold press has a texture to it and is fantastic for watercolor work. Hot press is smooth paper, and it's easier to draw on with pens but the watercolor will work slightly differently on it than on cold press. Many urban sketchers favor using ink and watercolor, and therefore tend to stay away from very rough watercolor paper as the texture is too difficult to use a pen on top of.

One type of paper is not better than the other—just more suitable for different things. Also, different brands have different levels of texture to their paper. As you can see, it really is a case of trying out different books over time.

I find the less expensive a sketchbook, the more freedom I feel. However, beware of very cheap paper or sketchbooks labeled as watercolor paper from budget brands. Choose a sketchbook from a brand you have heard of that is reputable. You want to give yourself the best chance of success to start with. Aim for something around the $15 to $20 (U.S. dollar) mark, and it should be of a decent enough quality. On the other end of the scale, I have expensive sketchbooks on the shelf that I am too scared to touch! Make sure to strike the right balance between quality and expense.

As you progress along your sketchy adventure, you will develop your own personal tastes and preferences for which sketchbook and paper you prefer to use.

ADDITIONAL SUPPLIES

Some final accessories you will find useful are:

- Eraser
- Sharpener
- Bulldog clips
- Cloth or paper towel
- Small water spray
- Water container

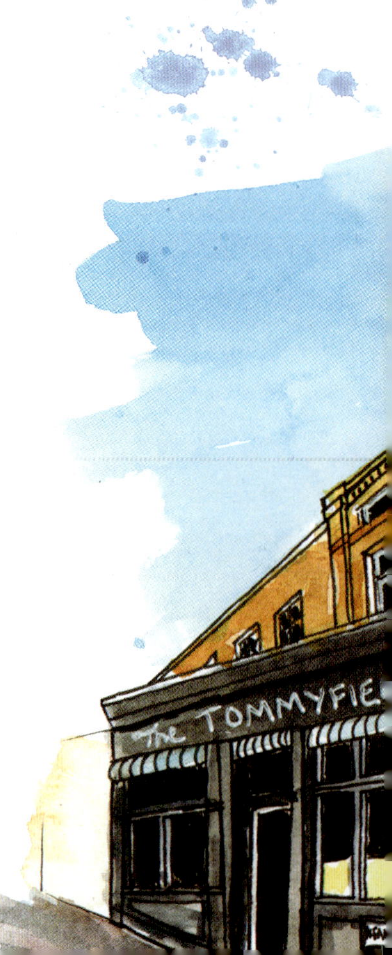

FUNDAMENTAL DRAWING & PAINTING TECHNIQUES

Understanding the fundamentals of drawing, as well as painting with watercolor, will set you up for maximum success when urban sketching. However, the only real way to understand the concepts that follow is to start using and practicing them within your sketch. I enjoy evaluating a sketch after I have done it to figure out what went well and what I may not necessarily have gotten right. I find this helps combat a negative mindset when you feel you haven't done a sketch you're happy with. Every sketch you do is a learning experience. Look at your sketch and evaluate what you may do differently next time. Or what it may be lacking that you could add in the moment. For example, if you feel your sketch does not have enough contrast, add some deep dark colors in areas. It may be all your sketch needs to improve it.

In this section, I will give a basic essential overview of the fundamentals specifically as they relate to urban sketching.

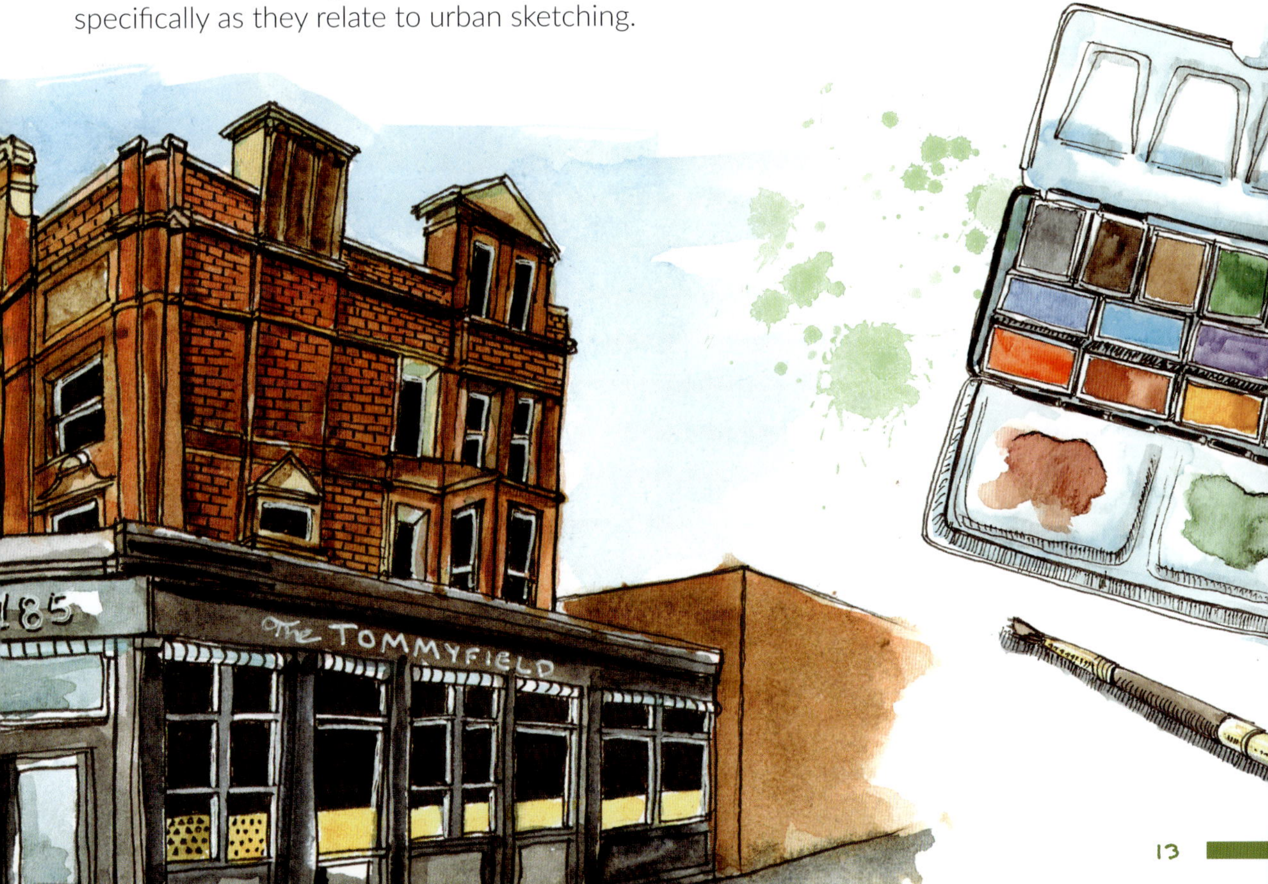

PROPORTION

Proportion is the key to making a sketch look believable. Even if your lines are wonky or you missed some details, if the proportion of your sketch is somewhat accurate, the sketch will look good.

Proportion means the scale of one thing in relation to another. Imagine if you drew a house and it had a tiny front door, one huge window and some medium-sized windows, a gigantic roof and a tiny chimney. If you saw a drawing like that, you would think all those elements are completely out of proportion. Likewise, if you draw a skyscraper yet the house next to it is the same height, again, it would look unbelievable because the proportion is all wrong. These are extreme examples, of course. When you sketch, the proportions of your subject matter will be far more nuanced than this and sometimes super hard to spot when you are drawing but if you step away from your sketch, perhaps you will be able to see what the problem is. For example, one common mistake is drawing buildings wider or narrower than you should, therefore throwing off the buildings' distribution of windows or ornamental features.

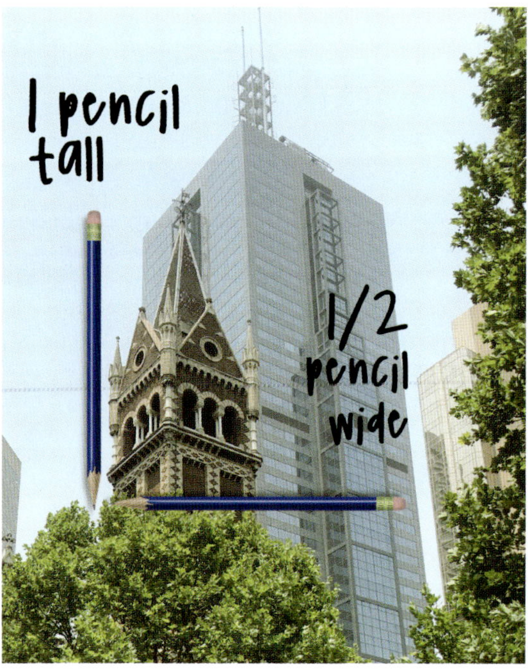

A

A common way to try to relay correct proportions on the page is to hold out your pencil or pen in front of you, lock your elbow and use it as a unit of measurement, turning it horizontally and vertically as you need. You have probably seen a stereotype of an artist holding out their brush, turning it this way and that, squinting at their subject matter.

The idea is that if the building you are drawing is one pencil tall and half a pencil wide (image A), you at least know the proportions of that building.

So when you draw the vertical line on your page for the height you want the building to be, you know that the width of it should be half of the height. Getting that first big shape on the page in the correct proportion is most of the battle won. You can now use that shape as a reference point for everything else in your sketch. These are called visual landmarks.

Most buildings or houses have clear divisions, perhaps rows of windows or even ornamental features. Once the big outer shape is drawn you can assess where the next biggest shapes are within it. Perhaps you can see three clear rectangles. This may be the roof, the top floor and the bottom floor. It doesn't matter that the roof is a different shape than a rectangle. Its height may still be equal to the two shapes below it. The important thing is to get the divisions in proportion to each other.

B

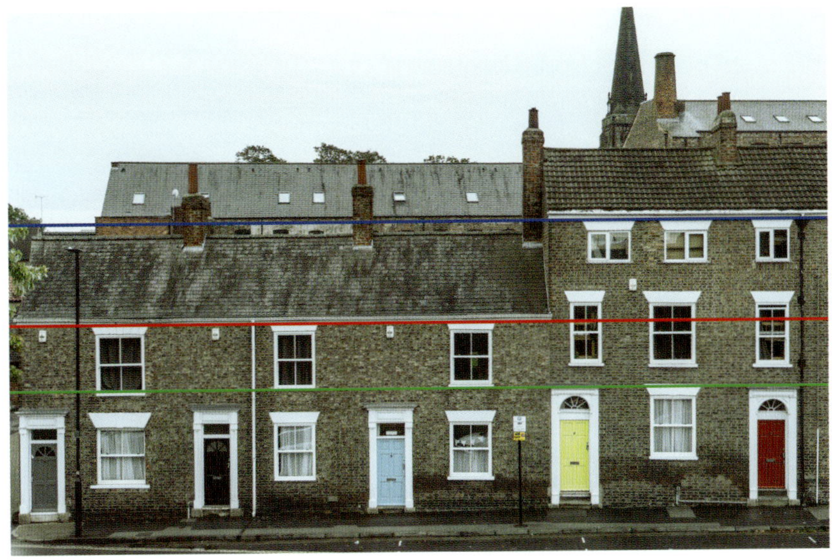

You may even see some vertical divisions too, although those usually come with putting in windows, which, after the floors, will probably be the next biggest shapes to add in. You can use this method of moving from bigger shapes down to the smaller shapes and continue to the finer details. There may be other buildings to add, as well. Now that you have your main building drawn, you have more visual landmarks to use to help you draw the rest of the scene. In the photo above (image B), the bottom edge of the roof on the right is just a tad higher than the top of the roof of the houses on the left (shown by the blue line). The bottom edge of the roof of the houses on the left is about 25 percent lower than the top of the second-story windows of the house on the right (shown by the red line). The bottom of the second-story windows on the left house line up with the top of the door on the right house (shown by the green line).

Don't worry about being 100 percent accurate. I find accuracy actually diminishes the personality and spirit of the sketch. I never use a ruler to measure anything or use a straight edge. Remember, this is urban sketching and some sketches you will want to do quickly and "in the moment." There's no time for rulers. Capturing the energy of a scene is far more important!

PERSPECTIVE

One of the other keys to a successful urban sketch is drawing elements in perspective. Perspective is a fundamental skill in drawing that allows objects on a 2D surface to appear 3D, which is super satisfying.

Once you understand the principles of perspective, you can gauge perspective by eye rather than using physical guidelines drawn on the page (especially if you prefer to be a bit looser and more casual about your sketch). You can also emphasize and exaggerate perspective to make your sketch look a bit more quirky like urban sketchers Ian Fennelly or Lapin (page 186).

TYPES OF PERSPECTIVE

The first distinction to make is between linear perspective and nonlinear perspective.

Linear perspective refers to a scene where there are parallel lines that recede off into the distance to something called a vanishing point located on the horizon line (sometimes referred to as the eye line).

If there is only one vanishing point on the horizon line and all the parallel lines in the scene meet (or converge) there, then this is known as a **one-point perspective**. This photo I took in London (image C) is a good example of a one-point perspective. Do you see how all the parallel lines in the photo seem to be sucked into a black hole in the distance?

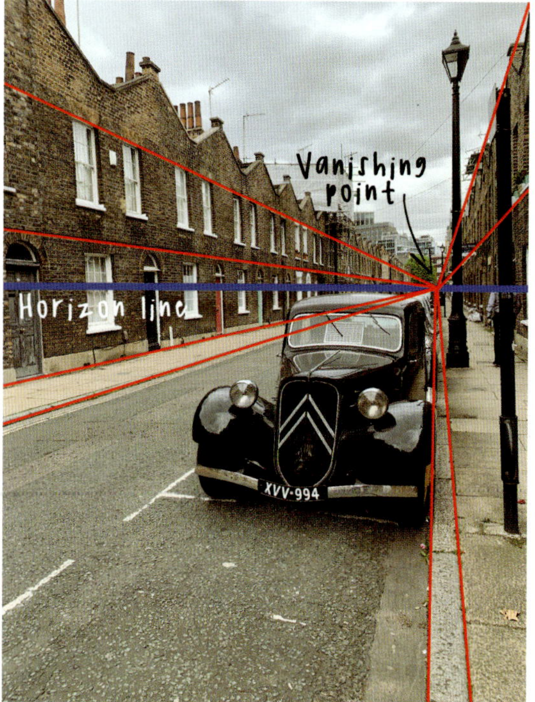

C

If there are two vanishing points on the horizon line, then it has a **two-point perspective**. In the photograph below (image D), you can see how the corner of the building is prominent, and you can see down both sides of the building. Both sides of the building have converging lines toward a vanishing point outside the page.

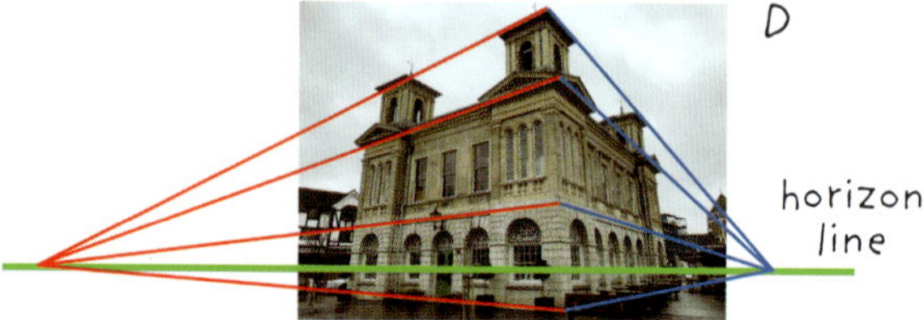

D

Note, you do not need to be dogmatic about perspective to still get a good enough sketch. I did the following sketch by eye, and while it's not perfectly accurate, it gives enough of a feeling to make you believe or understand what's going on.

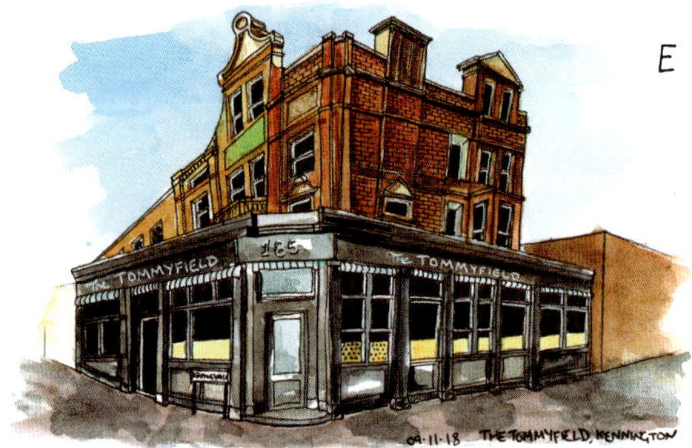

E

Three-point perspective is when the scene contains three vanishing points. Two of the vanishing points remain on the horizontal eye line, but the third vanishing point is on an imaginary vertical line and it could be near the top or near the bottom of the scene (image E).

You may have noticed this when you take photos and buildings seem to lean into each other as cameras dramatically exaggerate the perspective. If you are looking up and the walls appear to lean in toward each other, this is known as a "worm's-eye view," such as in the diagram below (image F).

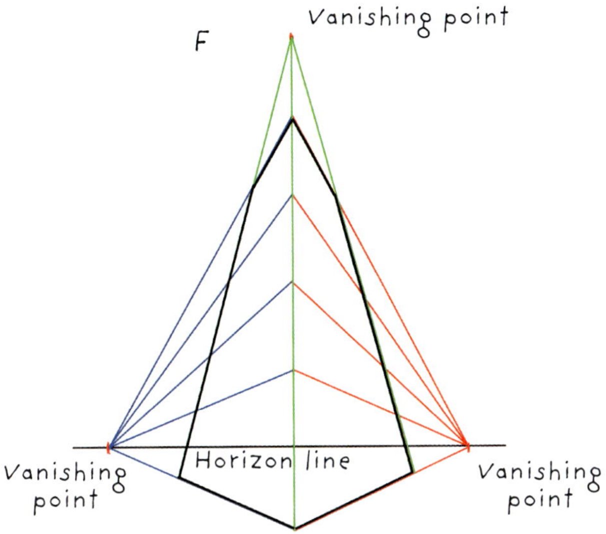

If, however, you are at the top of a skyscraper looking down and the bottoms of the buildings seem to lean in toward each other, this is known as a "bird's-eye view."

Linear perspective is what we usually find in architectural scenes, whether it's external views of buildings or interior spaces. There are lots of lines sloping off at various angles to indicate they have depth and are thus 3D.

Nonlinear perspective (also known as **zero-point perspective**) is when there are no parallel lines present that recede to a vanishing point. This kind of perspective is most common in natural scenes, landscapes and some interior scenes. Therefore, nonlinear perspective utilizes other principles to infer depth, distance and perspective.

There are some tips and tricks we can use to show perspective in a scene that does not have parallel lines converging to a vanishing point, like in image G.

G

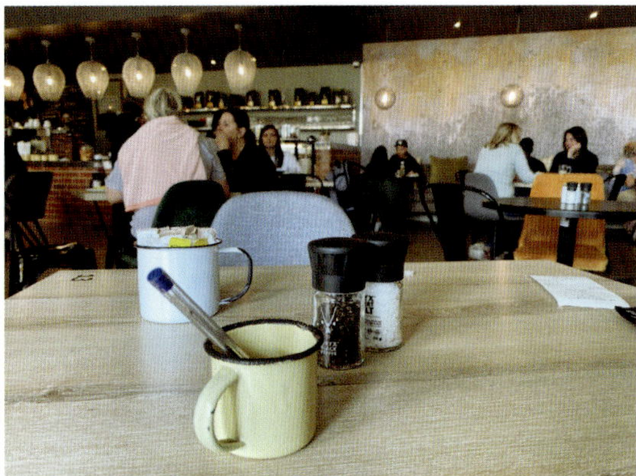

- **Relative Scale –** Draw objects farther away from the viewer much smaller than those in the foreground (and closer to the viewer). Notice how large the cup in the foreground is compared with the person sitting right in the background.
- **Overlapping –** Drawing objects one behind the other shows us the ones behind are farther away.
- **Value and Color –** Objects that are farther in the distance tend to have more of a blue tint. This is because of the effects of the atmosphere. This is not quite so apparent in an interior scene of only a few feet in depth but far more obvious when looking at distant mountains.

- **Clarity and Texture –** Objects in the foreground are clearer with more detail and texture, whereas objects in the distance should be less detailed. Notice how the items on the table I am sitting at are crystal clear in the photo on the previous page; however, the people sitting farthest away from me are quite blurry. This effect is exaggerated by the way the photo was taken, but if you apply this to your sketch, it will give a wonderful sense of depth.
- **Position of Objects –** If an object is placed higher on a flat surface, it tends to recede away from the viewer. This is most effective when combined with relative size, clarity and texture. Notice how the closest cup is also the lowest item in the photo.

You can also draw objects that are in the foreground with a thicker line and objects in the background with a finer line—it's a lot of fun to play with this and exaggerate it to make a stylized sketch.

One of the keys to urban sketching is selecting the view you want to sketch and then positioning yourself deliberately.

COMPOSITION

Composition is vital to make a pleasing sketch. It refers to how you organize and arrange elements on your page. There are some common systems you can use to ensure your sketch is composed well.

The most well-known system of composition is called the rule of thirds. The concept is used across all visual arts, such as photography, film and design, to create a harmonious and visually pleasing image.

You will most likely find a setting on your smartphone that allows you to switch "grids" on when taking a photo with the camera. The image will be split into thirds both vertically and horizontally. The idea is to place key elements where the lines intersect. For example, if you are taking a photo (or sketching) a landscape, you may place the horizon line on the bottom horizontal line. In this case, the bottom third will have land and the remaining two-thirds will be the sky like in image H. Or you could place the horizon line on the next line up, meaning the sky will take up one-third of the sketch and the land (or sea) will fill two-thirds of the image.

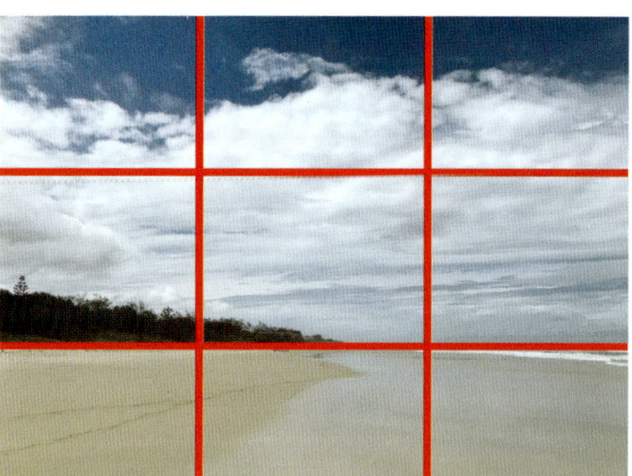

H

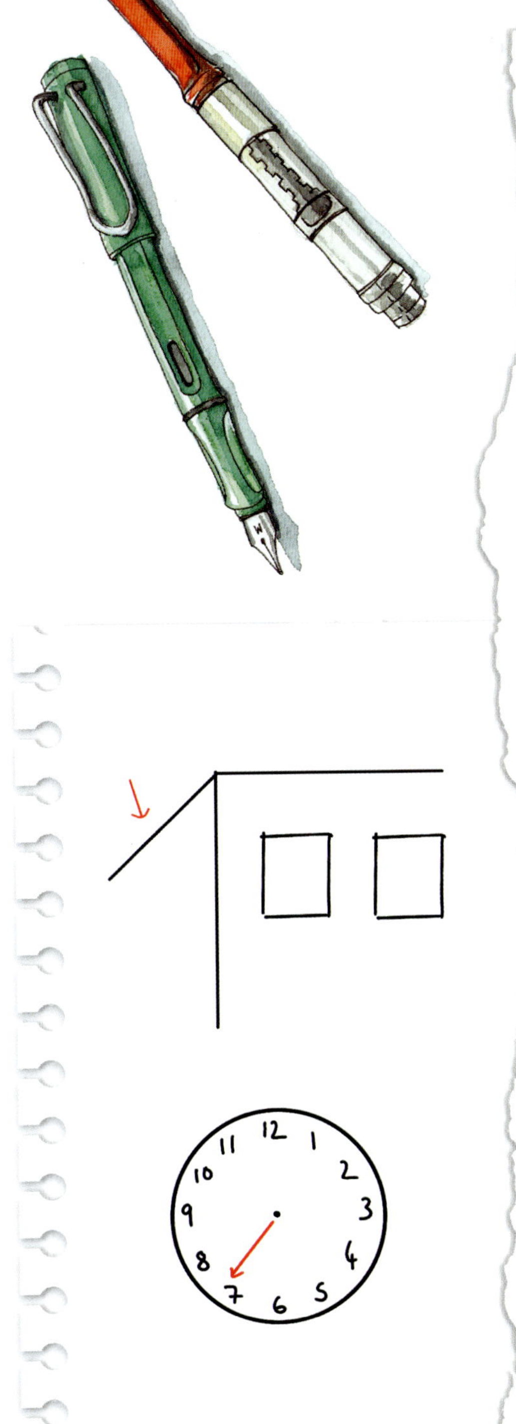

EXERCISE

Practice assessing perspective using photos:

1. **Find examples of images with different perspectives and print them out.**
2. **Get a ruler and a marker and follow the top and bottom edges of the buildings. The place where they all meet will tell you (a) where the vanishing point is and (b) where the horizon line is. Use these details to determine which kind of perspective the image has.**

Perspective is one of those things you naturally practice with each sketch.

If it's something you really want to focus on, then I encourage you to lightly draw the horizon line on your page, along with light construction lines in order for you to get your perspective more accurate. But I also give you permission NOT to do that and just eyeball it, which is what most people do.

Sometimes your vanishing points will be way off your page, so knowing how to draw linear perspective without horizon lines or vanishing points is a very useful skill.

Assessing angles accurately will enable you to eyeball and draw perspective more successfully. Using clock hands as a reference helps to envision angles. Think of the angle in terms of where it would point on a clock face.

Generally, I hold a pencil so it's flat and tilt it to the same angle I want to mirror, think about where it would point on the clock and then roughly draw it on my page. For example, the image on the side has an angle that is pointing down toward the left; this is roughly similar to the clock pointing at seven. I use this trick all the time to assess angles.

For the most dynamic composition, place the elements you wish to emphasize in one of the four areas where the lines intersect. Notice how the photo of the lighthouse below (image I) places the top of the lighthouse in the top left intersection, and the bottom of the wall, where it meets the road, is placed on the bottom left intersection.

I

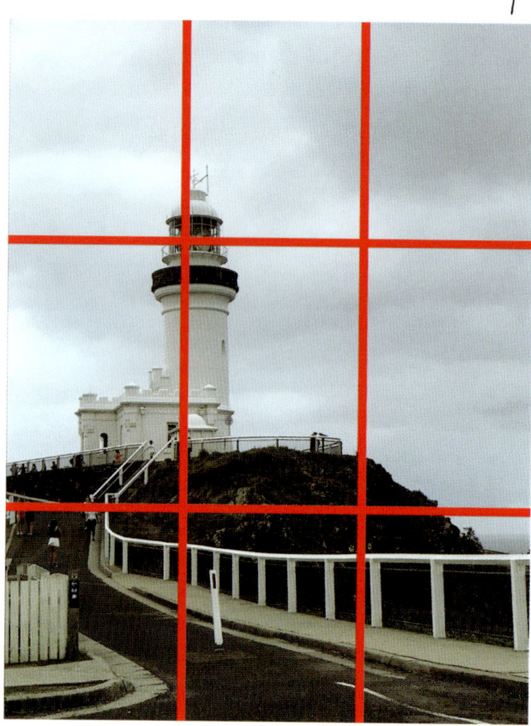

You do not have to place things in all four intersections; just one or two would work well.

Also, notice how the railing leads your eye in from the bottom right of the image to the bottom left intersection at the base of the lighthouse. Leading lines draw the eye into the picture and guide it around. This is also an important and widely used compositional tool.

When deciding where to place things on your page, the rule-of-thirds system is the simplest way to make your layout feel more harmonious. It also helps to prevent you from plonking things right in the center of the page. While sometimes that can work, more often than not, having elements placed according to the rule of thirds is going to look far more interesting.

DEPTH

The depth of a scene relates to creating the illusion of being able to step into a scene. as well as giving a thickness to things to make it feel like you could reach out and take hold of them. The first thing to consider is whether your scene has a clear foreground, middle ground and background. The foreground relates to the things closest to you. In a cafe scene, this could be your cup of tea, cutlery and anything else on the table that you're sitting at. The middle ground could be other people sitting at tables farther away from you and the background could be the counter where food and drink are being prepared. A sketch with clear layers of foreground, middle ground and background will draw in the viewer and make the scene more believable and captivating to look at. The viewer could imagine stepping into the scene.

Aside from foregrounds and backgrounds, adding depth to individual objects will also create a sense of dimensionality. For example, when you draw a chair or table (page 43), you need to draw the faces of each surface you can see from your viewpoint, as well as capture light and shadow.

CONTRAST

Contrast is a key element to making a sketch pop off the page. Contrast refers to the lights and darks in a picture. The bigger the range between the lightest and darkest parts of the picture, the more contrast it has. The white of the page is always going to be the lightest part of the picture and that's why using white or negative space effectively can make a sketch so striking. The darkest areas of a sketch will be black. I like to use a black brush pen in certain areas of a sketch. It leads to a stylized look but also adds extreme contrast. One of the biggest mistakes beginners make is that their sketch is all one tone—there are no bright brights and dark darks.

The easiest way to assess tone in your sketch—where the highlights, mid-tones and shadows are—is to squint your eyes as much as possible. This removes all the details from your scene and allows you to focus on tone. I find this particularly useful for finding the darkest areas of my scene.

TIP: ***A great way to practice seeing tone is to take a photo with your phone and edit it to make it black and white. This trains your eye to find the light and dark areas of a scene.***

A trick to emphasize contrast in areas of your sketch is to place your lightest colors (or indeed the white of the page) right next to your darkest color. If you can do this in one or two areas of your sketch, then this will give the illusion of maximum contrast. This is a more advanced tip, so not something to worry about right away, but as you progress, this may spring to mind and you can look out for when and where you can do this in your work.

WATERCOLOR TECHNIQUES

I want to touch on a few key techniques in more detail here that we will refer to throughout the book.

MIXING COLORS

In the art supplies section (page 10), I suggest that you get a watercolor set with twelve colors. Technically, you can mix most colors you need from primary colors. But as an urban sketcher, time is especially important, so it's nice to have already mixed colors ready to use, such as greens, browns, grays, etc. There are also some colors that you just wouldn't be able to mix up: bright turquoises and hot pinks for instance. As you move along your journey as an urban sketcher, you will naturally enjoy sketching particular things and therefore will gain a personal preference as to which colors you like to use.

However, mixing additional colors from the ones you have in your set is essential. This will give your sketch far more nuance.

I have found the very best way to learn your set and the colors you can produce from it is to make a watercolor mixing chart. Begin by drawing a grid on your watercolor paper with a pencil. If you have six colors in your set, draw six rows and six columns. The size of your paper will determine how big your squares should be; somewhere between 1 and 2 cm is good. Label each row with the name of your paint from top to bottom; do the same across the top of your columns from left to right. Make sure they are in the same order! The idea is to paint squares with a mixture of two colors: one listed on the left and one listed at the top. However, there are two pairs of each color, and we don't want them to be the same. I like to make a note to myself that the color listed on the top of each column should always be more than the color listed on the left. In that way we will get different mixtures for each combination.

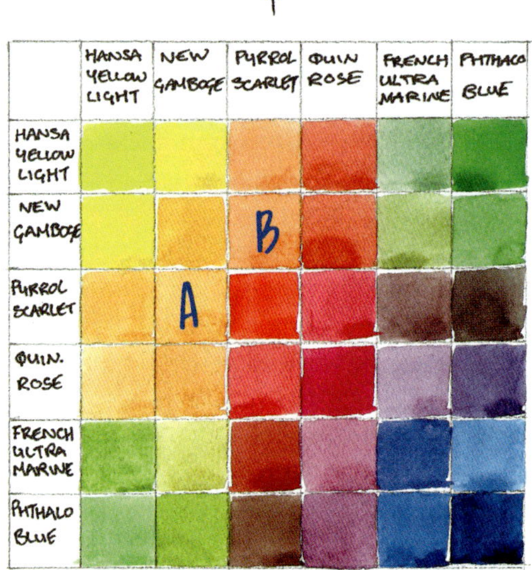

For example, in my 6 x 6 chart, where Pyrrol Scarlet is labeled on the left and New Gamboge is at the top, the mixture (marked A) has more New Gamboge than Pyrrol Scarlet. Therefore, it is more of a yellow-y orange. Conversely, where New Gamboge is labeled on the left and Pyrrol Scarlet at the top, there is more Pyrrol Scarlet in the mixture (marked B) and therefore it is a more red-orange.

Where the same colors intersect (diagonally from top left to bottom right), paint the pure color, not mixed with anything else.

If you would like to see a video demonstration, please visit learn.sketchyouradventures.com/workbook.

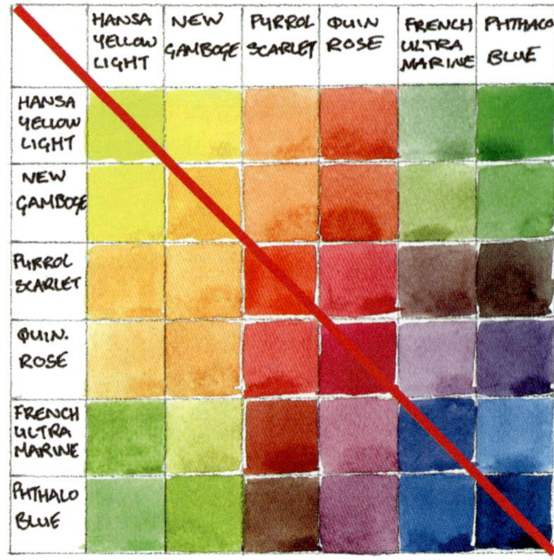

When using watercolor, if you need a lighter version of a color, you simply need to add more water—never add white as you might with acrylic or oil paint. Watercolor is a unique medium that is naturally translucent. Therefore, diluting the paint in combination with painting on the white of the page lightens the color.

It can be slightly more involved if you need a darker version of a color. Here are a few things you can try:

1. Use a thicker consistency of paint. As you may know, in watercolor, the more water you use, the lighter the color; the more pigment you use, the darker the color.
2. Add a touch of the complementary color and mix it in; for example, if you want a darker version of red, add a little green.
3. Add a darkish gray into the mix, such as Payne's Grey. This may not always work though, so be sure to test your color mix on a separate piece of paper.

As you become more experienced, you will have a better idea of which method will work for the particular sketch you are working on.

EXERCISE

Practice the three techniques on page 22 in your sketchbook to create darker versions of your paints. Which one gives you the most pleasing effect? Can you see how each is different and how they may be useful in different settings?

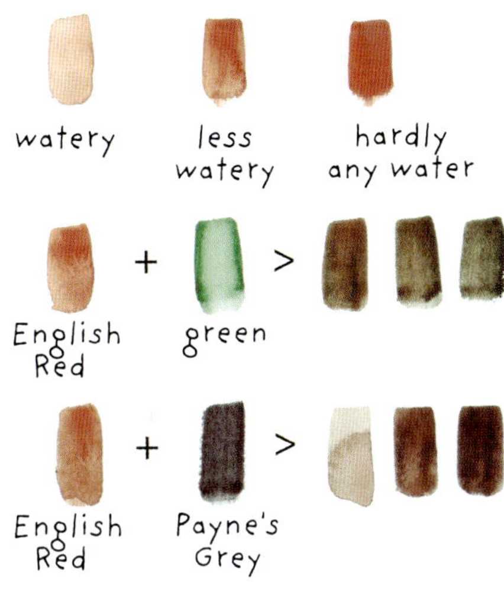

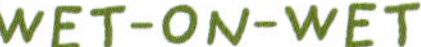

WET-ON-WET

Wet-on-wet technique is when wet paint is applied to a wet surface, whether it's simply wet paper or wet paint already on the paper.

Wet-on-wet is excellent for creating soft blends, a sense of haziness, backgrounds and texture such as weathering and rust.

The excitement of using wet-on-wet technique is that the results can be unpredictable as the technique itself is tricky to control. There are also a number of variables that can affect the outcome of wet-on-wet, such as:

- The paint will behave differently depending on which paper you are using. I find the most pleasing wet-on-wet effects are when the technique is used on 100 percent–cotton cold press paper.
- If you are in a hot, dry climate, the paint will dry far quicker, and therefore, the paint may not blend or spread in quite as much of a dramatic way.
- The amount of water versus pigment you use can dictate the spread and intensity of your results, as well.
- Different pigments may also behave slightly differently from one another depending on their chemical makeup.

Timing can have a significant impact on your results too. For subtle wet-on-wet that is very softly blended, add paint to the wet surface straight away. For a bolder and more defined result, such as when you want to add texture, don't add paint to the wet surface immediately; let it dry a tiny bit and then add paint.

In image A, I painted a strip of Naples Yellow and to the right of it I painted a thin strip of Indigo. I let the colors touch each other slightly as I painted the Indigo. I didn't use too much water so the blending of the colors where they touch is subtle.

Building on this, I used the same technique for image B (but with English Red and Indigo) and then spritzed the area with water from the little water spray bottle I keep with me. See how the edges splay out?

In image C, I laid down a clean stripe of water onto the page; I then dabbed in some English Red along the left edge of the strip of water. The paint and the water did the rest.

Building on this, I did the same thing for image D but then added a second color, Turquoise, on the right edge of the area of clean water.

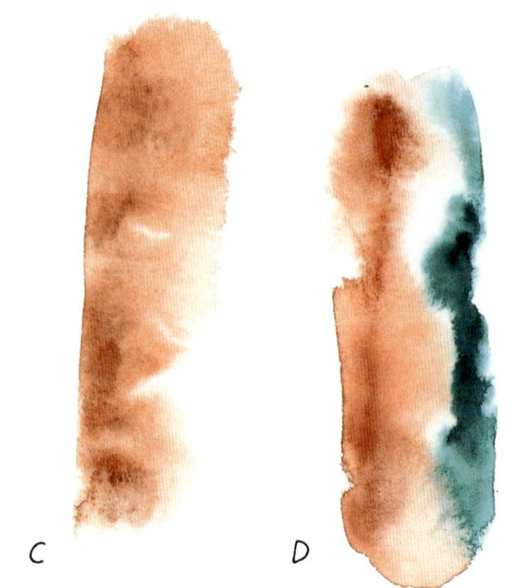

In this final example (image E), I put a clean area of water down on the page and added Payne's Grey to both the left and right side of the clean water. In the middle, I added some Quinacridone Gold. After this, I put clean water down again, and then randomly dabbed in English Red, followed by Payne's Grey and then Quinacridone Gold. I made sure I dabbed them all in separate areas, not on top of each other. Pigments behave differently. Even though I added the lightest color—Quinacridone Gold—last, it actually spread and moved the other two pigments aside as it interacted with the water. It's fun to watch.

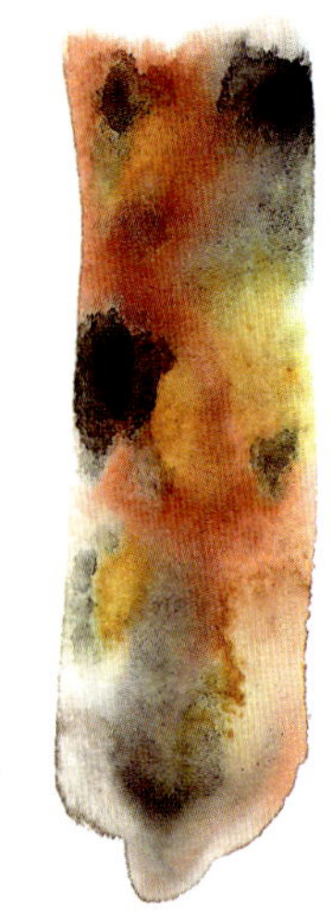

Wet-on-wet is such a dynamic technique and the effect cannot be exactly controlled. This makes it super interesting but unpredictable. Do some experiments in your own sketch-book so you can at least get an idea of how different pigments and amounts of water affect the outcome.

DRY BRUSH

The dry brush technique is used by water-color artists to show texture. It's particularly useful to show glistening water, as tiny pockets of the white page are left behind when a dry brush is dragged across the paper. The dry brush effect is best on textured paper (cold press) but you can still achieve a useful result on smooth paper (hot press) too.

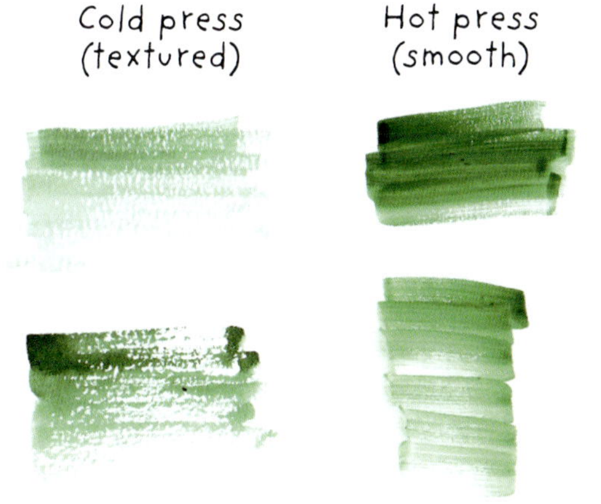

As the name suggests, it requires a dry brush in order to make these marks. The best way to achieve this is to pick up a nice amount of paint on a lightly wetted brush and then lightly dab it on your cloth or paper towel to absorb some of the moisture before dragging it across your paper. I find the dry brush technique is easier to apply with synthetic bristles rather than natural, as natural hair brushes tend to hold more water. Also, you won't mind scrubbing your synthetic bristles on the page, but when it comes to a natural hair brush, it's probably best to not abuse it in such a way as you may end up damaging it.

Dry brush technique is not a predictable technique but if you practice a little and get to know how your brush and paper behave, then you can get a degree of confidence with when and how to use it within your urban sketches.

BACK RUNS

Back runs, blooms or "cauliflowers," as they are sometimes known, are caused when certain parts of the painting dry more quickly than other parts. This can sometimes form a hard edge of paint that may have been added a little later than the initial area that was painted.

Climate can heavily affect the drying time of your watercolor. It's not something I take too seriously; as an urban sketcher, you will learn to roll with things and see what happens, but it's worth mentioning.

Although back runs often occur as an acci-dent, don't be disheartened by them. They still look interesting. You can even use them purposefully, in foliage for example. To cause a back run, paint an area and just as it starts to dry (when the surface is not as shiny), you can drop in some more paint. Paint flows to where the water is, so if an area of your paint has dried, it won't flow there and will instead cause a hard edge that looks like cauliflower (hence the name)!

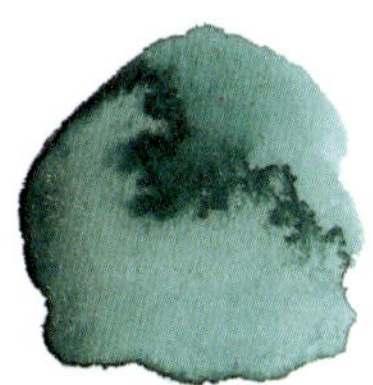

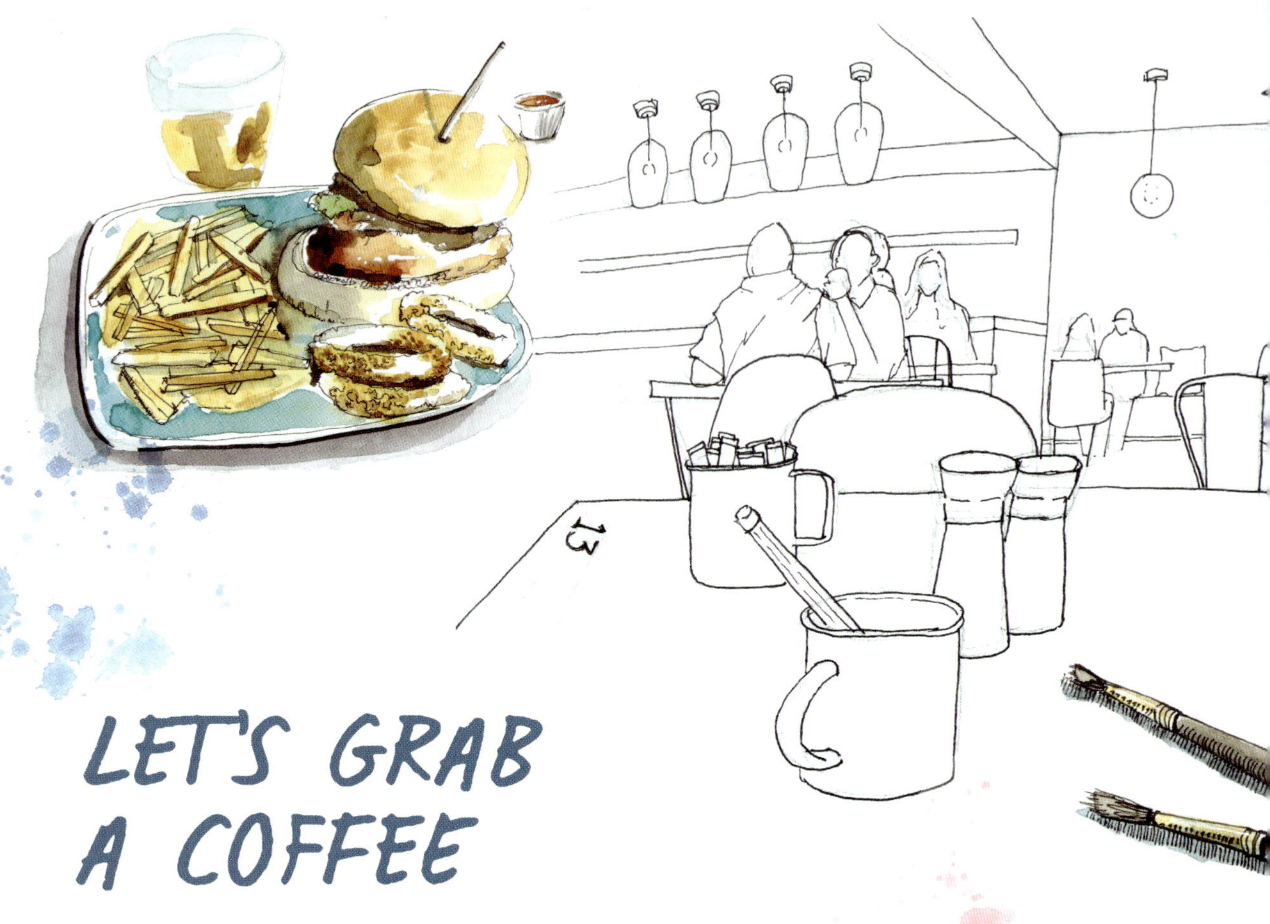

LET'S GRAB A COFFEE

A cafe is a great place to start your urban sketching adventures. Most people are busy chatting, eating or working and won't pay any attention to someone sitting in the corner scribbling away in their notebook. I prefer to have an A5 or smallish sketchbook for this kind of setting. As a beginner it allows you to be discreet, which is especially helpful if you are shy to sketch in public.

You don't have to worry too much about perspective, and you can simply draw what's right in front of you to start. What better way to get used to sketching in public?

Remember urban sketching is about telling stories of a place in time. What that story is, along with how big or small, is your call. Who's to say a sketch of your morning latte is any more or less important than the Victorian building over a road, or the people hanging out in the park? It's your sketchbook and your record of the world around *you*. In time, no subject will be off-limits.

SKETCH YOUR TABLE

We're going to start small, practicing with one item at a time, and then build outward. This is a good strategy for starting any sketch, and the techniques we use for each will assist you when you start to sketch more complex items and scenes.

You may hear advice to draw directly in ink, but I think this is very intimidating advice for beginners. So, feel free to ignore this and do what makes you feel comfortable. My advice is to stick with pencil for now, and I will show you how to use pencil to create skeletons from which to build on with ink.

With that in mind, let's consider some of the different items on your cafe table and how to sketch them.

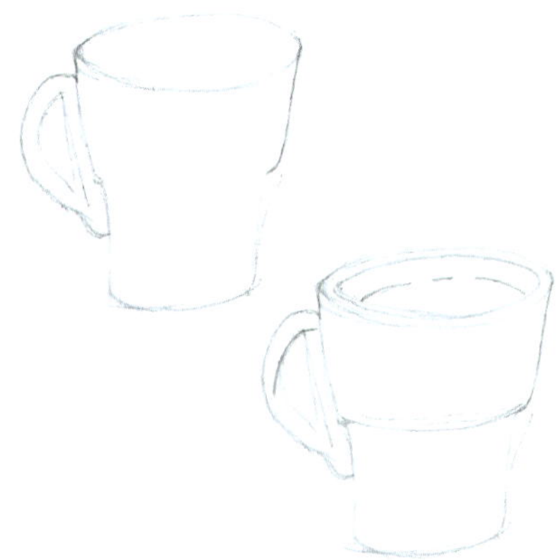

COFFEE CUPS

Start by drawing the outline shape of your coffee cup. This is known as a contour sketch. Don't fuss over any details; just get the basic shape and size drawn on your paper. Once your outline is drawn, you can add some more descriptive lines inside the shape.

Our aim is not to draw and paint the most realistic version of the thing in front of us. Sometimes we just have to "let go" if the thing we are drawing is not quite straight, proportional or in perspective. Trust me in saying that the sketches I find most full of life are not the ones that are perfect renditions or hyperrealistic. I am sure you will notice my drawing is not perfectly accurate but a stylized version of what I am seeing. I suspect this style is what attracted you to urban sketching in the first place.

Use your pencil outline to add ink over the top. Do not simply trace your pencil lines. The pencil lines are there as a rough basis of the shape and position of the object. When you draw in ink, you are committing to your lines so feel free to correct any pencil lines you don't think are quite right.

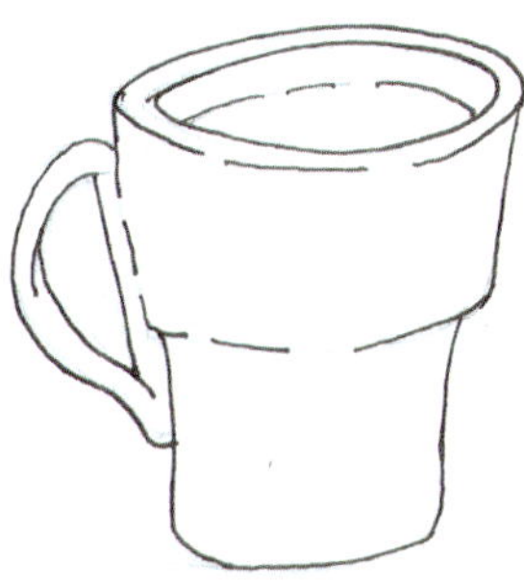

You may notice in my example, I used some solid lines and other lines with gaps in them. This is a tip I picked up from urban sketcher Steven B. Reddy (page 185). I find this a useful way to show which lines are the outline of a shape, i.e. an edge that can be physically felt, versus a broken line that is a descriptive line showing thickness or a slight change of "plane." For example, the broken line halfway down the coffee cup indicates where the cup goes from wider to narrower.

When painting a coffee cup, pay attention to where the lightest parts and darkest parts of the cup are. Indicating the shadows will help to communicate the 3D form of the cup.

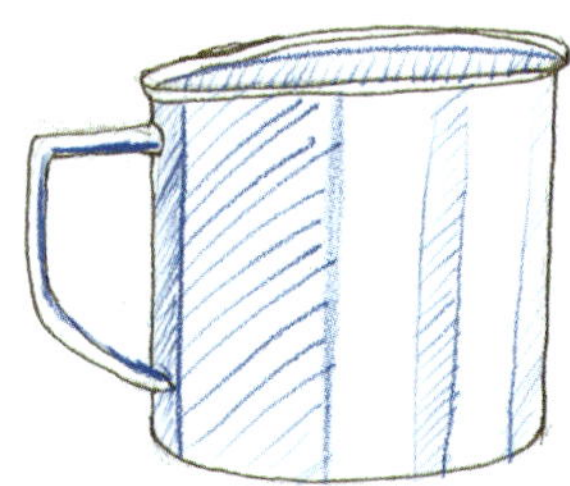

Above you can see a basic line drawing of a mug. I have identified where the shadows are on each cup using hatch lines. This is an example to demonstrate where the shadows are. I don't add the color hatch lines to my actual sketch, although you can add light pencil lines for where the shapes of shadows and highlights are. For areas of highlights, keep the white of the page. Then paint the rest of the mug one color. In my example, I painted the mug blue. Once dry, paint a darker version of the color in the shape you marked for the shadow areas.

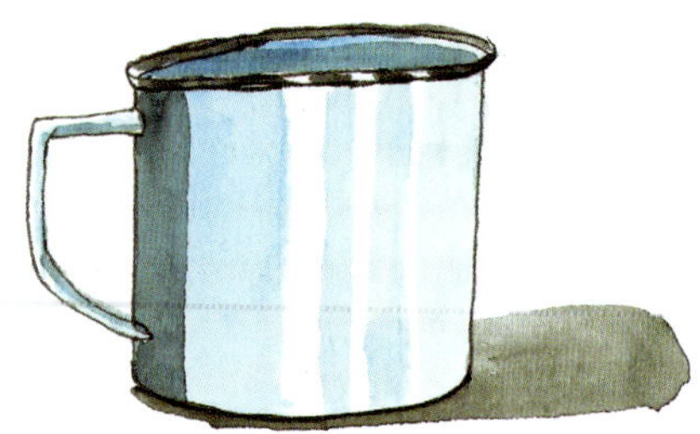

Don't forget to add a shadow underneath the mug too. This anchors the mug to a surface rather than it floating in space.

Don't overthink this process. Usually an item like this would be part of a scene anyway, so you don't need to add too much detail.

SAUCERS / PLATES

When it comes to saucers and plates, many are white in color. A reasonable question to ask is how do I paint a white plate? And the answer is, you don't!

The trick to painting a white plate (or indeed any white object) is to look for the ways to define the shape by using other colors.

Leave the shape of the plate white and paint a light blue or gray in areas where there are shadows. Adding a background around the white shape will also help to define it.

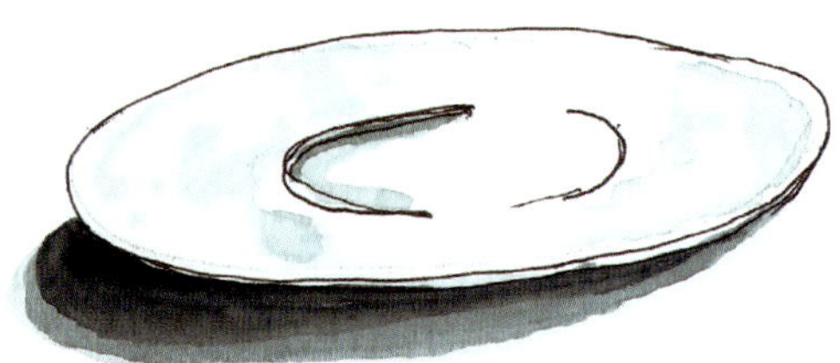

CUTLERY

When it comes to cutlery, one of the main difficulties is how to portray shiny metal. Once you have drawn the cutlery, look for the areas of white to preserve. The trick is to exaggerate what you see. Wherever there is a highlight, leave that part of the sketch unpainted, i.e. the white of the page. Paint the rest of the object in a light gray or blue. I prefer a blue as I feel it gives more character. I used a watery version of Indigo for my example.

Once this layer is dry, use a darker version of your color (less water, more paint) to paint in the shadow areas. Squint your eyes to see where the darkest parts are. Don't be afraid to go very dark, as this will give your sketch lots of contrast and make it more dramatic to look at.

This will take some practice. I encourage you to make some studies of cutlery in your sketchbook. This will help you practice sketching from life, as well as how to portray shiny and reflective surfaces using watercolor.

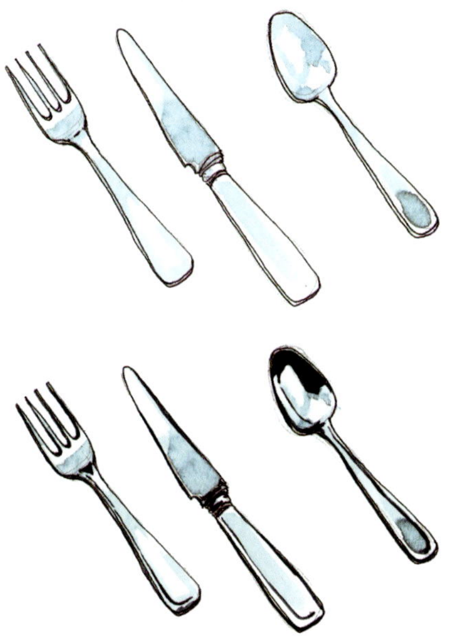

SALT, PEPPER & CONDIMENTS

Condiments are a fun to thing to add into the sketch of what's on your table. Many sauces come in brightly branded bottles, so it's a nice way to inject some bright colors into your sketch. Some condiments are harder than others to sketch, such as translucent salt and pepper shakers or sugar dispensers. Due to the translucent nature of watercolor, it's a great medium to use for translucent items.

Much like the saucer, the approach I take is to paint the shadows with pale blue to indicate any shadow areas of the glass. Also, take care to notice there is a thickness to glass, so the thing it contains won't go all the way to the edge. Tiny details such as this can make your sketch go from okay to great.

For the shiny metal part of the dispenser, follow the same process as with the cutlery. Exaggerate the highlights by preserving the shape of the highlight as the white of the page and paint the rest in a light version of your chosen color. Once dry, paint a much darker version of the color to indicate the shadows.

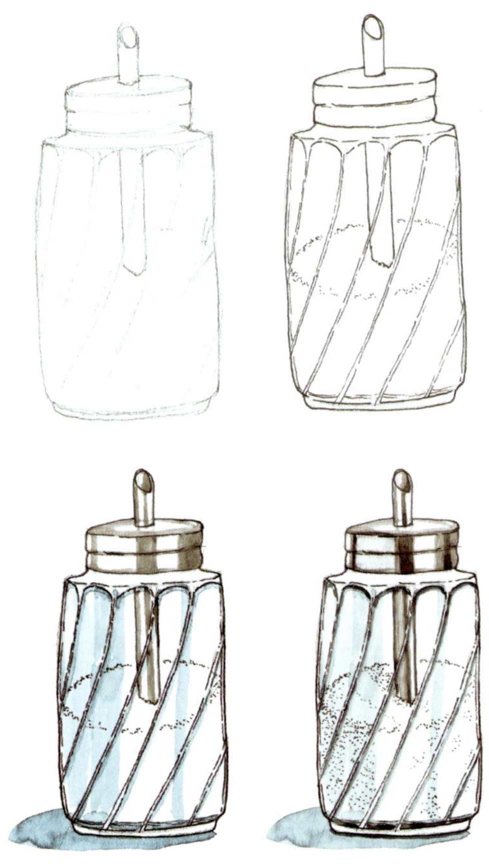

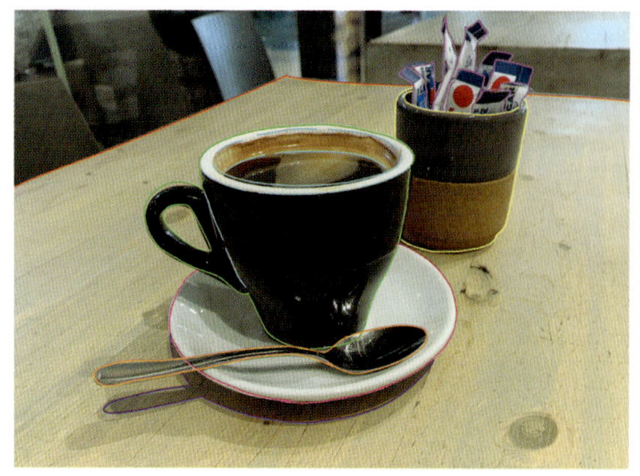

EXAMPLE SCENE

For this sketch, I drew the outline shape of the cup (the green lines in the image at left), followed by some descriptive lines inside the shape (light blue lines). Then I roughly sketched the saucer, the teaspoon and the packets of sugar behind the cup with my pencil. I also outlined the shadow shape underneath my cup (dark purple) as it's such a distinct shape. I didn't end up inking this line; I just kept a faint pencil line to show me where to paint. I also sketched in the edge of the table (orange) to add some background and context to the scene.

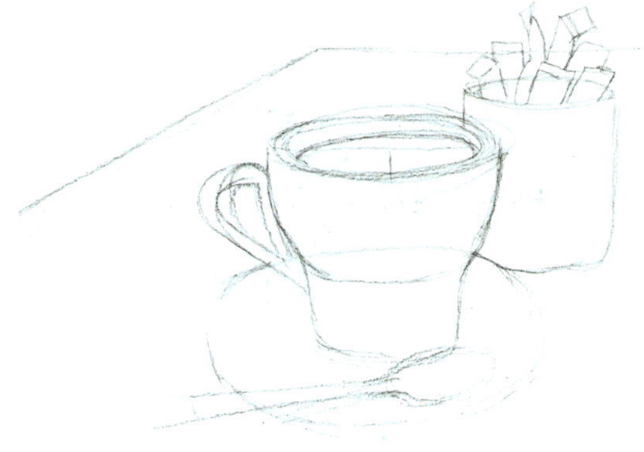

Next, I used a waterproof pen (0.1 Pigma Micron fineliner) to ink the permanent outline of the sketch, adding more details than the original pencil version. Note: I didn't trace my pencil lines exactly because that would have led to a stiff drawing; instead, I kept looking at the items while drawing with ink. The pencil lines are there as a guide. Eventually, you may not even use pencil lines, but as a beginner, I think it's a good idea to have some reference points on the page.

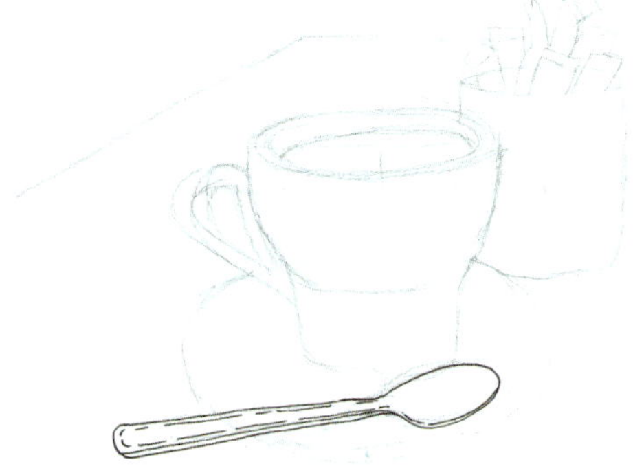

When inking a sketch, I start by drawing the items that are in front of others. In this example, I started with the teaspoon as the other items in the sketch sit behind it. When I drew the spoon, I not only drew its outline (the contour) but I carried on and drew extra little elements, like the edge of the handle to show its thickness. Small details like this help to show depth and dimension.

I then drew the coffee cup, the saucer, the pot of sugar packets and finally the edge of the table. Inking over your sketch offers the chance to refine the basic, sketchy lines of the pencil stage. In some areas I didn't follow my pencil lines at all, as I felt I had not gotten the right shape, angle or size of an object.

Similar to my advice regarding not tracing your pencil lines with your pen, try not to simply "color in" your sketch. You can be a bit "rough" in painting your shapes, leaving slight white gaps in areas. Notice how I did this on the inside of the coffee cup. The area is not one flat color. It's where coffee has been left behind, and there's some texture there.

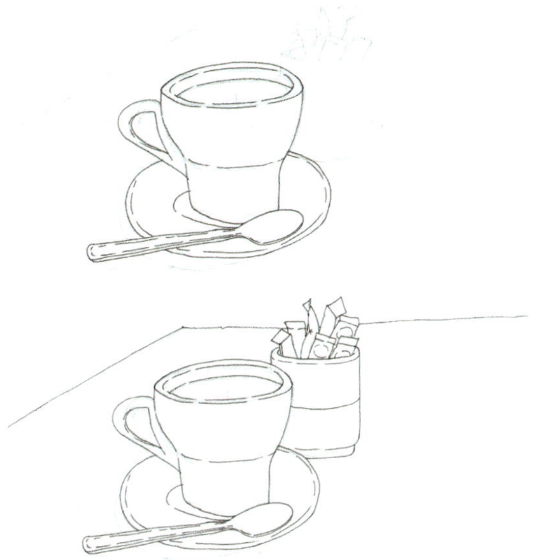

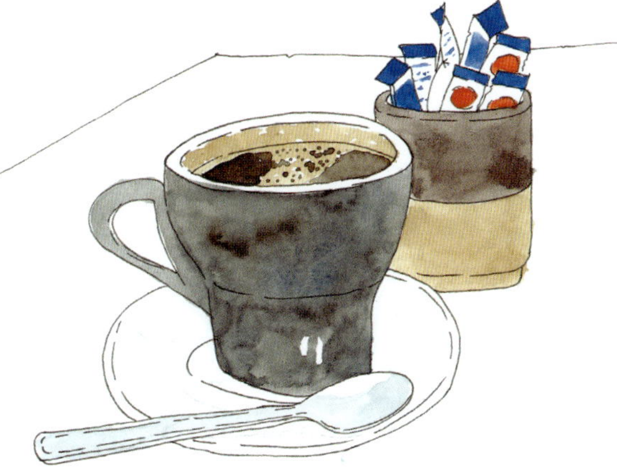

Before painting, I lightly penciled in some shapes of the key shadow areas because I didn't want to draw on top of my first layer of watercolor. This reminds me which areas to preserve and which to make darker. You can see them marked below in orange outlines.

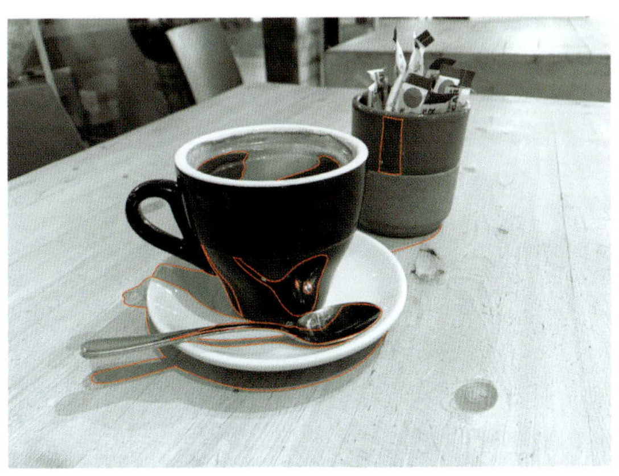

I started the watercolor stage by painting the lightest color. This is generally the rule when it comes to watercolor as you can always make things darker, but it's not easy to lighten something.

I put a very light (i.e. watery) wash of water-color over the saucer, except on the very edge, which I left white. I used Indigo in this instance but any blue-gray color will do.

I painted the teaspoon a slightly darker tone of blue-gray, painting around the left area of the spoon. I then moved on to the cup and painted the inner rim in a light brown, as well as the middle section of the coffee, leaving some tiny areas of white space.

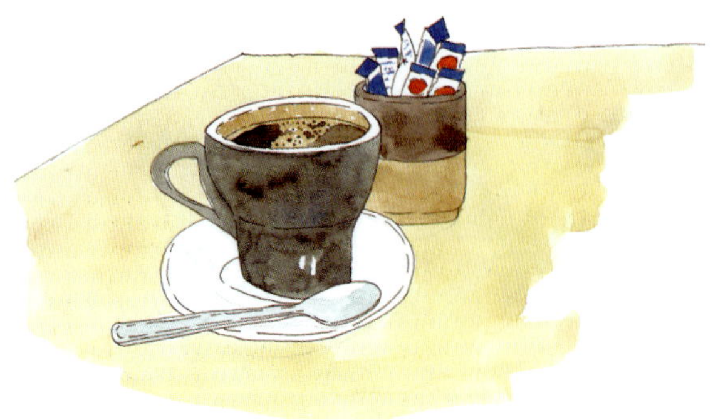

The bottom section of the sugar pot is more or less the same color, so I painted that at the same time. It's always good to paint every part of the sketch that is the same color in one go. It's an efficient way to paint and keeps your colors consistent across a scene. The top half of the pot is mid-gray, but I made mine warm (almost brown-gray) just for variation. I'm not too concerned with getting the exact colors.

When the light brown inside the coffee cup was dry, I painted the rest of the coffee with a dark brown color and put a few dots of dark brown on top of the light brown to show a bubbly texture.

I then moved on to the coffee cup itself, which is black. You will hear this advice countless amounts of time, but it's generally more interesting to not use black paint in watercolor. Instead, you can mix black from blue and brown. As you paint, the colors will separate in areas, and it creates a beautiful effect, far more interesting than flat black. My coffee cup initially looked gray, so I added another layer and darkened certain areas in my second stage of watercolor.

I left two small areas of white where there are a couple of highlights. You may not see bright white highlights in real life; the key is to exaggerate any areas where light is hitting your objects and leave those areas blank in your sketch. This will take some practice, so if you accidentally paint everything in a flat color at first, not to worry. There are other ways to add pops of white back into your sketch if you forget or can't leave the white of the paper for some reason.

I finished by painting the table surface. You could do this at the beginning if you prefer—there are no hard-and-fast rules. With larger areas like this, I recommend using a bigger brush to quickly cover the area to avoid any areas drying and resulting in "cauliflowers" (page 25).

Adding shadows is one of my favorite steps. When you add shadows, it starts to bring the flat 2D items to life. The easiest way to assess lights and shadows in your scene is to squint your eyes. This removes any details and allows you to focus on tone (i.e. the lights and darks).

To indicate a shadow on an object, mix a darker version of the object's color (page 22) and paint the shadow area with that darker color. For the shadow on the saucer, I used a slightly darker version of Indigo than in the first phase of painting (which was very light and watery). There are actually two stages of shadows that you can see in the photo. I don't want to get too granular with the details, but I think the tone shift between the hard cast shadow (the darkest shadow) and then the fainter shadow around the outside is interesting. I painted the largest area of faint shadow first, and once dry, I painted the darker shadow shape with a stronger mix of Indigo (i.e. less water, more pigment).

I used the same color for the shadow on the spoon. I painted the shape down the handle, leaving a couple of areas unpainted to show it is shiny, and then painted the dark shape on the spoon, leaving a sliver of the first color showing around the white unpainted highlight as there's a transition between the shadow and the bright white of the highlight.

There are some faint shadows on the white sugar packets in the jar, so while I had Indigo on my brush, I put a light watery mix on the packets to show a bit of form.

Next, I painted the shadow under the saucer (and teaspoon) and sugar pot as they are the same color. The shadow on the table has a brown tinge to it, so I used Sepia (dark brown) but added a tiny bit of Indigo (dark blue) just to neutralize the brown a little.

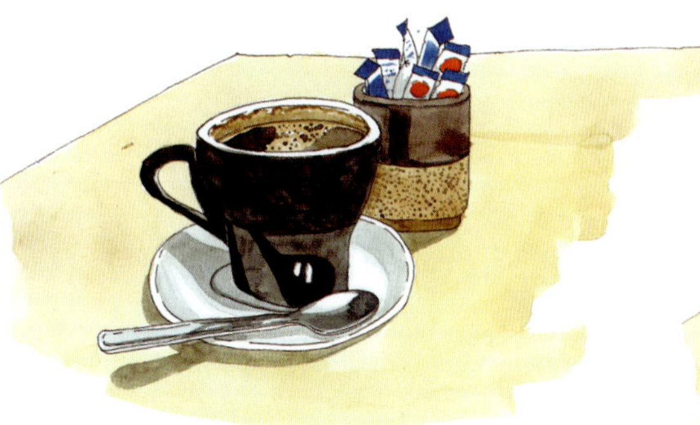

There's a tiny line of dark brown coffee residue on the inside rim of the coffee cup. While I had Sepia on my brush, I painted the very bottom of the sugar pot and added some dots to the bottom half of the pot as it's made from corklike material. A brush with a nice point like the dagger brush is very useful for something like this. You could also use a brown pen or watercolor pencil if you wanted to. I like how the texture of the cork on the bottom half of the sugar pot mirrors the bubbles of the coffee. A happy accident but I think it's interesting. I quickly added a dark strip of shadow on the top half of the sugar pot and around the rim.

I mixed a darker, thicker consistency of blue and brown than in the first stage to paint the coffee cup. I started with the top half of the cup and painted that whole section. On the bottom half of the cup, I only wanted to paint certain areas darker: the bits we marked in pencil earlier. I was careful to paint around the two highlights I wanted to leave white. I also painted the handle darker, reserving a thin slice on the inside of the handle where it's lighter. It was too tricky to reserve white paper for some of the tiny highlights on the handle, but I addressed this in a later stage of the sketch.

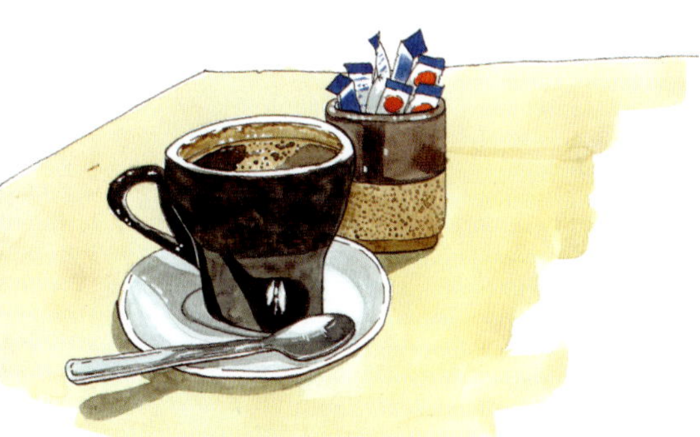

As discussed on page 21, having areas of extreme lights and extreme darks in your sketch will make it look so much more dynamic.

To add some visual interest and enhance depth and contrast, I added some thicker ink lines in certain areas: around the edge of the coffee cup to emphasize that it's sitting in front of the sugar pot, underneath the sugar pot where the pot meets the surface, the inner rim of the sugar pot to emphasize that the sugar packets are inside it and, finally, underneath the coffee cup, saucer and teaspoon to show they are all sitting on their respective surfaces. It's important not to overdo the thicker lines in your sketch. Before you know it, everything could be outlined in a thick black line! That's definitely not the effect we want to achieve.

Last, I added a few white highlights with a white gel pen: a few areas on the handle of the coffee cup, inside rim, saucer, rim of the sugar pot and the spoon, along with its reflection in the coffee cup. I left those two areas as white paper but notice how, with the aid of the gel pen, I reshaped or extended them as I felt necessary.

This may seem like a lot of information and stages in order to sketch a simple scene; however, the more you sketch, the more this process will become second nature, and you will do it without thinking.

FOOD SKETCHING

The food you experience in a place tells as much of a story as the people you meet and the architecture you see. I have sketches of camel stew from Somalia, platters to be eaten with your hands in Ethiopia, American smokehouse fare in South Africa and a burger and pint from England. Every time I look at those sketches, I remember eating the food, the people I shared the meal with, the look and feel of the restaurant—all from a sketch of the food itself.

I'm certainly not saying you have to sketch every single meal you have at a cafe or restaurant! But, from time to time, you may feel compelled to record your meal. Perhaps you are traveling or you are in a particularly unique cafe or just had time and felt like sketching your meal.

SPEED

Food sketching on location and from direct observation can be a challenge, especially if your food has just been served hot in a yummy restaurant and you want to eat it immediately.

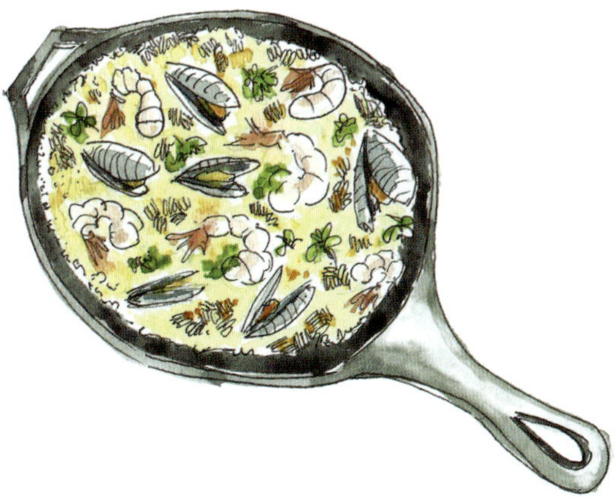

TIPS ON HOW TO SKETCH FASTER

- Use a pencil and do a loose sketch of your food. Get marks on the paper quickly. I find by using pencil rather than pen, the marks feel less permanent and therefore less scary. I think it's easier to loosen up.
- Hold your pencil farther back and tilted to the side. This will force you to not get too fiddly with sketching details using the point of the pencil but rather make big shapes with the side.
- Draw with your whole arm rather than your wrist. This is easier on larger paper.
- Try to look at your subject more than your paper while drawing on the page. This will take some getting used to but is a very important skill in strengthening your hand-eye coordination and learning to draw what's actually there rather than what you think is there.
- Let go of the need to be precise. Embrace the quick, sketchy results of this process and remember you will refine it later where necessary. At this stage you just want to get the essence of the food.
- You don't need to draw everything. Pick a few key items and infer the rest. That was my strategy when sketching this bowl of paella to the left. There are a few mussels and prawns that are recognizable—the rest was suggested. The viewer will be able to tell what the dish is.

There are two solutions to this challenge: Only sketch cold food or sketch faster! There's no better impetus to learn how to sketch quickly than very tasty food getting colder by the second.

Learning to sketch food quickly helps to develop your eye, teaching you how to capture the essence of your subject with minimal lines. Sketching food can also improve your observational skills as the food needs to be recognizable and appealing (well, if it looks appealing to start with)!

TIP: ***When sketching a hot meal, some urban sketchers draw a quick sketch of the food in pen (or pencil), then eat some; then they may paint some bits of the sketch for reference and then eat the rest of the meal and finish the painting afterward using what they already have on the page and their memory.***

TEXTURE

Texture is one of the most important elements of sketching food. By showing texture, we can communicate whether something is crunchy, smooth, creamy, gelatinous, rough, etc.

You can indicate texture with a pen or with watercolor, or both.

The quality of the line you draw can describe the surface, contour and texture of the item you are drawing. Continuous, even lines can indicate a smooth texture, whereas broken, erratic lines can indicate a rougher texture.

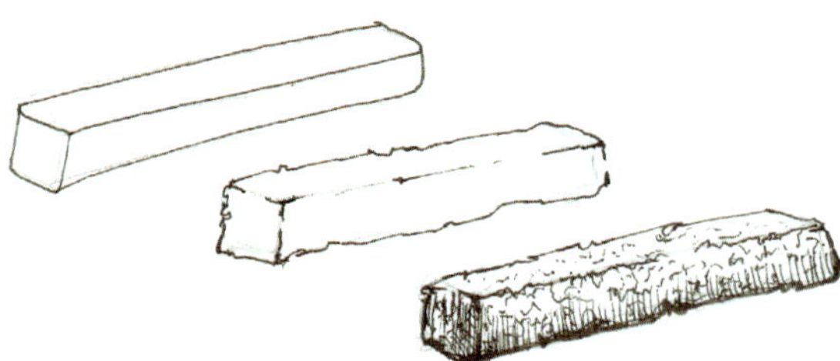

Just using ink, you can draw the texture of something porous like bread. In this example, I used a mixture of large and small irregular ovals to describe the surface. In the crust, I used light long lines to show the different type of surface. I used the pen at quite an extreme angle, tipped on its side. Explore the different marks your pen can make at different angles and by applying different pressure.

Adding a base layer of pale beige and then adding darker shades in the ovals helps to describe the texture even more.

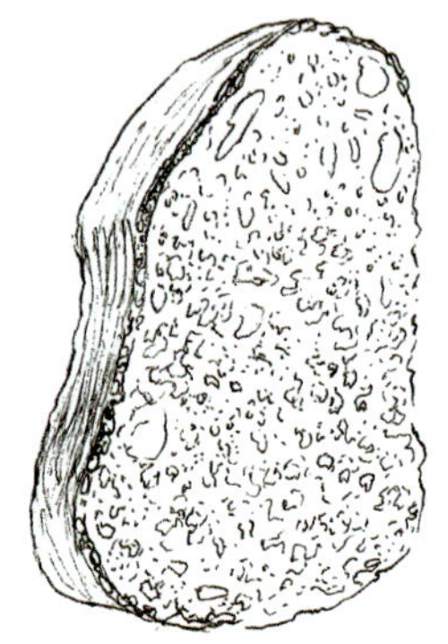

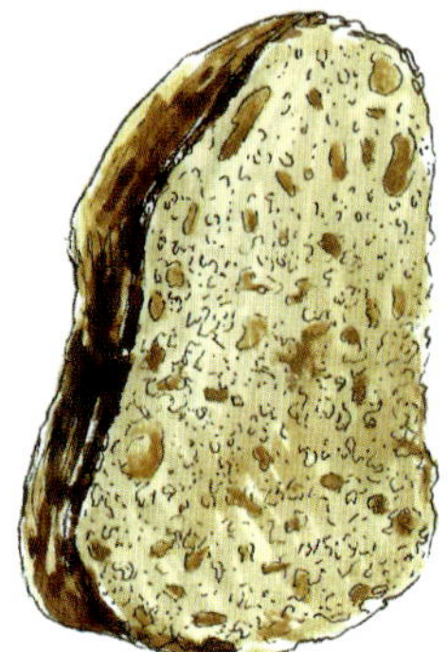

When painting with watercolor, you can exaggerate the highlights by leaving some areas completely unpainted to show something that's very smooth and shiny.

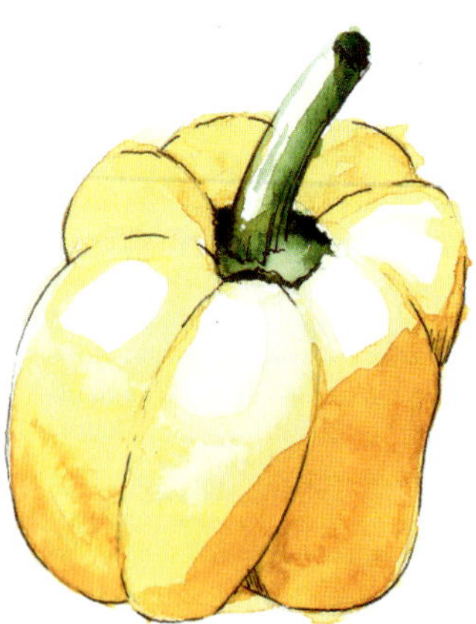

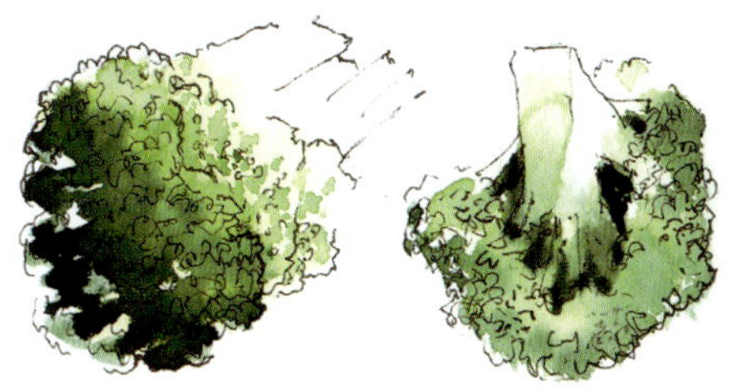

In this sketch of broccoli, notice how the areas of white have very little detail, yet the darker areas have much more textural detail.

This is a great way to emphasize darker and lighter areas, which gives more contrast and makes the sketch more interesting. You can make the pen and brush work together in creating texture. The pen is great for adding the rough circular squiggles and the brush point can be used to add dots of watercolor. Also, notice some tiny little gaps of white left even in the dark area of the broccoli. This adds more life to the area. It's much more interesting not to paint solid areas of color.

Dimpled fruit skins—such as oranges, lemons and limes—can be represented by using small curved lines. Don't feel you have to cover the entire surface with the same lines. In this example, I only drew the lines in part of the orange and didn't draw any texture in the lightest part of the orange. This is a way to suggest texture without having to draw everything. I also used my brush to create texture, as well. Dab the point of your brush on the page to make small marks emphasizing the marks made with your pen.

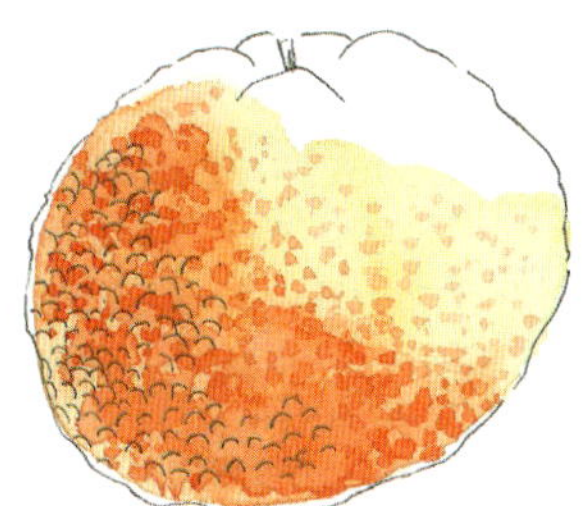

An item such as a gummy bear has a gelatinous texture. It's shiny, smooth and not completely opaque—it lets some light through. The key to emulating the texture is reserving strong shapes of the white paper to show the highlights. Paint a very light color around the areas of white and keep building up the darker tones until you reach the darkest last. Squint your eyes at the subject to help you see where the darkest and lightest parts are. This texture is much easier to represent with watercolor than with line.

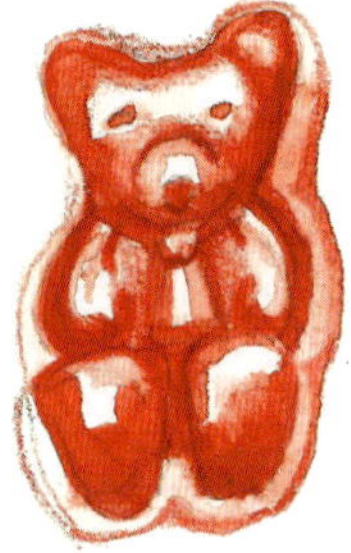

There are multiple textures in this sketch of a slice of cake.

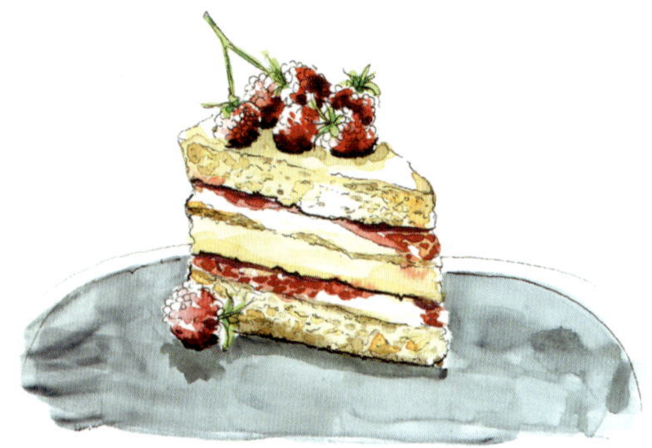

There's the leafy texture of the raspberry stems, the bumpy surface of the raspberries, the spongy texture of the cake and the creamy texture of the filling.

Learning how to represent different types of surfaces with both ink and watercolor to sketch small objects like food will be invaluable as you progress to more complex subjects.

STORYTELLING

How you sketch can also tell a story. You can add context, as well as personality, by exaggerating certain things, such as the lean of the burger or the perspective of the plate. The looseness of your lines can indicate the excitement of wanting to eat the meal or even the fast pace of the environment you were in. A more precise sketch with neat lines can tell a story that it was a long, lazy meal and you had lots of time to draw; maybe you were on holiday and you spent a couple of hours at your table.

In this sketch, I roughly drew the main shapes of the food in pencil, followed by a few choice ink lines.

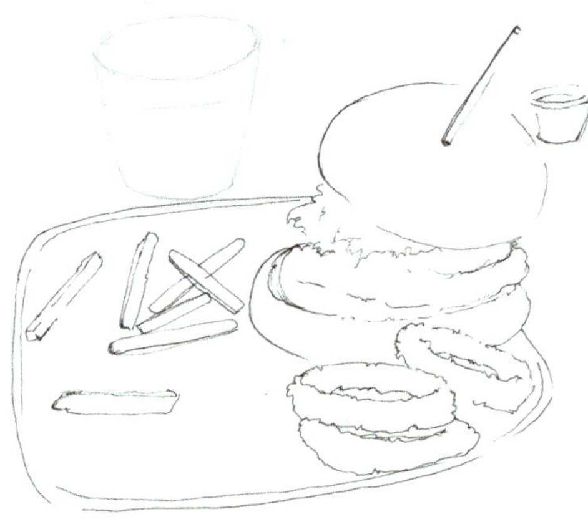

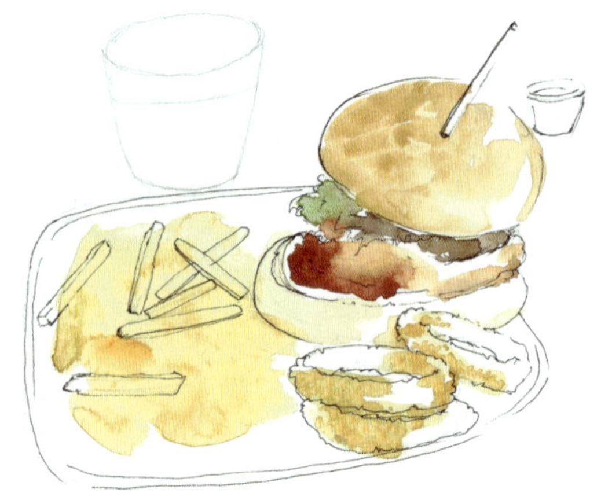

Notice I only sketched a few of the fries. There were a lot but I didn't need to draw every single one. A key skill of urban sketching, which you will see throughout this book, is how to hint at something without having to draw every last item or detail. This will help you draw quicker and capture moments that are fleeting. Plus I knew I could come back and add some more random fry shapes after I had eaten them.

I left the sketch at this point and ate my food!

Once I had eaten some of my meal, I went back and filled in my sketch. I added a few shadow shapes and brushstrokes to the onion rings to try to show the texture of the crispy batter.

I then put in some very quick color on the hot items of food. I wanted to eat the burger and fries while they were relatively hot so I focused on those details first. The other items—such as the drink, the plate and the pot of ketchup—could wait until afterward.

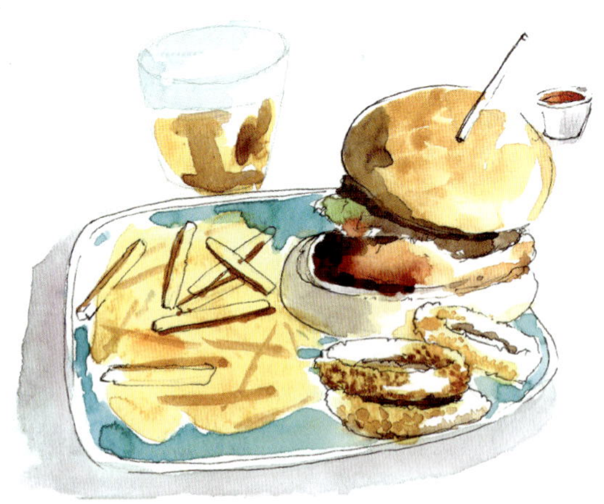

In the final stage of the sketch, I added some stronger shadows around the fries, under the onion rings and a little around the burger just to make those items look like they are sitting on the plate and have some dimension.

Did you notice how "loose" this sketch is? By loose I mean drawn quickly without focusing on details. I am trying to capture the essence of the thing rather than drawing every minute detail.

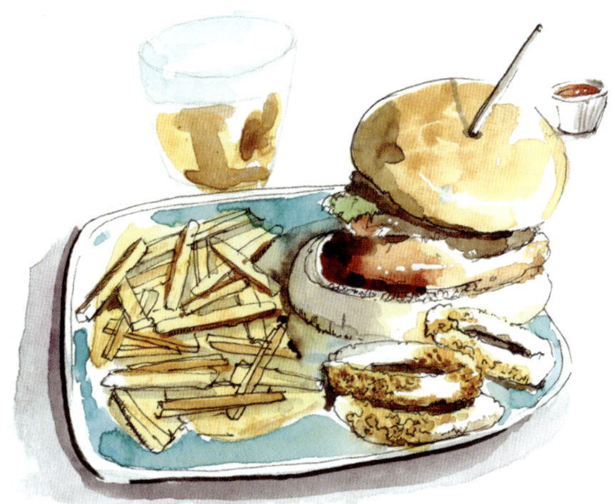

ADDING NOTES

I love adding little notes about what I ate, the things I was thinking or the conversations I had.

You may want to remember what you ate in more detail and record the ingredients of your dish or the elements on the plate. Perhaps you heard a funny snippet of conversation while you were eating and want to record it as part of the experience of your meal.

Or you could even record some notes on colors or techniques you used to sketch food. I always say every sketch is a learning experience. What better way to learn than to record what you did, what you were happy with and what you may do differently in the future.

Urban sketchers always make a note of the location of the sketch and the date, but you are welcome to add more notes as you see fit. Or not. The choice is yours!

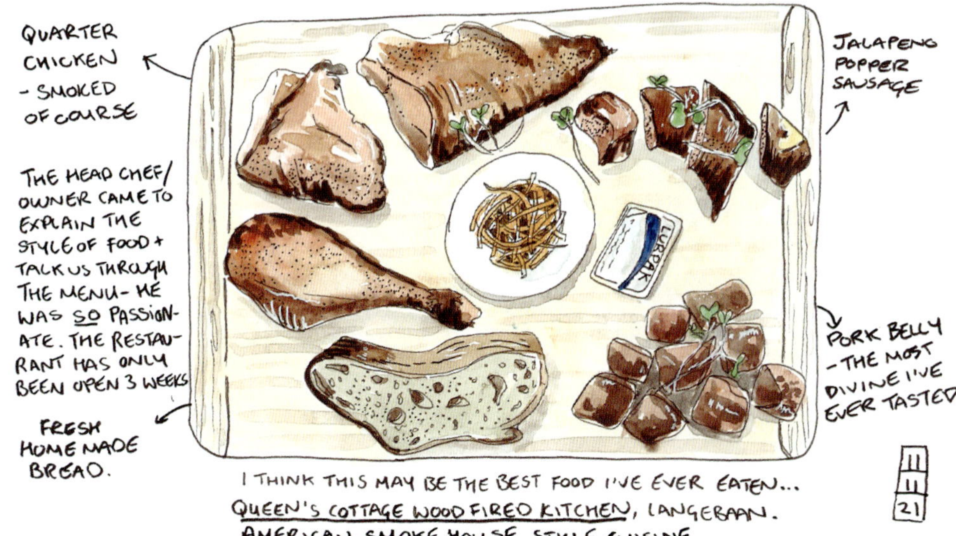

EXERCISE

1. Sketching—tight vs. loose

You can practice sketching food at home, as well as when you are out and about. Try sketching in different ways—tight or loose.

Draw an item of food slowly and carefully. You could sketch a sandwich or a slice of cake. This could be referred to as a tight drawing.

On another page sketch the same item fast and loose. Still keep your eye on the shapes and proportions but hold your pencil (or pen) farther back and use your whole arm to draw.

Notice the lighter, quicker lines of the loose sketch versus the slower, more considered lines of the tighter sketch.

Neither method of sketching is better than the other; it's a personal preference and taste. I personally draw in both ways depending on the subject matter and how much time I have available.

2. Refine some lines

Keep working on the loose sketch. You may have some wispy lines where you drew quickly; restate these with a more solid line, especially where there are distinct edges of your subject. Thicken your lines where there are shadows. If you did your loose sketch in pencil, switch to pen to do this stage. Don't worry about erasing your pencil marks—they add to the charm of the sketch.

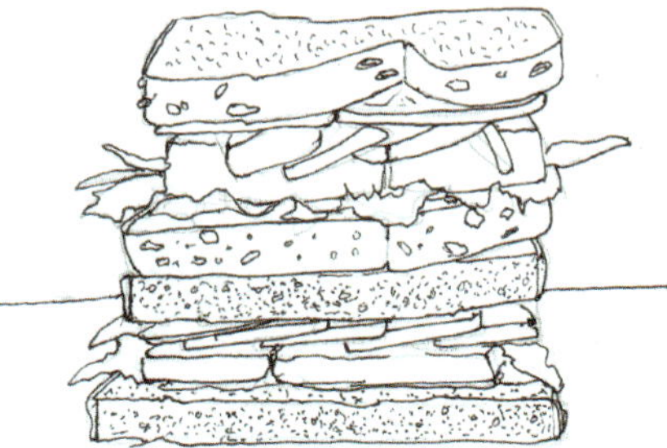

TIGHT

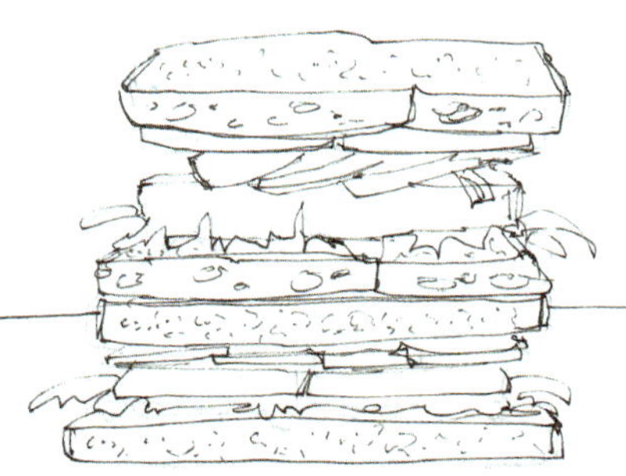

LOOSE

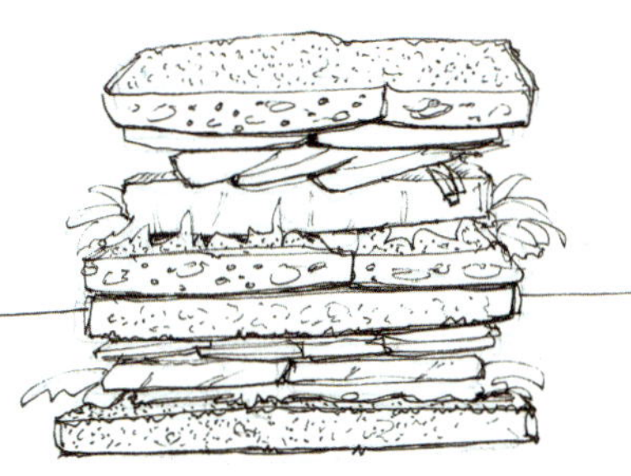

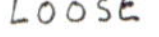

LOOSE

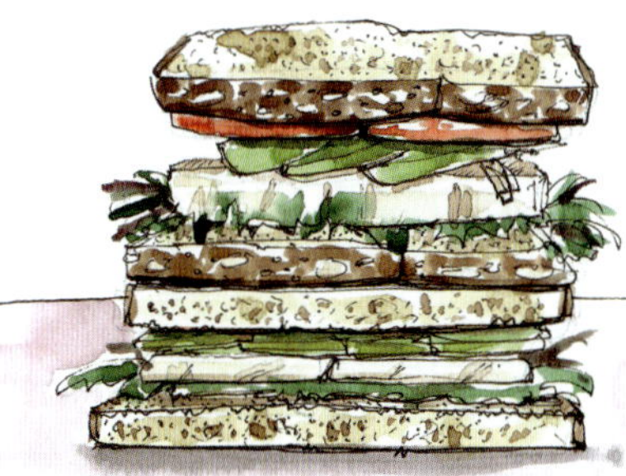

LOOSE

3. Add textural marks

Add some marks to indicate texture as we discussed earlier. These marks will bring the entire sketch to life and make it feel like you could eat the food right off the page!

I think the loose version has a bit more energy to it. What do you think? Which sketching style do you prefer?

Don't forget, when you paint your food, keep it loose too!

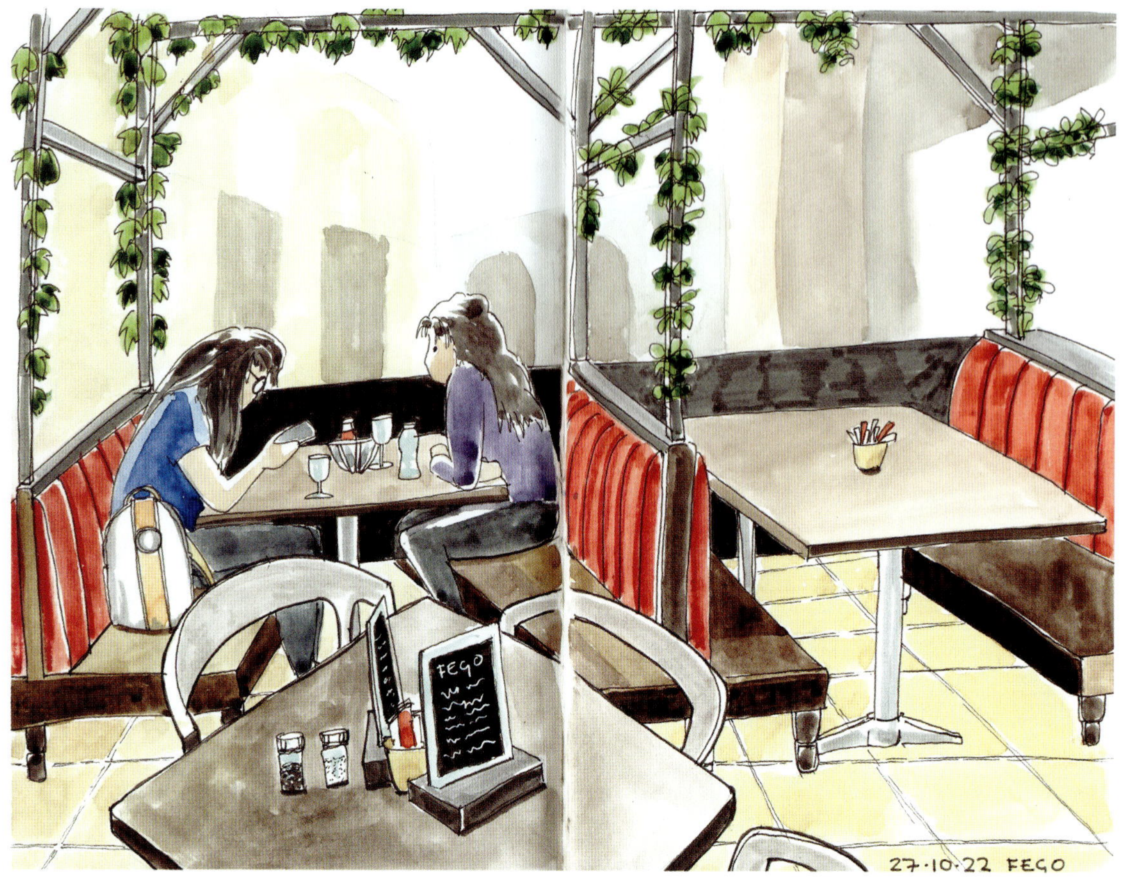

BEYOND YOUR TABLE

So far we have focused on the elements on your table, but what about the wider world of the cafe or restaurant environment?

Perhaps you don't want what's on your table to be the focus of your sketch, or you want to add some context to where you are.

COMPOSITION

When sketching an interior scene such as a cafe, think about the composition of your scene. The sketch will be more successful if you have a clear foreground, middle ground and background. This will help create a sense of depth and pull the viewer into the scene.

An easy way to establish a strong foreground is to use your table or something on your table and exaggerate its proportion in comparison to the rest of the scene. This is a tactic used when a scene doesn't have any strong parallel lines to show perspective, i.e. a zero-point perspective as discussed on page 17.

In the example image on the left, I deliberately sat at a table where the view wasn't too cluttered. There was only my table, a booth with two people and an empty booth to the right. There weren't multiple layers of tables and chairs to deal with.

TIP: ***Be strategic about where you sit. Set yourself up with the best vantage point so you can produce a sketch you can achieve.***

I started by sketching the foreground elements, which in this case were my table, the things on the table and the chairs surrounding it. After this, I moved farther back in the scene and sketched the table and the women, as well as the benches they sat on and then the metal frames with the foliage wrapped around. The background is exceptionally vague, and I only added it right at the end after drawing and painting everything else as the sketch looked too stark.

Notice that my foreground elements, the table and chairs, have a thicker black line around them than the elements farther back in the scene. I did this deliberately. Using a thicker line is an excellent way to pull elements to the forefront and to emphasize them. It creates a sense of depth.

TABLES & CHAIRS

Drawing tables and chairs in perspective is tricky, especially when they overlap each other. Start with the simplest view of something and build up from there.

In this example, I sat straight in front of a table and chairs that were parallel to me. I started with the table first so I could use it to try to situate the chairs in relation to it, creating a sense of realistic proportion.

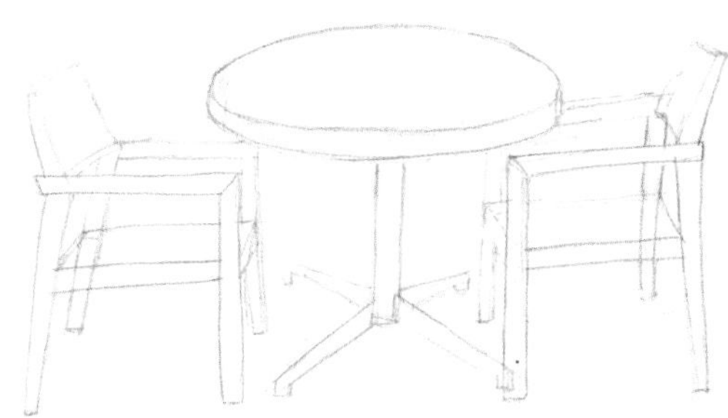

The table is circular, but in perspective, it appears to be an ellipse. I recommend using a pencil to draw light oval shapes, looking at your subject constantly. Don't be afraid to keep reinstating your pencil lines until you get a shape you're happy with. A tip to drawing circles or ellipses is to try to use your whole arm, from the shoulder to the wrist, rather than just your fingers. You can get a more fluid motion and therefore smoother shape by using your entire arm.

I held out my pencil and used it to measure the table. I established that the length of the visible part of the pole connected to the table surface is half the width of the table surface itself. It's easy to misjudge something like that. I measured it three times as the pole seemed so much longer to my naked eye.

After I drew the table, I moved on to the chairs. The arms of the chair tucked just underneath the table surface, so that's an easy visual landmark to translate to the page. I measured the length of the armrest, and it's the same as the height of the pole holding the table. I did not go over the top with accuracy, but having a rough idea of how wide or tall things are in relation to each other can go a long way toward making the sketch successful.

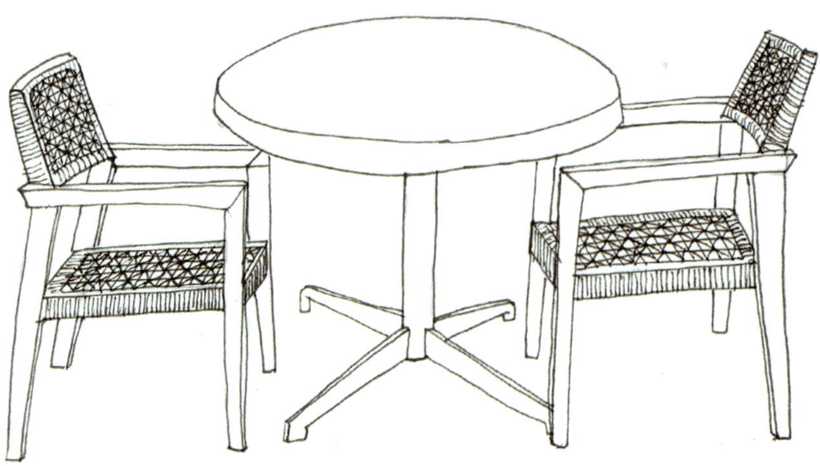

Another tip is to draw through things, especially when you are working in pencil as it can be erased afterward. It can be useful to draw something in its entirety that may be behind something else; then when you come to inking, you can draw one thing behind the other and simply erase the pencil line. Notice how I drew the rear legs of the chairs all the way through the seat (page 43). It's easier to get it to line up this way. Even though I have measured and taken some care, my sketch isn't perfectly accurate but that's okay. It doesn't need to be perfect.

Last, I inked the sketch and added all the finer details that bring it to life, such as the depth of the frame of the chair and the textures on the woven seat. I also corrected any bits that I felt weren't quite right when I drew in pencil. The table surface is a bit wobbly but I don't mind—it adds character!

PEOPLE

People can be a tricky subject matter, but there are simple ways to include people in your scene without worrying about knowing anatomy or capturing a likeness. People are essentially just another type of furniture in your scene!

In the cafe sketch on page 42, I drew the women in pencil and focused on their overall postures, using the furniture around them as visual landmarks in order to decide where certain body parts should go. Notice the complete lack of detail in their faces; ability is irrelevant in this kind of scene. The faces are too small to draw the details. I think it's far more important that the body itself is in proportion with the furniture and in a believable pose. Luckily, these women stayed in the same positions for a while so I could sketch them; however, they did leave before I finished painting my scene. They were both wearing black, but I thought for the sake of clarity in the sketch, I would change the color of their clothes.

TIP: *If someone leaves while you are still drawing them, look around and see if you can use another person who may be in a similar pose. You can borrow parts of them to finish off your initial sketch. Many urban sketchers do this.*

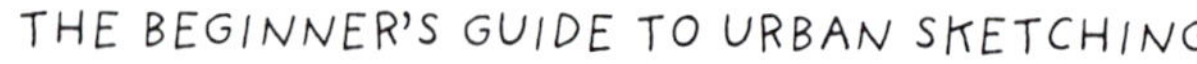

EXERCISE

1. Find a view in your local cafe where there aren't too many layers of tables and chairs.

As you become more experienced, you will be able to judge which viewpoint will make a successful sketch and a pleasing composition. For now, opt for a scene where you have a strong foreground (such as the things on your table), a mid-ground (one other table and chairs, perhaps some people) and a background that you will keep very vague.

2. Draw the foreground elements first.

If working in pencil first, remember when you ink your sketch to use thicker lines around these foreground elements. This is something I usually do at the end of the sketch, after I have painted.

3. Draw the mid-ground elements.

Remember, you can draw through other things if it makes it easier. Don't draw too much detail in pencil. You can draw details and textures later with ink.

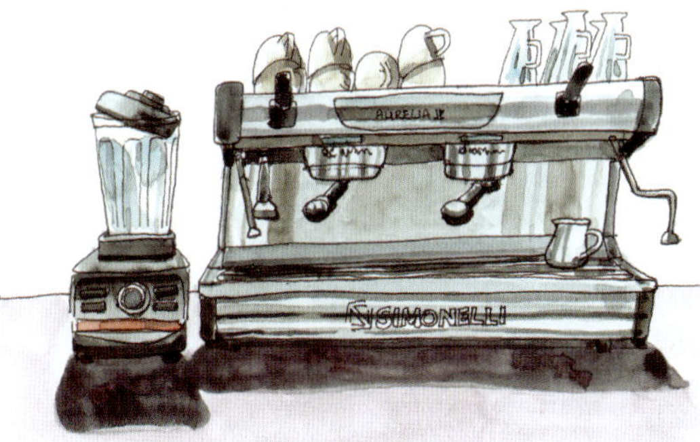

4. Pencil in any background elements.

Keep this vague. Reference my example on page 42. I painted vague shapes of color to indicate walls and buildings in the background.

5. Ink the sketch.

Once the ink is dry, you can erase your visible pencil lines. Don't worry too much about erasing every last bit of pencil. The watercolor will make it less noticeable.

6. Paint your sketch.

Do this in two stages. First, paint everything the color you want it. Try to paint everything that is the same color at the same time. Once the first layer is dry, add shadows by adding darker versions of the original colors. This will bring life to the sketch.

7. Finishing touches.

Thicken lines of the items in the foreground. In my cafe sketch, I also used a black brush pen to add an area of black behind the two women to make them more defined, and also on the menu in the foreground. This then allowed me to use a white gel pen on top of the black menu to add the name of the cafe and some squiggles to indicate text.

SKETCH A SCENE

PERSPECTIVE-LESS PERSPECTIVE

Let's put everything from the previous sections together and sketch an entire cafe scene.

PICKING A LOCATION

1. Look for a simple scene to start with.

Don't choose a place with lots of clutter and mayhem as it may overwhelm you. In my scene, there are only two layers of tables and chairs beyond my own table, with only a few people and a simple interior.

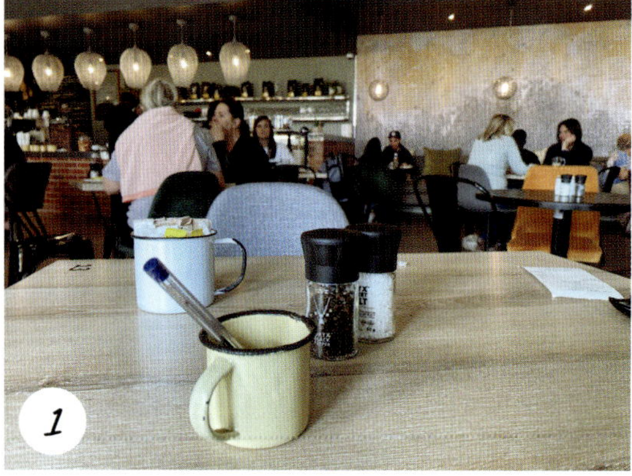

1

Of course, you can also edit what you see if the scene seems too busy. Don't be afraid of not including details if you think they are going to make your sketch too messy.

PERSPECTIVE

2. Determine which type of perspective your scene has.

Depending on where you are seated and what you have chosen to sketch, there may be a clear sense of perspective in your scene. Check for parallel lines in the floor tiles and/or the line of the ceiling.

I chose a scene with a zero-point perspective (page 17). Therefore, I will need to employ some of the techniques we discussed to imply depth, such as overlapping elements, scale and drawing distant objects higher on the page.

TIP: *If you are having trouble visualizing your scene as a flat 2D image, take a photo with your phone and study it. See how objects that are closer to you are much bigger and distant objects are smaller and higher up in the image? Do not draw from the photo. But study it for a while so you understand how a 3D scene works in 2D.*

PENCIL SKETCH

3. Take a few minutes and sketch some quick pencil marks so that you know where everything is.

This is especially important for a busy scene like this that includes people. They can and will move, or even leave. If you have a rough placeholder for where they were and the pose they were in, you can still fill them in using other people as reference. You can find more on people-sketching strategies on page 44.

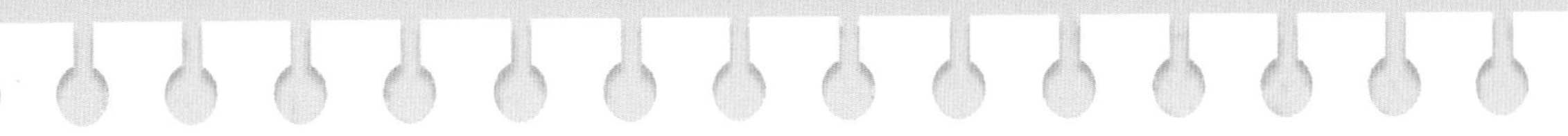

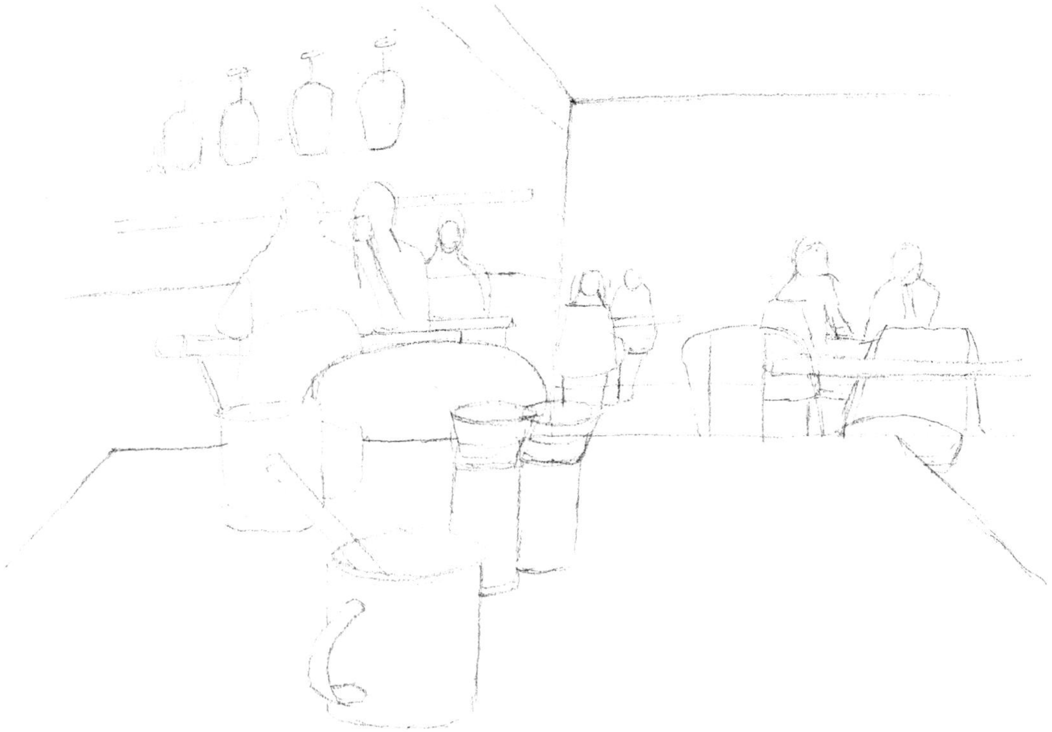

3

The pencil sketch is the skeleton, and it really helps with complex scenes. I started by drawing the cup with the pen because it's the closest object to me. To show depth, I made sure that it was larger than the cup behind it and drew it lower on the page. Using this first cup as a visual landmark, I drew the salt and pepper shakers and the second cup. I then drew the shape of the table followed by the seat tucked into it. After this, I drew the next closest items: the chair with the person sitting with their back to me, the person to the right of them and their table, as well as the empty table and chairs on the right of the scene. After this, I moved to things immediately behind them. In this way I built up the scene, layer by layer.

When you use pencil, only draw basic shapes, no details. The marks are placeholders just to make sure you get things on the page in the right place at roughly the right size.

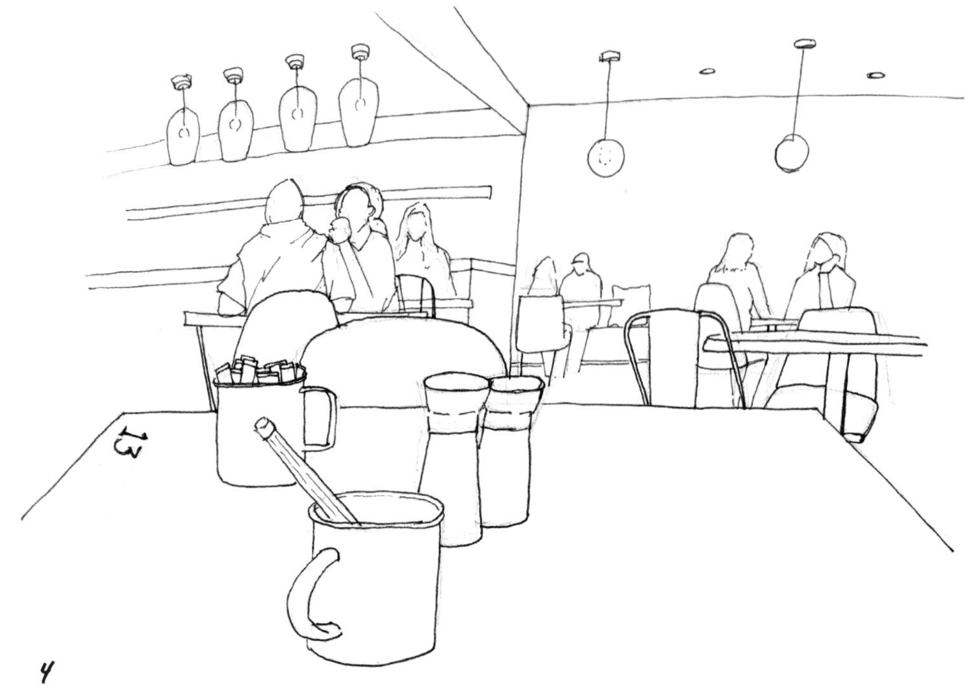

INK DETAILS

4. Use your pencil sketch as a guideline to ink the scene, correcting anything you may have gotten wrong and adding more details as you go.

I used a 0.2 fineliner to draw this scene. Much like the pencil stage, I started with the objects closest to me and then continued to draw the things behind, layer by layer. I drew both the outlines of objects as well as the details. Don't worry about wonky lines. They are unavoidable, and by the end of the sketch, you won't even notice them.

Once I had drawn everything, I decided to put some deep blacks in my sketch. I used a black brush pen to add the black poles of some of the tables and chairs.

TIP: *Notice I have not drawn the faces of the people. In this kind of scene, I didn't feel it was relevant. I actually enjoyed the effect of faceless people so I decided to keep them this way. I thought it was more important to capture their poses and interactions with the environment around them rather than their faces.*

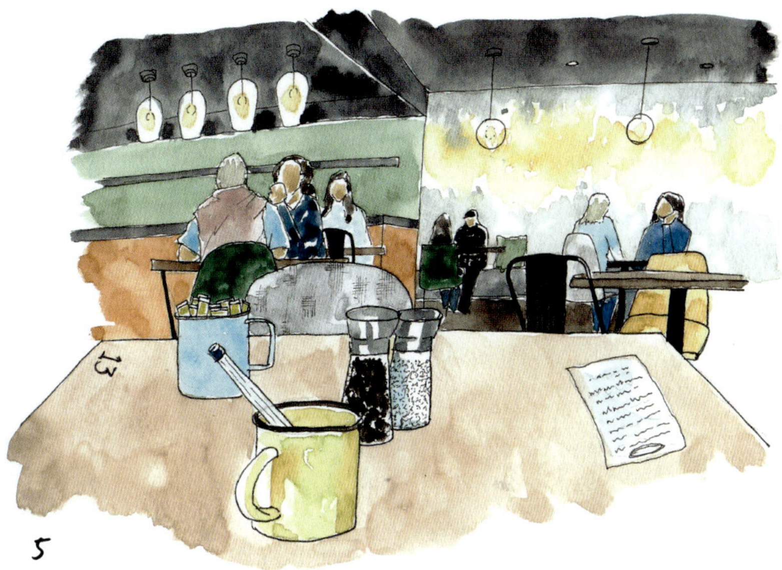

FIRST WATERCOLOR WASH

5. Start your first layer of watercolor with the biggest shapes and the lightest colors.

For my scene, that was the table in front of me. I kept the table fairly plain so I could draw some wood grain on it toward the end. Always start lighter; if you need to make things darker later, you can. Painting a second layer is completely fine and something I often do if I feel my first layer was too wishy-washy. Sometimes you need to see more of the sketch come together before you can make these decisions.

I continued painting the base color for the rest of the scene, trying to paint things that were the same color at the same time. Remember, you do not have to paint the exact colors as what you see in front of you. It's better to use consistent colors throughout your sketch as the results will be more pleasing to look at.

The wall at the back on the right of the sketch had an interesting pattern and texture to it. I wondered whether it would overpower my sketch if I added it but then I decided that since it's such a distinguishing feature of the location, I should try my best to indicate it. Notice I said indicate not replicate. I used the wet-on-wet technique (page 23) and put a clear strip of water across the middle of the wall, dabbing some Yellow Ochre in and letting it spread. I let this dry a little bit before adding some light gray to either side of it, letting a little bit mix with the Yellow Ochre but otherwise keeping a slight band of white between the two colors. I think this does the job without going into too much detail and inadvertently making the wall the focus of the sketch.

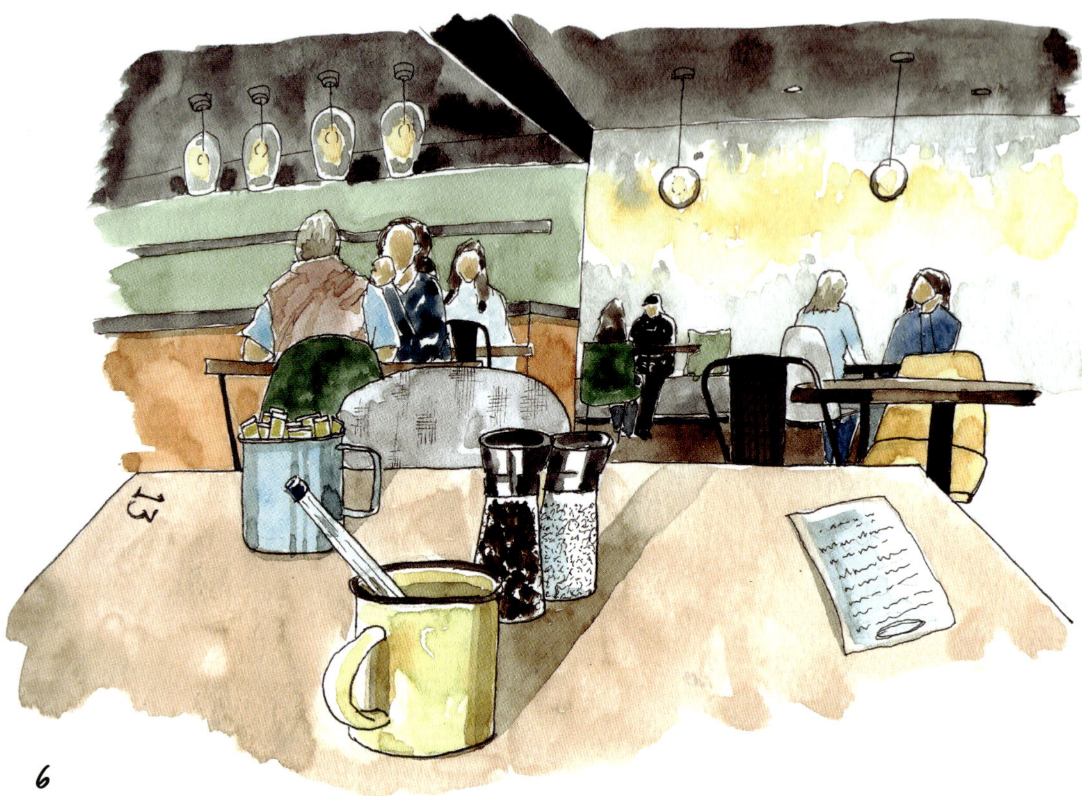

I encourage you not to be too tight with your painting. Leave some small gaps of white and don't worry if you don't go up to the lines. It will give the sketch a more relaxed look. The white gaps can be used to indicate highlights and light reflecting off things. This will make the end result far more interesting to look at than if you paint flat layers of color.

SHADOWS

6. Once your first layer is dry, refine your scene with a second layer of watercolor by making certain areas darker and adding shadows.

This is where the sketch starts to come together. There's actually not too much to add in my particular scene. I made the edge of the drop ceiling much darker; I also added some light shadows on the table in front of me—cast by the cups, condiments and the receipt—and added some more details to the glass light fittings.

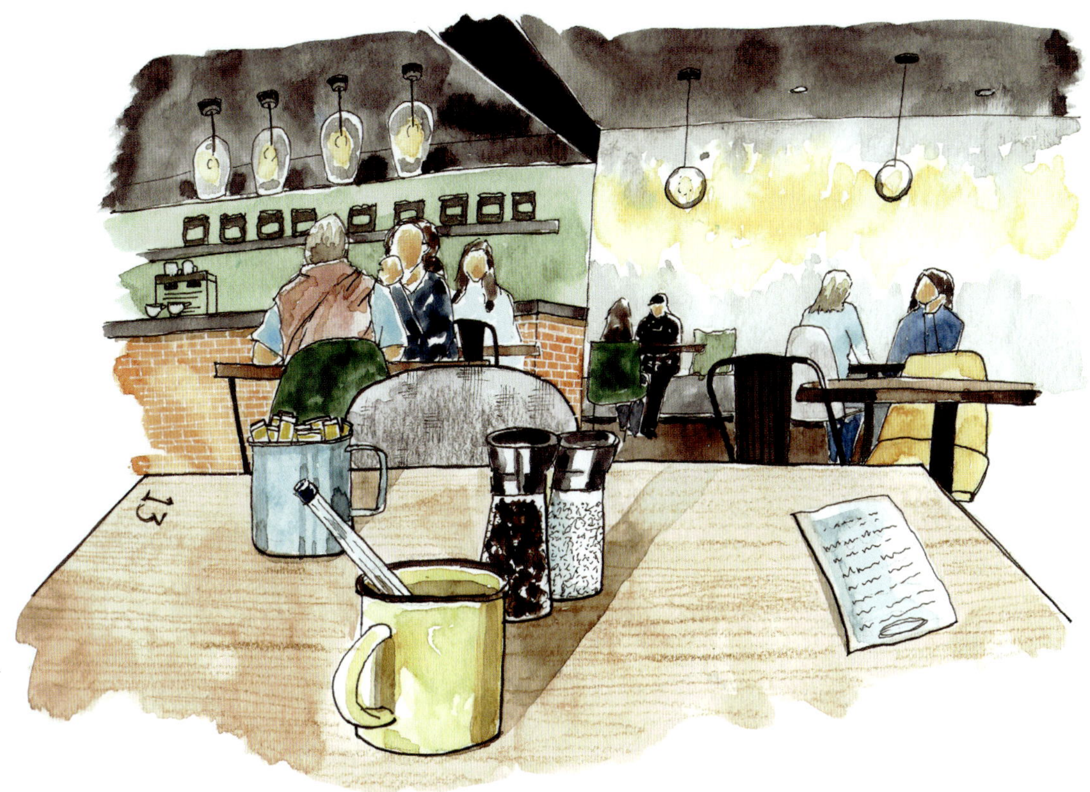

FINISHING TOUCHES

In the final stage of the sketch, I thickened some lines to emphasize my foreground objects and separate them from the background as well. I also realized I needed to add some objects on the shelf in the background. Sometimes you miss small details like this. It's fine to draw them at the end. Luckily the bags of coffee were a dark color so I could paint over the top of the green wall. I also added a subtle brick pattern under the counter. Finally, I decided to add some wood grain to the table in front of me as I felt there was too much flat color in the foreground that made it look boring. I used a brown color pencil and lightly drew lines across the table's surface. The pencil picks up the slight texture of the page to give the idea of wood grain. In fact, I liked the effect so much I decided to use the same technique again on the chair in front of me but used soft shading with a gray color pencil instead. This indicates the texture of the material on the chair. For more on creating texture, see page 36.

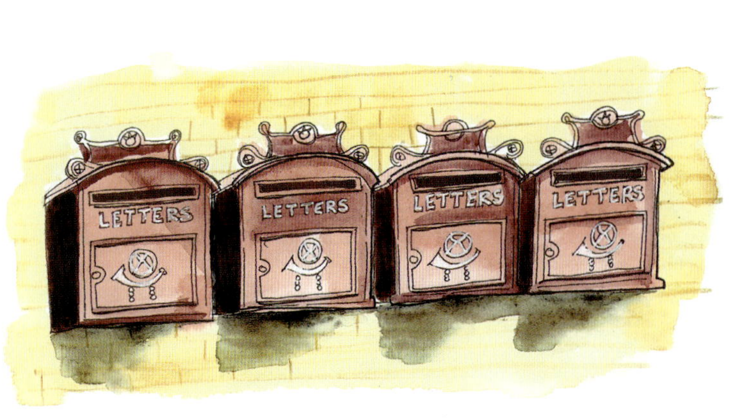

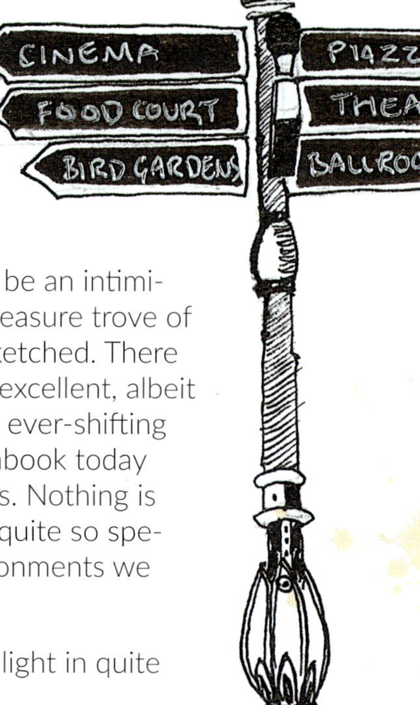

TAKE IT TO THE STREET

The street is an urban sketching mecca. It can be an intimidating place filled with clutter, or it can be a treasure trove of interesting shapes and colors begging to be sketched. There are a number of items in the street that make excellent, albeit unexpected, subjects to draw. The street is an ever-shifting landscape, and what you record in your sketchbook today may be gone the next month or next few years. Nothing is permanent, and that's why urban sketching is quite so special; it is a record of the transitory urban environments we inhabit.

After this chapter, you'll never look at a traffic light in quite the same way.

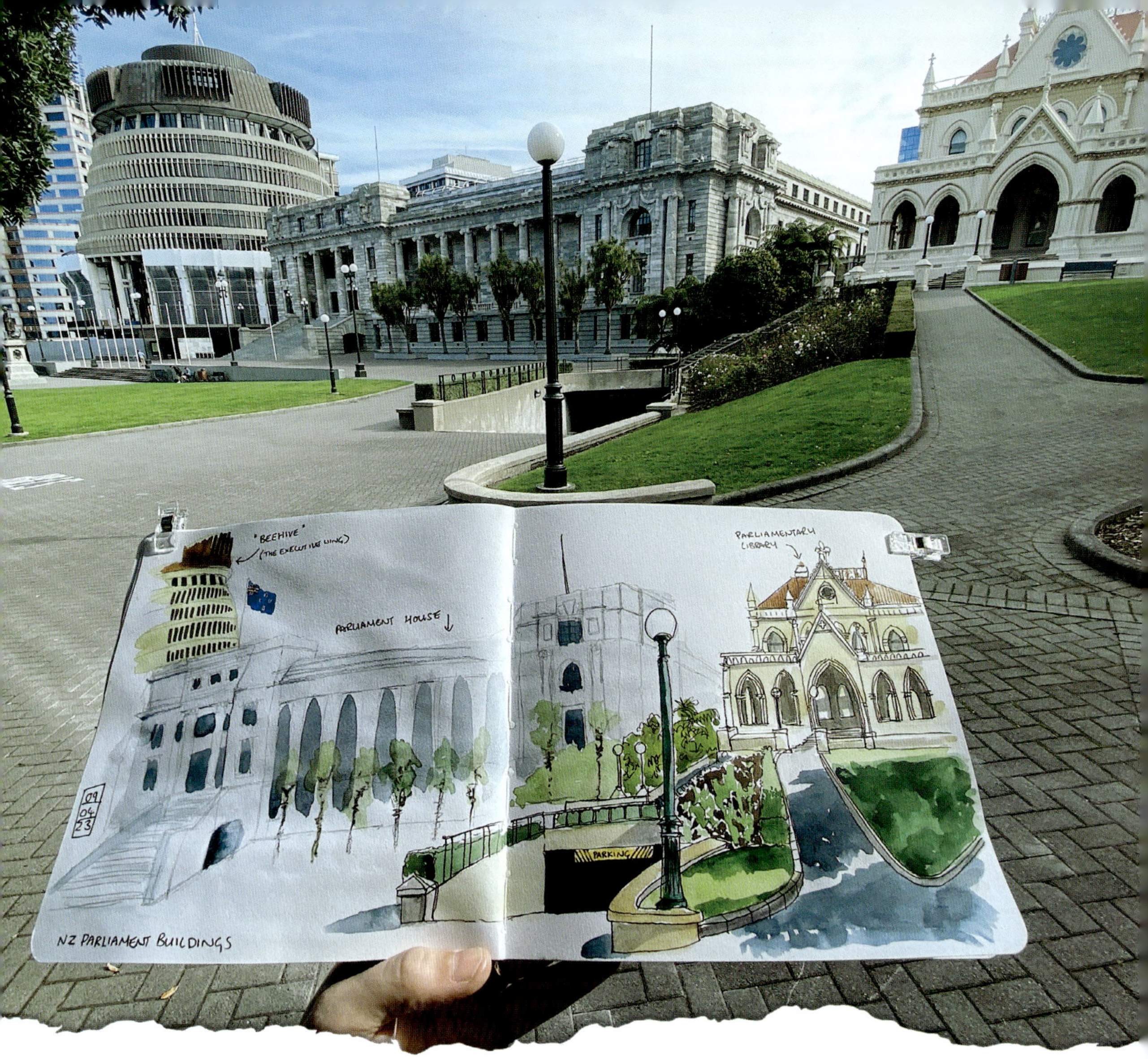

STREET FURNITURE

It may come as a surprise but street signs can make great sketches in their own right. The way you choose to interpret your subject matter can take a mundane item and turn it into an exciting piece of art.

For example, urban sketcher Pete Scully "collects" sketches of fire hydrants. Not the most exciting subject matter, but when you see the fire hydrants through Pete's eyes (and his sketches), you can't help but find them fascinating to look at.

What pieces of street furniture can you collect in your neighborhood? Look out for different types of benches, lampposts, street signs, phone booths, etc.

Admittedly, some neighborhoods may have more ornate street furniture than others but the point here is to see mundane items as exciting subjects to draw. No matter how plain they are, when they are captured in your sketchbook, they become fascinating.

ROAD SIGNS

An easy way to get started sketching outside is focusing on simple items with simple shapes: enter the humble road sign. It may not seem so exciting but road signs, traffic lights and general street clutter can be super fun to sketch. They have simple shapes and bright colors. You can sit on a bench on the pavement or perhaps at a bus stop or even in a parked car and observe the street signs. You do not have to draw everything in the scene.

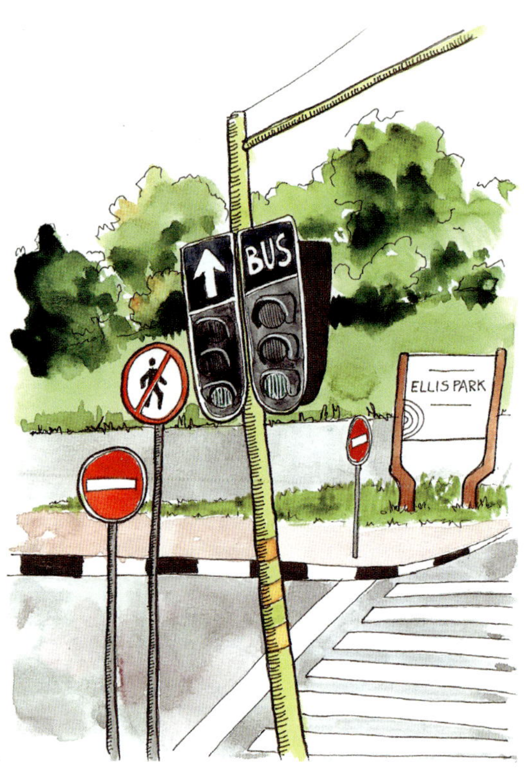

In this scene, I wanted to focus on the traffic lights and then build out with the other clutter of signs. I drew the pole holding the traffic lights at a jaunty angle. They were leaning slightly in real life, but I decided I would like to exaggerate this a little to make the sketch a bit more dynamic. Unfortunately, the traffic lights of Johannesburg are regular victims to cars. Many are severely bent or knocked over altogether!

The traffic lights and two other signs next to it are the foreground elements. The stop sign, Ellis Park sign and pavement are the mid-ground elements and the foliage at the back is the background.

I made the foreground elements bigger to show they are closer to the viewer. I also added thicker lines around them at the end of my sketch to make them bolder too. I then added some small hatch lines on the shadow side of the poles. This is not something I often do; however, I thought it added some interest in this particular sketch, and I like how it turned out. Notice that my lines that make up the poles are not completely straight and the round signs are not perfectly circular. Things like this really don't matter, yet they can cause beginners such anxiety. I doubt anyone can draw a straight line or a perfect circle freehand.

Another element of this sketch I really liked was the markings on the road. Without them there, I don't think the sketch would be so interesting. Notice how the road is not a flat gray color; when I painted it with Payne's Grey and the paint was still wet, I dabbed a tiny amount of Quinacridone Rose (reddish pink) in places. The pigment spread and softened as it dried, and it gave a little more visual interest.

Remember to be bold with these kinds of scenes. I think the more contrast (strong lights and darks) you can include, the more striking the scene. This helps to overcome the banality of the subject matter too. I didn't add a sky in this sketch as I wanted the large open area of white to balance with the dark area in the traffic lights. I thought the sketch would look more graphic that way. Experiment with this and see what you think. Take a photo of your sketch without the sky and then add a sky and take another photo. Assess which you think looks better. This may change depending on your scene, subject matter and how the sky looks.

LETTERING

Lettering on street signs tends to be blocky and very clear to read, so it can be easier to replicate than more ornate signs you find on shops and restaurants.

Urban sketcher Ian Fennelly doesn't even try to replicate the lettering he actually sees; he just does it in his own way, which I love. You can choose to be as accurate as you like with your lettering.

Either way, adding signs with lettering to an overall scene can help to add context of where you are. Don't be afraid to add even the most mundane road signs to your sketch. They add so much life to a sketch. Urban scenes can be mundane to the uninitiated but finding the magic in them is part of your role as an urban sketcher.

When I want to accurately portray lettering (as well as fit words into a certain amount of space), I find it helpful to draw some guidelines in pencil for the top and bottom of where the letters will sit. I do this roughly by hand and draw each letter in pencil too. I then thicken each letter by using a technique called "drawing through" to help me get the letter as even as possible. Drawing through refers to drawing every line, even though they don't need to be there or will be covered up when I fill the shape of the letter in. This is most evident in the "B" in image 2 below. Do you see how I have drawn the two curved parts of the "B" straight through the vertical shape? This helps to line everything up, and I know it will be covered up later by black ink or I could simply erase the pencil lines once I have drawn the outline of the letter in ink. By drawing a consistent thickness of each letter, it will help the sign look more legible. This process works well for all types of block lettering.

Some letters are trickier than others. An "S" for example, is a little more difficult because there are no straight lines. I draw the shape with a single line and then try to thicken either side of it evenly as I move around the shape. It takes a little practice.

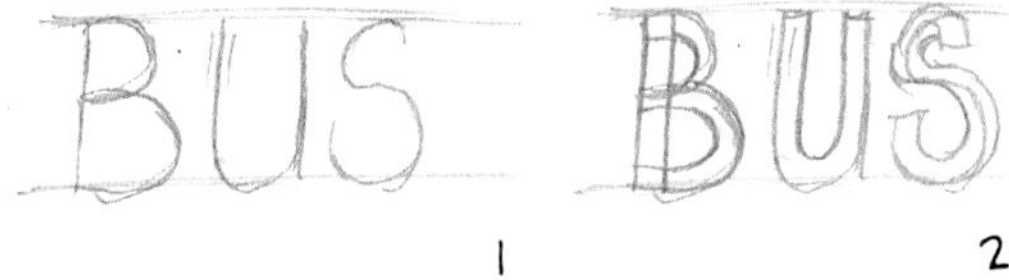

The other thing to watch out for is the spacing between each letter (image 3). In the example, you can see that the space between the "B" and the "U" is a little too large and knocks the word out of balance.

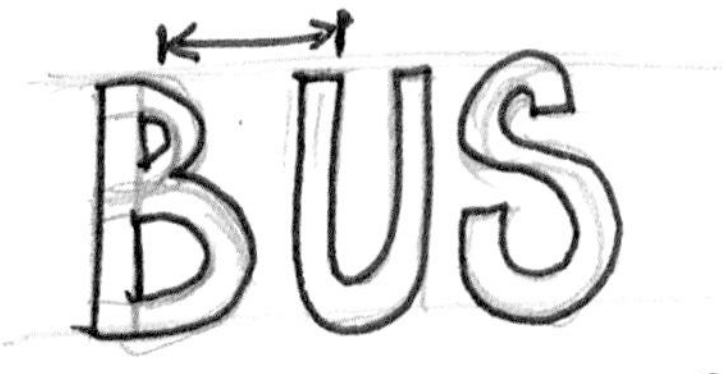

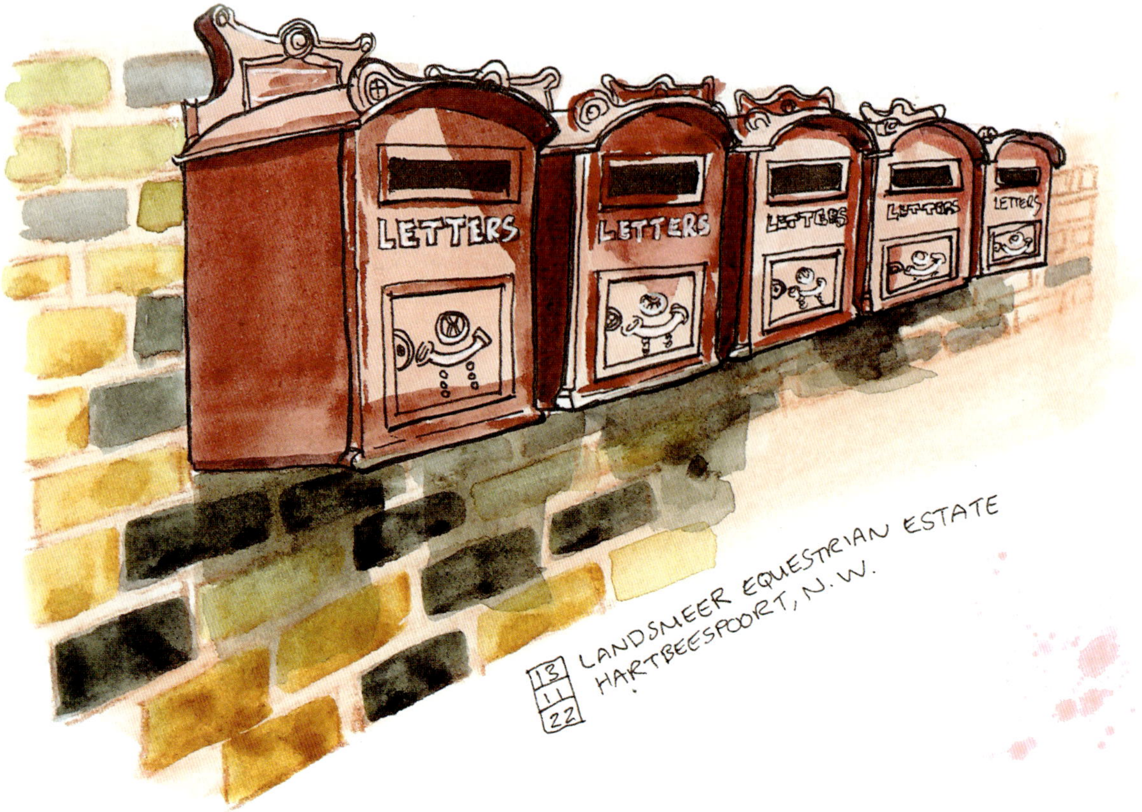

13/11/22 LANDSMEER EQUESTRIAN ESTATE
HARTBEESPOORT, N.W.

Of course, not all letters are blocks and sometimes you may have cursive fonts to deal with. In that case, I find it helpful to think of "drawing" letters (rather than writing) like they're just another element of your sketch. You can use pencil guidelines still and even draw the angle the letters slant on, along with the spacing. This will help you get a reasonable approximation.

MUNDANE TO MAGICAL

I came across this row of red post boxes. Seemingly mundane, yet they offered a beautiful sketching opportunity. These kinds of post boxes are actually not something you see in Johannesburg naturally, and I thought they were an interesting ornamental touch outside the housing complex they were attached to. I didn't want to spend too much time sketching them. The most important thing to me was to capture the essence of the first post box and to represent the perspective of them.

Can you see how sketching the post boxes at this angle (above) is far more interesting and engaging than if I had sketched them straight on (below)?

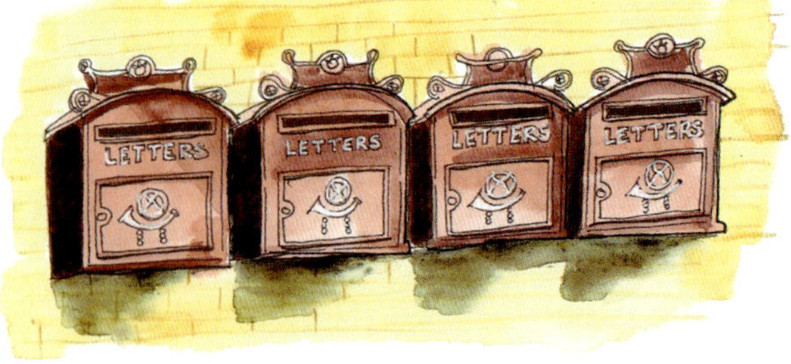

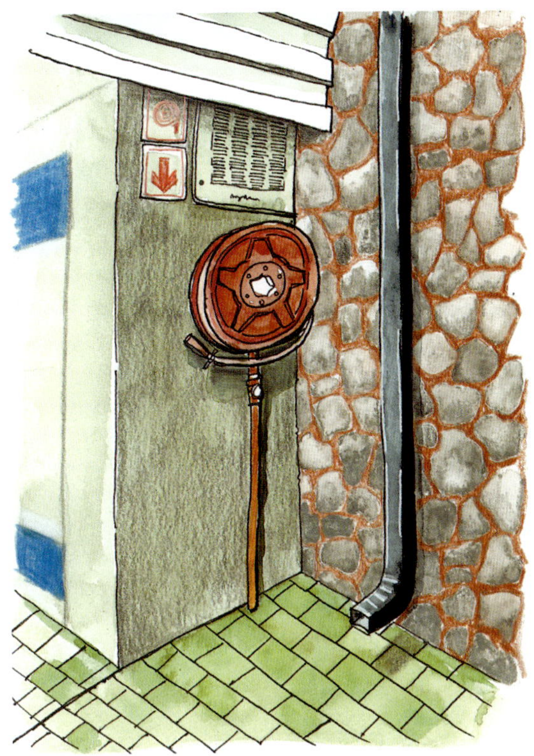

Another thing that caught my eye was this fire hose on the wall. Sometimes you just see very boring things like this, but your creative brain snaps to attention and calls you to sketch it. I really enjoyed sketching the wall texture in this scene. I decided to use a couple of watercolor pencils, one reddish brown and one gray. I created texture in the gray stones themselves with the watercolor pencils. On some stones, I wet the stone first and then colored over it with the watercolor pencil, and on others, I colored lightly with the pencil and then wet the area. I found I could get a nice variation like this. I also added watercolor pencil over the top of the dried watercolor layer of the wall the fire hose is attached to. By shading over the top of the watercolor layer, even on this smooth hot press paper, I achieved a nice texture to indicate the roughness of the wall. Watercolor pencils can be a useful addition to your urban sketching kit but are not essential.

The most boring of things can be turned into an interesting sketch. You can practice this skill around your home. I have sketched a dish sponge, plug extension boards, a pot of cooking utensils and even wind chimes. I make a game of it to see what different styles or weird colors I can use to make the subject more interesting. This is an excellent way of practicing sketching from observation, as well as experimenting with different styles.

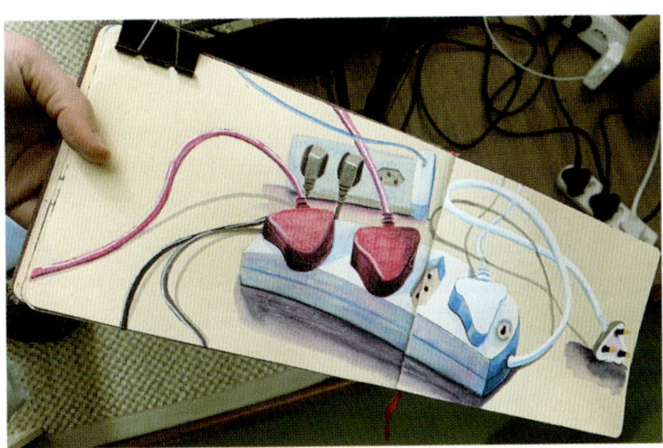

As you can see, you don't need to live somewhere like London, Rome or Paris to find inspiration for sketching. The art of urban sketching is to sketch whatever you see in front of you and tell a story, recording that specific moment in time.

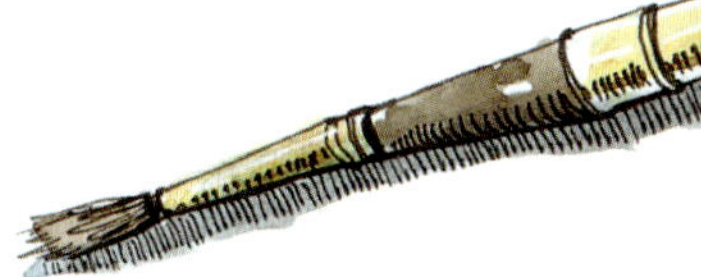

EXERCISE

1. **Get out in the street. Find a place you feel safe, whether at a bus stop or in your car, and assess the scene.**

I actually keep a note (whether mentally or physically) of places I see that I want to sketch. It can really help to eliminate aimless wandering if you already have a few locations in mind when you head out to urban sketch. It's great to have your sketching stuff with you at all times, but there's not always an opportunity to stop and sketch when you are going about your day. Having a little log for when you do have time is useful.

2. **Choose what you want to draw and decide what to leave out.**

I recommend focusing on singular objects to start with. If you have time and the inclination, you can add context afterward (other objects nearby and a background). It is up to you. Sometimes it may depend on how much time you have available.

How about sketching a streetlamp? Ornate streetlamps can be really fun to draw. While they can't be found everywhere, when you come across them, see if you can carve out some time to sketch them.

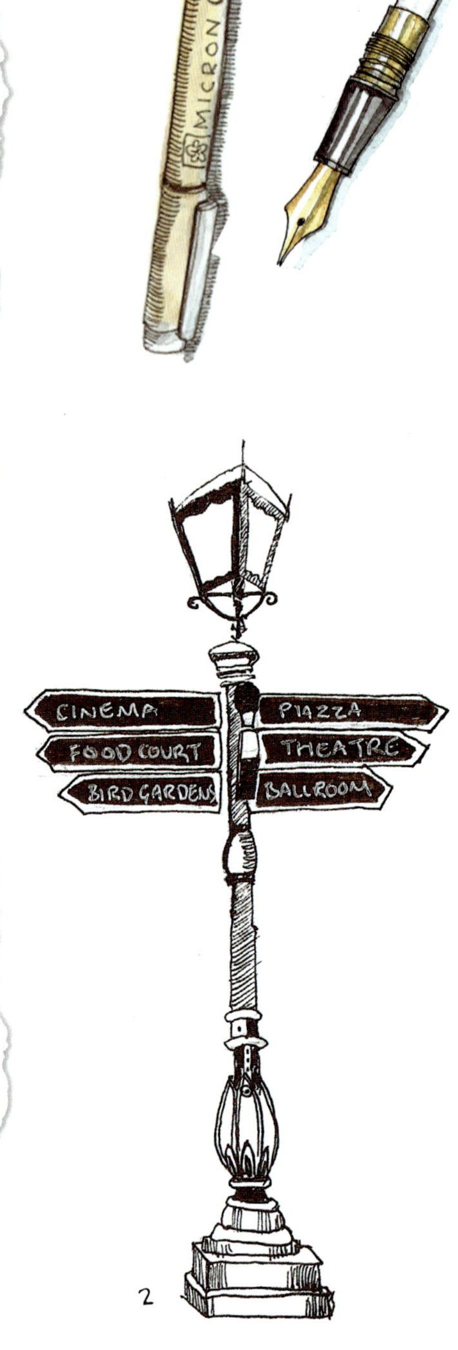

3. **Create a collection or collage (page 177) of similar items.**

This is a great way to record the differences of the same item from place to place. It also offers an opportunity for creative experimentation. The more comfortable you get with sketching an item, the more inclined you may be to try different ways of representing the subject.

And remember, you don't have to draw everything, just the bits that interest you. I really liked the ornate metal frame of the bench on the left, but didn't feel like drawing all of it. Next, I added a close-up of the ornamental armrest of another bench to fill in the rest of my page (3).

4. **Find inspiration wherever you look, even in the most mundane of items.**

You will start noticing and appreciating far more than the average person now that you are on the hunt for things to sketch.

In the UK, we have the iconic red telephone boxes. There is one in the village where I grew up, right outside the local pub. Although, it no longer has a telephone inside but a defibrillator instead (4)! I love how this sketch now tells a story of turning old into new, something useless into useful.

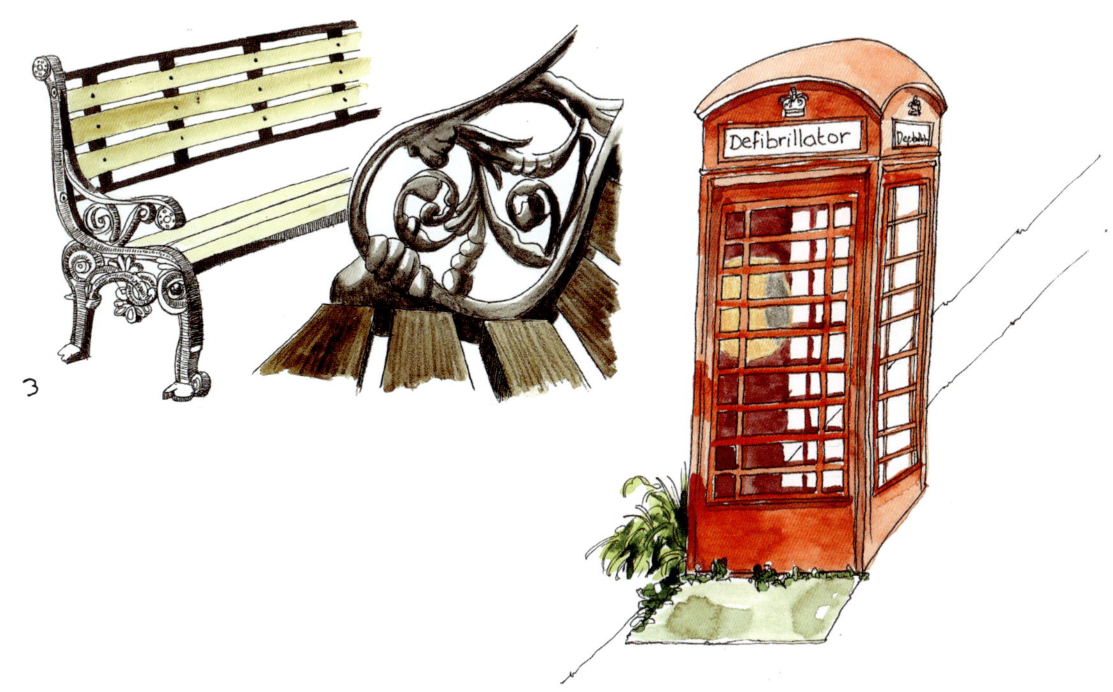

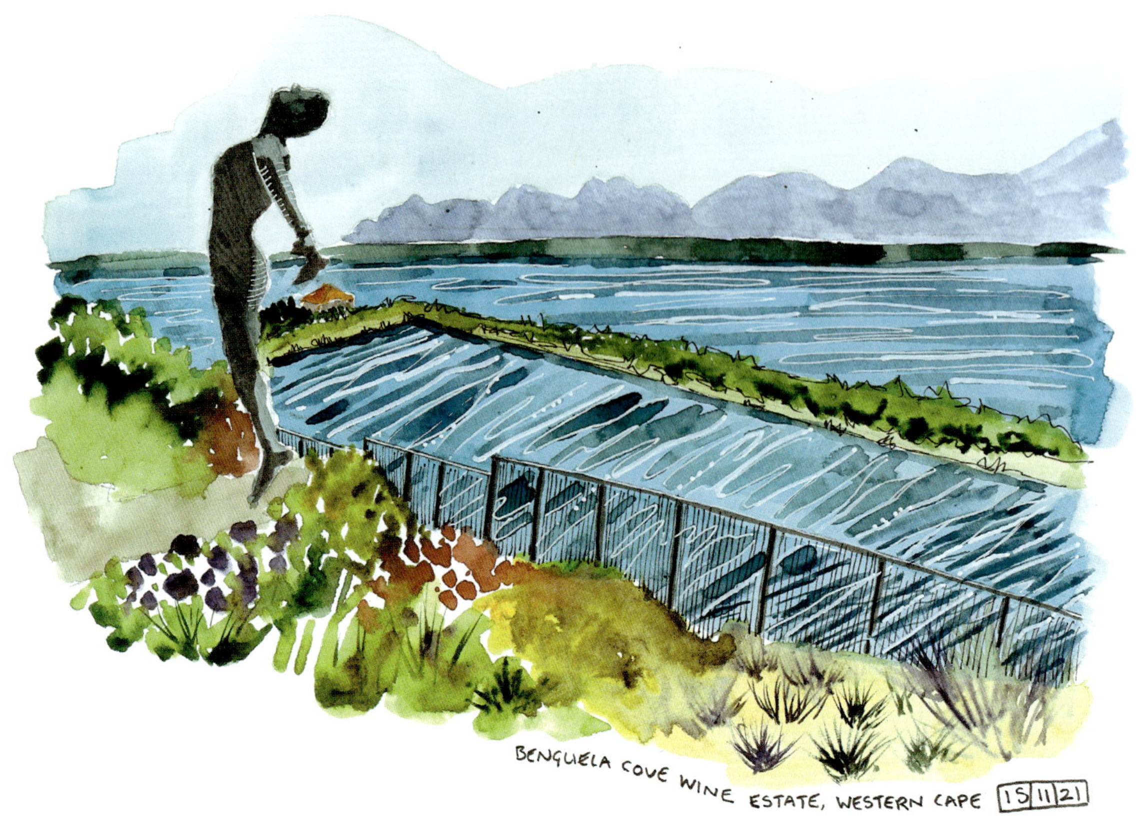

STATUES

Statues offer a great range of subjects to practice with, from objects to people to animals (or even people sitting on animals), with details such as folds of clothes, faces, hands and hair. As such, they can be difficult to sketch.

I recommend deliberately practicing statues as they can be challenging yet they're stationary so you can spend as much time sketching them as you want. Sketching statues can also help in other situations, such as sketching in museums (page 168) or sketching ornate architecture (page 126).

In the above example, I wanted to sketch the statue, but I didn't want it to be the main focus of the scene. I wanted to show the gorgeous surroundings of the Benguela Cove Wine Estate in the Western Cape of South Africa.

CONTOUR DRAWING

The best way to deal with statues is to simplify what you see.

In the following example, I tried to ignore what my logical brain was telling me: This is a man holding a child. I blocked out those thoughts and focused on drawing the overall outside shape (contour) of the statue. Draw the lines you actually see, not what you think you see.

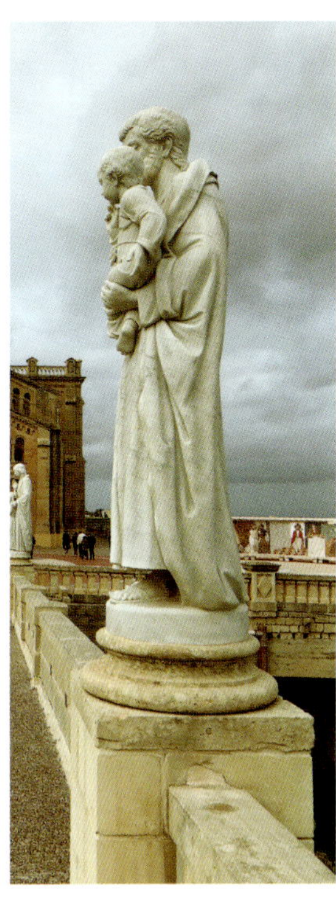

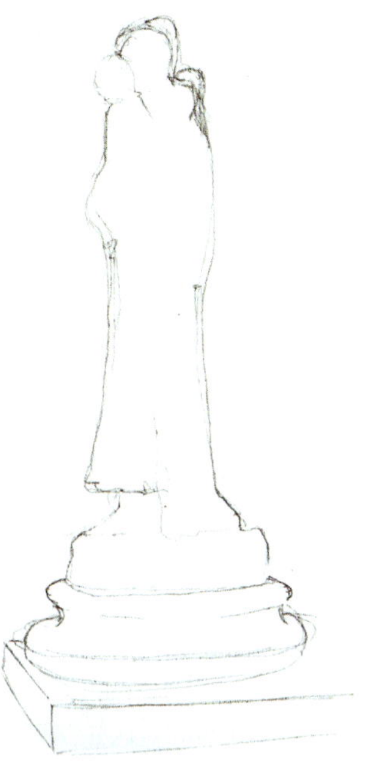

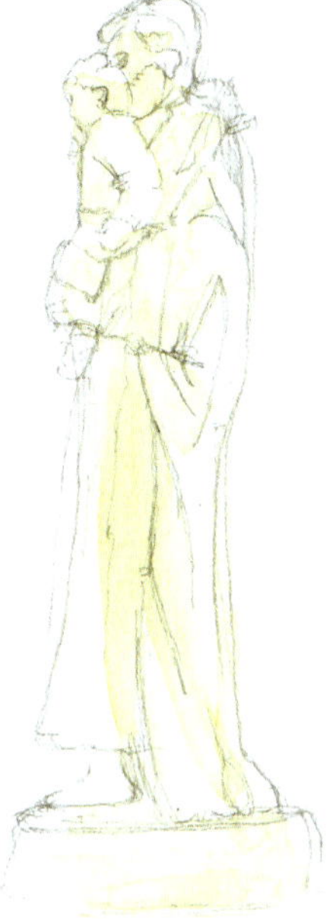

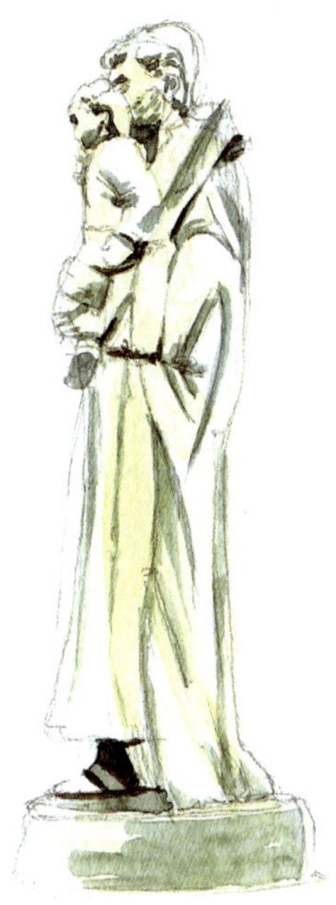

Once I drew the contour of the statue, I moved inside the shape and drew the details, correcting the contour as needed. This is a complex statue, and it's easy to get overwhelmed. However, by ignoring the subject matter and simply focusing on line and shape, along with where those lines and shapes meet and intersect, I built up the sketch of the statue.

At this stage, I could have inked the sketch and erased the pencil marks, but I decided I liked the sketchy pencil lines, so I simply painted watercolor over the top to see what it would look like.

Breaking a statue down into shapes of tone is a great way to start. As such, it is ideal to sketch a statue when it has strong lighting on it, i.e. strong highlights and shadows. This will make it much easier to paint the areas of tone.

I painted the statue with a base color of Naples Yellow, being careful to reserve some white of the page in certain areas where the highlights were. There wasn't extreme contrast on the statue, but I exaggerated the areas of highlights I saw so my sketch looked more dramatic.

My statue had highlights (the white of the page) and some mid-tones (the Naples Yellow I just painted), so I moved on to painting the shadow areas. Rather than use black or even Payne's Grey, I decided to use blue for the shadows. This makes the sketch more interesting. As the majority of the statue is Naples Yellow, blue will work well as a shadow color as it is a complementary color (i.e. opposite yellow on the color wheel). Ultramarine felt a little too bold, so I decided to dull it down slightly with some brown.

Blue and brown in equal parts do make black—and a far more nuanced and interesting black than if you were to use black straight from your set. Here are some example swatches. Can you see both pigments in some of the swatches and how much more exciting it looks than just using a flat gray or black? Test the blues and browns you have in your watercolor set to see what mixes you can achieve.

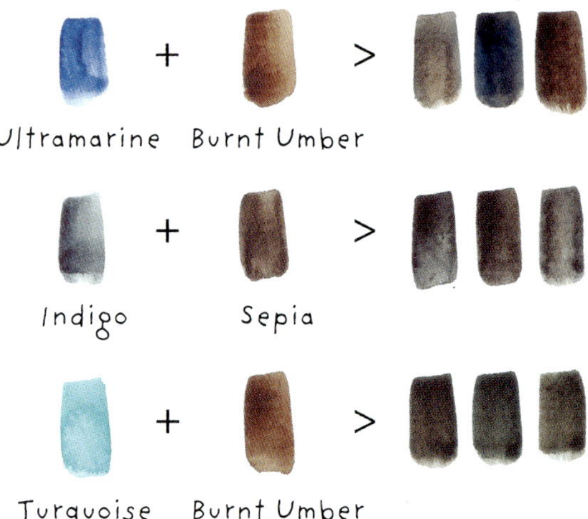

ADDING BLACKS FIRST

Another strategy I enjoy using is to draw the contour of the statue but then add areas of black with a brush pen for the shadows, followed by watercolor. I used this strategy when I sketched these sculptures in the William Ricketts Sanctuary in Victoria, Australia.

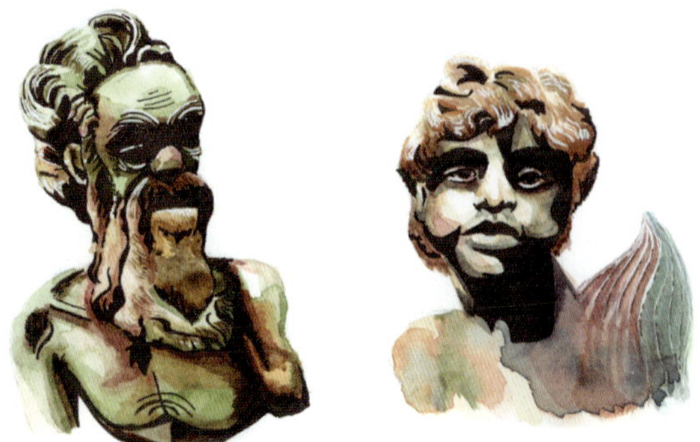

WILLIAM RICKETTS SANCTUARY, VICTORIA

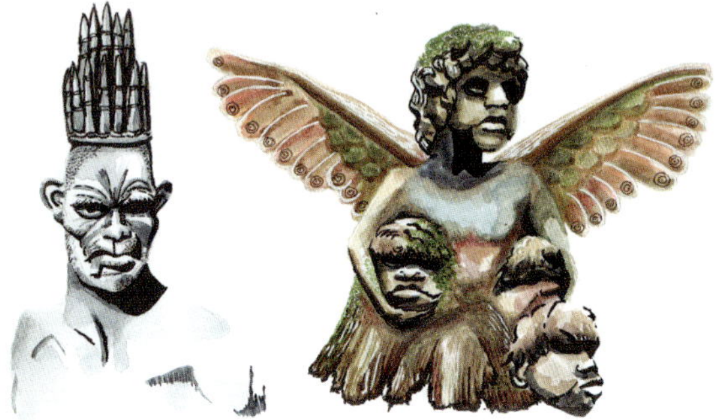

In this next example, the elephant statue holds such a dynamic pose, it seems as though it's mid-action.

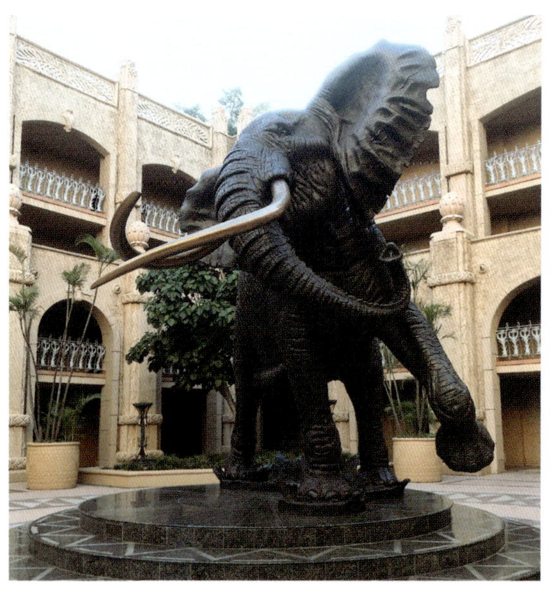

While quite an intimidating subject, I started in the same way as the previous example. I ignored my brain shouting, "It's an elephant!" and that it should be drawn in a certain way.

I think it actually helps that the statue is not in an orthodox pose and recommend picking statues with more unique poses because it forces you to look much harder to figure out the shape rather than letting your brain guess what the shape should be. I focused on the contour of the statue; however, there were some key elements of the statue inside the contour shape, so I also drew some of the details inside the big shape to help me. For example, I needed to put the trunk in, even though it doesn't really form the outer shape from the angle I was looking. Putting the trunk in helped me establish visual landmarks so I could draw the tusks and, in fact, the entire bottom half of the statue.

I concentrated on where the lines should go in relation to the other lines. I didn't think to myself, "That's a leg" and then draw what I think an elephant leg looks like. We don't realize we do this when we draw; it happens automatically. A major clue that you are doing this is that you are looking at your page far more than your subject matter.

After I drew the outside shape and the smaller details inside, I added areas of black with a brush pen. This can be a very helpful way to establish shadow shapes. It feels like you are sculpting the statue on the page. It's a very stylized way of sketching a statue.

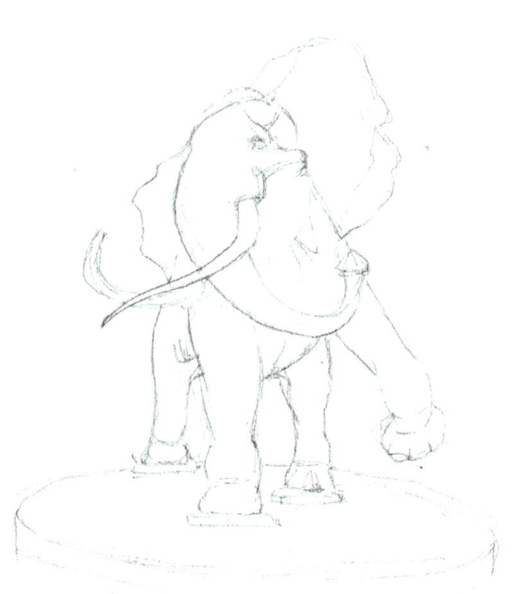

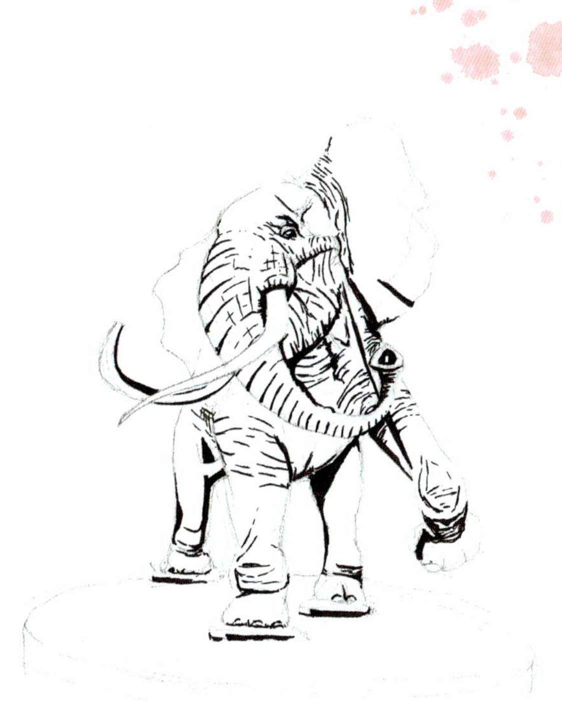

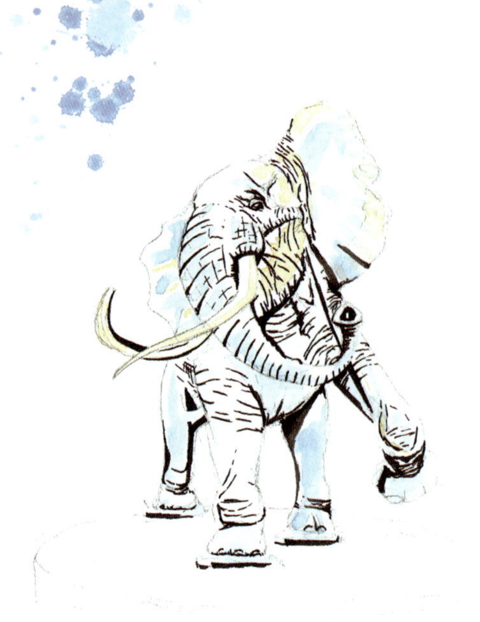

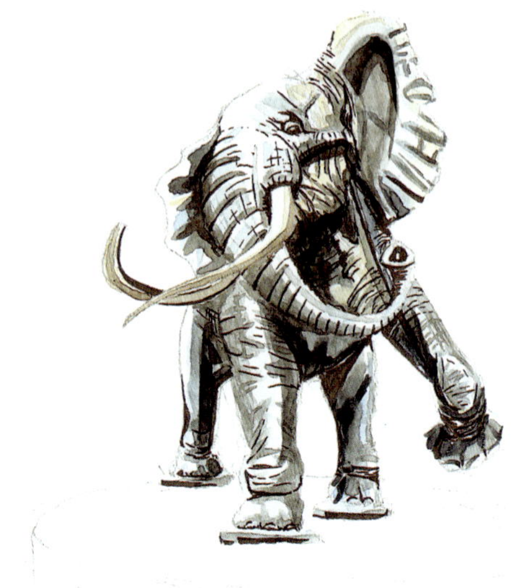

I added some light Yellow Ochre and blues to map in some of the mid-tones. The statue is black, but if you really look at it, you can see golden tones where the surrounding buildings are reflected in the shiny surface, as well as blues.

Avoid painting something a flat color (unless it really is a completely flat color). When you observe closely, you will find a variety of colors in something that seems as though it's one color.

In the final stage, I mixed some Ultramarine (blue) and Burnt Umber (brown) to make a more nuanced version of black. I squinted my eyes to try to find the darkest areas of the statue. As I used the same color mix for this entire stage, I increased the amount of water (instead of pigment) on my brush to give me lighter tones. I focused on the shapes of tone I could see and slowly built the sketch up. I also added some indications of texture, such as the folds and wrinkles of the skin, with the point of my brush.

This is a bit of a different technique but it's one that may resonate with you or something you may find useful for sketching a particular statue or scene.

ADDING SURROUNDINGS

So far we have considered statues as the focus of our sketch. Now let's look at how we can add context.

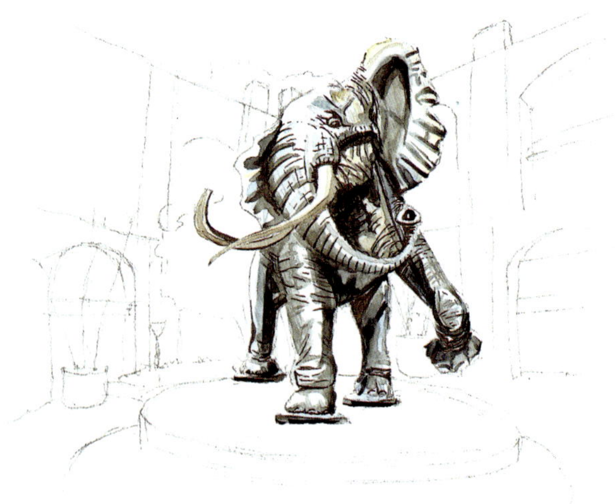

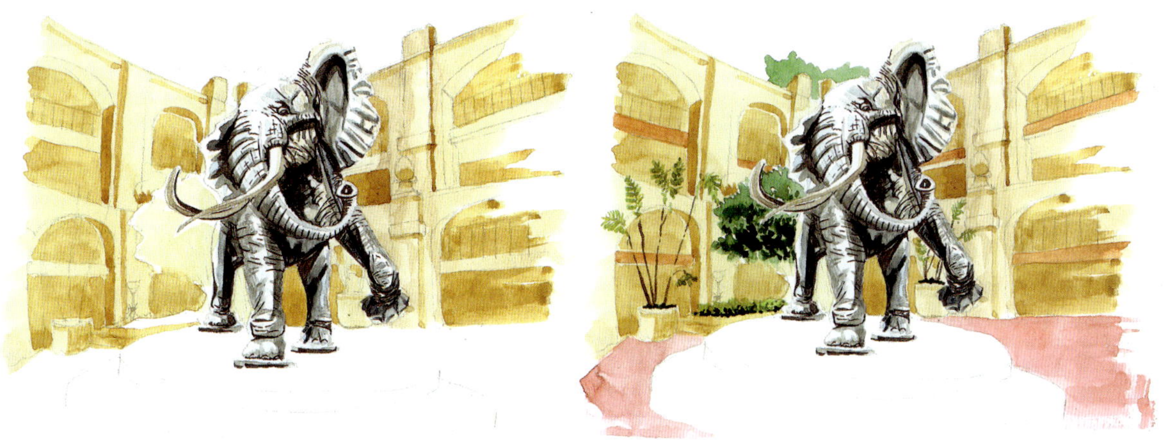

I placed the elephant statue in the center of my page, which is often not the most interesting composition; however, the statue is so striking and the somewhat symmetrical buildings behind it lend themselves well to this type of composition. Remember, rules are there to be broken . . . sometimes.

If the statue is a key feature of your scene, make sure it's clearly in the foreground. Sketch it first and then build the background around it afterward.

In this particular example, I already painted the elephant. You don't need to paint the statue first in your scene. You can draw it first and then paint the whole scene at the same time.

The most important thing at this stage is not to overpower the elephant statue. It's the "hero" of the sketch. I don't want to get too busy with all the background details, as it will entirely detract from the elephant. Notice I haven't gone overboard drawing all the details in the buildings. I have kept them very simple, and I have trailed the background off on either side of the sketch.

As the elephant was drawn in pencil, with no ink, I kept the background entirely in pencil too. It's not something I do all the time but it felt natural for this sketch, and I didn't want to draw the background in ink when the elephant isn't, as it would make the background too prominent. The background needs to stay vague so as to infer a sense of depth, as well as focus.

I painted the warm stone color of the buildings first as that's the lightest color, and I could overlay the green of the foliage and any shadows over the top. Try to mix up enough color to paint the whole area. I wasn't too concerned about getting a smooth, flat wash of color, as the buildings have some texture in them anyway.

Once this first layer was dry, I added a darker version of the base color for the areas of gentle shadow. Following that, I added some other details, such as the foliage and a light pink on the ground. In reality, there are some geometric designs on the floor, but I decided to leave them out, again not wanting to detract from the subject of the sketch.

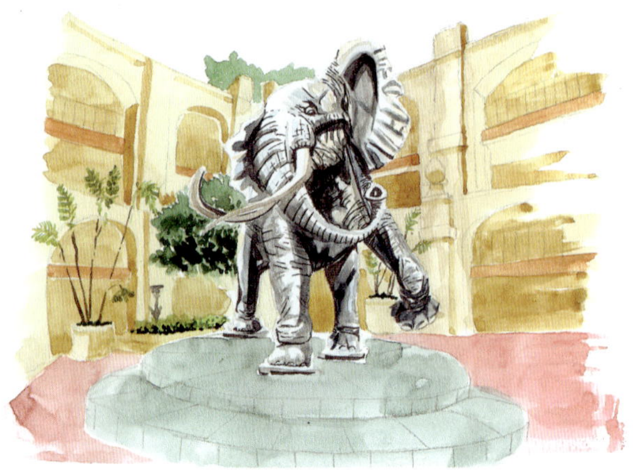

The final stage is to add the darkest colors: the stepped plinth the statue stands on and the darker shadows in the background. Again, I didn't want to add too much detail to the tiled plinth the elephant is standing on, but I didn't want it to be one color either. I settled on drawing a simplified version of where the tiles are and then painted a fractionally darker shade in between those lines, purposefully leaving a sliver of the base color shining through. I did the same on the vertical part of the step but with a darker shade, as those areas are slightly more in shadow. This gives a nice soft effect but still indicates a little detail.

I decided not to add a sky; I felt like it would look better without.

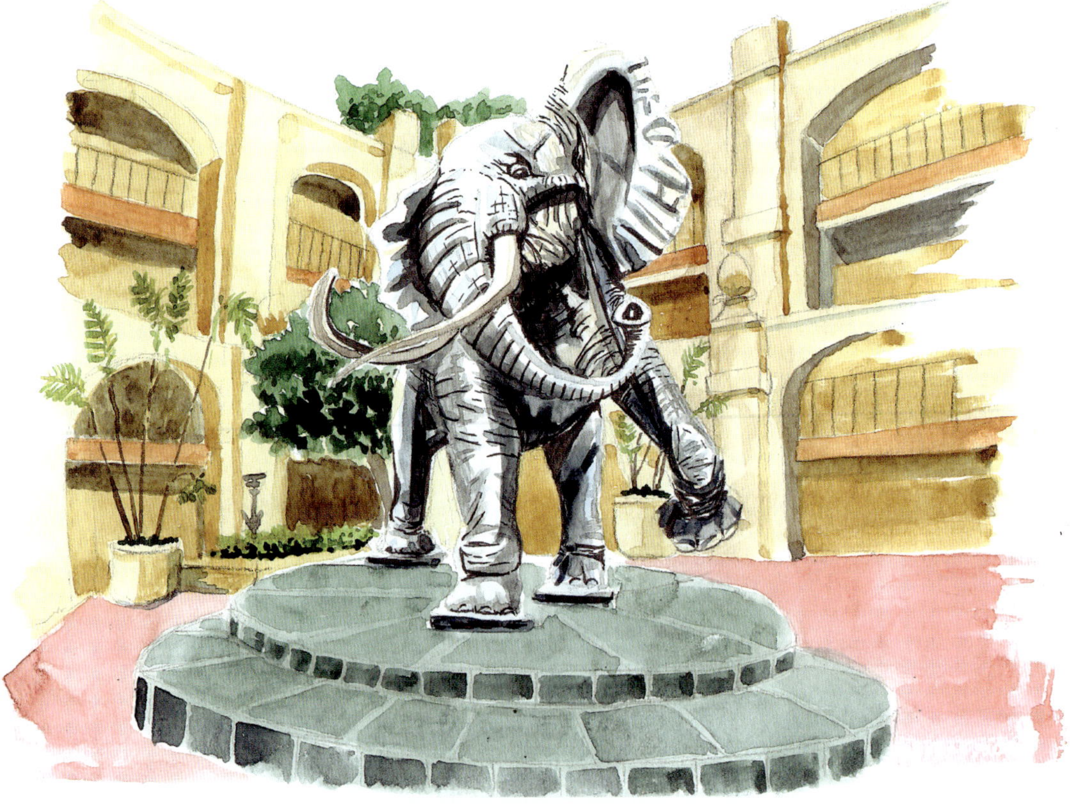

EXERCISE

1. **Find a simple statue to draw.**

You can build up to more complex subjects over time but try to find a statue that's a single subject (rather than multiple people, someone riding a horse, etc.). Also, look for a subject in strong lighting where there are defined shadows.

Draw the big shapes first. Focus on the proportion of the statue and how each element relates to itself in terms of size.

TIP: *You can find statues of any scale in many different contexts. One of my favorite places to sketch is the cemetery. I know that sounds odd, but old cemeteries contain an incredible collection of interesting statues, from well-kept to decaying. There's so much variety, and generally, they are very peaceful, beautiful places to spend a few hours drawing. They are also a great place to go if you are a little shy to sketch in public currently.*

I have a YouTube video of me sketching this scene on location. In case you would like to watch it, I have included the link in the PDF workbook you can download for free from learn.sketchyouradventures.com/workbook.

2. **Isolate the shadow shapes of your statue.**

Draw your statue in pencil and mark the shapes of the shadow areas lightly. Use a dark blue and paint the shadows first. Or you can be more extreme and use a black brush pen like I did in the sculptures on page 62.

Explore how painting the shadow shapes helps define the rest of the statue. Use this as an exercise and don't worry too much about the finished result. This will train you to think in shapes of tone (i.e. shadows, mid-tones and highlights) rather than literally drawing the subject in front of you. Not every sketch has to start with drawing lines.

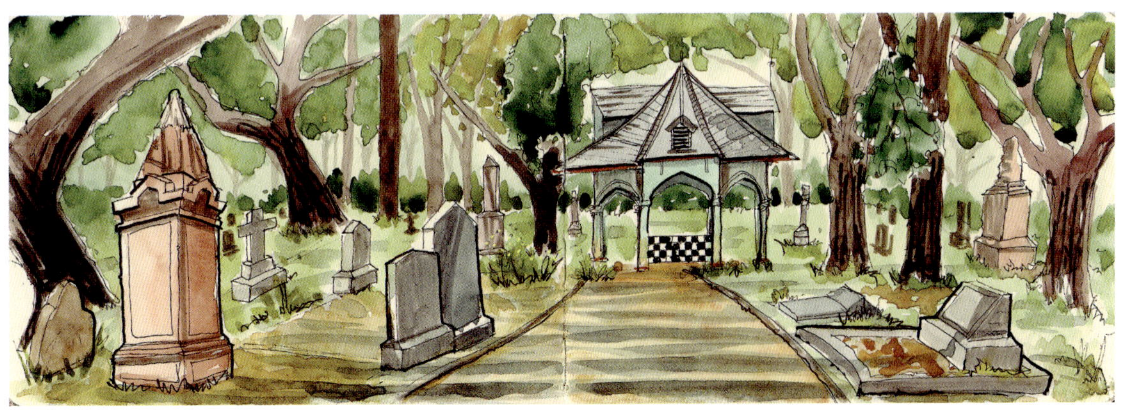

SKETCH A SCENE

WHAT'S THE FOCUS?

Sketching an entire street scene is naturally going to be a subject you will want to draw as an urban sketcher. However, there is usually so much going on and so many details to catch it can get overwhelming quite quickly.

In previous sections, we have covered how zooming in on particular details of a street can lead to just as much satisfaction as sketching an entire street scene. In this section, let's explore how we could sketch the entire scene.

COMPOSITION

1. In this first example, let's forget about perspective. Look for a scene with a main focal point or point of interest—something that inspires you to sketch.

Make sure when you select a scene to sketch that you are setting yourself up for maximum success. There has to be something to pin the drawing on, a focal point, even if it's a sign or traffic light in the very foreground.

The distinct point of interest in this scene (for me) was not just the building but more specifically the yellow and brown tower part with the glass windows on top and the roof, which in my mind looks like a hat! I also liked the way the road cuts through the foreground part of my composition (1A).

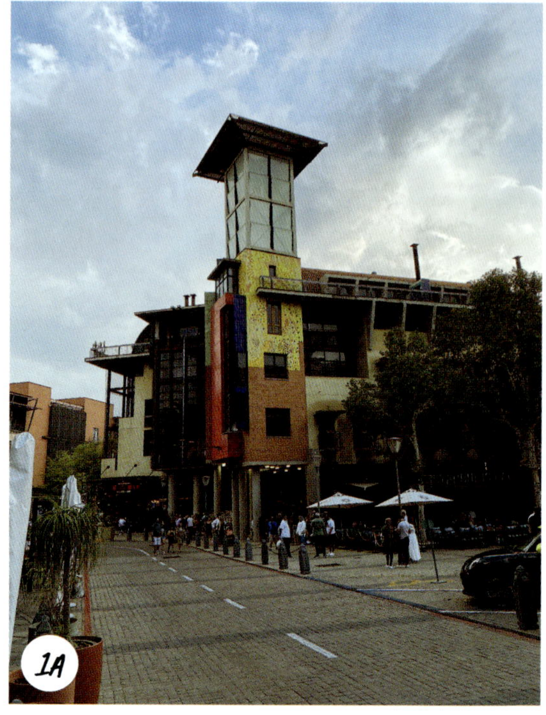
1A

Even though we are not focusing on perspective, the road helps show some depth to the scene (1B). I had to make sure there was a clear foreground, so I chose to emphasize some of the plants on the left. Remember, it's totally okay to edit what you see. You can skip some things you don't want to draw, but you can also emphasize things. It's your sketch, and you are at liberty to bend reality to make it more fun for yourself.

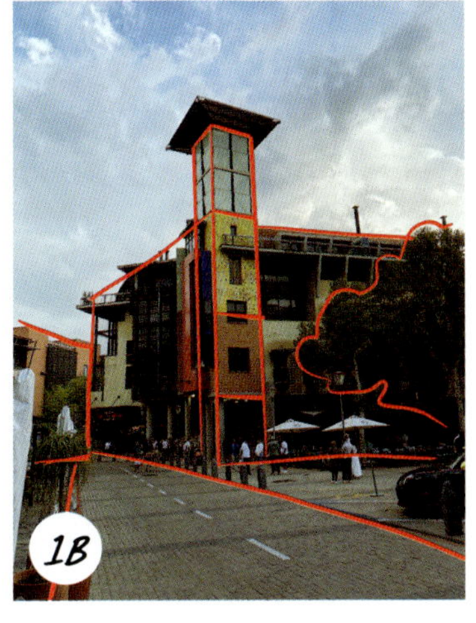

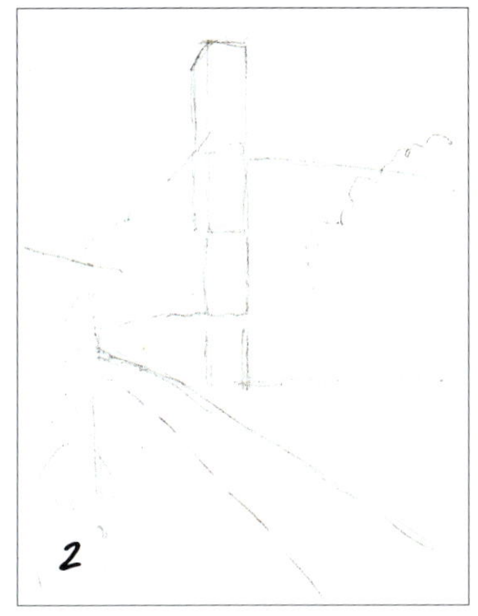

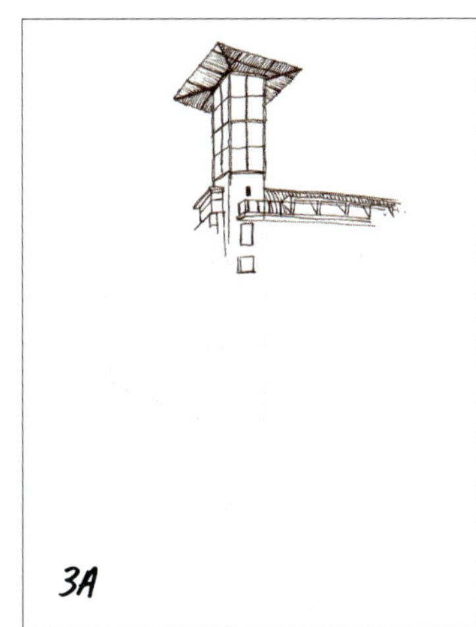

PENCIL SKETCH

2. Start by mapping the big shapes in pencil.

Simplify what you see as much as possible and just get the basic shapes on the page to make sure everything fits.

INK DETAILS

3. Add ink details on top of the pencil sketch, starting with your area of focus.

A great way to create emphasis is to not add detail to every single area of your sketch. Put lots of detail in your area of focus and less detail in other areas, especially in the background (3A). I have trailed my sketch off on the right side significantly, and there's not too much detail on the left either, aside from the foreground plants (3B). I finished off by adding some very basic marks to indicate people in and around the restaurant areas. For more information on how to sketch people in a scene, see page 44.

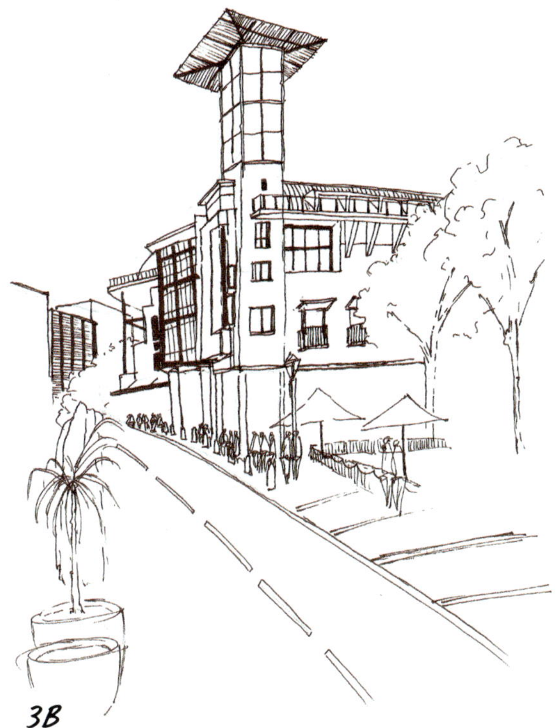

TIP: A good way to get a mixture of thin and thick lines in your inking stage is to use a fountain pen with a fude nib. These nibs are bent and allow you to make different weighted lines depending on which angle you draw with, leading to a very expressive line quality. As you progress, you may want to explore these pens further. You can find more information at:

learn.sketchyouradventures.com/workbook

FIRST WATERCOLOR WASH

4. Paint the lightest base colors of your scene.

When you mix a color, paint everything in your sketch that is the same color. It's economical but also ensures consistency throughout the sketch.

I started with a Yellow Ochre for some of the building. I used a flat brush because it's easier to paint objects with straight edges. I added a tiny bit of Ultramarine blue to the Yellow Ochre to tone it down in order to paint the cement posts under the building.

I continued by painting a lot of the neutral tones in the scene, varying my mixture of Ultramarine and Burnt Sienna to achieve different grays.

TIP: When painting windows, don't paint them a solid color. A lot of the time the sky and clouds are reflected in the glass. It looks much more interesting if you leave some tiny areas of white peeking through to hint at this.

I finished off by painting a purple-gray on the pavement area of the ground (4A). I did this by adding a tiny bit of Quinacridone Rose into my existing gray mixture (Ultramarine + Burnt Sienna). I hadn't painted the road yet because I was considering leaving it unpainted. I painted more of the scene to see how it looked before making that decision.

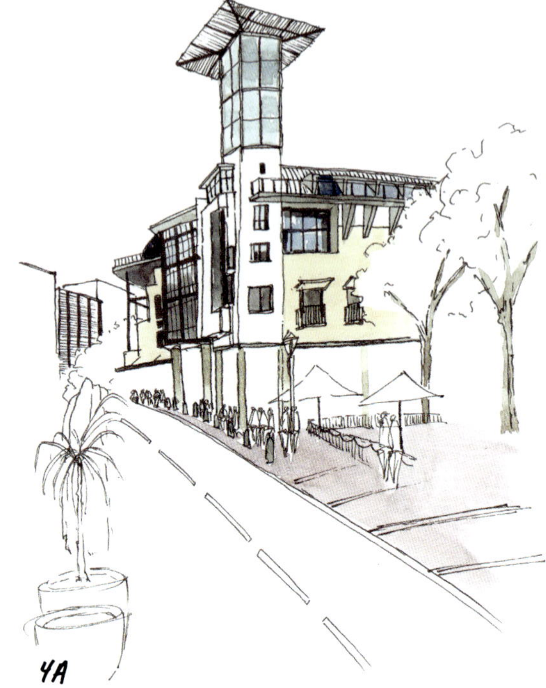
4A

When painting foliage, similar to the tip about the windows, don't paint it a solid color. Leave tiny flecks of white here and there to infer light shining through the leaves (4B). For the foliage in this particular sketch, I used a mixture of Lemon Yellow and Ultramarine. Once the base layer of green was dry, I made the mixture darker by picking up more pigment than water on my brush but also adding more blue than yellow into my mixture.

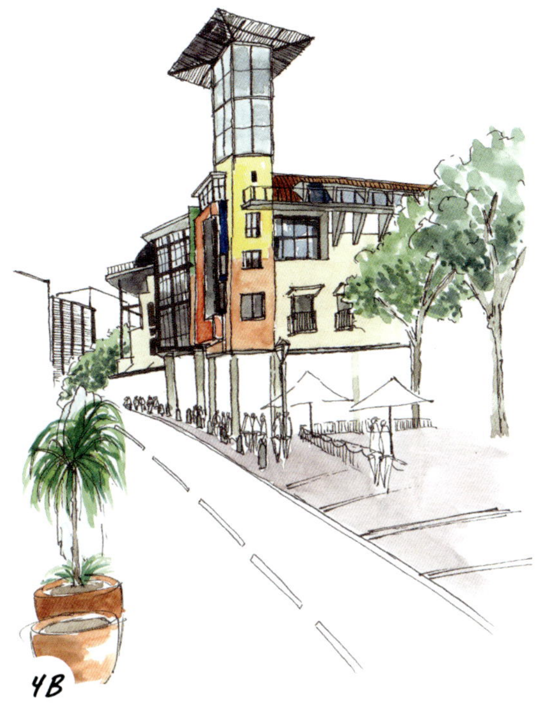

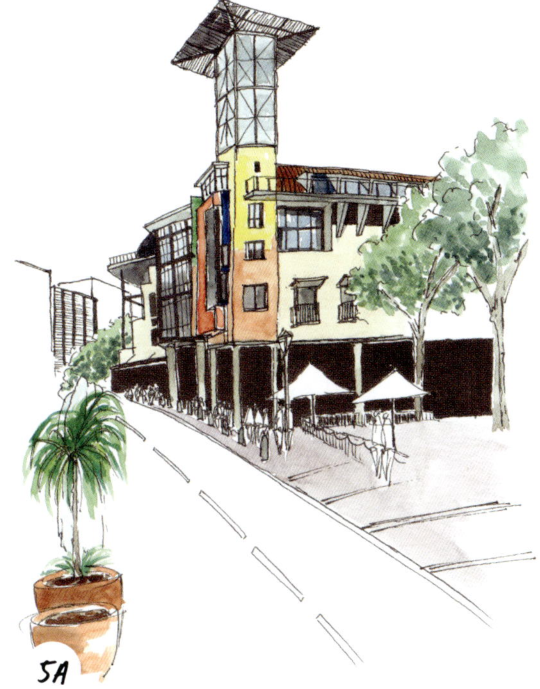

FINISHING TOUCHES

5. Add solid areas of black with a brush pen.

The solid black areas emphasize the people, as do the white umbrellas (5A). This is a stylistic decision, but I think it gives the sketch more contrast and therefore makes it look more exciting.

After adding the areas of black, I decided it would look strange to keep the road unpainted (5B). The large area of white paper was distracting and leading the eye away from the area of focus.

Don't be afraid to take liberties with the colors you use; you do not have to be true to life. I have kept the background buildings on the left side of the page unpainted, as I didn't want any emphasis taken away from the main building that is my focal point.

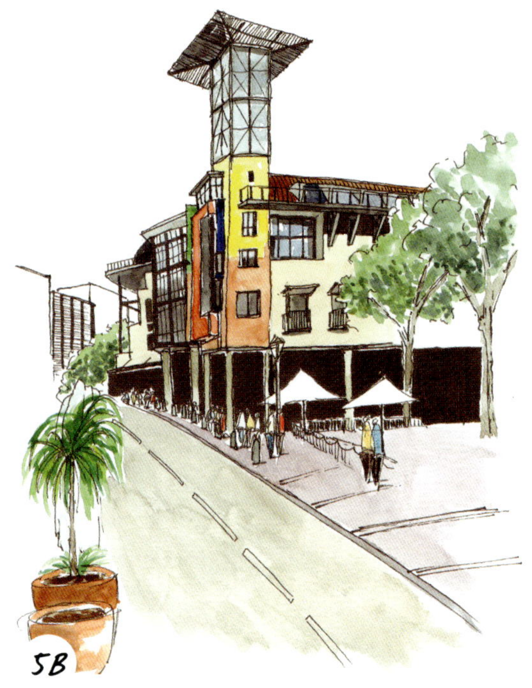

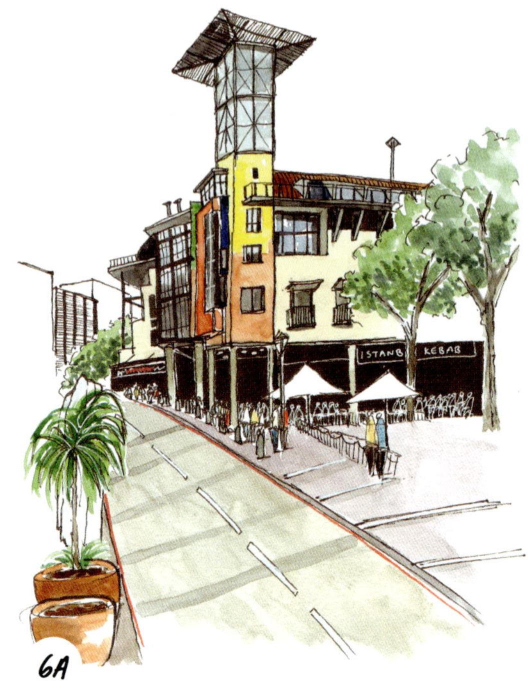

6. Add some finishing touches.

Once the black areas were dry, I used a white gel pen to draw some of the signs over the top. I also decided to draw some people in certain areas to emphasize how busy the area was and to indicate there were people inside some of the restaurants. As you can see, the figures I drew are extremely basic and quick.

I then used a red paint marker to put in the "no stopping/parking" lines at the edge of the road (6A). I wanted to put this pop of color in for interest but also to make it a little more clear what was going on in the left side of the sketch. If you don't have a paint marker, you could use a red color pencil or even red watercolor paint. A lot of bright red pigments are very strong, and if you use lots of pigment and barely any water, you can get a very strong color. You will need a brush with a good point and a steady hand to paint the thin lines!

As the final step, I decided to paint the sky (6B). I often find I paint the sky last as sometimes I think sketches look better without a sky, but with this particular scene, I feel the light blue area pulls the whole piece together.

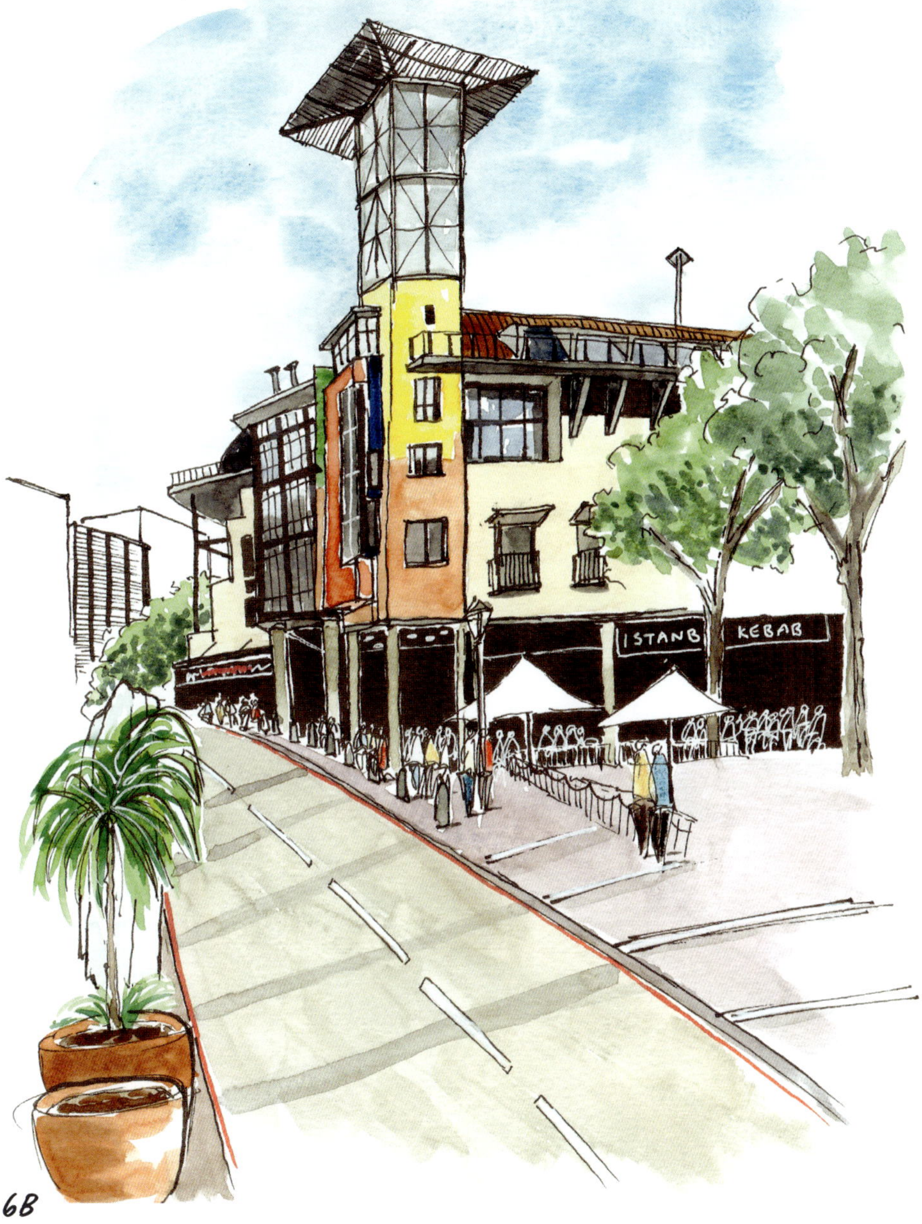

SKETCH A SCENE

ONE-POINT PERSPECTIVE

There may be street scenes that you want to sketch more deliberately than the process we used in the preceding section. I very rarely draw perspective lines on my paper, but I do try to visualize them. I think it's useful to understand where the horizon line is in the scene and how the parallel lines slope toward it.

PERSPECTIVE

1. **Assess your scene and identify where the horizon line is.**

In this photo of a street in London, you may think the horizon line is where the road meets the building at the end of the street. It's easy to be mistaken as it seems such a prominent horizontal line in the scene (1A). Remember two things: You may not always be able to physically see the horizon line (like you can when you look out at the ocean), and second, the horizon line is also known as the eye line. If you think about it logically, your eye line would not be where the building meets the street (unless you are looking uphill). If you are standing up, as I was when I took this photo, and the road is flat, your eye line is somewhere midway up the shop window.

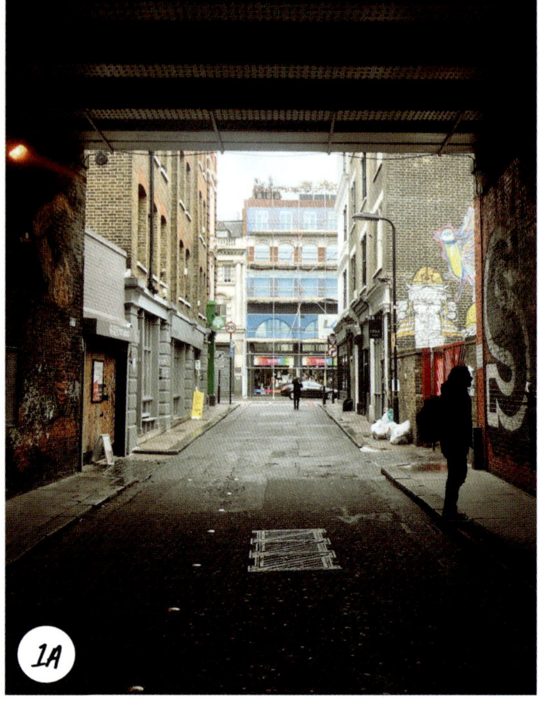
1A

If you are not sure how to find the horizon line, follow the angles of the parallel lines you can see in the buildings on either side of the street. Where they intersect is where the horizon line is.

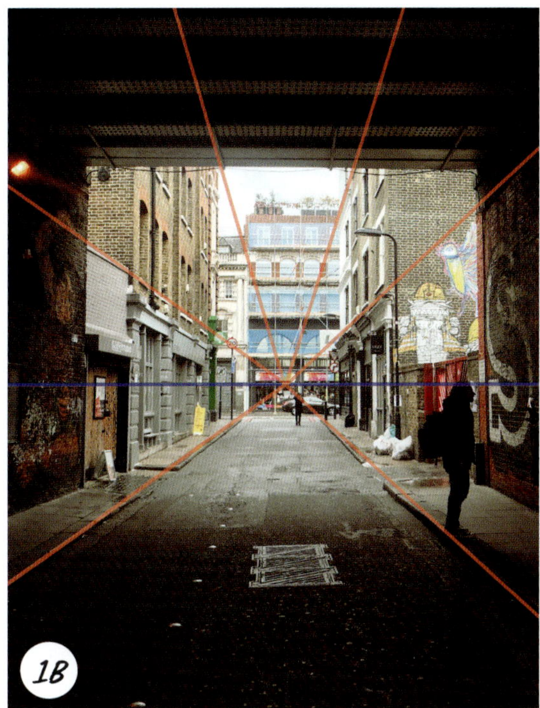

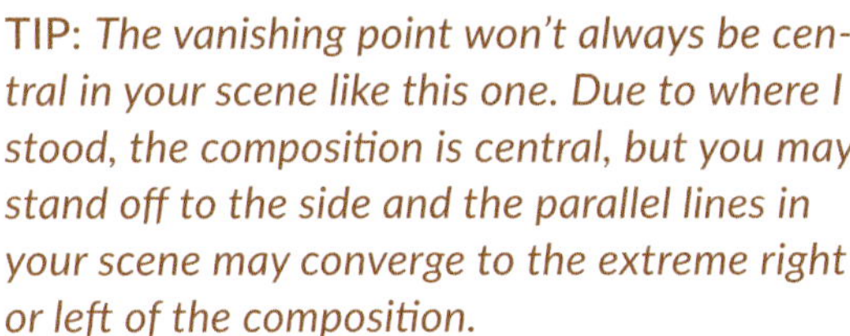

TIP: *The vanishing point won't always be central in your scene like this one. Due to where I stood, the composition is central, but you may stand off to the side and the parallel lines in your scene may converge to the extreme right or left of the composition.*

2. Draw the horizon line across your page very lightly in pencil.

You can also add some lines that radiate from it, like in the photo (1B). Remember, we are not cameras, and our sketches will naturally be a little wonky or inaccurate but that's ok. Let go of the need for perfection and embrace the creative sketching process.

As you can see, I drew the lines faintly and loosely on my page. I didn't use a ruler; if you feel you would like to then go ahead. Urban sketcher Alicia Aradilla carries an expired store card with her and uses it as a straight edge when she needs. As you probably know by now, I like wonky lines so I don't do this.

In street scenes like this, it can be a little difficult to discern exactly what's going on, but that's where our ability to simplify and interpret a scene comes into play.

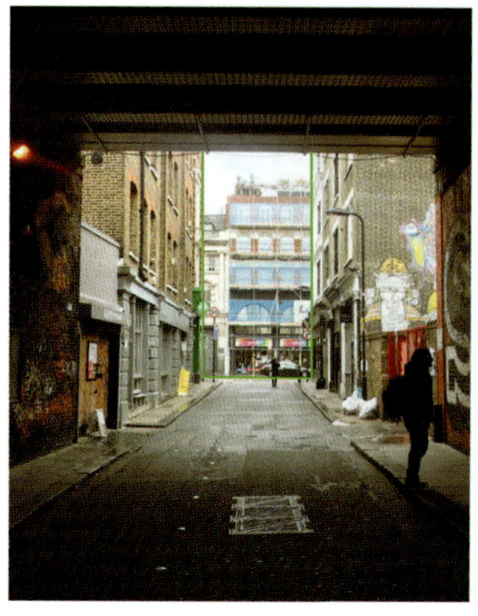

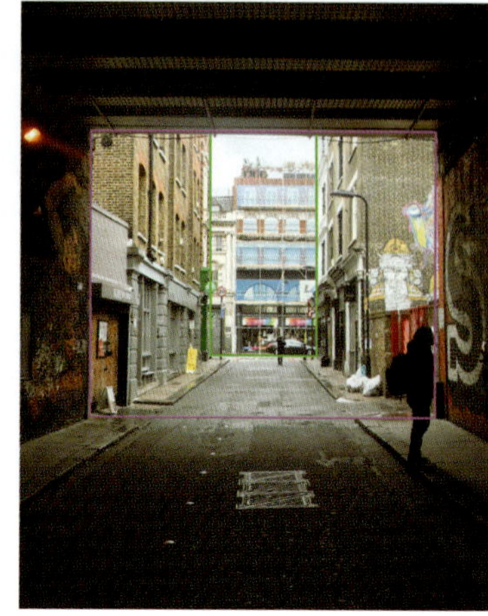

PENCIL SKETCH

3. Look for the most defined horizontal and vertical edges in the scene.

As I started to draw, I looked for the most defined edges in the scene to add to my grid. Where the surface of the road meets the bottom of the buildings creates a strong horizontal line. I decided how wide to make the road; from there, I drew the strong vertical lines of the edge of the buildings on the left and right.

At first I drew this box shape too narrow, so I erased and widened it. The space needs to be big enough to draw the buildings we can see right at the end of the scene. After drawing this first box, I drew diagonal lines to indicate the pavement on either side, making sure they are radiating from the vanishing point, following the grid.

From there, you can see there is another box shape: where the sides and underside of the bridge meet, as well as a gap in the pavement where it stops and restarts. Using the lines we have already drawn, plus our grid, it's easy to pencil this box in too.

With these marks drawn, we have everything we need to complete the scene. It's like completing a jigsaw puzzle and finding the pieces that work based on what you already have down.

4. Continue drawing the big shapes of the scene in pencil.

I drew the tops of the buildings facing the tunnel using the negative shape of the sky as my guideline. I drew a vertical line where the building on the left stops and consequently so does the pavement beneath. A new shorter section of a building follows it, and we see the brick facing us. Notice the bricks are horizontal; they do not conform to the perspective grid. Why is that? It is because they are not parallel with the other lines in our scene that we are using for perspective. I also

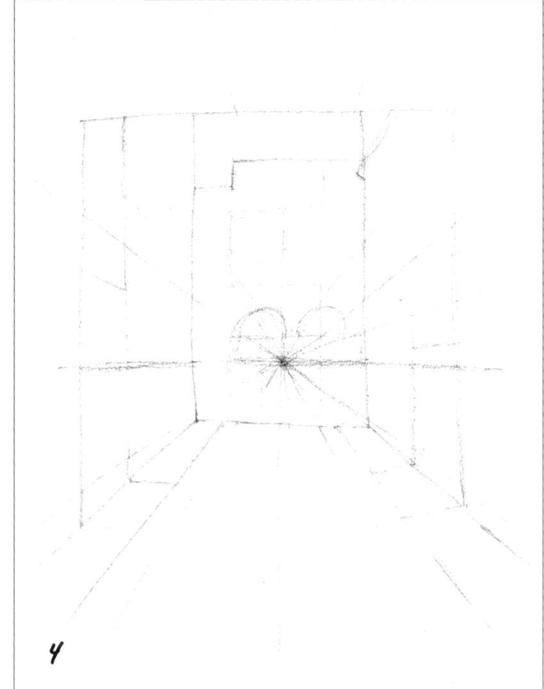

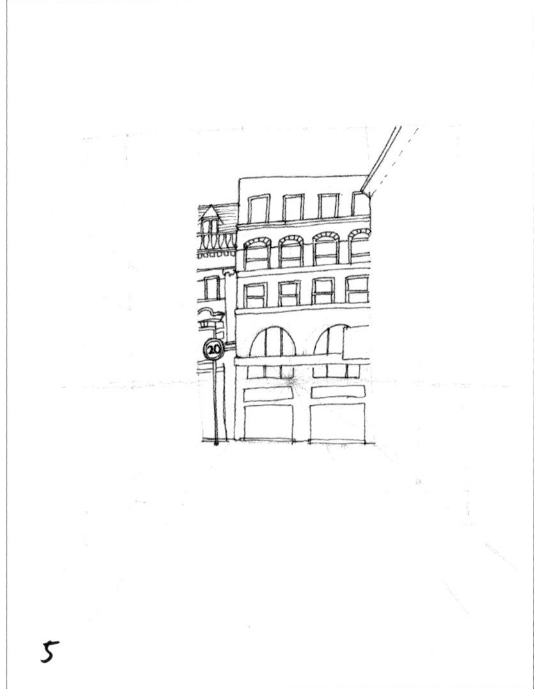

noticed that I can see the top of the building on the right side as the edge of its roof slopes down toward the vanishing point.

I have put some horizontal and vertical divisions on the building at the end of the street, including the big arch windows. It's not very clear what's going on, but I indicate what I think I can see to give the feel of the scene.

INK DETAILS

5. Complete the drawing using ink, correcting any pencil guidelines as you go.

I felt I had enough information on my page to start adding details with ink. Remember: Don't feel the need to stick to your pencil lines. They are just guidelines. If you want to change something with ink, do it. For example, I almost immediately abandoned the vertical guidelines on the building at the back as I realized they were not in the right place for where the windows should be.

This is a strange scene in that our "background elements" contain more details than the foreground. I think the focus of this sketch is the feeling of being in a tunnel and looking out. In this instance, I think it's wise to add detail to the distant objects as there's not all that much detail in the foreground.

I made an executive decision not to draw the scaffolding on the front of the building, although I could add it at the end.

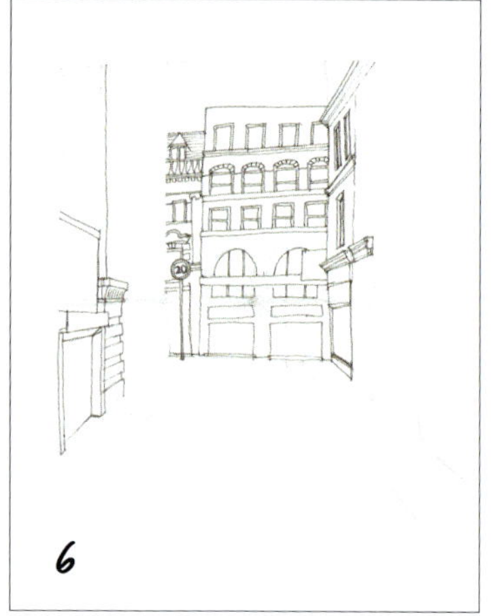
6

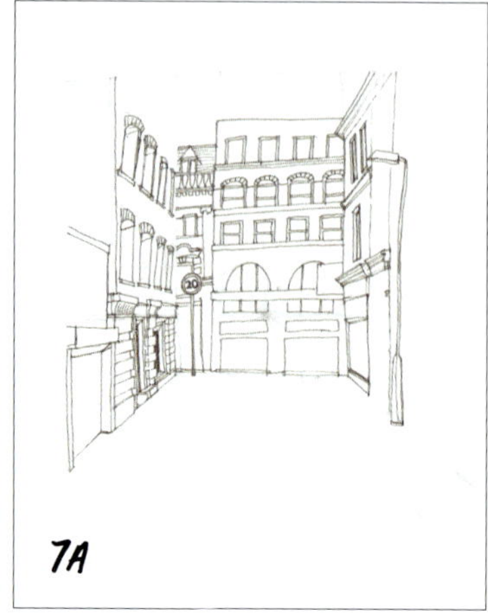
7A

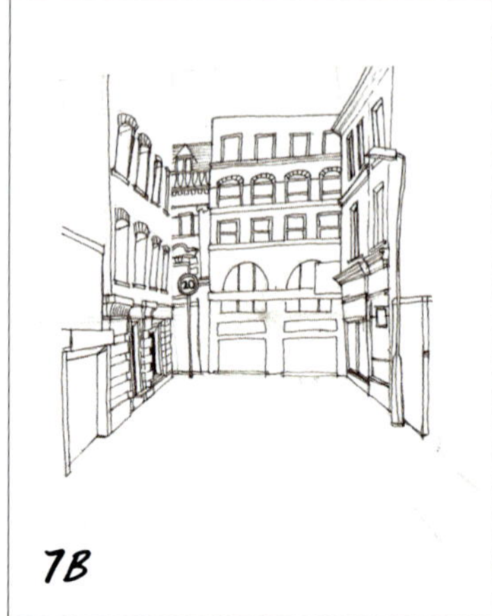
7B

I started by drawing the building at the back first because there are no perspective issues in this part; everything is either horizontal or vertical. By drawing this first, it helped me fill in the rest of the scene as I had lots of visual landmarks to reference. As a general rule, I draw from foreground to background, but this is an example where it seems more intuitive to draw the distant subjects first.

I edited as I drew this scene. I didn't draw all the signs—just one or two that are the clearest. I haven't drawn the buildings in perfect proportion, so I know I won't fit every single window in but that's no problem. This part is definitely tricky. We can see there are windows and we know they are there. However, in most instances the perspective is so extreme we can't actually see them properly.

6. Return to pencil if you need to where there are difficult areas of perspective.

You may want to return to a pencil to place certain details in your scene. In this scene, I used a pencil to place the windows before drawing them in ink.

TIP: *Remember, when dealing with architectural details such as windows, the top and bottom edges must follow the perspective grid. The top line is at a different angle to the bottom.*

7. Draw the areas of the scene you feel most comfortable with.

There's no right or wrong place to start and stop drawing. Don't be afraid to jump around different areas of your scene as you need. In this scene, I found it easiest to draw the ledges that divide the buildings horizontally and then add the windows after that. I stopped on the right as I realized there was a lamppost I wanted to include that was in front of the building (7A).

I then started in a completely different place on the left side of the sketch, drawing the buildings immediately after the tunnel and adding more details (7B). I found this to be the easiest place to start in order for me to understand where to draw other elements on that side of the sketch.

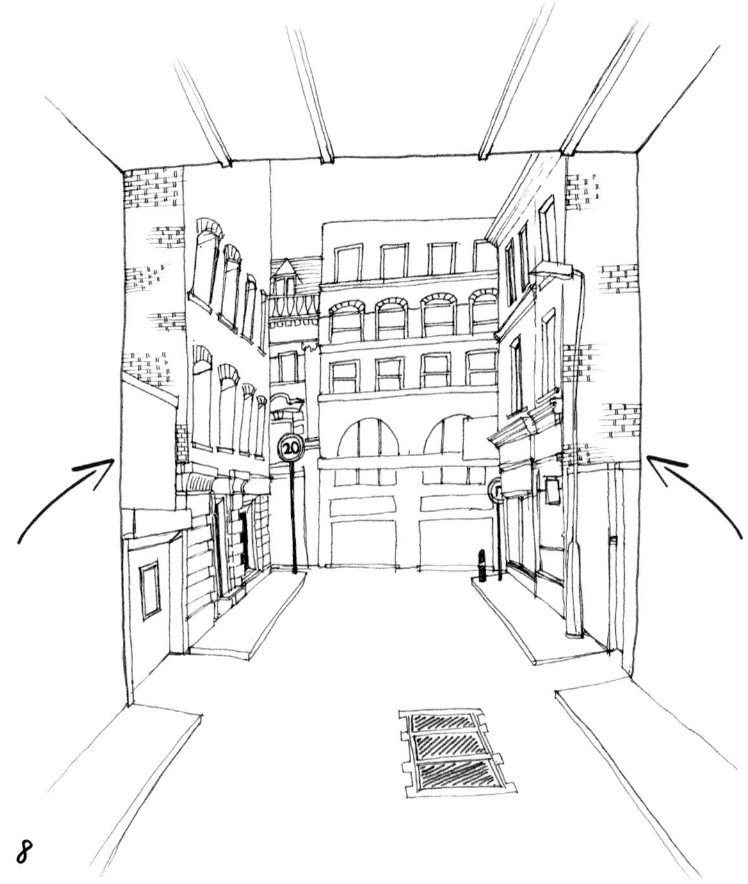

8. **Use thicker lines for emphasis.**

Varying line width can create a sense of depth in a scene. I had been using a 0.1 fineliner for this drawing but I switched to a 0.8 fineliner to draw the walls of the tunnel, as I wanted to exaggerate them due to them being much closer to the foreground.

I also added the drain in the foreground. It breaks up the road and also adds some more perspective to pull the viewer into the scene.

I took quite a few liberties with this drawing and simplified a lot of the complicated details, but the scene is still recognizable. Sometimes, if you try to draw every last detail exactly as you see it, the drawing can become cluttered and lost. Also, it would take an exceptionally long time to draw every detail perfectly accurately. Capturing a scene with less information is my preferred strategy for urban sketching.

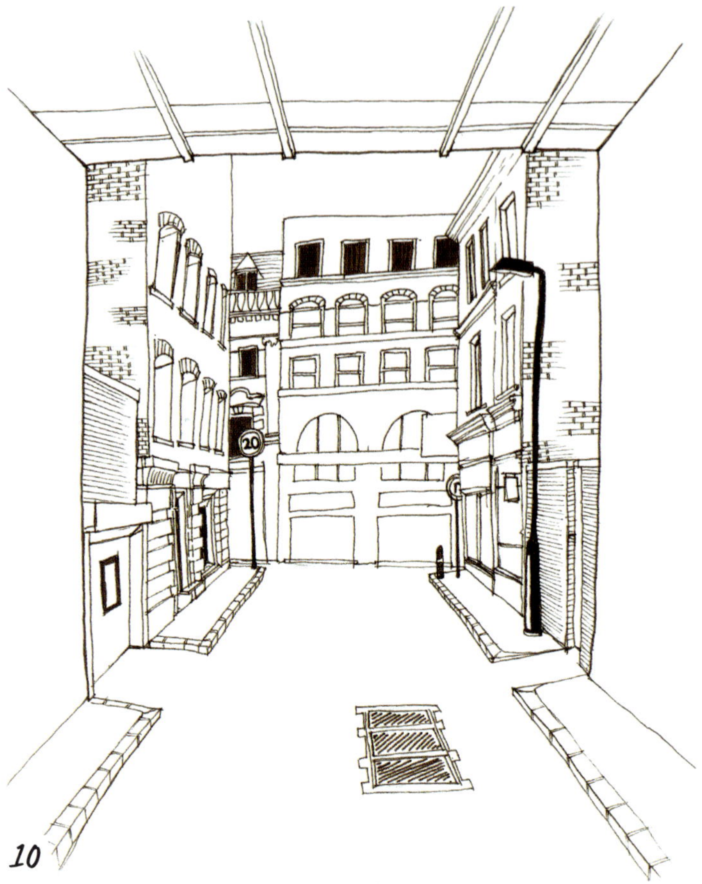

9. **Erase obvious pencil marks.**

If there is a lot of pencil on your page, do your best to erase as much as you can. A kneadable eraser usually works well. Don't worry if some of it still shows. You don't want to scrub too hard and damage the surface of your paper.

ADD CONTRAST

10. **Add areas of black with a waterproof brush pen.**

Be bold and add areas of solid black with your brush pen. It's fun to see something so striking at this early stage of a sketch. The contrast between the white of the page and the black of the pen can be inspirational. It may lead you to make some decisions you may not have otherwise made simply by doing this step now rather than after applying watercolor paint.

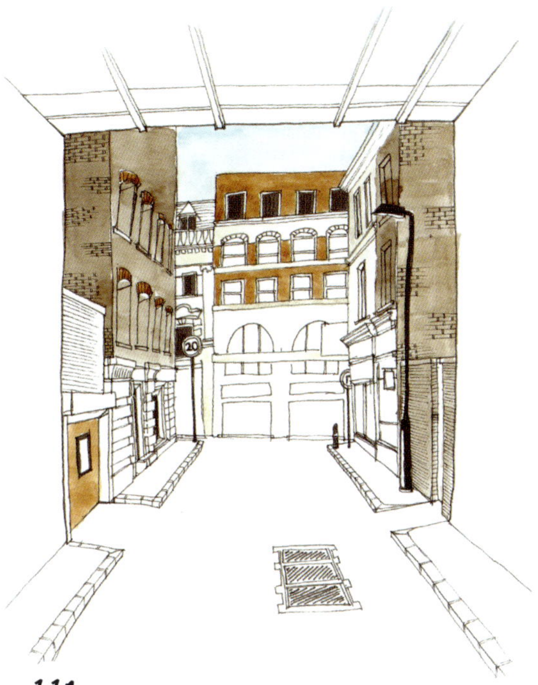

11A

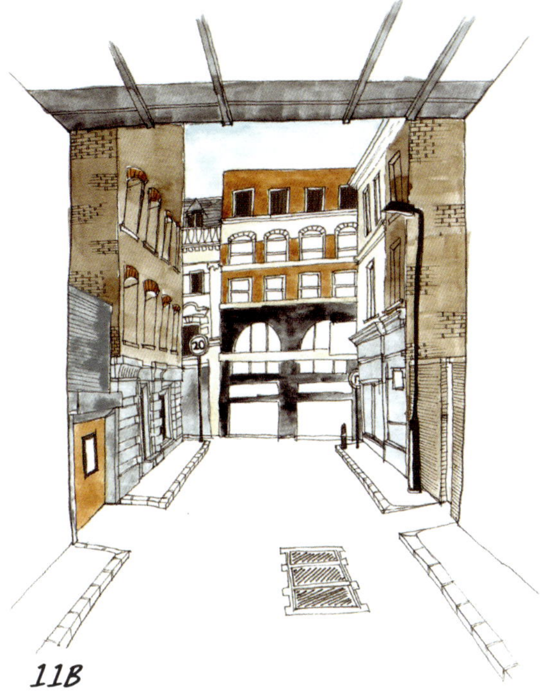

11B

FIRST WATERCOLOR WASH

11. Add the base colors across the scene.

As you can see from the reference photo, the background is bright and light and the foreground is very dark. I wanted to capture this in my sketch to show I was standing under a bridge looking out toward the light.

I started with a light layer of color all over the scene. Cerulean Blue (light blue) for the small shape of sky, Buff Titanium (or you can use a watery Yellow Ochre) for the beige parts of the buildings, Burnt Umber for the reddish brown parts and Sepia for the dark brown walls (11A).

To make the very flat man-made gray painted on the wall and shop fronts on the left of the image, I mixed Payne's Grey with a tiny bit of white (11B). This is an example where white can be useful. White is an opaque watercolor, so use it with caution. It is easy to mix muddy colors. It's useful when you are trying to make a man-made or pastel color. I added other darker grays in the scene with Payne's Grey but no white.

TIP: *As white is opaque, it will obscure some of your ink lines, so you will most likely have to redraw over the top once the paint is dry.*

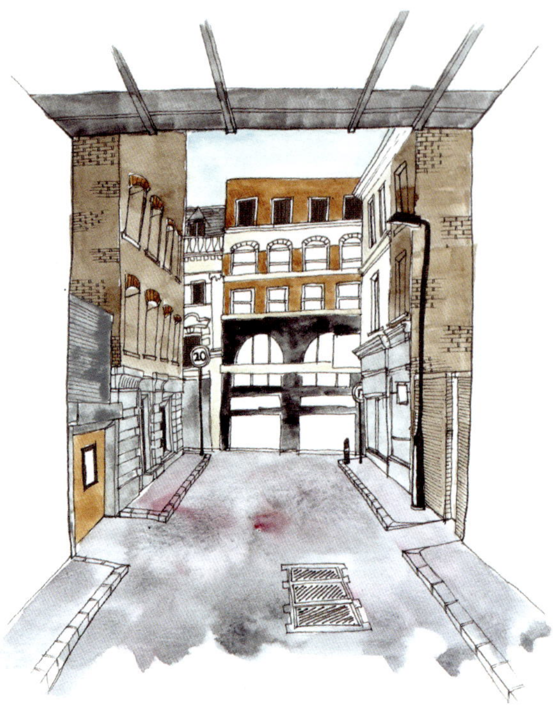

11C

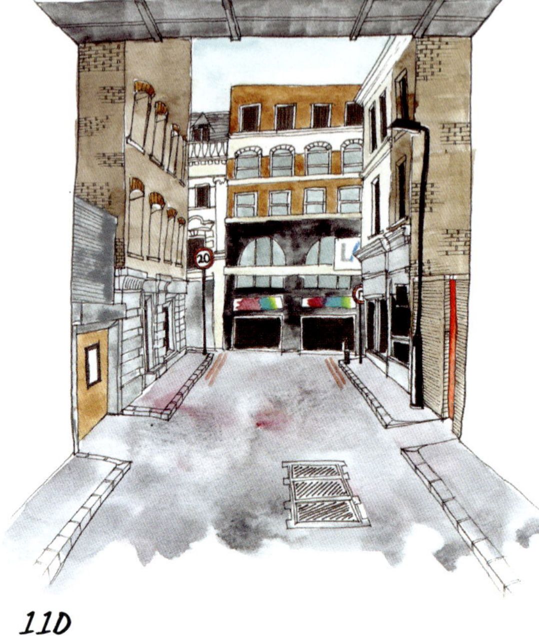

11D

I then painted the ground. I could have done this first; there's no real order you must paint things in. Do whatever feels natural. I thought the scene was a little dull at the moment, so I wanted the ground to be a little more dynamic. I used one of my favorite color combinations, which is Payne's Grey with a little bit of Quinacridone Rose. Make sure to use a larger brush for covering areas like this to avoid any streaking and to cover the area in paint quickly.

You may notice the paint on the ground has a speckly texture to it (11C). This is called granulation. Some pigments granulate more than others. Also, colors in different brands granulate more than others. Some people don't like the effect of granulation, but I think it adds interest and texture to a scene. I don't use the effect deliberately, but I also don't mind it when it happens.

Notice I didn't end the ground in a perfect straight line across the page. I think it's far more interesting for it to finish with random strokes like this.

Once the base colors for most of the sketch are down, I continue to add details such as the pops of red on the road signs and the colorful signs on the shops at the back (11D).

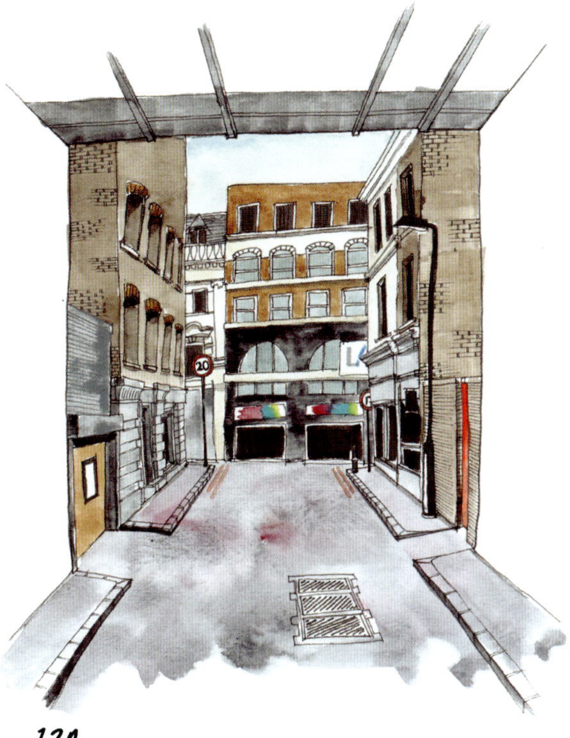

12A

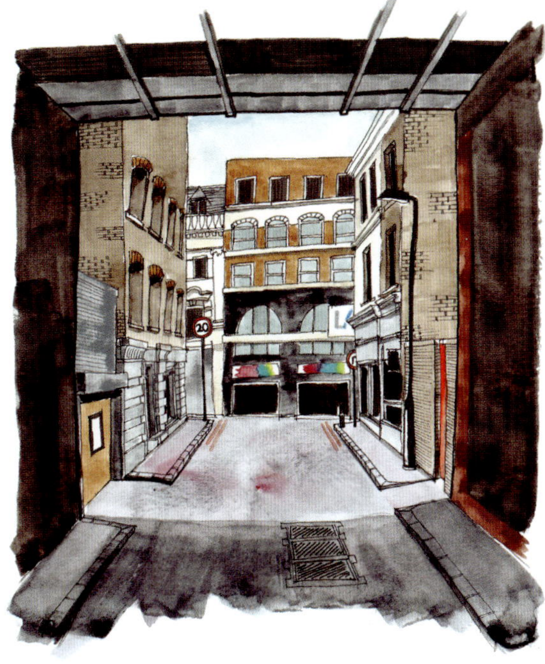

12B

SHADOWS

12. Add the shadow areas to the scene.

I then painted the shadows under the windows, along the pavement, under the ledges of windows and roofs (12A). For shadows on brown surfaces, I simply used a dark brown as my shadow color. Similarly, on any of the gray areas, I used a darker gray for the shadow.

I then emphasized the dark edges of the scene: the walls and underside of the bridge. This gives a lot of drama to the scene. I painted a mixture of Payne's Grey and Sepia on the walls and used a black brush pen for the underside of the bridge. Even though it's not so defined in the photograph, I decided to paint the road underneath the bridge a darker shade too (12B). This completes the effect of looking out from a dark tunnel to a bright scene beyond.

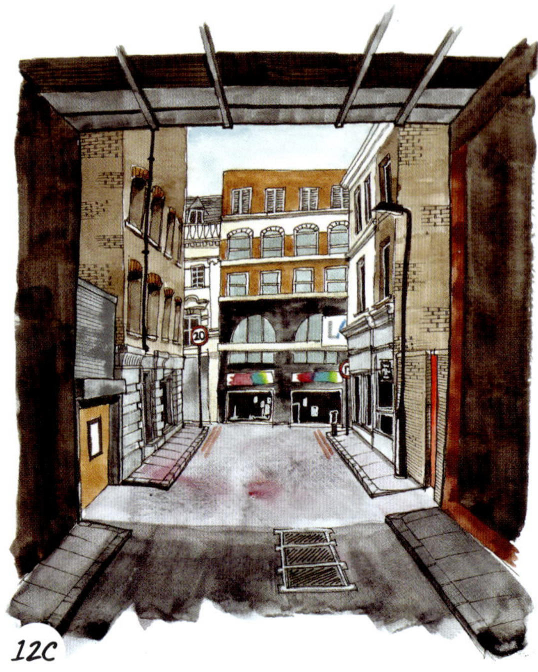

12C

The final step is to add some white gel pen in some of the windows (12C) and tighten up some of my ink lines that were hidden by the opaque white earlier in the sketch.

FIXING MISTAKES

There are definitely some things I didn't get right in this scene and some things I deliberately simplified. That's ok. Every sketch is a learning opportunity. The beauty of urban sketching is that you are not trying to produce some perfect piece of art to hang on the wall. The sketchbook becomes your visual diary of the places you have been to and things you have seen. If you make a mistake or get something wrong, it's no big deal. In fact, it's a part of the story of your sketch and the record of your personal journey as an urban sketcher.

I have realized I am missing a crucial building at the end of the row on the left. In my mind, it's crucial because it brings color into the scene and breaks up the grays and browns. To fix it I am going to add a thin strip of green and brown with a paint marker to indicate the building. Of course, you may not have materials like this with you when you urban sketch, but I am just raising this as a possibility. Paint markers have become something I now carry around with me as I really enjoy using them and having the flexibility to draw over the top of watercolor with opaque colors.

In my initial sketch, I skipped a few parts of the scene like the street art and the scaffolding. As you become more comfortable, you can draw more and more of the details in a scene like this (if you want to) but don't be afraid to get the basic scene on paper and skip any parts that you don't feel like including. Drawing the basic scene is far better than drawing nothing at all!

You can always add things in at the end. Again, paint markers are super useful for this. In this sketch, I added the silhouette of the person looking at the wall with a black brush pen. I also added some simplified versions of the street art too. Finally, I decided to add the scaffolding with a white gel pen and lightly colored over the areas where there are blue materials with a colored pencil.

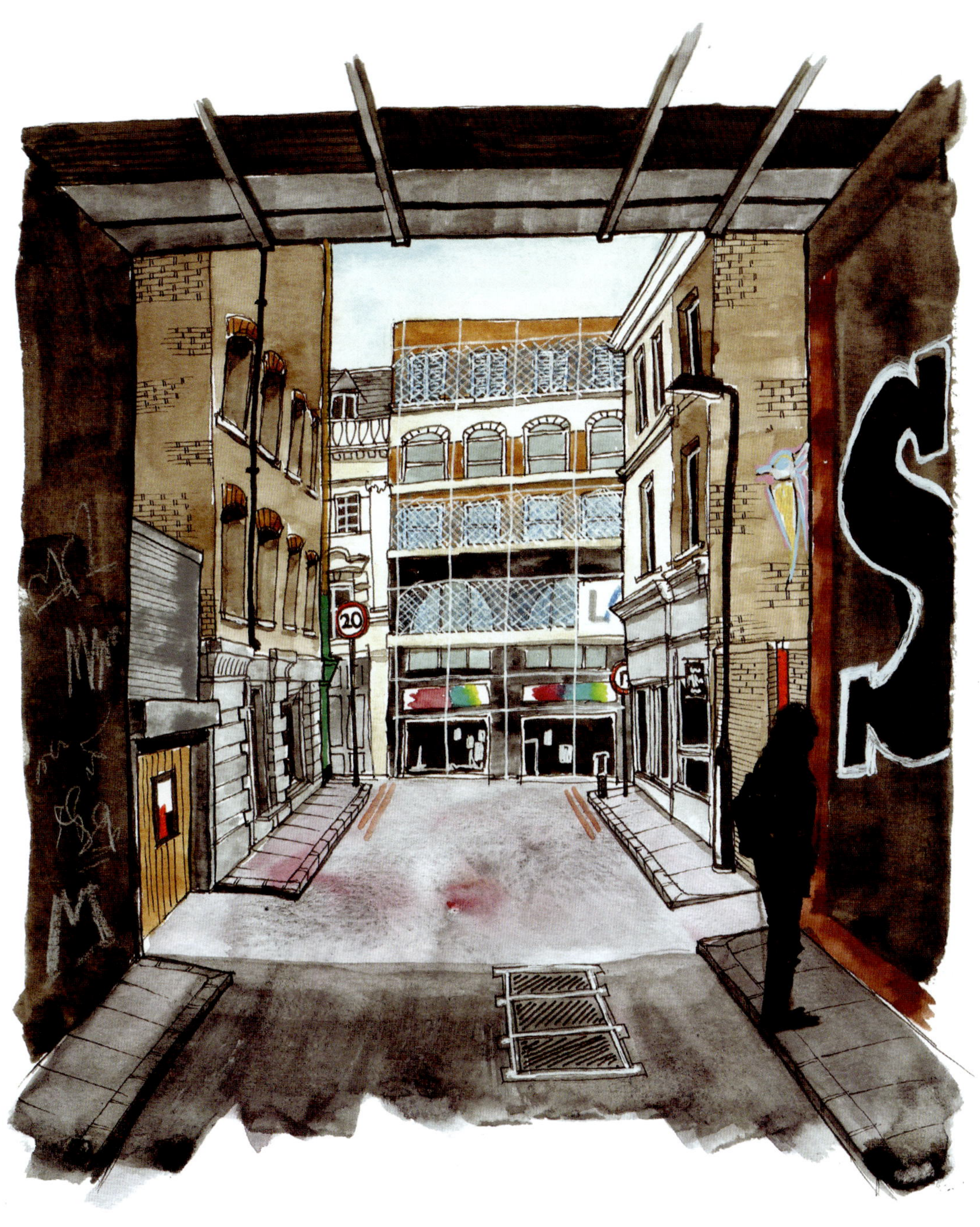
20

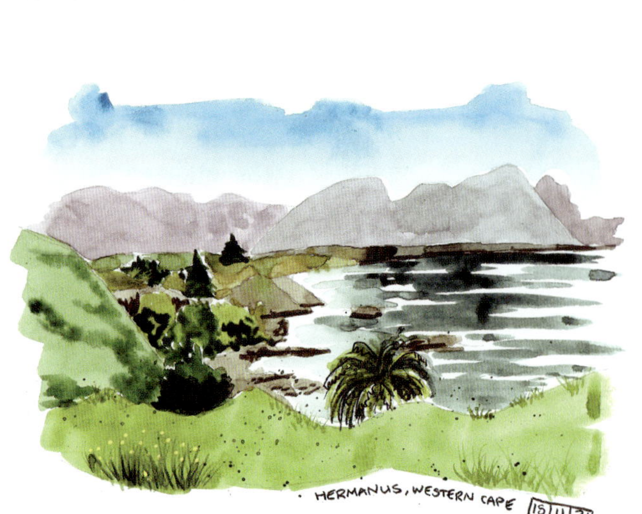

PARK LIFE

Green spaces within the urban environment provide a welcome refuge from the noise and bustle. City parks and gardens are a great place to sit back and relax to sketch. In England, in the summertime, every square inch of grass is covered in bodies seeking a slice of nature to indulge in. Parks offer an entirely fresh set of sketching opportunities. Straight, hard edges of the city streets transform into intangible organic shapes. While there still may be some structures to draw, the new challenge is how to portray so much foliage, so many shades of nature and the ultimate challenge: things in motion, such as birds and dogs.

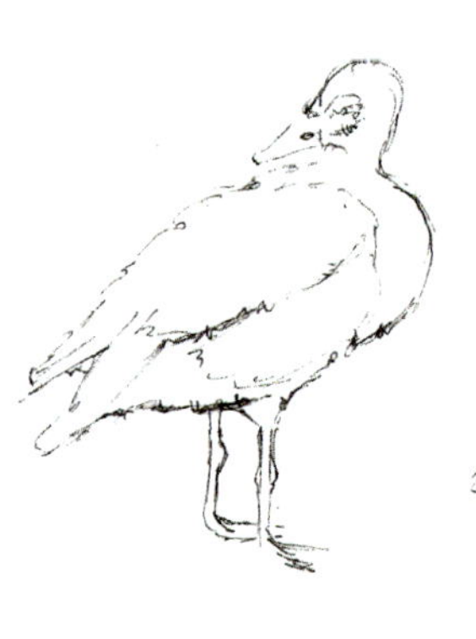

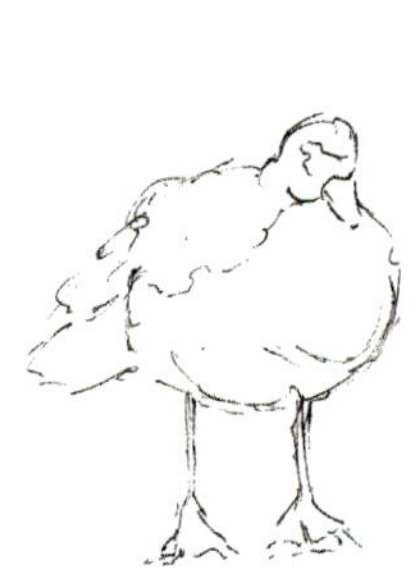

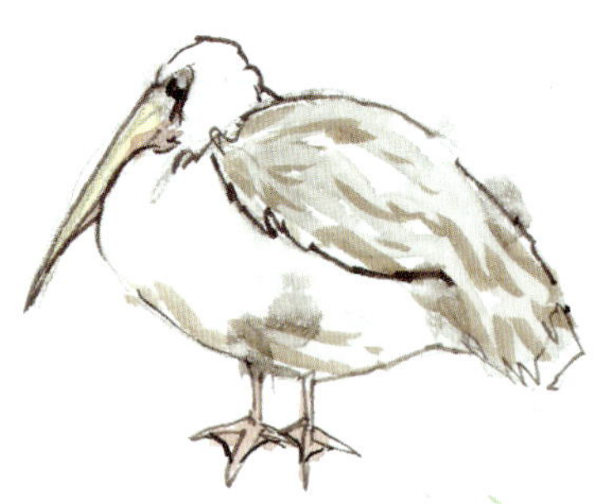

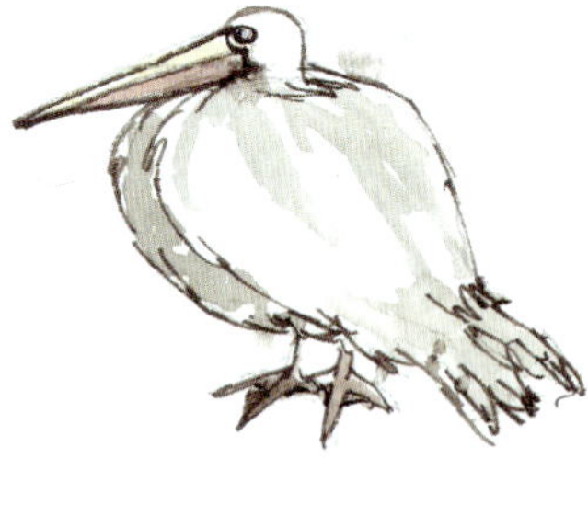

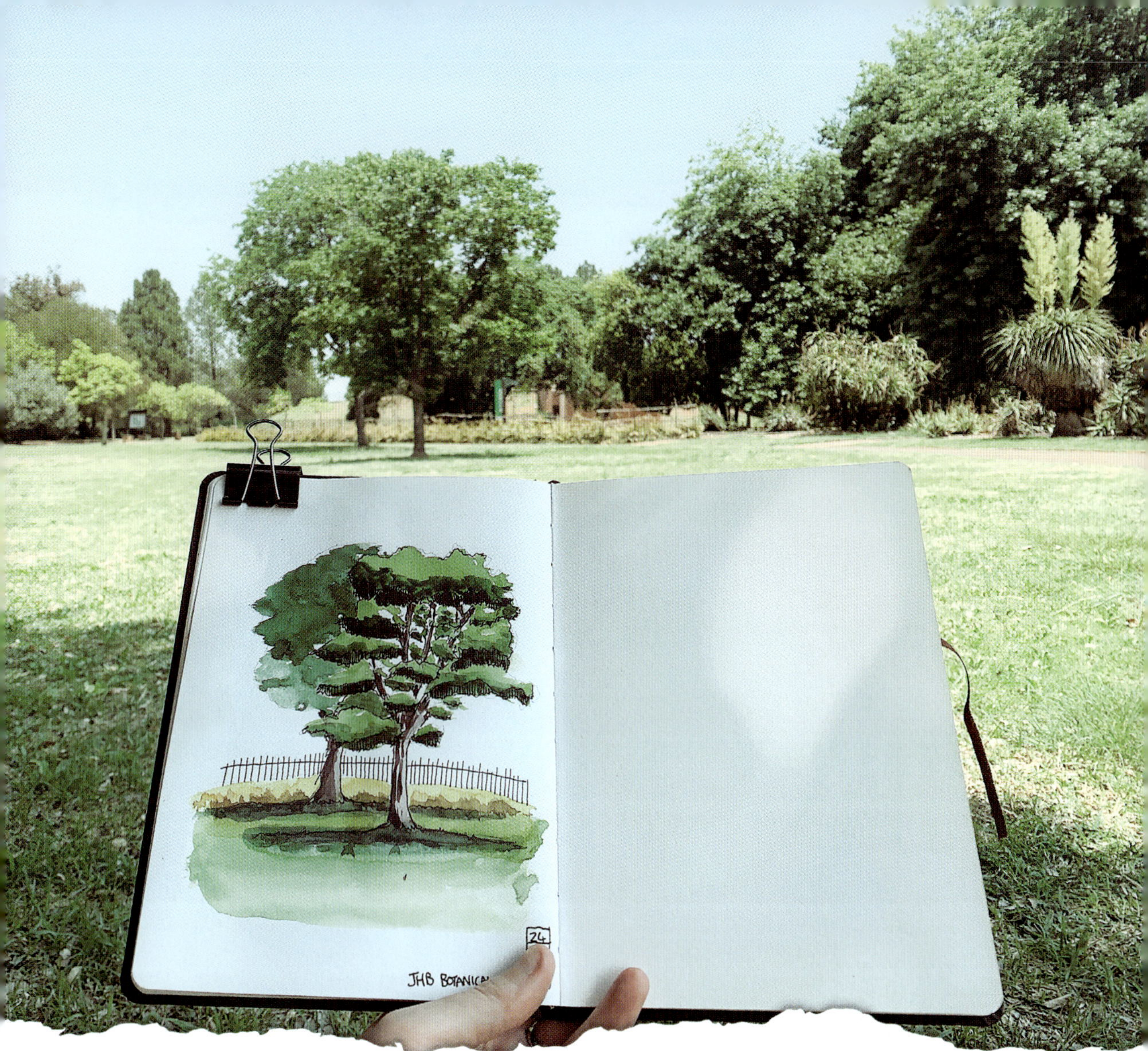

FOLIAGE

From sprawling cemeteries to leafy pub gardens to hanging planters outside (and inside) shops and restaurants, foliage is intertwined with man-made structures wherever you look and is an essential element of the urban landscape.

The shapes of trees alone can tell a lot about the location you are sketching. In colder climates, we may see more fir tree shapes yet in tropical climates, we see palm tree shapes. This is an extreme example but foliage can be a great storytelling device.

Let's look at the various elements to consider when sketching foliage. The goal is to understand how to incorporate foliage within our urban sketches, not sketch plants and flowers in fine detail. The following exercises will provide you the building blocks to enable you to add convincing foliage to your urban sketches.

SHAPES

The shape of a bush, tree, leaf or flower is a key indicator of what kind of plant it is. We are not botanical illustrators, so laboring over every detail is not what's called for. Try to block out details (remember our squinting trick on page 21) and draw the rough outline or silhouette of a tree, for example (1A). This will help you produce a convincing sketch.

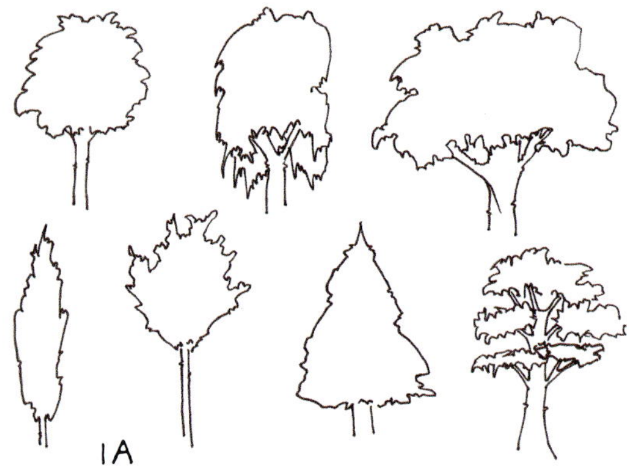

1A

You can draw the outline shape of the tree with your pen or block in the shape with watercolor (1B).

1B

COLOR

There are many shades of green and many ways to mix green in watercolor. Not all foliage is green, but if you can nail some different mixes of green, it will go a long way to help you describe the foliage you're looking at. This also helps to indicate what kind of foliage is present as color can also tell us about the time of year.

You can buy shades of green premixed, but as urban sketchers, we want to travel lightly and carting ten different greens around with us "just in case" isn't very practical. Especially if you can learn to mix a few shades from the small set you already have. As mentioned on page 21, you should ideally have warm and cool versions of the primary colors.

Mixing variations of warm and cool yellows and blues together will give an interesting array of greens. If you followed my advice on page 22 and made a watercolor chart from your watercolor paints, you may have already discovered this.

Let's take a look at a few color-mixing variations so you can see what I mean (2A).

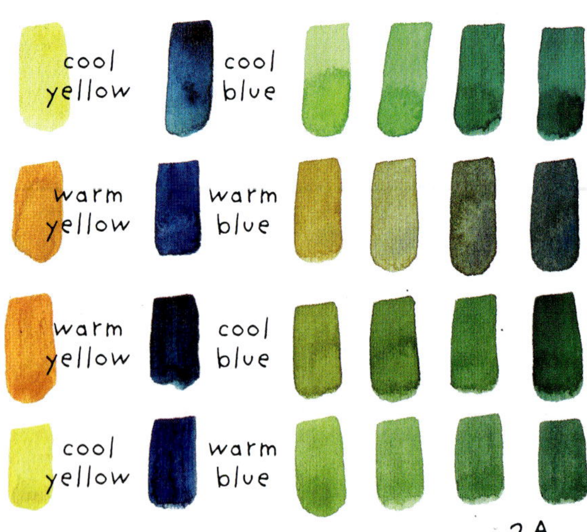

2A

The shifting of the seasons also affects the color of foliage, so you can practice some color mixes for warm oranges and reds, as well (2B). Here are some example color mixes for autumnal foliage:

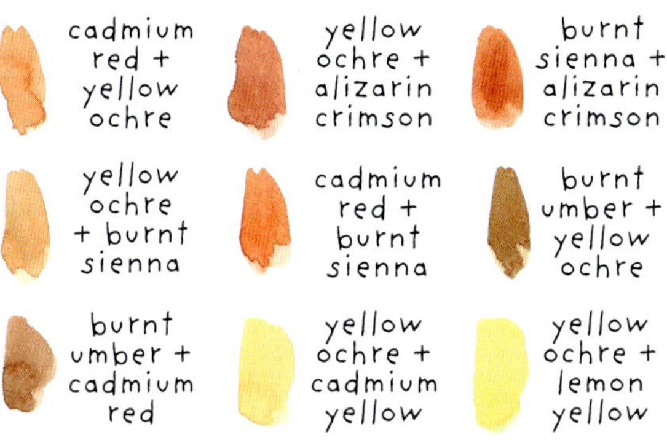

2B

I encourage you to play with the colors in your set, make swatches and keep notes about which colors you mixed together.

TEXTURE

You can use pen lines, as well as brushstrokes, to capture the texture of foliage. Adding texture to foliage that has convincing shape and color conveys that next level of depth and interest to a sketch.

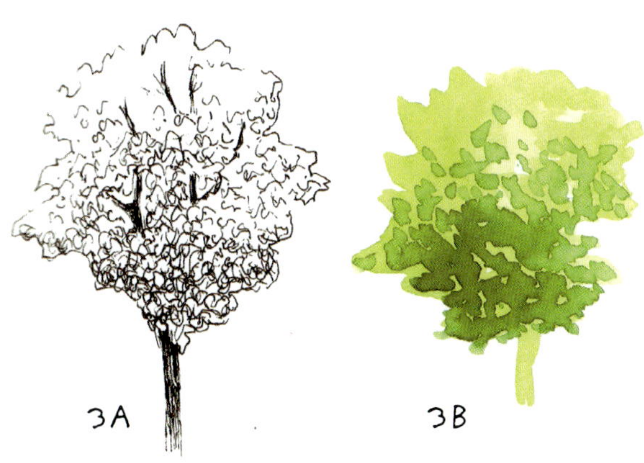

3A 3B

I used random small squiggles with a 0.2 fineliner in image 3A to indicate the texture of leaves with a pen, increasing density in the shadow areas and keeping it sparser in the lighter areas.

After my watercolor shape dried, I added some darker brushstrokes on top with the point of a round brush (image 3B). You can also try wet-on-wet for a softer effect. These broken brushstrokes indicate the texture of leaves, as well as the feeling that light is shining through parts of the tree.

Different textures can be achieved by varying your choice of brush and even paper.

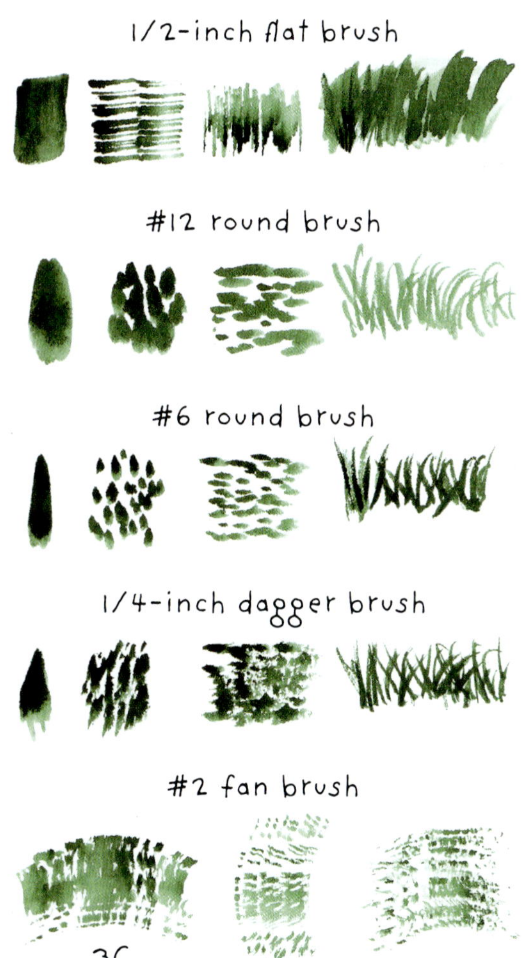

3C

You can see the range of marks different brushes can make in image 3C (page 89) when used at various angles.

As well as using different brushes, you can also use a dry brush to vary your marks as discussed on page 25.

Can you see how the vertical dry-brush mark could work well to indicate a tree trunk? Or the horizontal dry brush could indicate a field of grass? Experiment with the marks you can make in your sketchbook with the brushes you have.

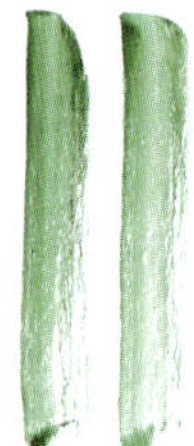

VOLUME

Adding volume to your sketch of foliage will help you move the shape from a flat 2D shape to a 3D-looking object. You can do this by adding thicker lines and denser marks in areas of the foliage.

I used a thicker fineliner with a line weight of 0.5 to add some more textural lines and slightly thicker lines where the heavy shadows are in the tree area (image 4A). You can exaggerate the shadows you see for a more stylistic result.

You can also use watercolor to add darker areas to your foliage to indicate shadows (image 4B).

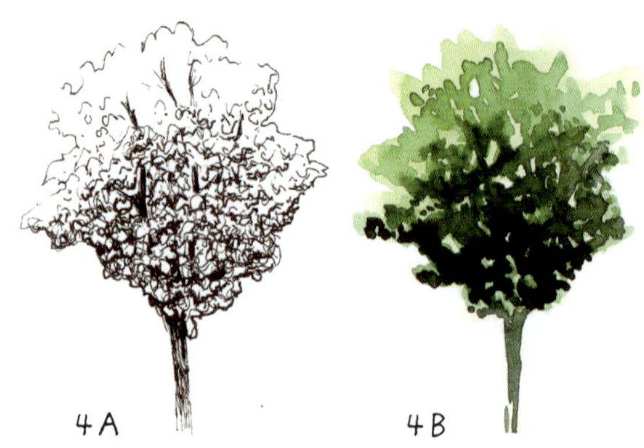

EXERCISE 1: PEN SKETCH

1. Select a tree or bush and outline the shape of it with your pen (see image 1A, page 88).

Keep it loose and wiggly! I didn't draw a continuous, hard line around the edge of the shape of the tree I chose. Feel free to use broken lines. The most important thing is to look at the overall shape and don't get caught up in the details.

2. Use pen lines to capture the texture of the foliage (see image 3A, page 89).

Remember to increase the density of your pen marks in the shadow areas and to keep them sparse in the lighter areas.

3. Add volume to your sketch with thicker lines and denser marks in the shadow areas of the foliage (see image 4A).

Look at your chosen bush or tree, squint your eyes to find the darkest parts and add thicker lines or a darker color to the respective areas of your sketch. Usually, the darkest areas will be toward the bottom of the foliage and the top will be lighter as this is where the sun is hitting.

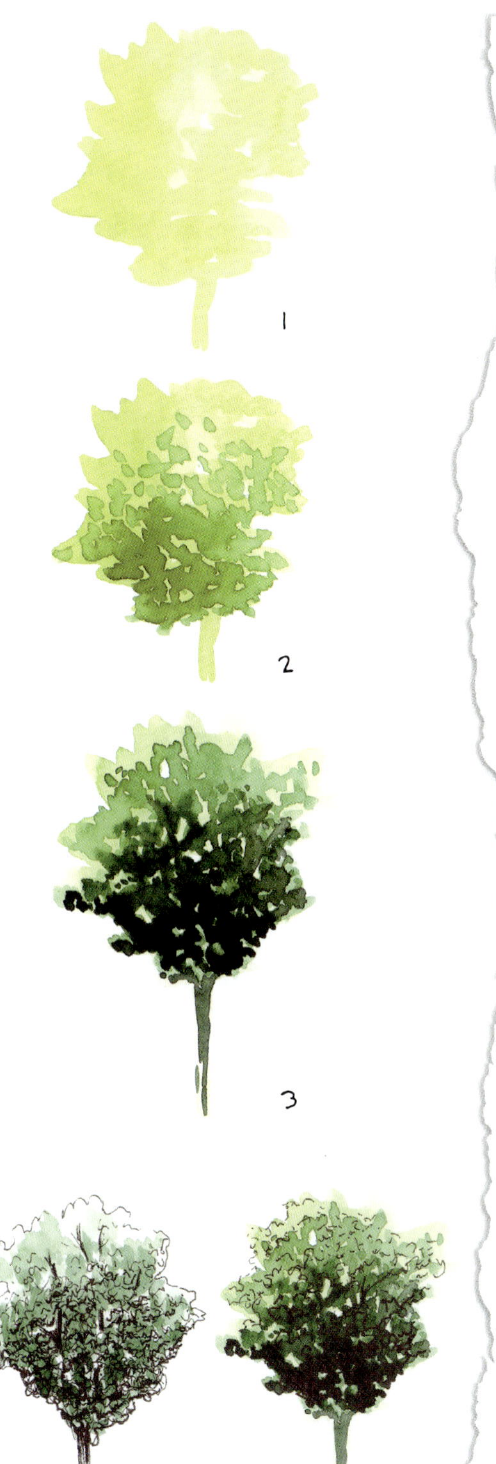

EXERCISE 2: WATERCOLOR SKETCH

1. Using the same tree or bush as reference, paint the shape of it.

Use one color for now—the lightest one you can see in your chosen bush or tree. It doesn't have to be exact. I chose a yellow-green for my example as that was the lightest color I could see in my tree.

2. Use brushstrokes to capture the texture of the foliage.

Use broken brushstrokes to indicate texture, and leave some little areas of white paper to give the feeling that light is shining through parts of the tree.

3. Add volume to your sketch with darker brushstrokes in the shadow areas of the foliage.

Don't be afraid to use a very dark version of the color of the tree to indicate the shadows. Lots of contrast (i.e. light lights and dark darks) can really make your sketch pop.

As you experiment, further mix and match ink line sketching with watercolor painting (known as line and wash) and see what happens. I recommend using watercolor lightly over the sketch that is in line and vice versa. If you mix both techniques to their fullest capabilities in one sketch, the effect may not be as successful.

WINTER TREES

Without the leaves, trees are still super fun to draw. It can be quite complex to draw every single branch, but as long as you can capture the essence of the tree, there's no need.

You can capture winter trees in ink, watercolor or both together.

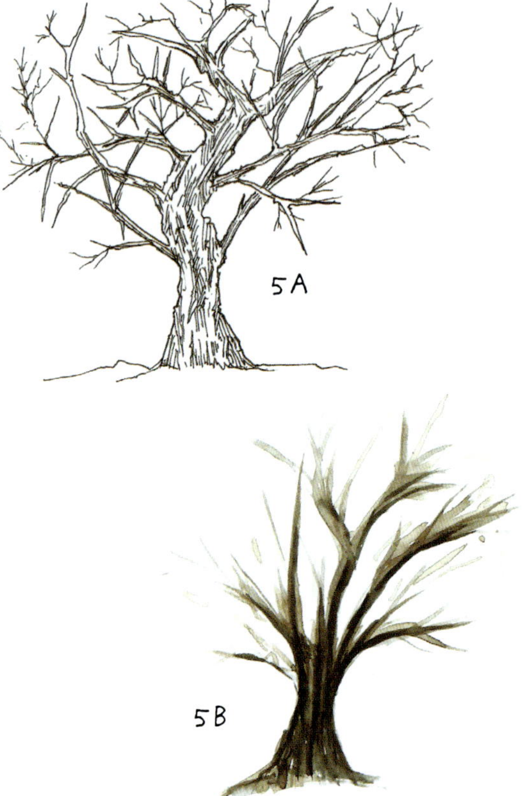

PLANTERS

Planters are fun to draw as they have a nice mixture of structure and organic shapes. I find it easiest to draw the shape of the planter first, followed by the shape of the plant inside it.

In this example, I drew the basic shape of the planter in pencil and then some loose, wiggly lines to indicate the foliage on top (image 6A).

When I drew over the top in ink, I realized the foliage line came down below the straight edge of the planter (image 6B).

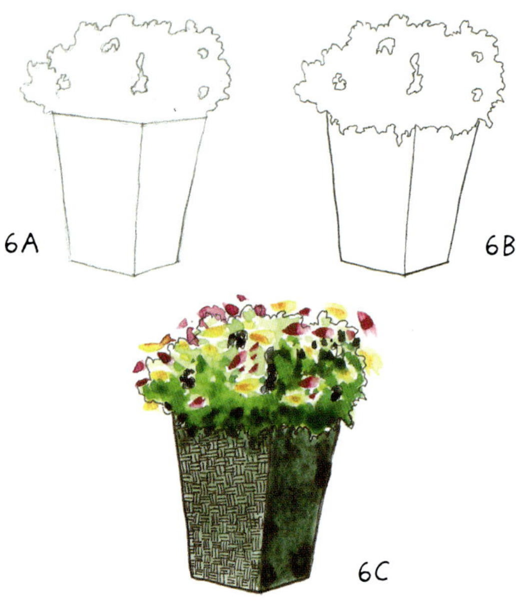

First, I painted the flowers, then the foliage around it. If I tried to paint the flowers on top of the foliage, it wouldn't have worked as the light yellow and pink colors wouldn't layer well over the top of the greens. I also added some texture with my pen on the lighter side of the planter to show the woven material. Little ink details like this will show up better if drawn on top of the watercolor, so it's always best to add them after (image 6C).

Planters come in all shapes, sizes and materials. As you add them in to a scene, be aware of how they interact with each other and the scene around them. The less in focus the planters are in the scene, the less detail you need to add to them.

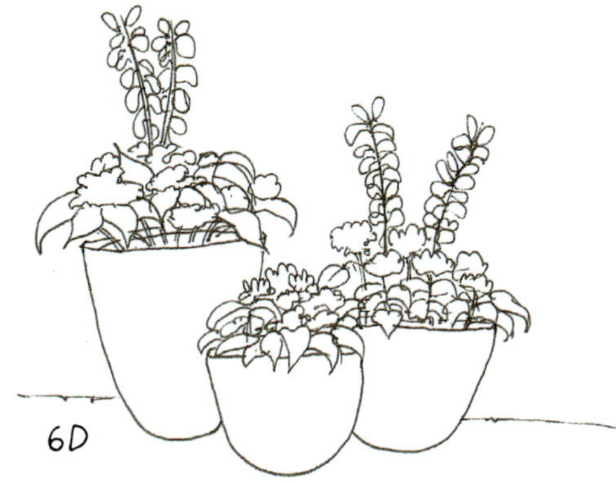

In this example, notice how the planter in front overlaps the two behind it (6D). I didn't draw the plants in any great detail. I just tried my best to focus on the basic shapes of the flowers and leaves. I used lighter colors on top of the flowers and leaves where the light hits and mixed a darker color for the base of the plant to indicate the shadows (6E).

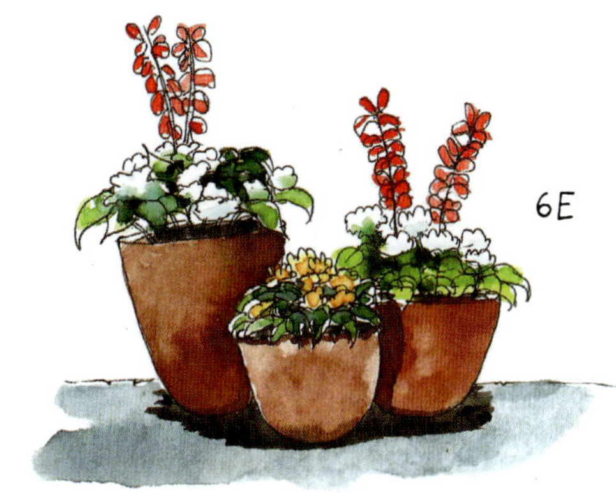

This is a very quick sketch, and when including planters in a larger scene, it's not necessary to go any further than this.

HANGING BASKETS

Much like planters, hanging baskets are fun to include in your urban sketch. I find many old pubs in England are adorned with hanging baskets! Take into consideration that perspective will apply to your hanging baskets. Therefore, the baskets will get smaller the farther away they are and will follow the line of the building they are attached to (7). As they recede into the distance, they will have less detail. It's fun to exaggerate this effect in your sketch to emphasize the perspective.

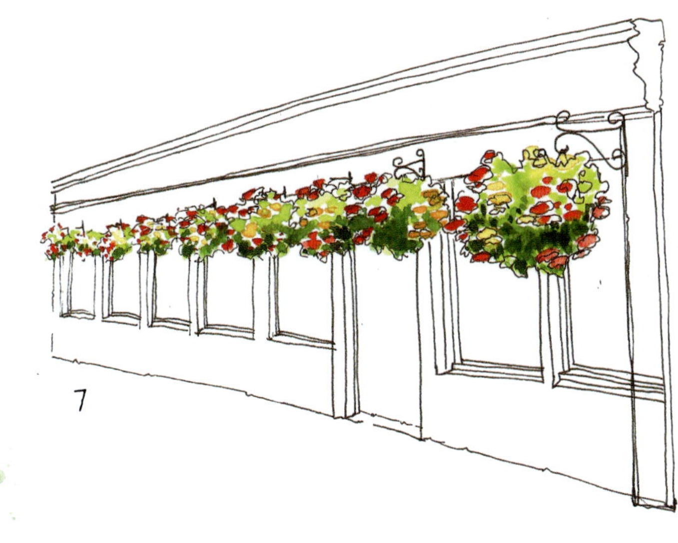

BUSHES & SHRUBS

Bushes and shrubs aren't too different from how you would draw or paint the top of a tree. Focus on the shape of the outline to start with. Color is another important factor to differentiate a group of bushes and shrubs from each other. Often bushes and shrubs will overlap each other in a scene.

I recommend drawing the outline shape and then painting the shapes in the lightest tone of color you can see, which will act as the highlights (1). Then, I use a mid-tone version of the same color for the main body of the leaves (2), followed by the darkest tone for the shadows (3).

It's easier to sketch a collection of shrubs and bushes when they vary in shape and color, like the example below.

In this sketch, I penciled all the shapes in lightly and loosely. I then worked from shape to shape as there were so many different colors going on. I started with the lightest green bushes I could find and painted any that I felt were the same color. I then made my color a little darker, adding some more pigment and using slightly less water to paint the mid-tones. Once dry, I made my color even darker to paint the base of the bush. I would then move on to the next collection of bushes or shrubs that were a similar color and this way built up the scene.

Utilize the texture of the brush to make and replicate the shapes of the foliage.

Don't paint the shape in a flat, solid color; leaving little pockets of white will give the effect of light shining through the leaves.

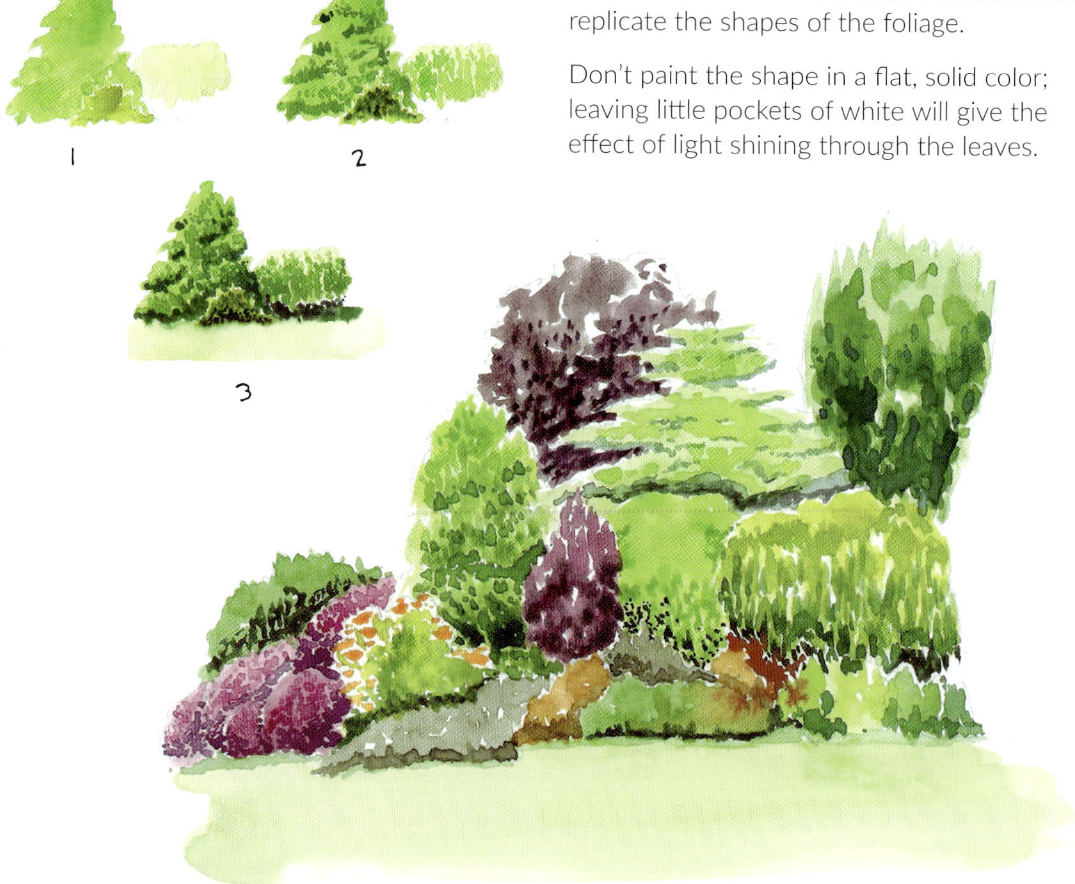

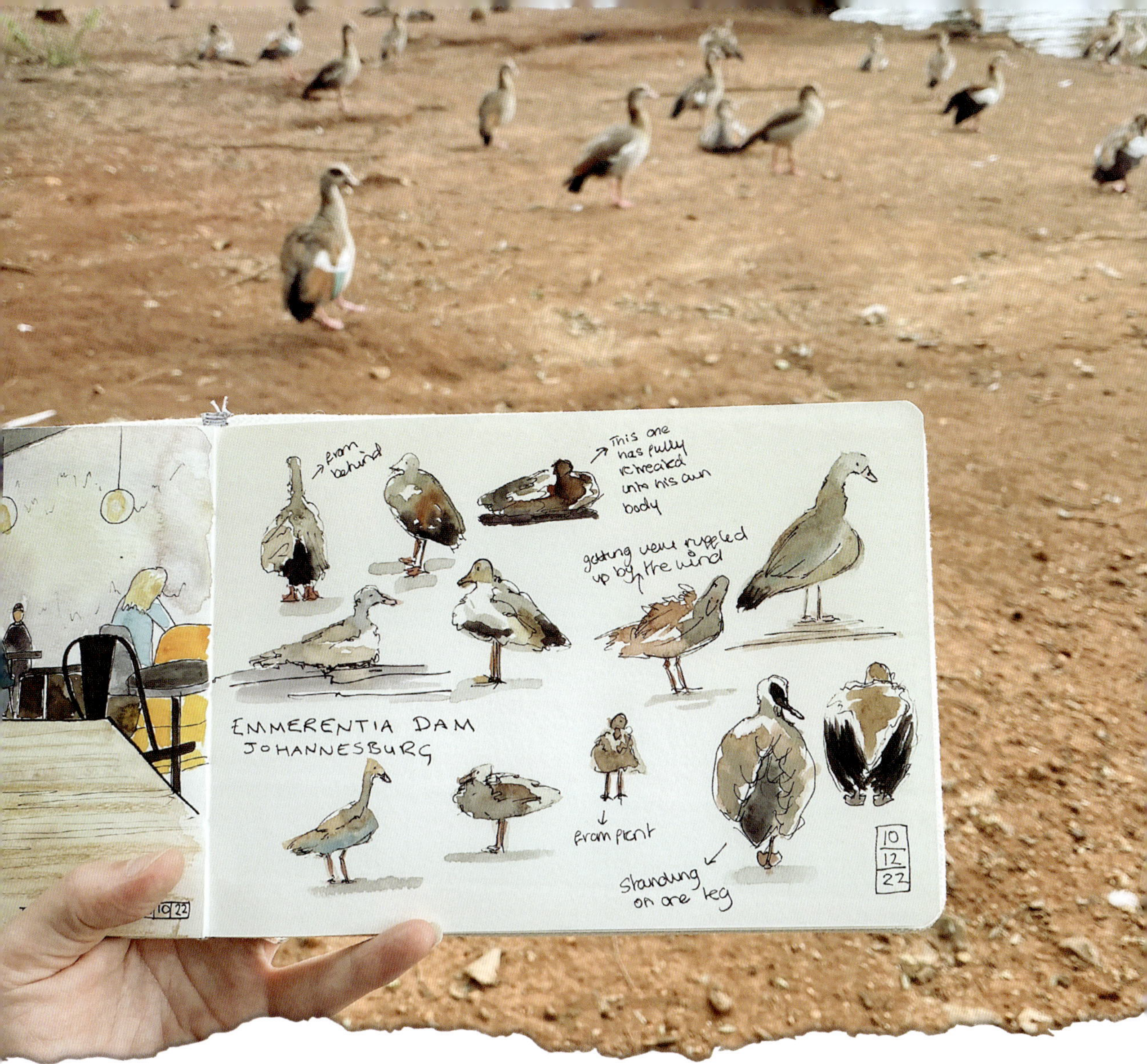

URBAN WILDLIFE

Birds are a readily available subject matter when it comes to wildlife, no matter where you live. They can be found around us whether at home, on the street or in the park. However, it can be tricky to sketch them as they move quickly, sometimes frantically. There are some strategies to deal with sketching things that are moving constantly, which we shall explore in this section.

Blind contour drawing is a fun way to warm up when you sketch and a perfect technique to try when you are sketching things that are always on the move. Blind contour drawing is when you sketch the contour (meaning the outline) of the subject while looking at your subject and not at your page. Pick a point to start and then follow the shape of the subject slowly with your eyes, mirroring what you see with your pencil or pen on the page. When you are finished, you can look at your page.

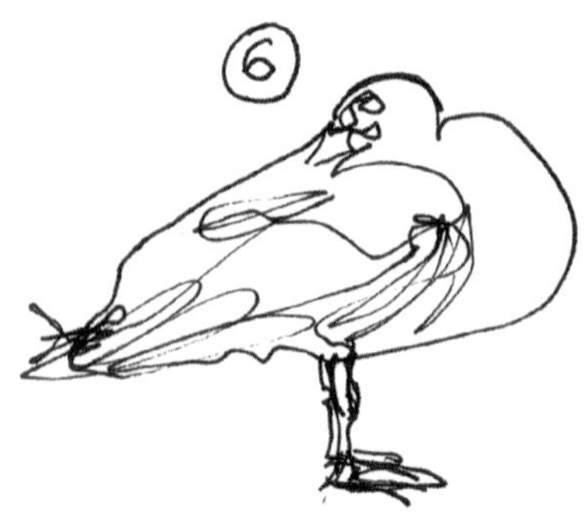

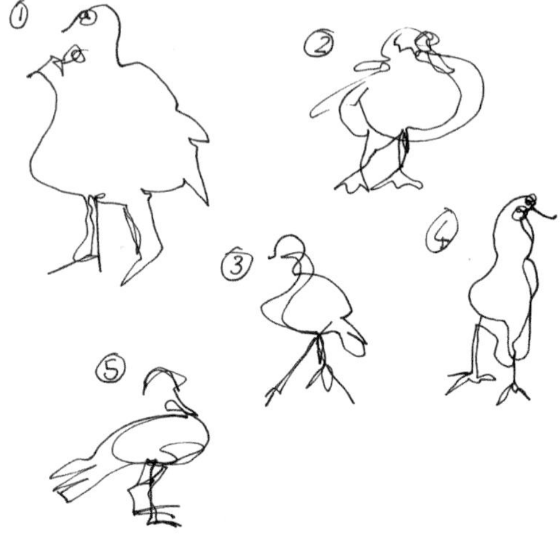

The results are usually hilarious, but the point is not to draw an accurate rendition of your subject; it is to loosen you up, strengthen your hand-eye coordination and get you over the fear of the blank page.

Once you have done a few totally blind drawings, allow yourself to look at the page every once in a while when you draw. Now see what a difference it makes! I am actually quite pleased with the looseness of drawing number 6.

As you become more confident with your sketching, you should find yourself looking more at your subject than at the page whenever you sit down to draw. This type of exercise can help instill that habit.

BIRDS AND DUCKS

I love sketching birds, especially at our local bird sanctuary, where there are countless varieties. I especially enjoy sketching ducks. They are a very forgiving subject as they move a bit slower. You can sketch many of them in different positions across your page.

I have two main strategies for getting the shape of the duck onto your page very quickly.

Strategy 1: Paint a very light color in the general shape of the duck and perhaps add some other colors while the first color is still wet. This is a fun time to play with the wet-on-wet technique (page 23). I use a light color as the base shape, so that if I get it a bit wrong, I can correct it by restating the shape either with a darker color or in the ink stage. The very light color that may be wrong won't show up much at all.

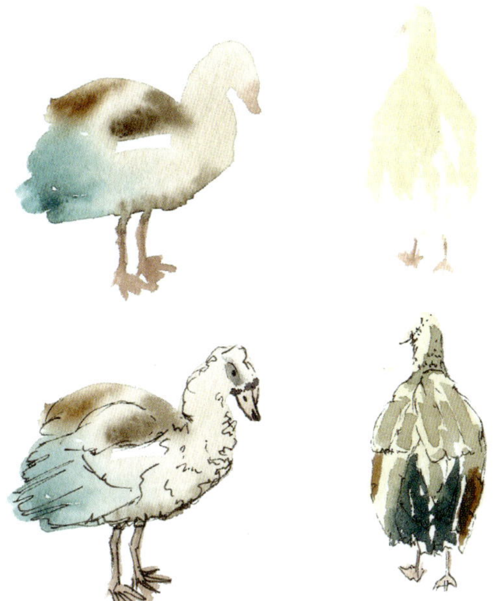

TIP: *When doing quick, little sketches like these, I love using a water brush (page 11). It reduces the fuss for needing a brush and container of water. I find I am more agile and can capture things that move far quicker with this setup.*

Strategy 2: A second strategy is to draw some quick marks in ink. Keep your lines very loose and gestural. Don't try to draw the details or features of the bird—just draw some lines of the overall shape or action. Perhaps draw some directional lines of a few feathers you can see clearly or the overall shape of a group of feathers. I kept my lines light and feathery as I can always restate them later to give it a stronger form if I want to.

When the paint is dry, draw the details on top in ink. In the meantime, while waiting a minute or two for the paint to dry, start another small sketch. The great thing about birds is that if your subject moved while you were waiting for the paint to dry, usually there are many around and one of them will most likely be in a similar position. Don't be afraid to merge multiple subjects together to create your sketches.

When it comes to drawing, look for the main shapes, rather than at individual feathers. I think the most important feature to get right is the shape of the bill. Notice that my lines in the rest of the sketches above are light and broken; there are no solid, heavy lines outlining anything. The watercolor is providing the shape, so I just used the ink to define a ruffled texture and a few feathers. In my second example, I added some more watercolor after drawing in ink, as my base layer was all one color. You can bounce between watercolor and ink as you like but don't overwork the sketch. Try to keep it quick and minimal.

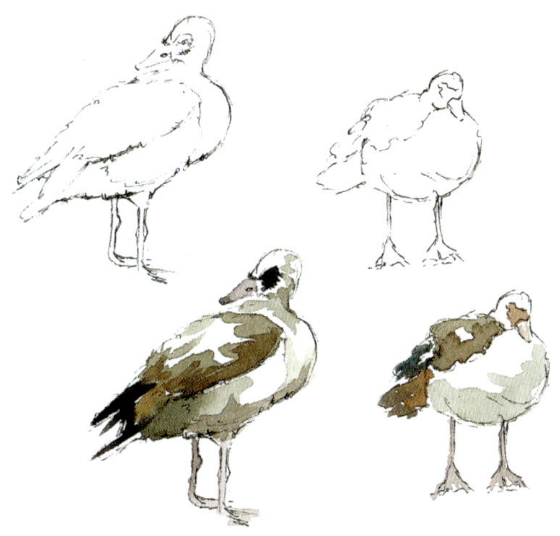

TIP: *Notice where the legs are attached to the bird's body. It's easy to assume you know and just draw them how you think they should be. The more you really look at your subject, the more you will notice small details like this that will help your sketch (no matter how loose) look more realistic.*

Then add some loose watercolor over the top. Just roughly paint areas of color. Don't get granular with any details. Keep the colors minimal and focus on where the light parts and the shadow areas are. Exaggerate them for a more stylized effect.

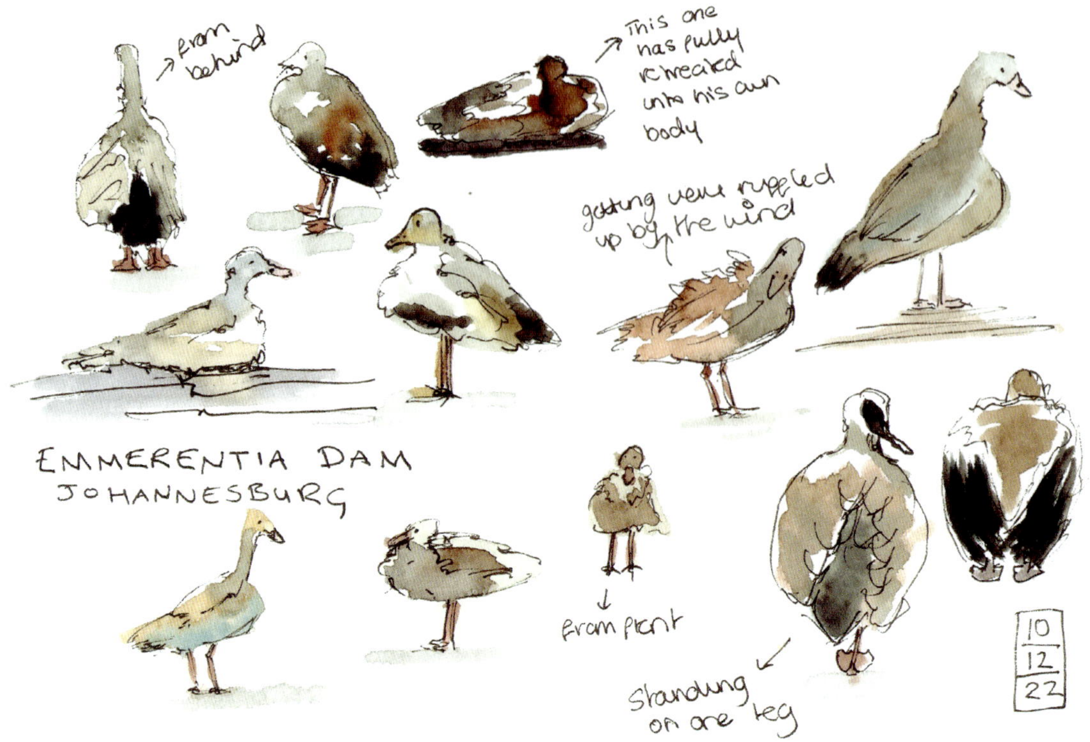

Sometimes I like to add little notes to my sketches, just to aid the memory of the moment, or record something funny or of note.

This is the best way to capture anything in motion, be it animals or humans. You just want to capture the impression of the thing—there's no time to add details. That's why I like to create lots of small sketches. It's quicker, you can draw a wide variety of different positions and poses, and you capture a sense of the number of ducks, for example, around you.

No matter which strategy I use, I add a shadow shape underneath the subject that anchors it to the ground (or water).

These sketches take between 2 and 5 minutes. This means you can make many sketches. Don't worry about realistic renditions of the birds. It's far better to stay loose and capture the pose and character of your subject. Just keep going until you are worn out! It's surprisingly fun to see quite how quickly and loosely you can sketch while still maintaining a degree of recognizability. You will end up with so many quirky little sketches. I encourage you to visit your local duck pond or bird park and have a go.

URBAN FARMS OR CITY ZOOS

While not something you would necessarily see in the park, you may have an urban farm or city zoo in your neighborhood. If you live in the countryside, perhaps you have a real farm nearby.

As mentioned earlier, we have a bird sanctuary close to our house that's also home to a few other types of wildlife. I absolutely love sketching there. It can be a challenge, but it is so much fun to try to sketch some of the birds and other animals. Some stay more still than others. It's a good idea to get warmed up on the slow-moving animals (like this iguana) before moving on to the ones that race or fly around a lot.

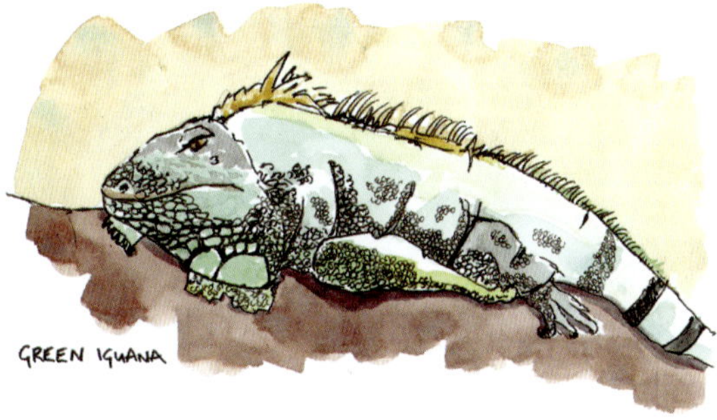

Notice how "tight" the drawing is of the subject that didn't move (the iguana) versus the looseness of some of these bird sketches where the birds' movement varied from frantic to moderate.

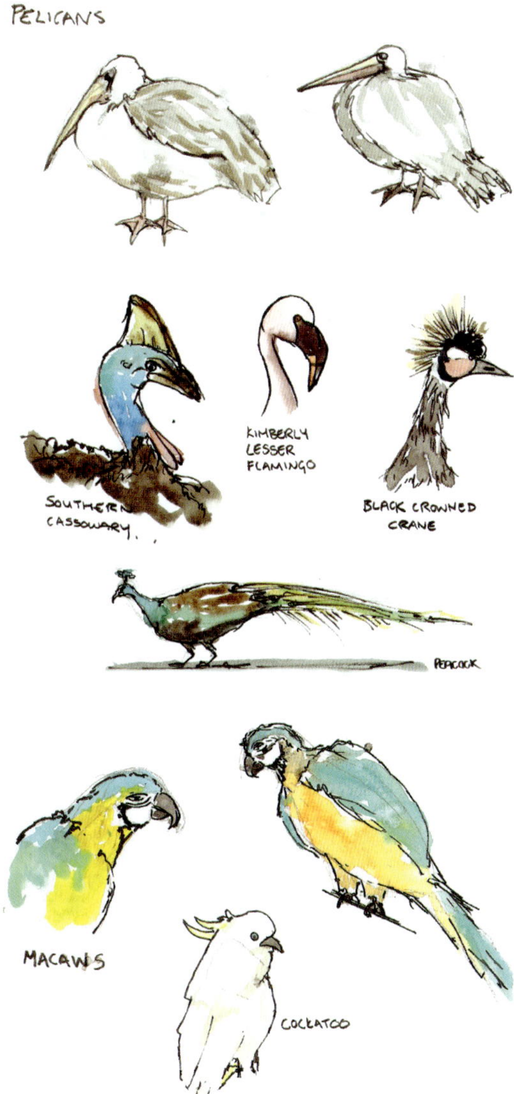

As mentioned earlier in the book, there is no right or wrong approach to sketching. My process and outcome seem to largely depend on the subject I am drawing.

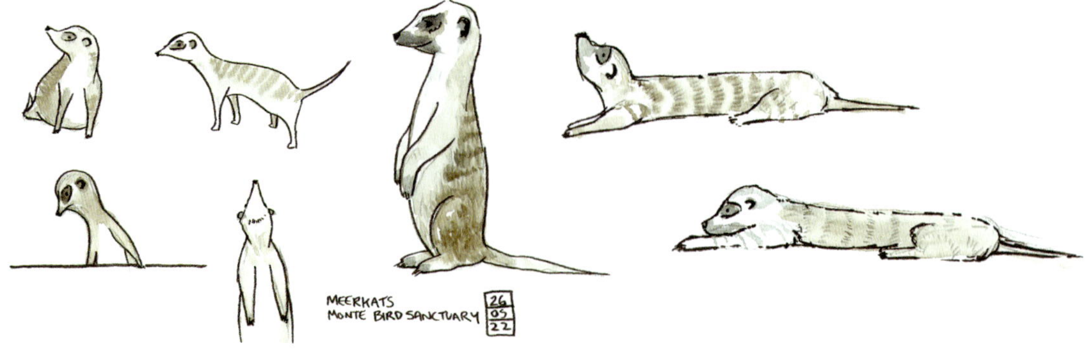

These meerkats would not stop moving while I was sketching them. I kept my marks as minimal as possible and tried to catch the essence and personality of the animal.

I tried two different strategies when I sketched the meerkats. The first strategy was to capture the main shape of the animal in pencil. I just drew a contour line, no further details. I then added some detail with watercolor paint only. I could use any of the meerkats for this stage.

The second strategy was to capture the main shape and posture of the meerkat with a very light color of watercolor, one you can barely see on the page. This is a very quick way to get a shape of something that is constantly moving.

I noticed that the meerkats would often return to the same sorts of poses (just at high speed). There were several of them so my sketches became an amalgamation of a few different ones. Just as urban sketchers do when sketching people, which we discuss on page 44.

Of course, as soon as I left the meerkats, I turned back, and they were sunbathing—completely still! So, I went back and managed another couple of quick sketches before finally leaving.

I started sketching on the left side of the sketchbook and worked across to the right. Do you notice how the sketches become better from left to right? I encourage you to do multiple small sketches of any animals in motion. I can guarantee your sketches will improve with the repetition of trying to capture their pose and character.

DOGS

Dogs can be very tricky; they rarely stay still, especially in the park. But if one is sitting or, even better, lying on the ground, grab the opportunity!

I went with Urban Sketchers Johannesburg to sketch at a dog-training session, and it was extremely challenging. I found that my most successful sketches were those that I kept very simple.

I used a few different processes in these sketches. I was exploring which tools and mark making may help me to capture the chaos of an owner and their dog training each other (that's what it seemed like to me)!

In sketch (A), I decided to use a black brush marker to quickly draw the very basic shape of the owner and dog. The owner was a large man with a big coat on, so it made his body a big triangle. The dog seemed like a smaller

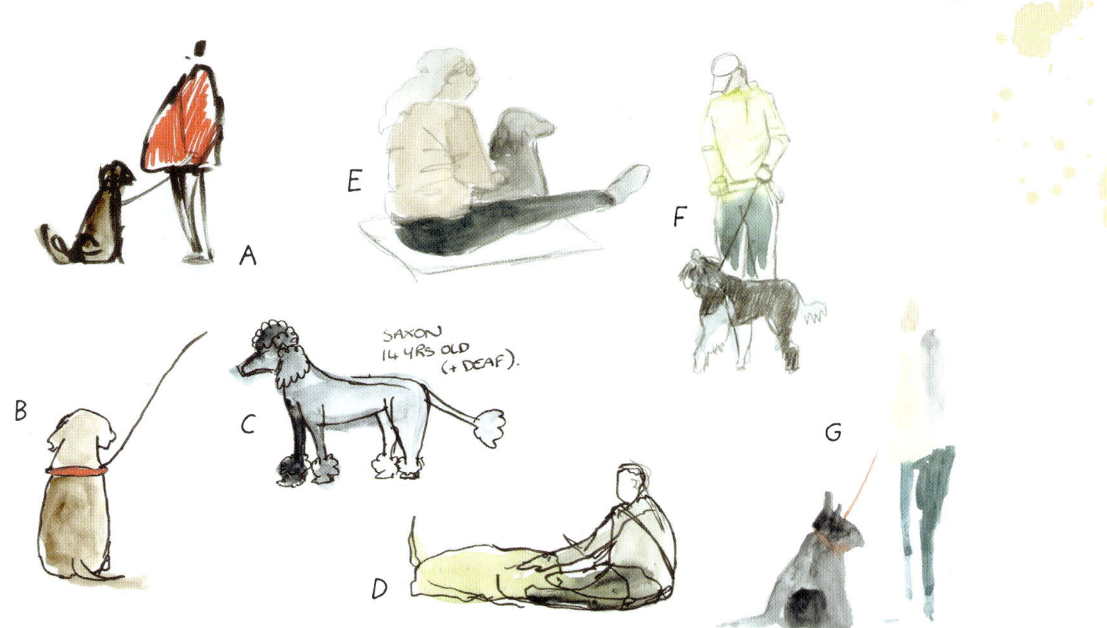

triangle. That's as complicated as it got in this sketch. I really like the floating black mark for the man's head, as well as his overall gesture, i.e. the way he is holding himself.

TIP: ***When you are making small sketches like this and experimenting, make a note (physically or mentally) on what worked and what you liked. That way you can build upon these discoveries in future sketches. Evaluations like these, no matter how casual, will really help you to progress.***

I think sketch (B) is a great example of how a small, simple sketch can still capture the moment. It's a simple contour drawing from the rear of the dog while sitting. I like that the line of the dog's leash disappears into the blank page. We know there must be an owner there, but it's left up to the imagination.

Sketch (C) was also a rough contour drawing in ink with some loose watercolor applied, taking note of where the shadows and highlights were. Poodles are a great subject due to their distinctive look.

Sketch (D) wasn't quite a blind contour sketch, but I deliberately kept it loose and looked at my subject as much as possible rather than the page. The dog and owner seemed to blend into one shape and so does the application of watercolor. I actually really like the overall effect even though someone may not necessarily know what the sketch is of!

I approached sketches (E) and (F) in a similar way. I used a black oil-based pencil (therefore not erasable) and sketched the shapes of the owner and their dog. Much like my advice when sketching ducks, I kept the lines and shapes simple and minimal. I then painted them loosely with watercolor. Remember to leave the white of the page in some areas where the light is hitting your subject. It gives a very pleasing effect.

In sketch (G), I shunned the use of lines altogether! I painted directly with watercolor, using minimal paint strokes to describe the scene. I encourage you to try this; it's really fun and can turn out beautifully. It forces you to look and pick the most important shapes to paint.

EXERCISE

1. Loosen up with blind contour drawings.

At your chosen location, start by doing some blind contour exercises of your subjects, whether they're birds, ducks, dogs or any other kind of wildlife. I recommend ducks and geese to start with though. Once you have done several blind contours, try some more but allow yourself to look at your page once in a while. Compare your sketches. Do you notice how much life these kinds of drawings have versus when you are rigidly trying to draw every detail of something?

TIP: *If you are concerned about using up your nice sketchbook pages, take some printer paper with you for these exercises and just use a pencil or pen.*

2. Start a new sketch and paint the shape of your subject in light watercolor.

Do your best to observe and paint the shape you see but don't agonize over it, because it can be readjusted if need be. Once dry, add some loose pen lines on top to give some more details.

3. Start afresh and draw your subject loosely in ink.

Start by drawing in ink first, and then once dry, paint loosely on top. Don't try to stay inside the lines but do observe where the shadows are versus the highlights. If the animal moves, use another one to finish your sketch or wait for it to return to a similar pose.

4. Experiment!

Use watercolor only, with no lines before or after. Make lots of small, quick sketches. Make notes on the bits of the sketches you like so you know what to repeat in the future.

TIP: *If you or your friends or family have a pet then you can practice your sketching skills with them, so you feel more confident when you're out in the world. You can make a collage over time.* *See page 173 for more information on sketchbook spreads.*

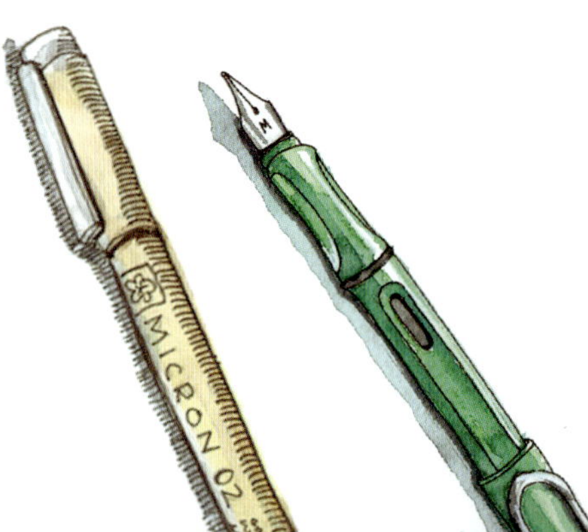

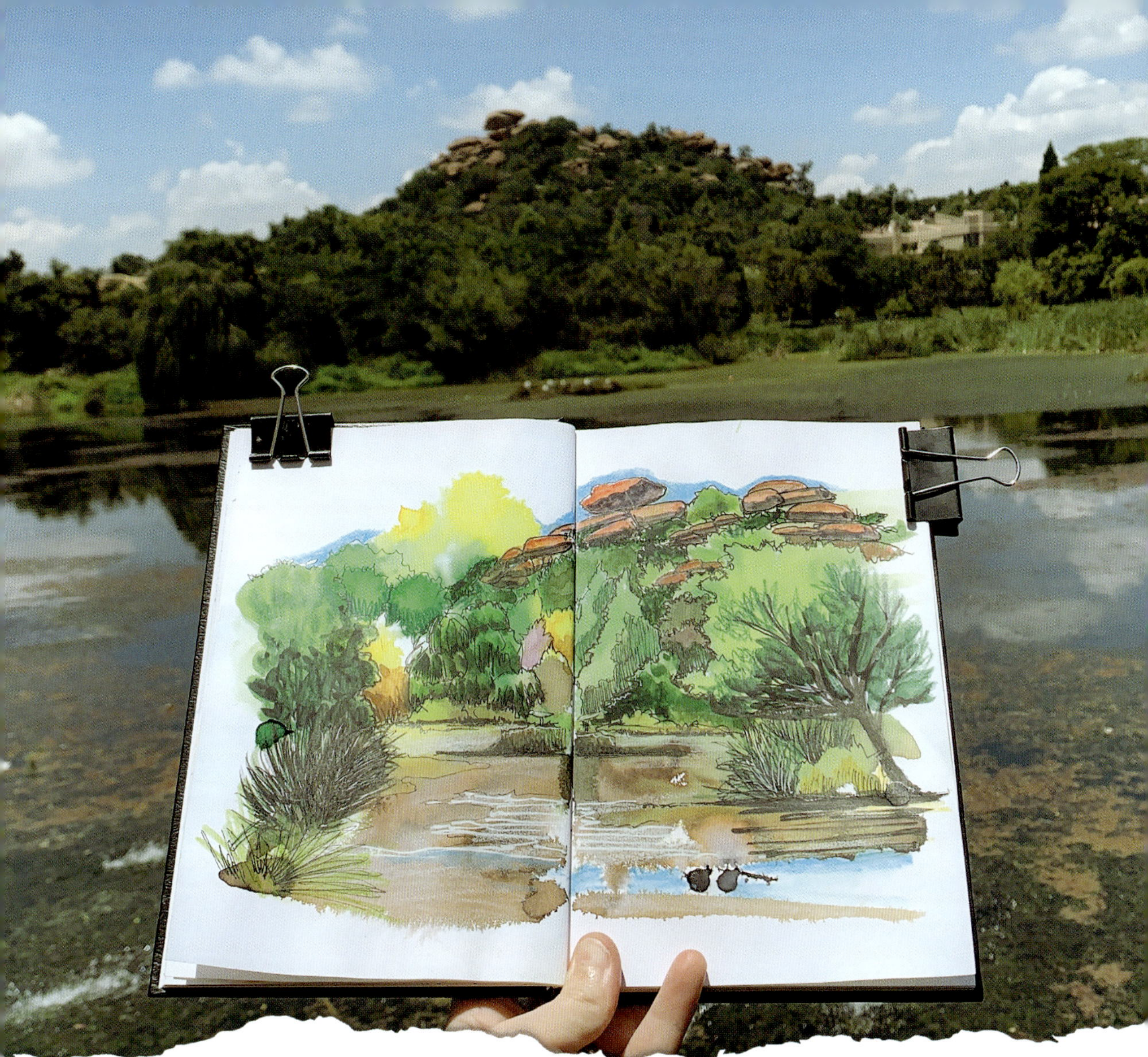

WATER & REFLECTIONS

Many parks have ponds or lakes, and learning how to represent water quickly and authentically is a useful skill to develop. I avoided sketching water for a long time. It scared me.

Over time though, I knew I had to try and, step by step, I found some strategies for how to indicate it in its various forms.

There is a dam in our local park, along with a rocky outcrop known in South Africa as a "koppie." I have sketched this scene so many times, always trying to play with how I represent both the rocks and the water.

In the sketch on page 103, I actually started off with a watercolor abstract background I had painted a few days before.

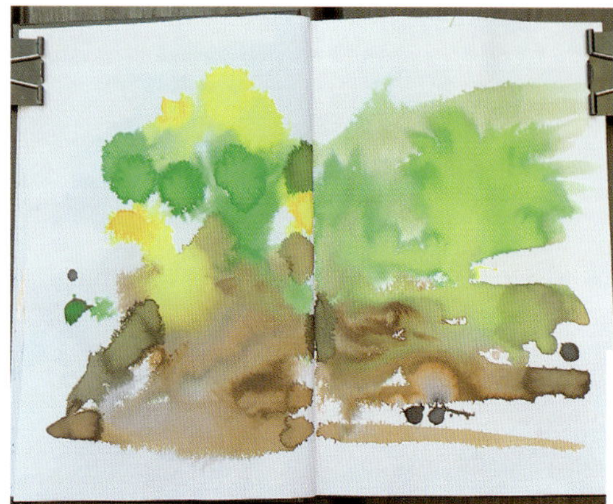

I had no idea what I would sketch on top of it when I painted it. However, when I sat in front of this scene, I knew it could work. So I sketched this outcrop on top. If you would like more information on this advanced technique, I have a full-length online course dedicated to teaching it, which you can find at this link:

https://learn.sketchyouradventures.com/awb

Notice how the water is brown in my sketch. This was largely dictated by the abstract background that had already been prepared, but it still works. This shows the way you represent water does not have to be literal. We shall explore color mixing for water later in this section.

Different types of bodies of water may require slightly different treatment; for example, the way you represent water from a waterfall will be different than the still water of a pond surface.

FALLING WATER

This waterfall is in a town called Kuruman in the Northern Cape of South Africa. The waterfall is known as the Eye of Kuruman, or The Eye, a natural fountain delivering twenty to thirty million liters of crystal-clear water a day. According to the sign in the park, The Eye is the biggest natural fountain in the Southern Hemisphere. I only wanted to capture the fountain itself, not the surrounding area. This made the sketch more manageable and quicker.

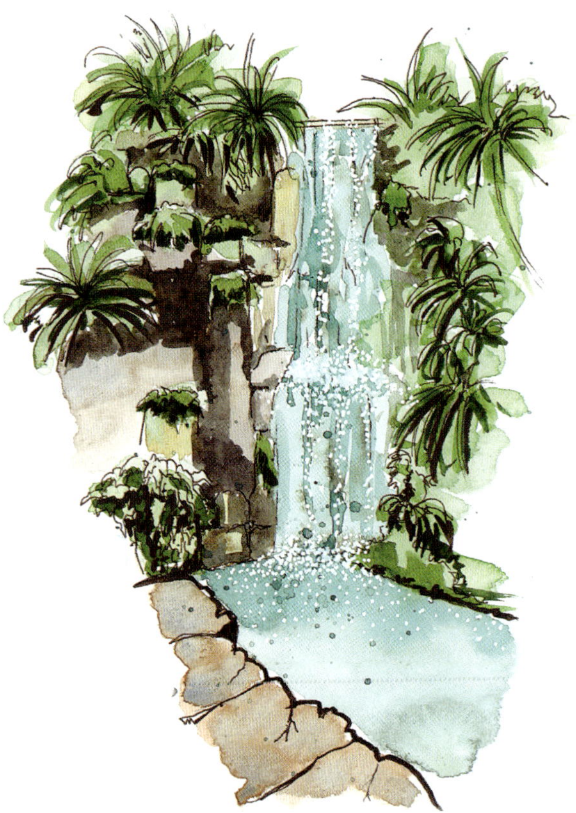

TIP: *Don't be afraid to pick one detail of a scene and zoom in on it, especially if you don't have too much time.*

I quickly sketched the overall shape of The Eye in pencil, very loosely mapping in the rocks and foliage. As you can see, there's not a huge amount of detail here. Natural objects can be hard to draw as the shapes are so organic and sometimes hard to distinguish. I think one of the most important yet subtle details is the shape of the water itself and how it looks like it is falling in stages. You can't always capture an effect like that with lines, so I utilized watercolor to help. After painting an initial wash of light blue, I added a deeper, darker blue on top to indicate some shadows, with a tiny bit of brown in areas (using wet-on-wet) to perhaps give the effect there are rocks behind the water. It's subtle but tiny details like that can bring so much more interest to a sketch.

The final element that brought the whole sketch together was a white paint marker. I used it to indicate spray from the waterfall in key areas. The dots are placed closer together in areas where the water is hitting a surface, such as in the middle of the fountain where the water hits some rocks and then where the water hits the surface of the pool that has formed beneath it.

Man-made fountains also feature falling water and may even incorporate a statue.

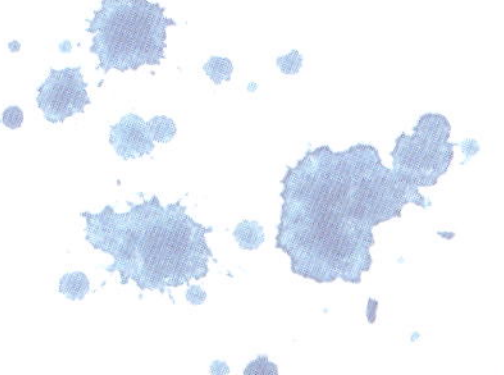

This is an example of a fountain I sketched. I left the background quite vague and just focused on the fountain itself. I added dots of white paint marker to indicate the water falling from each tier.

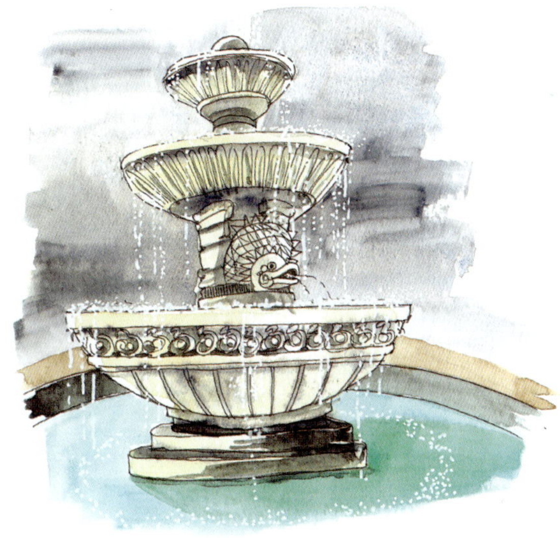

Another art supply you can use instead of a white paint marker is white gouache. Gouache is effectively opaque watercolor. A lot of urban sketchers carry a small tube of white gouache in their sketch kit in case they need to add some opaque white to a sketch.

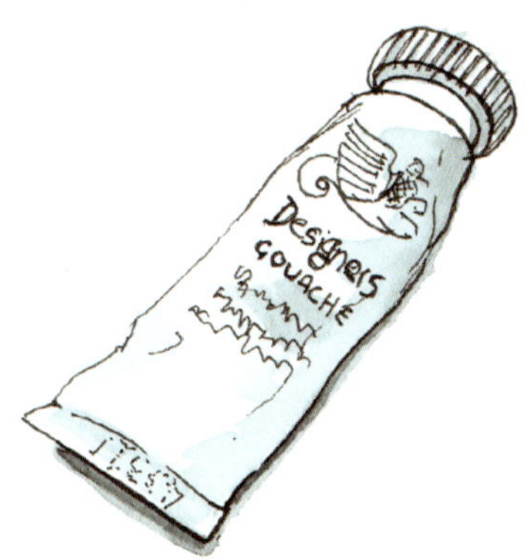

White gouache

OCEAN WATER

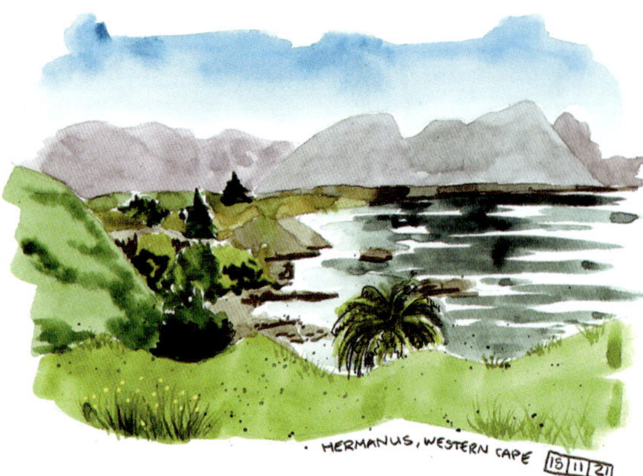

In this sketch, I captured the view from a town called Hermanus in the Western Cape of South Africa. It's hard to imagine I was standing on the edge of the town center with this view across the ocean to the mountains in the background. As you can see, this is another very simple sketch, but I particularly love how the water came out in this. First, I think the color is very beautiful (I will explain my color-mixing approach to water in the next section), and second, the play of light is represented very simply by placing a darker version of the color in the middle of the ocean and fading it out toward the shore by simply adding more water to the paint. The broken brushstrokes on the right of the sketch indicate light reflected from the surface of the ocean. The dry brush technique (page 25) is useful for capturing the light glistening on water very quickly and beautifully, as seen in the image below.

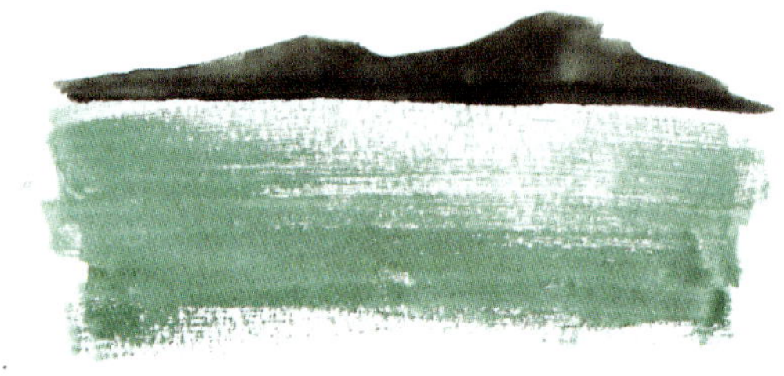

COLOR MIXING

I find just using a pure blue (such as Ultramarine) from my paint set doesn't give me the nuanced color of water that I would like, especially for lakes and ponds. I encourage you to try mixing a more interesting color. One of my favorite mixtures for water is Ultramarine Blue, Sap Green and Burnt Umber.

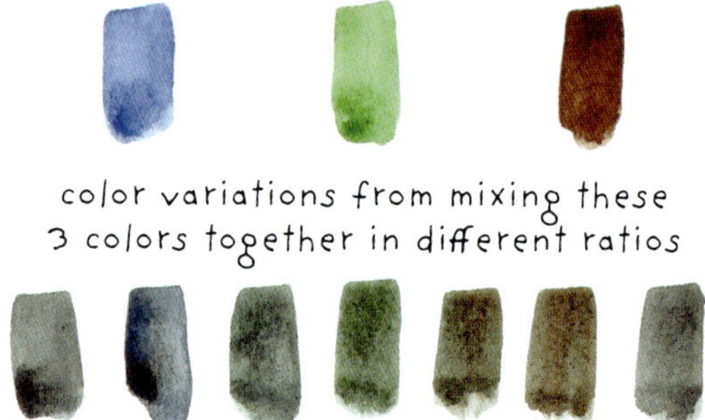

Experiment with color mixing. If the water is more blue, then add only add a tiny little bit of green and brown. If the water seems browner, then use more brown than green and blue. Make some swatches in your sketchbook and keep a note of which colors you have used. Don't worry if you don't have the same colors as I mentioned above. Just use the blue, green and brown you have. Sometimes I like to drop in Phthalo Blue or a Turquoise—just to make the mix a little more lively. As you experiment and swatch you own color mixes, you will develop color preferences for certain subject matter.

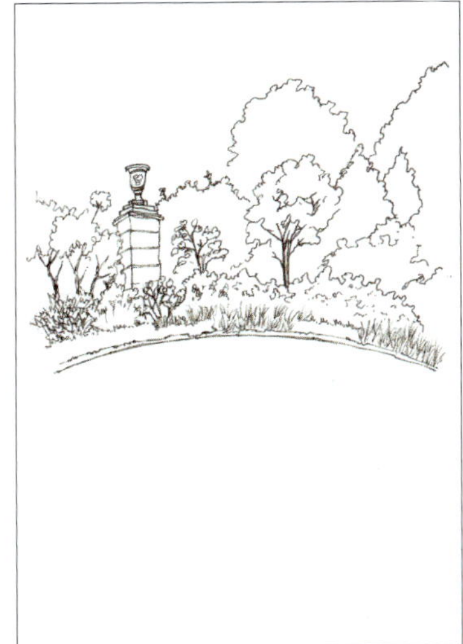

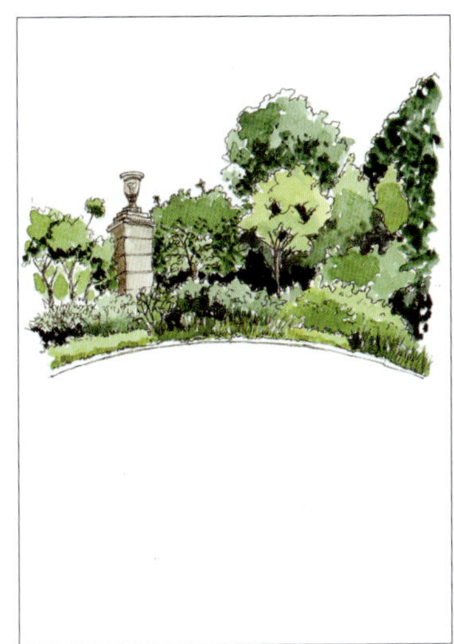

WATER REFLECTIONS

In this example, we're going to take what we learned in the Foliage section (page 87) and add some water to the scene.

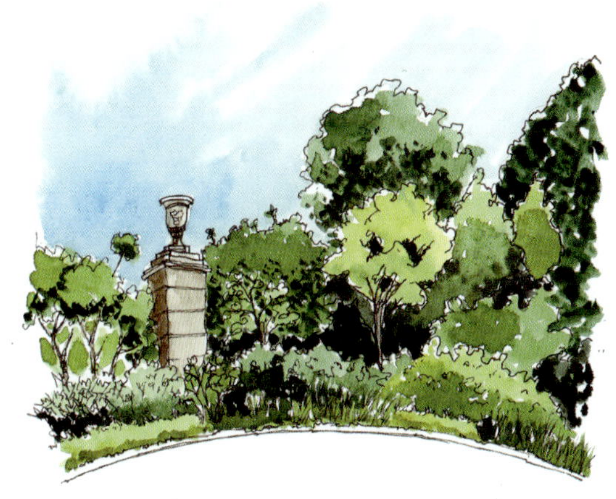

I started by sketching the basic shapes and composition on my page. I then added details with ink and painted the top half with watercolor.

After this, I moved on to add the sky. There were some interesting cloud streaks in the sky that were reflected in the water below. After the sky, I put in my initial water ripples in the same color as the sky. The water had ripples from the breeze that day; the surface wasn't completely still, so I emulated the movement of the ripples with my brushstrokes.

I drew shapes extremely lightly in pencil where the foliage is reflected in the water. So, I put my initial brushstrokes of green within them.

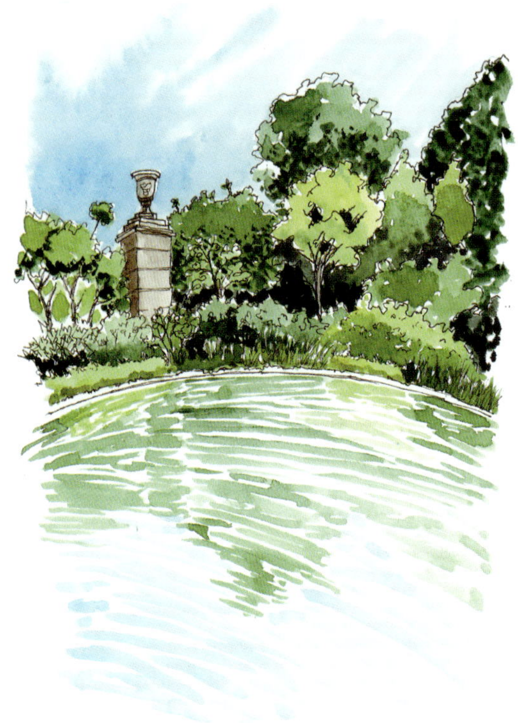

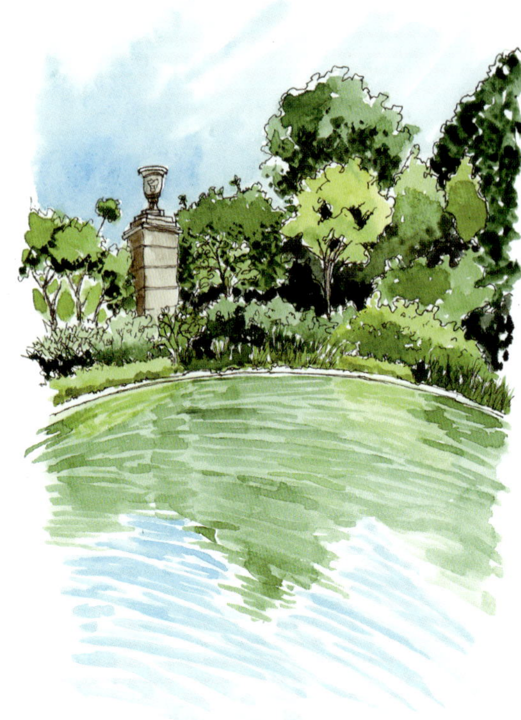

Once the basic colors of all the reflections were dry, I started working on adding shadows to bring some more life to the reflections. I didn't want the reflections to overpower the foliage in the top half of the sketch, as they are the objects causing the reflections. They had to be the stronger, starker shapes so the sketch made sense.

The key to reflections is to leave small white space between brushstrokes to indicate the light reflection from the water, as well as the broken nature of the reflection. In this case, I felt I had gone a bit too far with the white gaps, and it looked a bit too chaotic, so I toned it down by putting a very light wash of green over the green reflections nearest the edge that meets the ground.

I also darkened a few areas of the blue ripples to give a bit more interest and variety to the strokes on the surface.

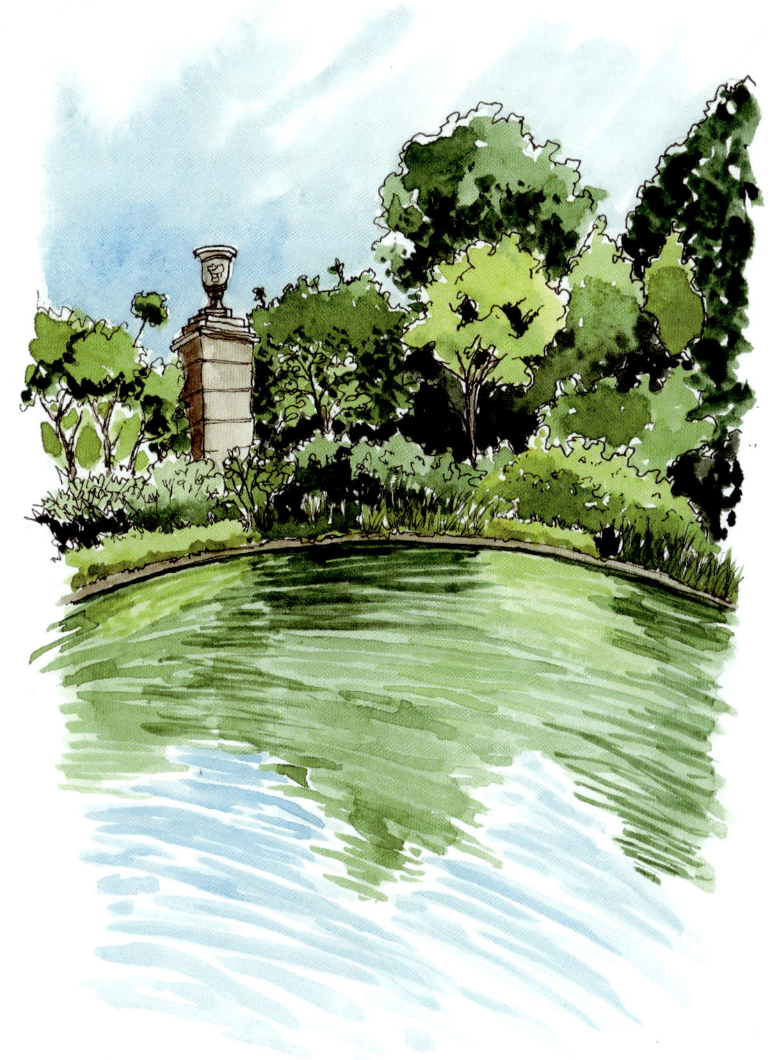

For the finishing touches, I painted the edge of the ground, along with its corresponding shadow. This emphasized the division between land and water.

I then added a few more shadow areas in the water where the foliage was particularly dark. I was careful not to overdo it; otherwise, the sketch could end up looking confused and messy.

This is a stylized version of what I was looking at in real life. I injected a bit of wonkiness (not overly intentional—ha!) and as such, a bit of personality.

SKETCH A SCENE

PUTTING IT ALL TOGETHER

Let's put everything we have learned from the previous sections into practice. There's a real freedom to just plonking yourself down and drawing whatever happens to be in front of you. However, there's a danger your sketch will fall very flat without considering composition. This is especially true of a park scene, as there may not be any clear perspective lines to indicate depth. Make sure you set yourself up for success before you even start drawing. A great way to explore a few different compositions quickly is to make some thumbnail sketches. These can be small credit card–sized drawings in pencil to help you discover some important aspects of what you want to draw. These do not have to take long—2 minutes maximum. Don't be afraid to move things in your sketch or to leave out things that you don't want to draw. Many urban sketchers bend and contort the scenes they sketch, as well as edit what they see.

COMPOSITION

1. Find a location with points of interest.

If your view includes nothing but grass and trees, it may be tricky to find a pleasing composition, especially as a beginner. Look for a scene that has a clear foreground, mid-ground and background.

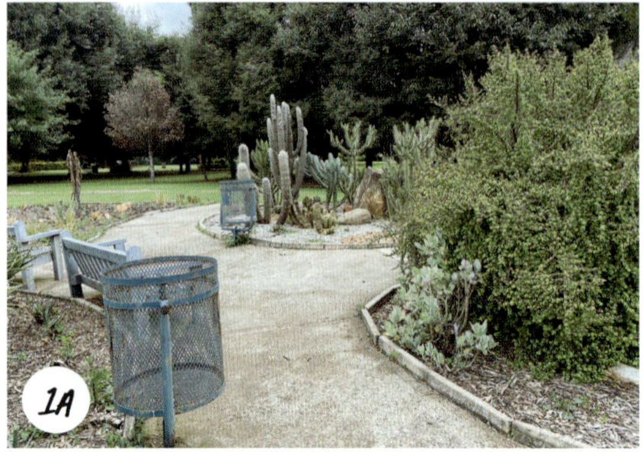

In this photo, there are clear layers in the scene. In the foreground, there is a trash can (not the most exciting subject matter but it will still work); in the mid-ground, there's an interesting range of succulents and in the background, there are some very dark trees standing on bright green grass (1A). Also, the curve of the pathway from foreground to mid-ground leads the eye into the scene. This would make a good composition.

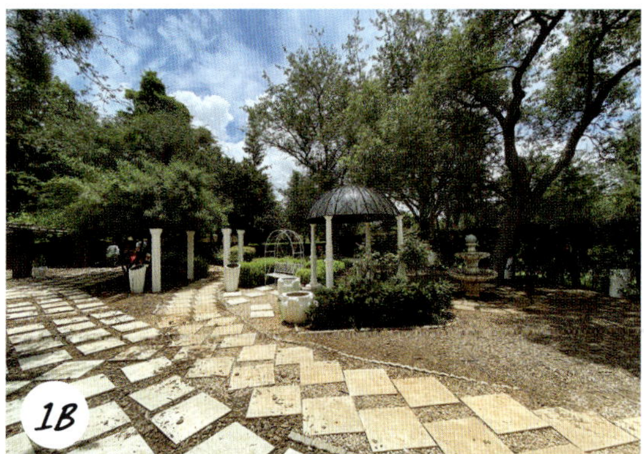

In this photo, there are a number of interesting items in the shot; however, all the interesting objects are in the mid-ground, and as such, it makes the scene appear very flat. There are also far too many paving stones taking up the foreground (1B).

2. **Make between two and four thumbnail sketches of the scene.**

By making some small thumbnails, you can establish which composition you think will work best for your sketch. You can have a lot of fun with this process—go wild with your ideas! They are only small 2-minute sketches, so there is no pressure and who knows! You may come up with something completely unexpected. Don't forget to try your thumbnails in landscape and portrait format.

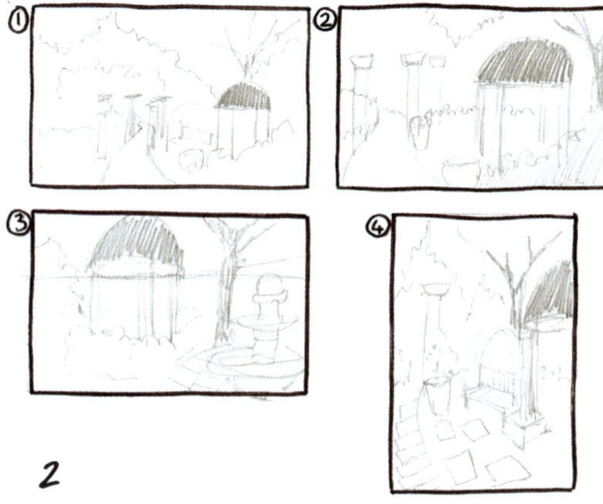

2

Once you have chosen your composition, you can move on to your final sketch and draw the big shapes in pencil. Don't worry about any of the details at this stage. Just draw big basic shapes to identify where things will be placed on the page and to make sure everything fits as you would like it to.

PENCIL SKETCH

3. **Identify what to draw first.**

For image 1B, I would start with the decorative pagoda and build out from there. It is the strongest shape in the scene, and it makes sense to start with placing it where you want on the page. You can use it as a reference point to draw the rest of the scene.

Some scenes may require a different strategy.

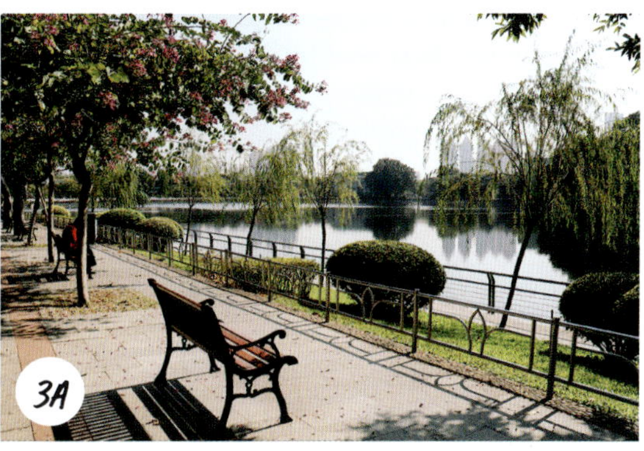

In this photo, there are very strong lines of the horizon and also the pathway that cuts across the bottom section of the scene (3A). In this case, I would start by drawing the horizontal line of the horizon and from there, the diagonal line of the pathway. The foreground element in this scene is the bench, but if we drew it first, it wouldn't really help to complete the rest of the scene.

Assess your scene and think about what would help you complete your pencil sketch. Look for strong horizontal or vertical lines that divide your scene (3B). If you do not have these, look for the largest objects that need to fit on the page.

There are no rules as to where to start drawing with ink, but I started on the left side of my page as I am right-handed, and it helps to draw from left to right so I don't smudge anything.

4. Think about the separation between foreground and background.

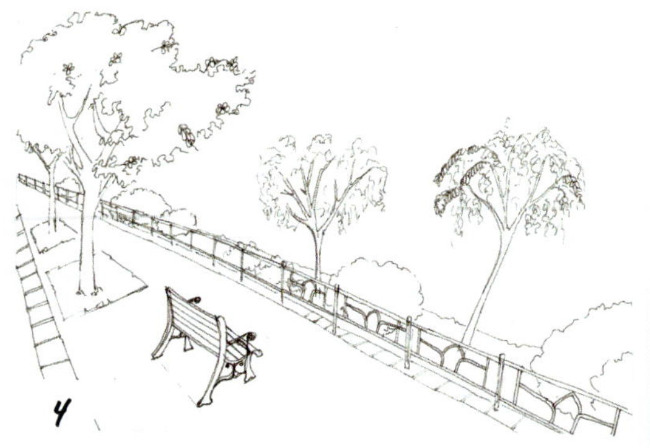

Notice that I didn't draw everything in ink. I left the background in pencil. If you look at the photo, you can see how soft the buildings are right in the background. If I drew them in ink, it would've ruined the depth of the sketch. Look at your scene; would it be better to leave some background elements in pencil, rather than draw them in ink, to make them softer?

FIRST WATERCOLOR WASH

5. Paint the large background elements first.

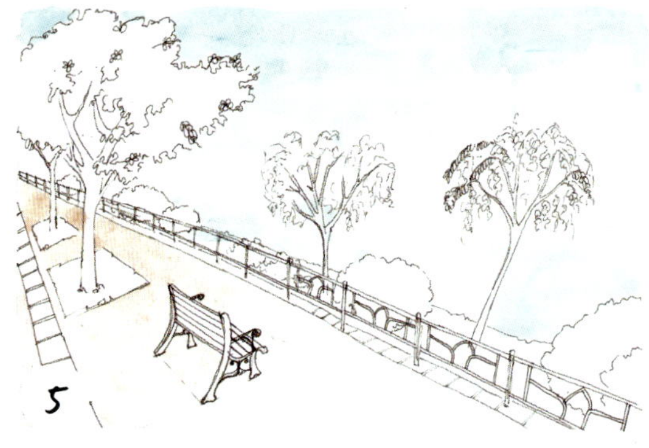

In the photo, the sky is not blue; however, this may have to do with the camera rather than how the scene looked in real life. I added a very pale blue to the sky. I also kept the reflection in the water extremely pale to assist with the contrast in the scene.

The sky and water were still wet, so I didn't want to paint anything that touched these areas so I painted the pathway next.

6. **Paint the rest of the lightest colors in your scene.**

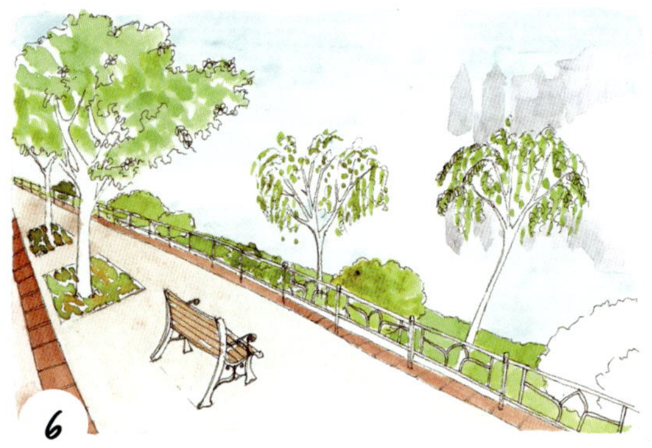

Once these areas were dry, I painted the base colors of the foliage and grass in the foreground, the bench and the paving on the pathway. I also painted the buildings in the distance and their corresponding reflections in the water.

SECOND WATERCOLOR WASH

7. **Add a second layer of darker watercolor once your first layer is dry.**

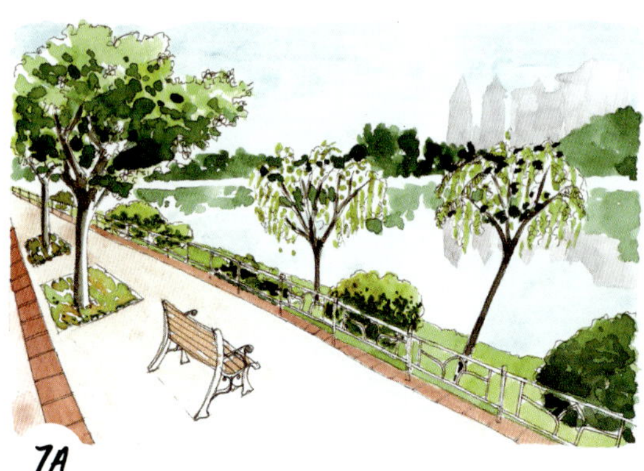

Once you have painted all the basic colors in your scene and it's dry, add darker areas on top to give objects more depth and shape. For example, I added a darker green on the foliage (7A). With the same color, I also painted the foliage along the water in the background, as well as its corresponding reflection in the water. I tried my best to match the shapes with each other to make it convincing.

Do you notice the dramatic difference from just adding basic light colors to now having some darker colors? Many beginners just add a single layer of paint to indicate the colors they see and call it done. But if you persevere a little longer to add a second layer of darker shades, it makes a significant difference.

A secret weapon that I very much enjoy using alongside watercolors are Faber-Castell Pitt Artist brush pens in a range of warm and cool grays.

FABER-CASTELL PITT ARTIST PENS

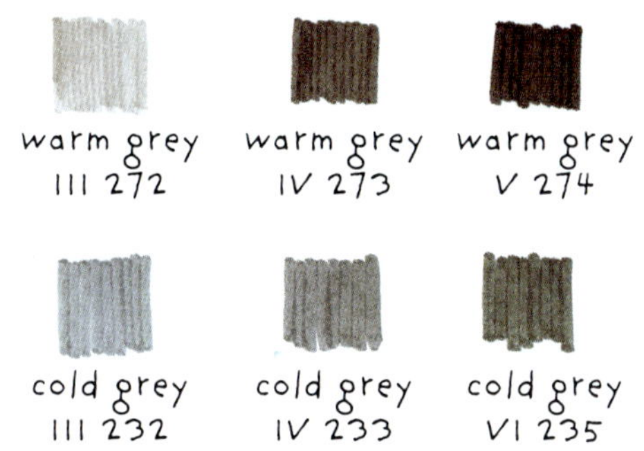

I have three shades of each: light, medium and dark. The pens contain India ink and are translucent, so they layer on top of watercolor beautifully and are an excellent tool for adding shadows, especially in small or tight areas.

I used a mid-cool gray to fill in the metal railings and a dark warm gray to color the metal frame of the bench (7B). I find I can be a little more accurate with the pens in tight areas such as these than I can with a brush and watercolor.

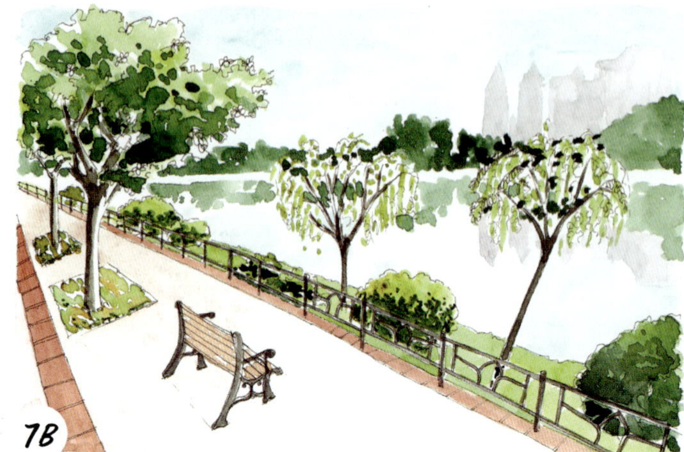

FINISHING TOUCHES

8. Look for the final details needed in your scene to bring it to life.

I added the shadows on the ground cast by the trees, the bench and the metal railing. I used a mixture of Indigo and Payne's Grey. I used a flat brush for the shadow of the bench and also the railing. It is much easier to get crisp, straight lines by using the edge of a flat brush.

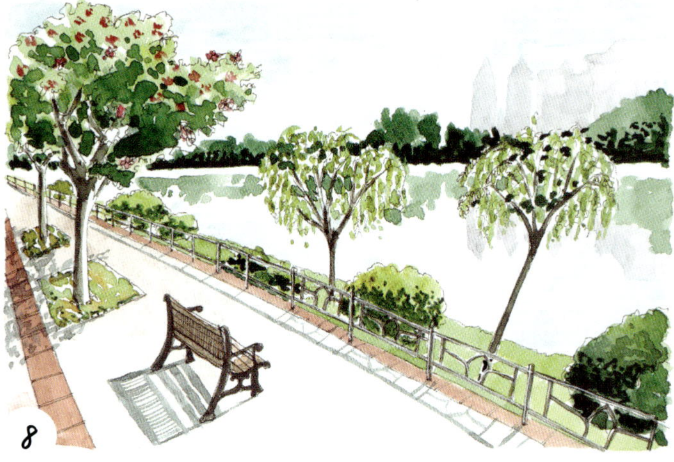

I also noticed I hadn't added some of the pink flowers on the tree yet, so I added those in. I added a darker green at the base of the foliage that meets the water in the background. I used a white gel pen on top of the railing I colored with a gray pen earlier. It's a quick shorthand way to indicate the railing has a bit of a shine to it.

I also made the shadow on the tree trunks much darker. It's fine to start off painting too lightly, as you can always make things darker. But don't be afraid to add very dark paint where it needs to be. This enhances the contrast and makes the sketch look so much more dramatic and interesting.

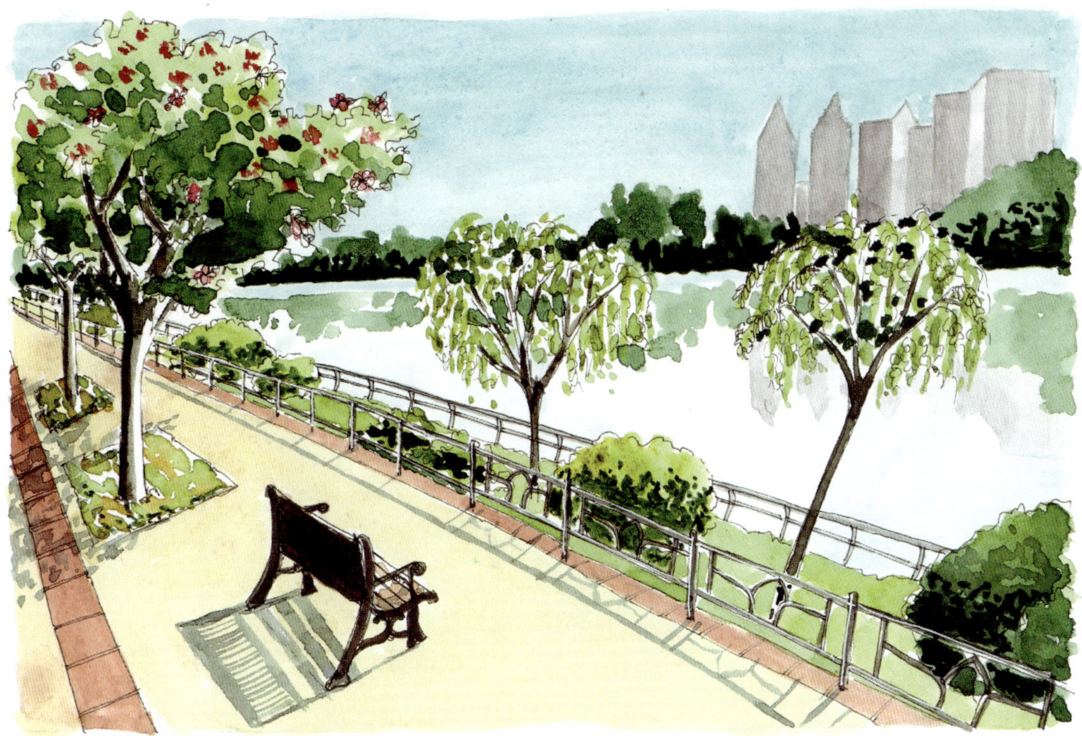

FIXING THINGS

I felt like something was not quite right with this sketch. It didn't have the level of drama I wanted. Therefore, I tried a few things to see if I could make myself happier about the scene.

1. I added the guardrail on the other side of the grass before the water. I drew it with a gray Pitt Artist pen, but it looked like a shadow, so outlined it with a 0.1 fineliner and it looked much better.
2. I painted the pathway a stronger color. It felt far too pale. I overlaid it with a second wash of Yellow Ochre.
3. I made the sky a stronger shade of blue.
4. I tightened up the buildings in the background; they looked a little too sloppy.

I feel like these small tweaks improved this sketch. Evaluate your sketch, step back and try to identify what works and what doesn't work. This self-evaluation process is one of the best ways to learn and improve. Don't be afraid to try to correct things. If it doesn't work out, there's no real loss. By trying things for yourself on your own sketch, you will start to figure out what works and what doesn't. Nothing compares to firsthand experience.

EXPLORING THE CITY

Architecture is my absolute passion when it comes to urban sketching. I admit, I know very little about the subject of architecture. However, this is unimportant when it comes to visual appreciation and the desire to draw. Over time, out of curiosity, your knowledge of historical periods and architectural terms may develop but don't let any perceived lack in that area put you off sketching. We need nothing but our eyes and hands (and hearts) to capture the beauty we see in buildings. And not necessarily an entire building or scene but architectural details, such as doors and windows, can be equally satisfying to draw in their own right and can provide just as much context.

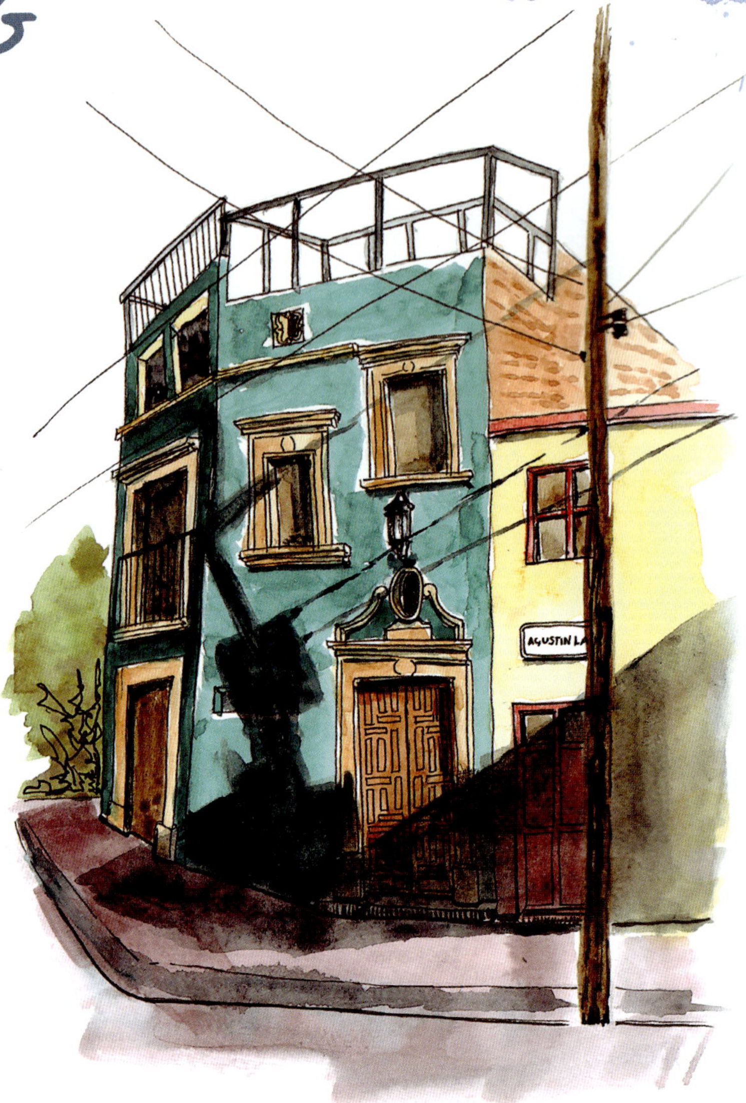

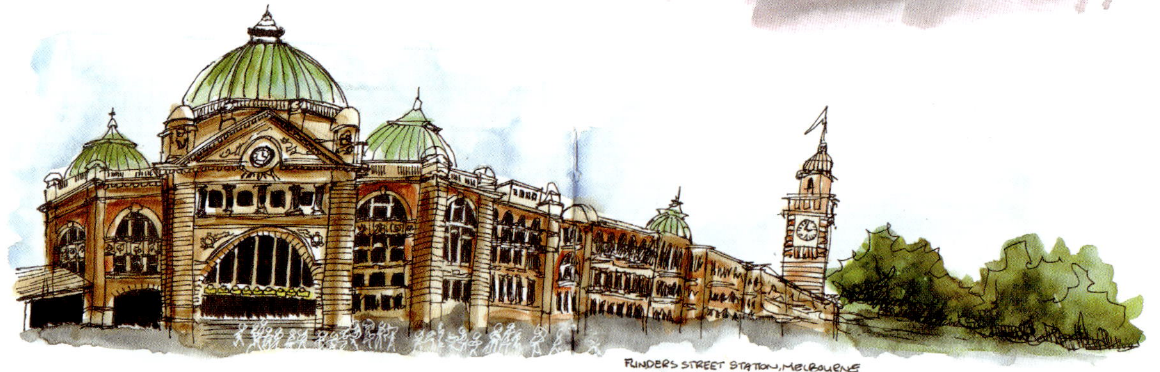

FLINDERS STREET STATION, MELBOURNE

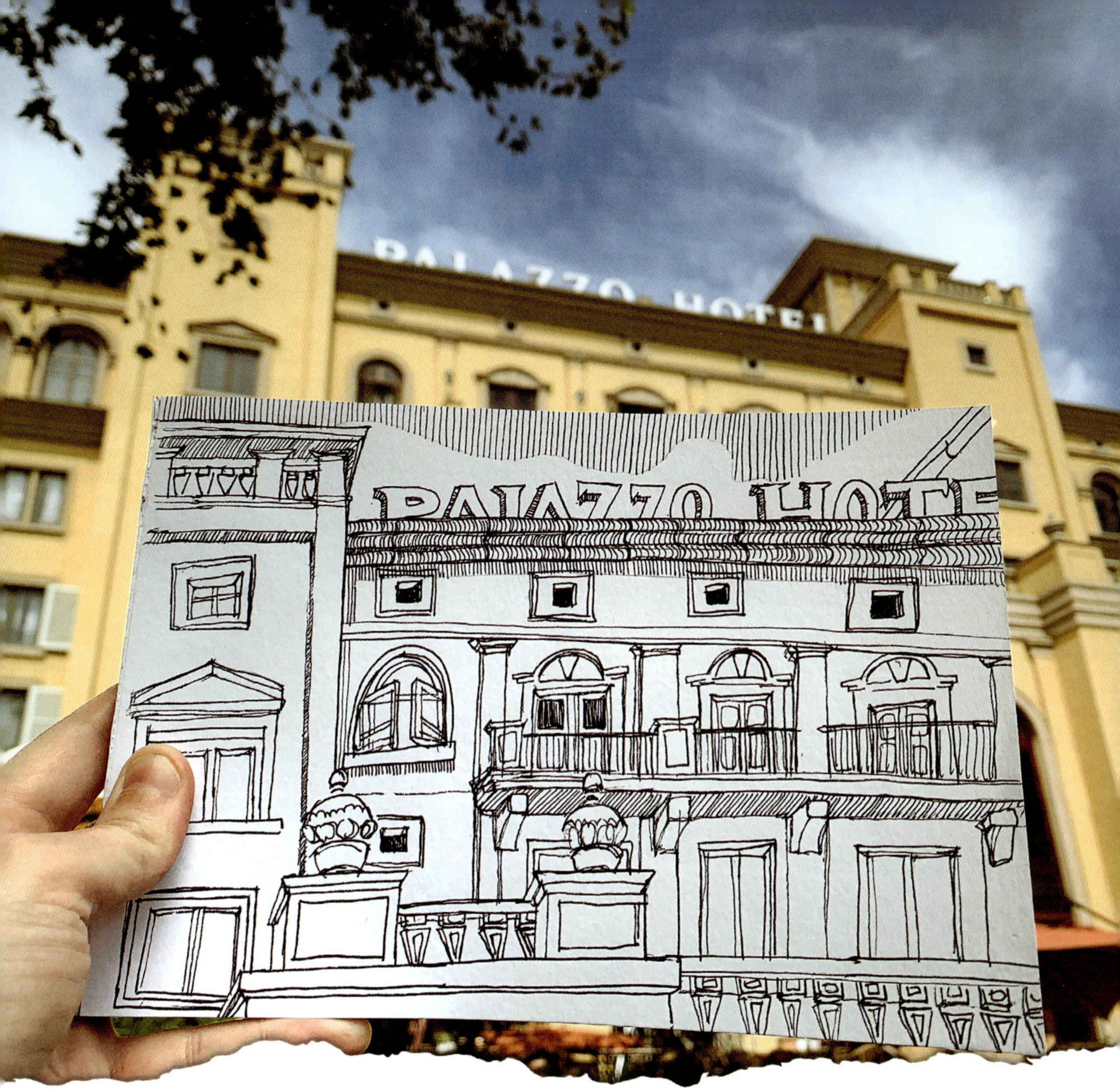

ORNATE WINDOWS & DOORWAYS

One of my all-time favorite things to sketch are old, ornate doors. I never knew this fascination lurked within me until I took a trip to Malta and visited the city of Valletta. The city is forever etched in my mind as the city of doors.

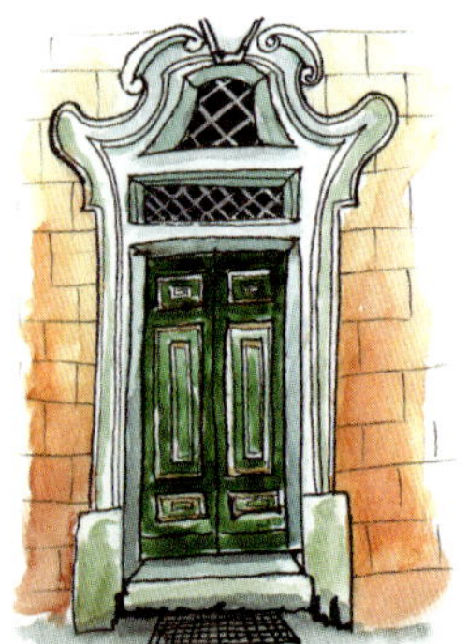

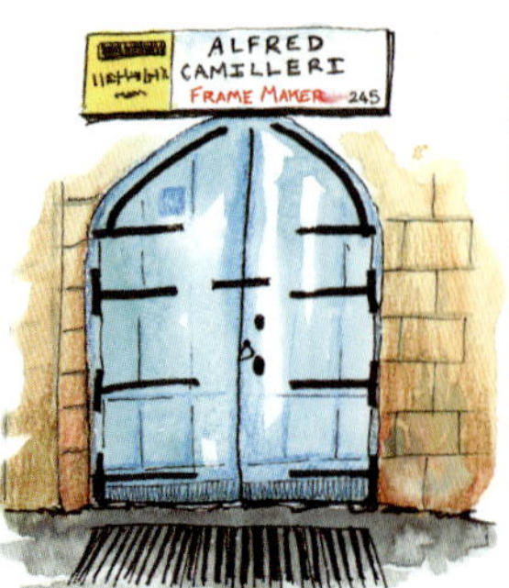

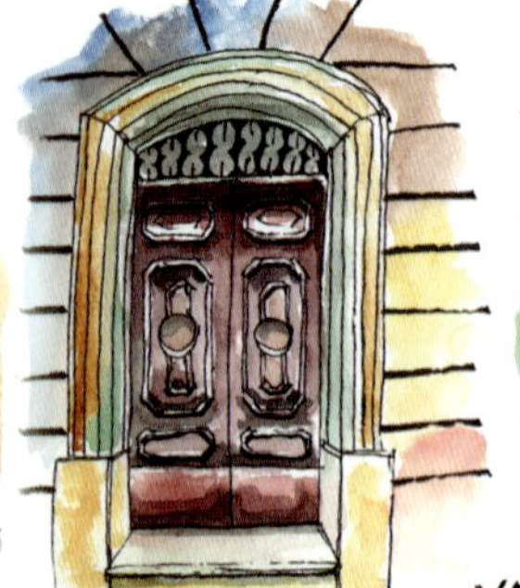

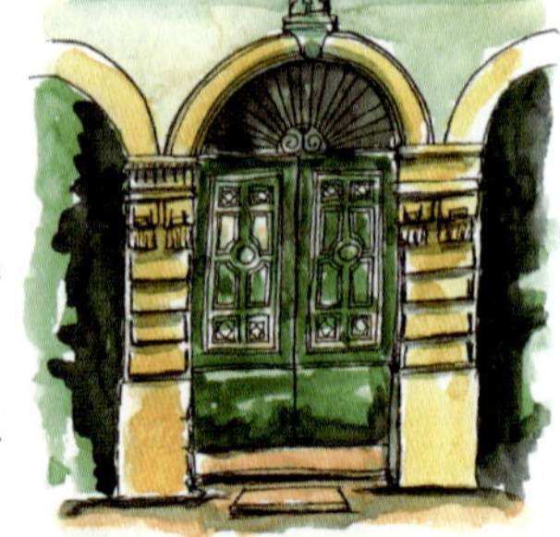

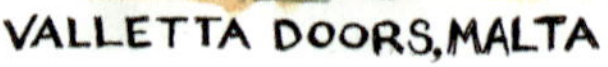
VALLETTA DOORS, MALTA

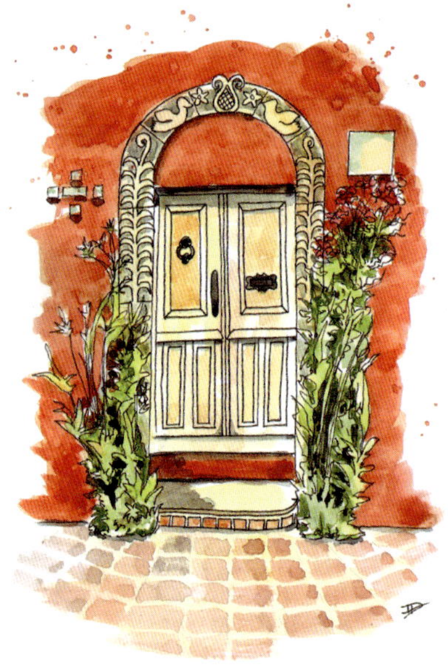

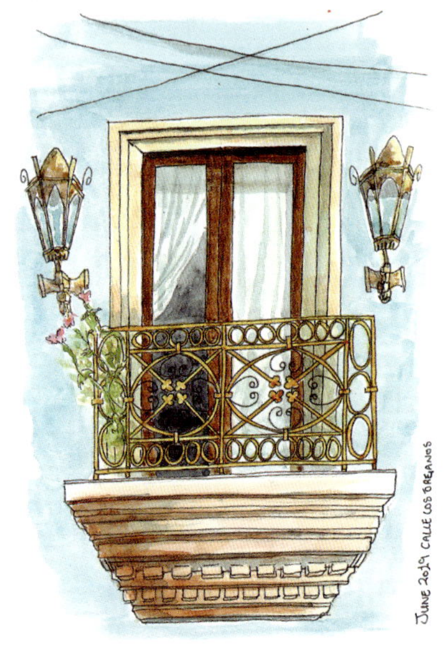

Ever since then, I find myself always noticing doors and imagine sketching them in my head.

The obsession continued in Mexico, specifically in the town of San Miguel de Allende and the city of Guanajuato. Aside from the spectacularly colored houses themselves, the doors (and windows) on every street are pieces of art in themselves.

I've found I'm certainly not the only one with this mild obsession, and the incredible photos you can find scattered around the internet (such as on Pinterest) are a testament to this. Even mildly decorative windows and doors are interesting to me. I also find the more weathered, the better.

Windows and doors are a fantastic way to start sketching elements of architecture without overwhelming yourself.

EDITING

Choosing what to leave out is as important as what you choose to sketch. You won't always have the time or inclination to sketch everything you see in front of you. In addition to that, some of the most exciting sketches I see (and indeed that I feel I have done myself) are those that have a healthy dose of white space or that only hint at things rather than have explicitly sketched every last detail. There's something far more interesting about what a sketcher chooses to leave "unsaid." If you think about it, this extends to many types of art. Books and films that leave some details up to the imagination or interpretation of the audience are far more intriguing.

SYMMETRY

Most windows and doors are symmetrical. When you look at a door front-on, the symmetry helps make it an easier shape to draw on the page.

Drawing the initial proportion of the door correctly is most of the battle won. From there, it's a matter of using the door as a visual reference to fill out all the other details, such as an arch at the top.

Most instructional art books will tell you to hold your pencil out in front of you, lock your elbow and measure your subject matter using the pencil as a unit of measurement (see page 14). This is super useful, but of course, there's still room for error when trying to translate this on the page. I supplement this technique by looking for squares.

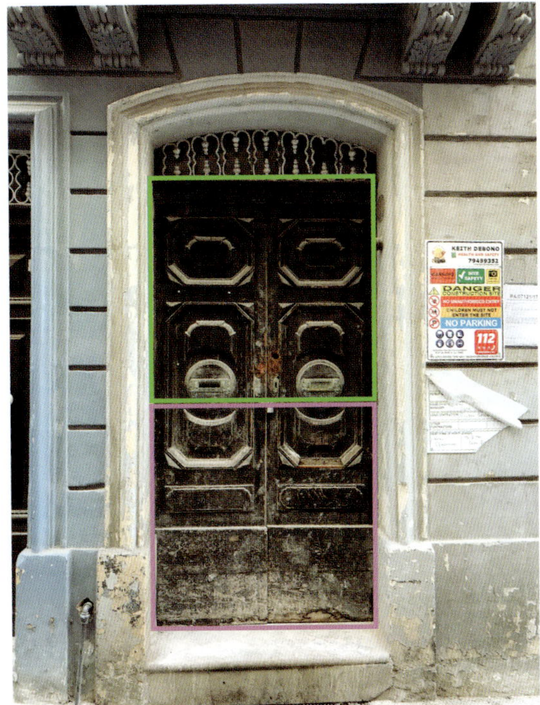

In this example, the door is roughly two squares tall. I can draw the door at any size I like, as long as I know that two squares fit into it. I can then add the slightly arched bit on top to complete the main shape of the door.

The other thing I tend to do is put a center line through the entire shape. I need this anyway to show the parting between the two doors. However, I usually extend it a little farther above and below the door. This helps when sketching something symmetrical so you can keep each side as even as possible. I am a massive proponent of wonky lines; most of my sketches also lean to one side. I never even noticed this until a family member pointed it out. I think it adds charm. I find proportion is much more important than straight lines.

DEPTH

Aside from sketching the shape of the door proportionally, one of the key elements to a successful door or window sketch is to show depth. You can do this with the lines you draw, as well as indicate light and dark areas with your watercolors.

The doorframe is one of the key areas that we can show depth. The actual door is receded compared to the mouldings around it. We want to convey that you have to step onto the doorstep to even reach the door from the street. It's easy to get lost in all the lines of the mouldings. In fact, I made a mistake and missed the blocks at the bottom in my initial sketch. Rather than abandoning the sketch, I restated the correct lines over the top and was able to save the sketch.

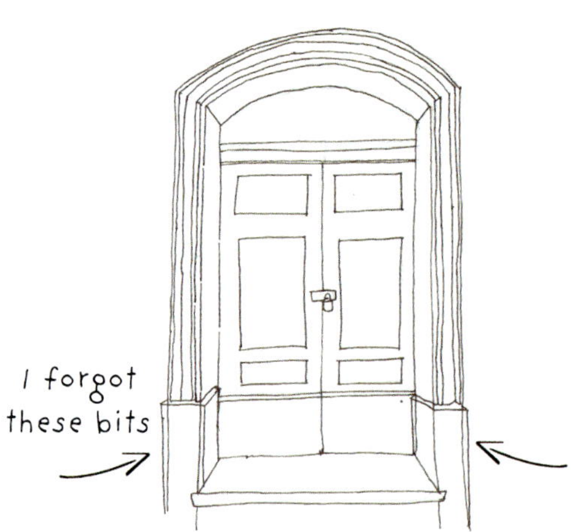

I think it's important to know that you will make mistakes, and rather than getting disheartened and scrapping your sketch, learn to embrace the mistakes and the spirit of urban sketching in the moment, and just roll with it.

As this sketch progresses, you'll find that those incorrect lines aren't even that noticeable in the end.

The panels on the door itself are a great way to show a little depth and dimension. We want to create the illusion that the panels are standing proud from the main body of the door and that they are extruding.

Here is a close-up of one of the door panels. I sketched it much larger, so you can see how I would portray it in line. The watercolor is what's really going to make the depth obvious in this example.

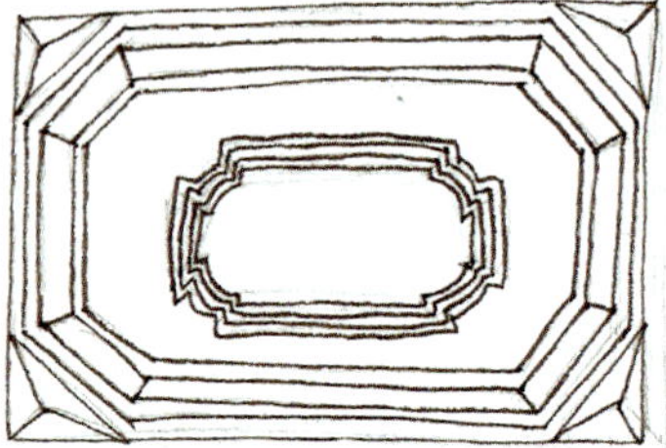

I used two colors in this example: Naples Yellow (for the light yellow areas) and Sepia for everything brown. I painted the lightest color first, using the Naples Yellow.

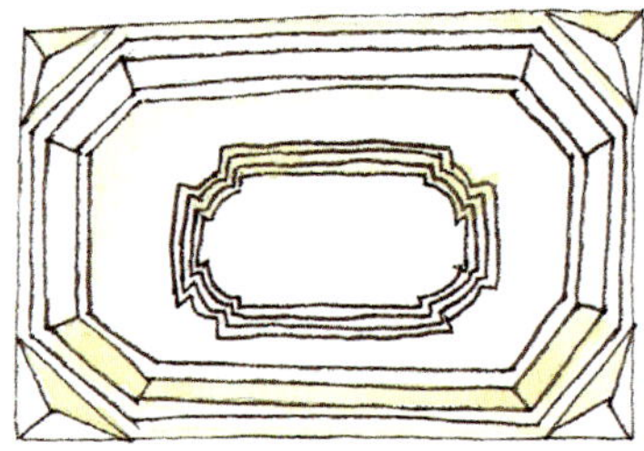

It's easy to paint a dark color over a light color, but there's no way to paint a light color over a dark one in watercolor. I then painted all the brown areas with Sepia.

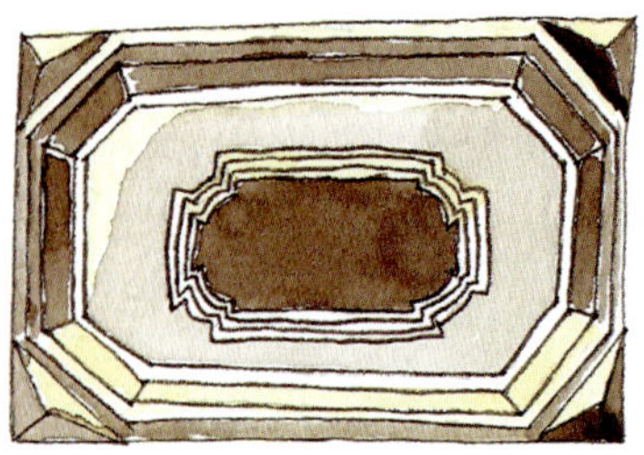

On my second pass of watercolor, I painted the darkest areas.

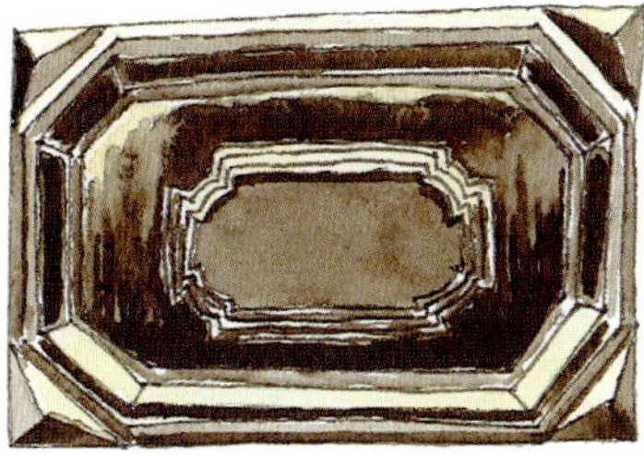

Water control is key. I didn't mix any other colors with Sepia to make it darker. I just varied the amount of water I used. The first pass of Sepia was more watery and therefore lighter. On the second pass, I used the Sepia with less water and far more pigment. This produced a much darker shade of brown. This is all I needed in order to show the depth of the panel.

I kept in mind the concept of placing the darkest color (darker version of Sepia) next to the lightest color (Naples Yellow) in order to maximize contrast (discussed on page 21).

ORNAMENTATION

My sketch of the whole door (page 120) was drawn too small to get that level of detail into the panel. So, I hinted at it. The size you sketch will determine how much detail you are able to render in your sketch. The sketchbook I was using is 5 by 7.5 inches (13 x 19 cm) (a bit smaller than A5). I switched to a 0.1 fineliner to draw the decorative panels on the door.

I simplified what I saw and drew the basic shapes with repetitive lines to show the undulating frame around each of the panels. In my previous example where I focused solely on one of the panels, I could draw the ornamentation more accurately.

Do not get bogged down with all the details you see. Just indicate intricate shapes with simpler versions or squiggles, like I did in this sketch.

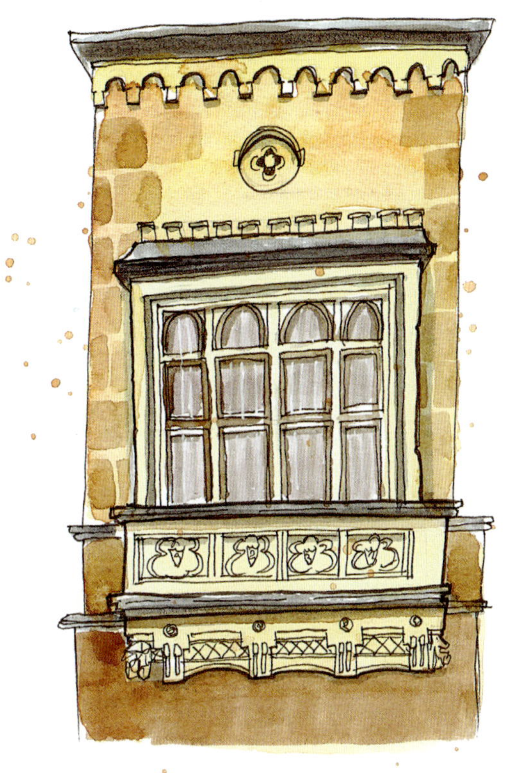

When it comes to the more decorative elements, I simplify the shapes. On the upper section of the balcony wall of this window, I interpreted the decoration as two "3s" facing each other with some kind of shield shape in the middle. In the lower section of the balcony wall, I drew each of the four dividing blocks with basic patterns that somewhat looked like what I was seeing. In a sketch of this size (5 x 7.5 inches [13 x 19 cm]), there's no room for intricate detail anyway. When you step back from your squiggles, you'll find it doesn't look too far off from your subject matter!

TEXTURE

Texture is a very important element in urban sketching. When it comes to old doors, many are weathered, scraped and have paint chipping off. The walls sometimes have a bumpy stone texture; they can have chunks out of them, as well as weathered paint. It can be challenging to show on the page, but there are some tips and tricks we can use to create the illusion of texture.

A lot of watercolor paper has at least a slight texture to it (depending on which sketchbook and paper you choose) and that makes it a little easier to show texture than on completely smooth paper. But it's not impossible on smooth paper—it just needs a little extra work.

WOOD

On some doors you will be able to see wood grain showing through. It's one of my favorite textures to sketch.

Adding the grain of wood can be as simple as adding a few choice lines with your pen in areas. A finer pen, such as a 0.1 fineliner, would be a good choice for this.

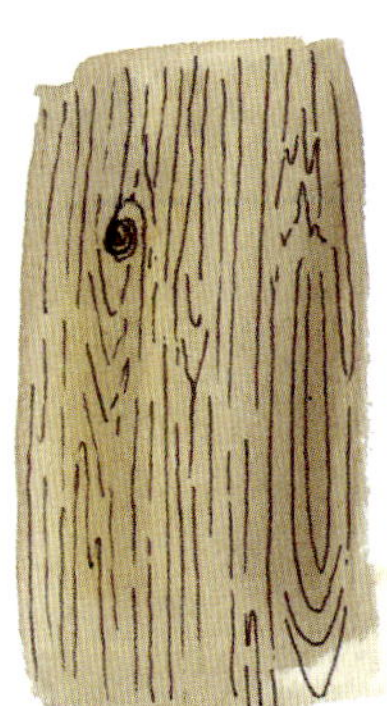

Or you could use a colored or watercolor pencil if you have one. This really enhances the texture, especially if your paper has some "tooth" (texture) to it already. Use the colored or watercolor pencil tilted slightly on its side, and gently rub over the paper to achieve maximum texture on the page.

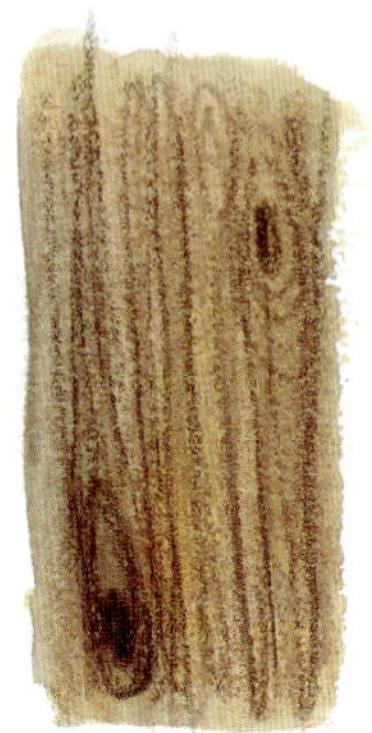

I encourage you to find some different examples of wood grain and make a few small studies. Experiment with different tools to see how you can translate the texture to your page.

BRICKS

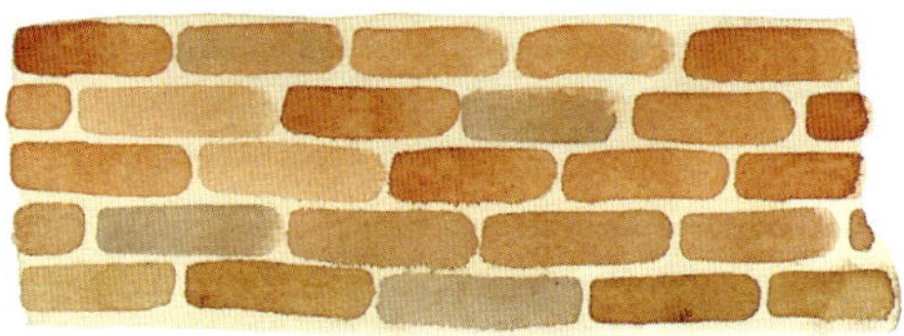

There are multiple ways to portray bricks, but one of my favorites is laying down a light yellow-and-brown wash where I want the bricks to be. This serves as the grout. Once dry, you can paint rectangles of darker watercolor over the top in a brick pattern. Remember, bricks aren't always the same color, so vary your colors now and again throughout the wall for maximum visual interest.

TIP: *If you have one or want to get one, use a small flat brush to get even rectangles every time. If you want to paint bricks like this often, then it will be a worthy investment. You can just get a cheap synthetic brush for this duty. You definitely don't need anything fancy.*

You can also draw bricks if you prefer. Remember, you don't have to draw every single brick (unless you particularly want to). You can just draw or paint areas of bricks and your eye fills in the rest. In this example, I was demonstrating the difference between tight and loose sketching, but you can also see the difference between drawing all the bricks and only drawing a few here and there.

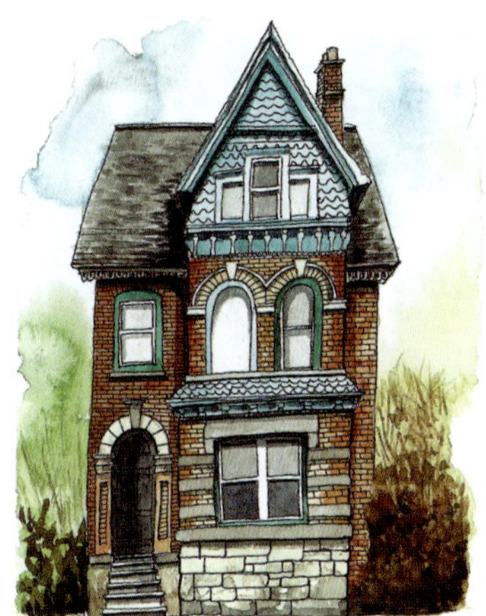

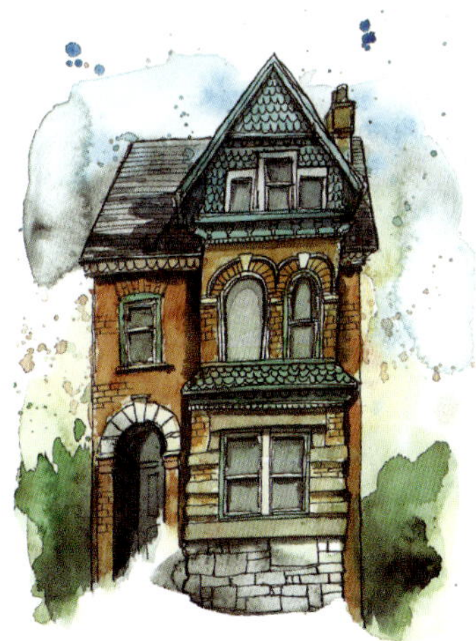

STONE

Similarly, there are many ways to approach drawing stone walls. I like the irregular shapes found within stone walls; it makes them fun and interesting to draw.

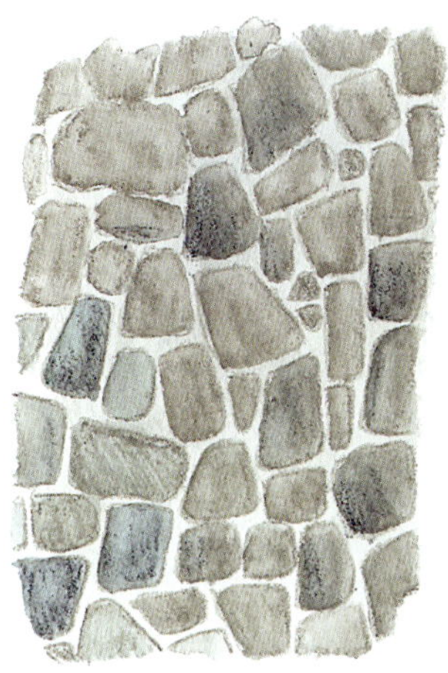

In this particular example, I painted a very light wash of gray first. Once dry, I drew the stones in pencil on top. I then colored each stone with a gray watercolor pencil, occasionally putting a little bit of dark blue into the mix. I then painted with water over the top to blend the colors together and achieve a more painted effect. The water won't erase the pencil strokes altogether. This is useful as you get the best of both worlds: a watercolor effect plus the texture of the pencil strokes. I think watercolor pencil on slightly textured paper can imitate the roughness of stone convincingly. But you can absolutely use watercolor paint or any other medium of your choice.

WEATHERING

Wet-on-wet (page 23) and dry brush (page 25) techniques are both effective ways to show a weathered texture on a door or wall. You can use them in conjunction with each other, as they both give different effects.

For the weathering on the doorframe, I used the wet-on-wet technique, being careful to blend the Naples Yellow and Indigo in certain areas, but then letting go to the will of the water and the paint mixing on the page. Wet-on-wet is an unwieldy technique, but keep practicing and experimenting as discussed on page 24, and you will get the hang of it—as much as one can, anyway!

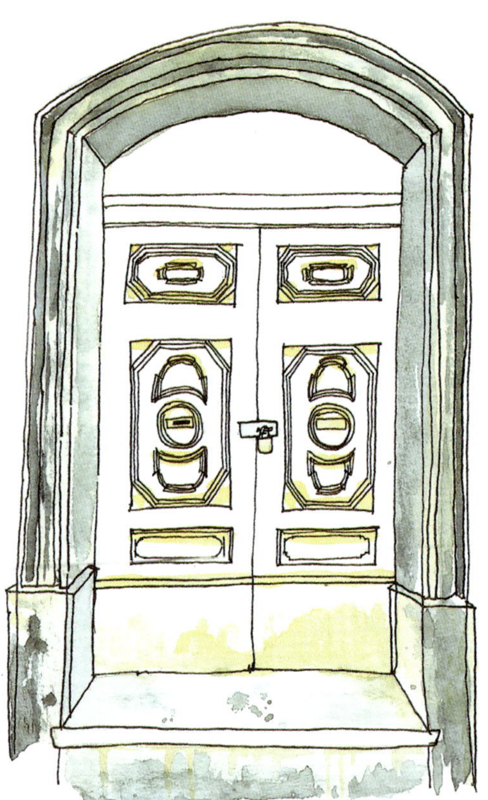

For the weathering on the door, I painted the light areas of the door first. I noticed that the top part of the door was much darker than the bottom of the door. I used a dry brush technique on the bottom panels of the door to make them appear extra weathered.

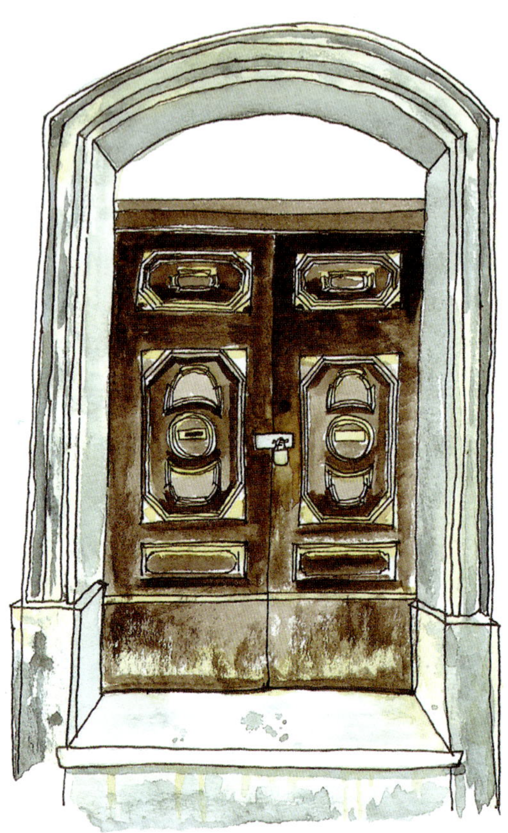

STYLIZED ELEMENTS

I painted the top part, above the door, black. But I didn't use black watercolor. I used two of the three colors I have used throughout the entire sketch: Indigo and Sepia (dark blue and dark brown). Mixed together they make an interesting black. By varying the amounts of Indigo or Sepia in the mix, you can make your black lean more toward blue or more

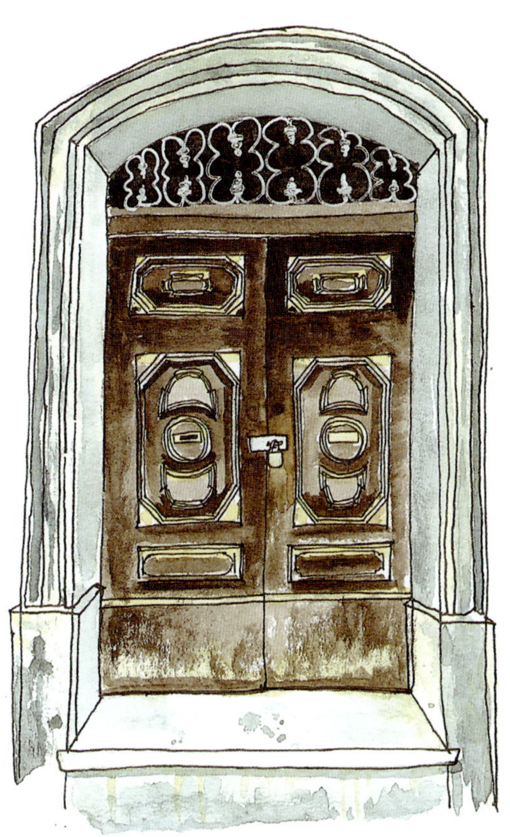

toward brown. Sometimes the two pigments separate, leaving little areas of blue or brown. It makes the overall effect extremely interesting to look at.

Once this area was dry, I used a white 0.8 Sakura Gelly Roll pen to draw the ornamental metal details over the top. I could have filled the area of black in with a black brush pen, which I do sometimes. For this sketch though, I liked the fact that I had used the same three colors throughout, so I wanted to stick to that self-imposed "restriction." Using the same colors throughout your sketch lends a sense of cohesion. Using too many colors can lead to the sketch looking muddy. Where possible, use fewer colors rather than more.

To finish the sketch, I added thicker lines with a 0.5 fineliner. Restating choice lines at the end of the sketch gives it some more dimension. I don't thicken every line, just those I feel I should. This is usually anywhere where there is a dark shadow, such as under the door and under the ledge of the step. I also add thick lines where there is a change of plane or if there's an edge that you would be able to put your hand behind.

EXERCISE

Draw an old door, and next to it, draw a close-up of some of the ornamentation you find interesting. You could even write some notes around it to point out what you found interesting and/or record the colors or techniques you used in the sketch. I talk more about sketchbook spreads on page 175.

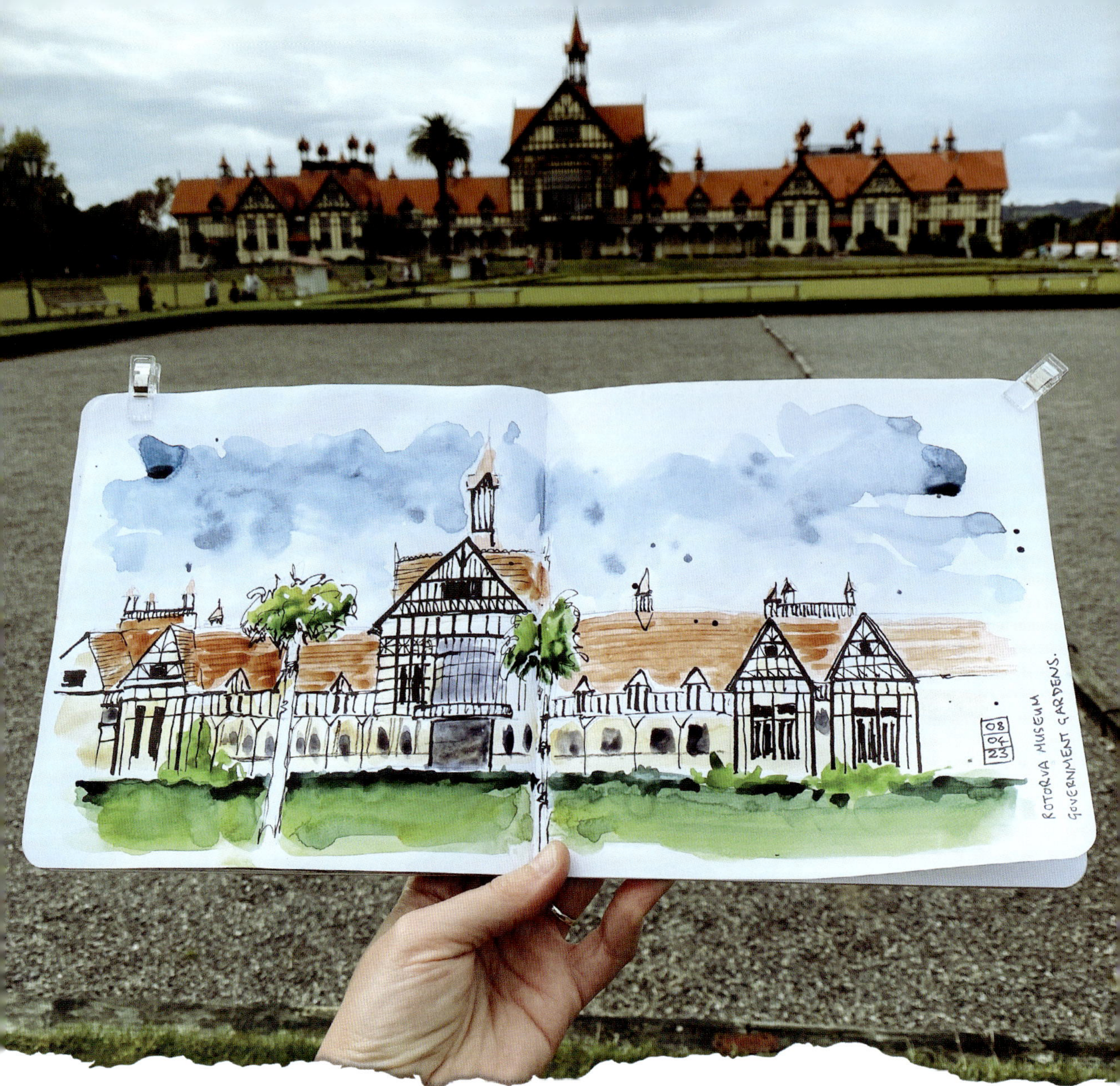

ARCHITECTURE MADE SIMPLE

One of the most common and exciting subjects for an urban sketcher is architecture. Some are blessed with having incredible architecture in their local area and some of us have to travel farther afield. The ability to sketch ornate architecture is certainly something worthwhile to develop as it is fun and extremely satisfying.

I have had the great fortune to sketch many beautiful ornate buildings on my travels. My first major breakthrough came in 2018 when I attempted to sketch the gothic behemoth that is Cologne Cathedral in Germany. That's when I really started to understand how to capture something so complicated in a representational way.

It's easy to look at complicated architecture and believe you could never produce a decent sketch of it, or that it would just take far too many hours.

After learning a few strategies, I managed to break through this belief and become more confident that I can sketch tricky architecture to a standard I'm happy with.

The aim of sketching is to make a quick representation of the thing in front of you. When urban sketching, speed is a useful skill to have as the environment shifts and our time can be constrained.

In my opinion, the most pleasing and successful sketches are the ones that represent the subject just enough so you can recognize it, but use the least amount of detail.

I think it's useful to know what you want to achieve with your sketch before getting started. Do you want to do a quick, loose representational sketch or a more detailed illustration? Knowing what you want to achieve at the end can help with where to start and the route you take.

When I started the sketch of Cologne Cathedral, I just wanted to do a quick and loose sketch that somewhat resembled the famous structure. I didn't have much time, but I wanted to be confident and see what I could achieve. This was my breakthrough moment. As long as the overall proportions and shape of the building are "right enough," then all of the ornamentation can be indicated with shorthand marks, and the building will still feel recognizable and detailed.

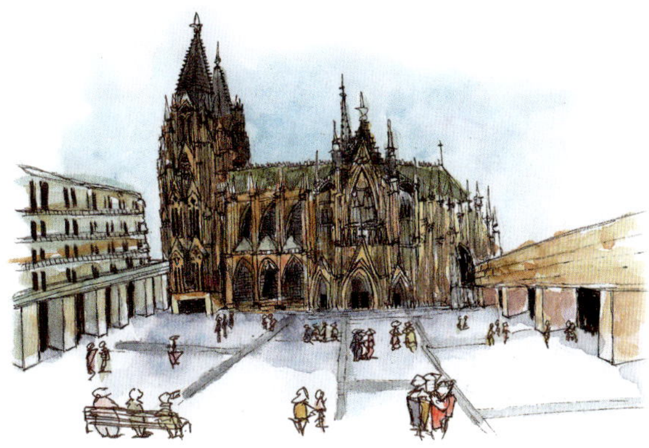

KEEP IT LOOSE

Keeping it loose is the best approach to sketching any overly ornate subject matter. It's quicker and looks more dynamic.

The idea of sketching loosely is to not worry about the details but to capture the "bigger picture," the essence of the subject.

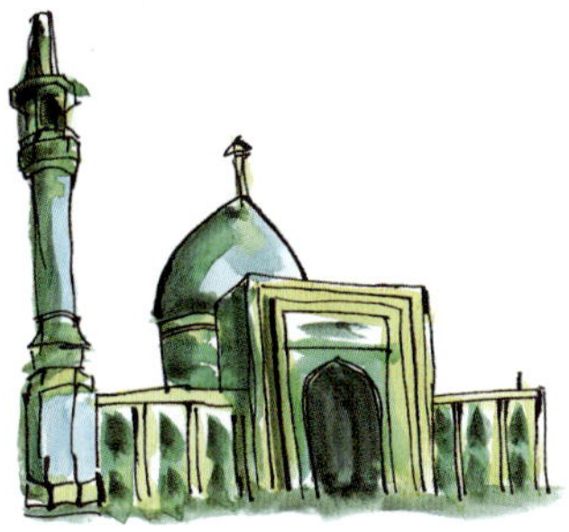

This mosque in Tehran, Iran, was very detailed and ornate; however, I feel I captured the essence of the building quickly and loosely. I drew directly in ink and added loose watercolor on top. This took 10 minutes (if that), yet it's one of my favorite sketches from the trip.

I am a big fan of sketching directly in pen when it comes to sketching loosely. However, I encourage you to map out the big shapes of your scene with pencil first, which I often do as well. This will help you ensure the building fits on the page and give you the basic idea of proportion so that you are more confident to continue drawing loose details directly in ink as the skeleton of your drawing is already on the page.

COMPOSITION

When starting to sketch complicated buildings, I strongly advise you to sit directly in front of the building to start with. This means there won't be any perspective issues to deal with, and you can focus on the building itself and its ornamentation.

Feel free to make the building you are drawing the sole focus of your sketch. You don't need to draw everything around it too. A sketch of an interesting building with white space around it can be very striking and something I often do. This is a particularly useful approach if you don't have enough time or if you simply aren't interested in drawing anything other than the building you're looking at or, as in this case, just one side of a building.

PROPORTION

The first thing to focus on is the proportions of the building. In pencil, mark where you expect the top and bottom of your building will ideally be on your page so it fits comfortably, and work from there. Only draw the large basic shapes of the building: rectangles, squares, triangles and circles. Do not get hung up on any details at this point.

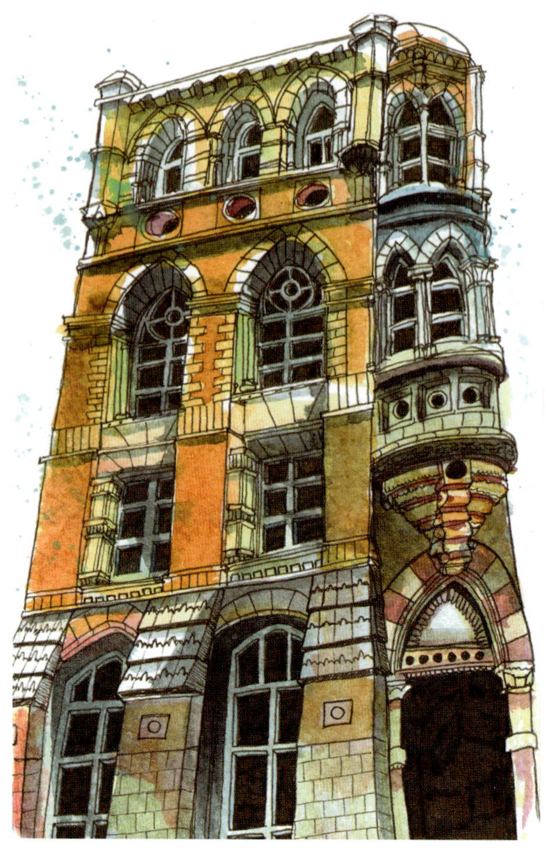

Once you have drawn the biggest shape, you can reference it to sketch your next largest shape, and then the next one and so on and so forth.

You will find buildings have a lot of clear reference points you can use to make sure your drawing is in proportion with itself. Look for natural dividing lines. The building may easily split into multiple sections. Features such as windows or ornamentation can help you see where to divide the building. These sections may run vertically or horizontally, or both.

In the sketch below, you can see three main horizontal areas: one at the top, one in the middle and one at the bottom (in red). As well as these, there are three main vertical sections too—a wide middle area and two narrower sections, one on each side (in purple).

Once your big shapes are mapped onto the page and you know everything is going to fit in and you're happy with your proportions, you can move to sketching the details with ink.

DETAILS

Squint your eyes, or if your eyesight is not so great like mine, take your glasses off and draw an impression of what you're seeing. It's easier to do this when you can't see all the details in the first place.

Is there an intricate relief on a panel? Just draw squiggly lines in the general shape of what you see.

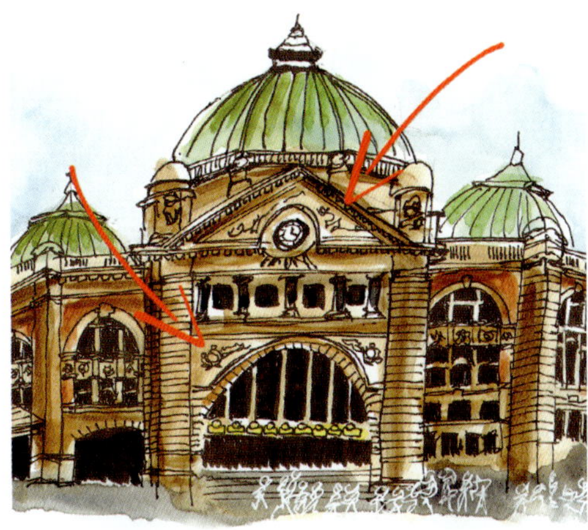

Are there ornate statues on the building? In that case, just focus on what shape they are making. If a statue is sitting on the corner of a roof, then think about the negative space the sky is making around it.

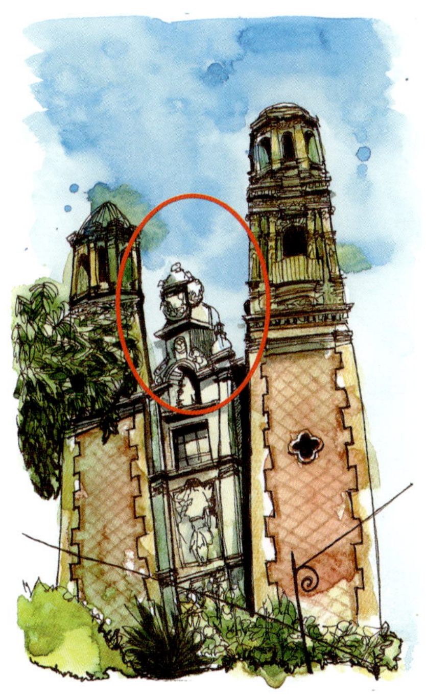

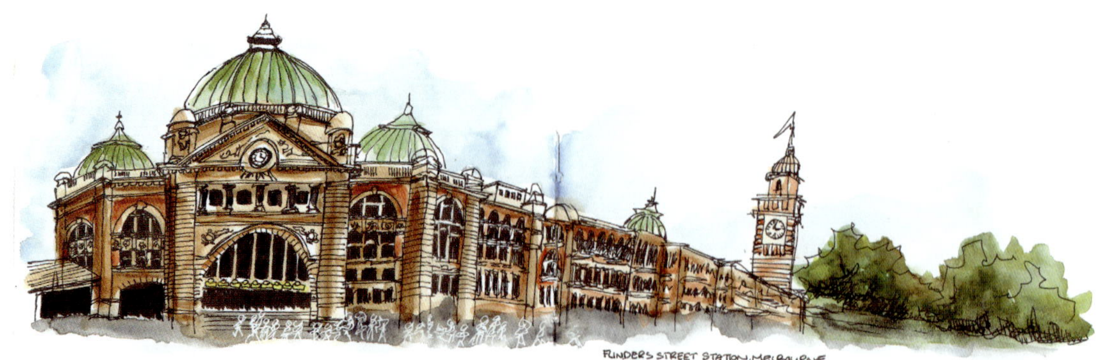

Try not to rationalize what you are seeing or draw what you think it should look like. Forget the subject you are drawing entirely and closely observe the actual shapes you are seeing. This is absolutely key. It sounds so easy but it isn't. You need to train your mind out of identifying objects and then just drawing what you think they look like. This is so ingrained that you do not realize what you are doing. Once you start to intentionally practice shutting off that behavior and focusing on only drawing the shapes you observe, your sketching will begin to improve. With continued practice, it will then become a skill you no longer need to focus on quite so hard. It will become natural.

When you step back from the sketch, you'll find that even though a lot of the details have been indicated by squiggles, the overall effect is recognizable and indicative of the ornate nature of the building.

Once I have completed the details of my sketch, I like to squint my eyes at the subject and just move around my sketch, thickening lines where there should more emphasis. This creates a sense of depth.

For example, the building may be facing you square-on, but there may be sections that are closer to you and other sections of the buildings that are recessed. Adding thicker lines to the walls that are farther forward will help create that sense of depth.

Also, use thicker lines where there are heavier shadows, for example, under window ledges.

Getting a sense for where your lines should be finer or thicker will come with developing your observational skill, as well as practice.

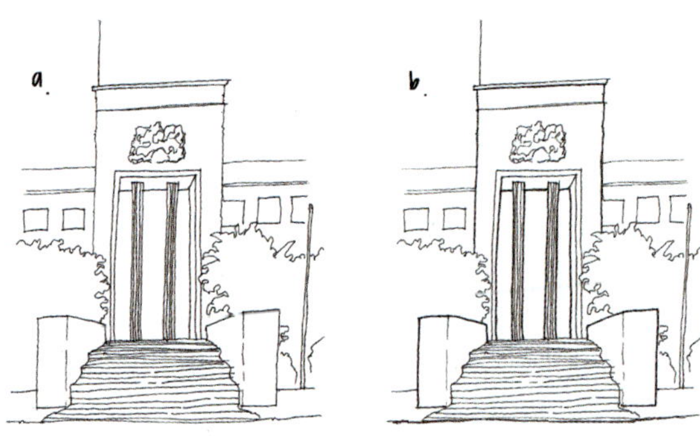

This is an extreme example but shows how much emphasis thicker lines can create within your sketch.

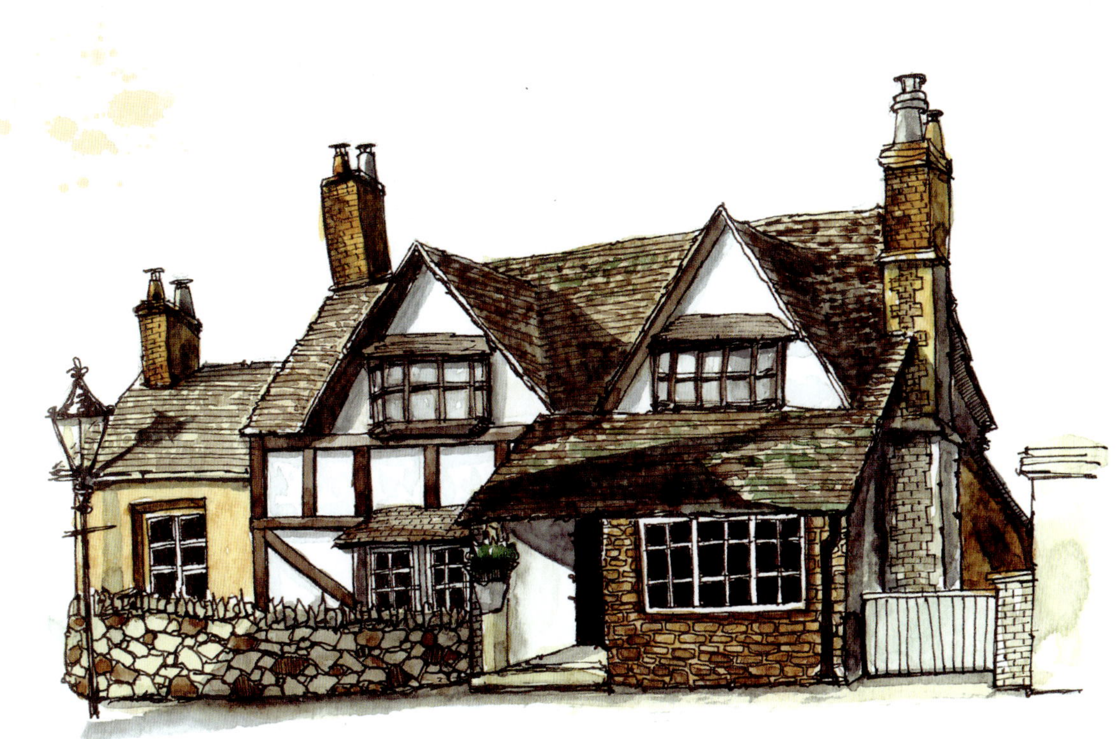

MATERIALS & TEXTURES

Instead of drawing a straight flat line, look at the texture of the building. It may be brick or rough stone, in which case you can indicate this with the quality of the line you draw. If anything, this really helps take the pressure off of trying to draw straight, perfect lines.

In the sketch above, I tried my hardest to pay attention to capturing texture as this cottage has different materials all over the place. Focusing on details such as texture will really take your sketch to the next level.

LIGHT & SHADOWS

Capturing light and shadow in your sketch is essential to making a 3D object look convincing when drawn on a 2D surface. In the same sketch of the house above, notice the strong shadow shapes across the roof and that the streetlamp is casting. Light and shadow also convey an atmosphere and mood—without these details the sketch wouldn't come to life on the page.

It's far easier to convey light and shadow when you are sketching a high contrast scene. What I mean by "high contrast" is when there is a huge difference between the darkest darks and the lightest lights. Sketching on location at midday is tricky for this very reason; the sun is right above you, and therefore, it does not cast lovely strong shadows that can make even the most mundane subject that bit more magical. Photographers almost always aim to work inside the golden hours, just after dawn and before dusk, as this is when the light is at its best. I am not suggesting you can only sketch at specific times of day, but it's just something to be aware of.

If the scene in front of you is not high contrast, or if it was but now the light has changed, then you can, to some extent, invent the light and shade. Decide on where your light source is coming from. You may even want to draw a faint arrow in one corner of your sketch so it reminds you. You can then keep one side of your scene very light where the sun is, and on the opposing side where the light doesn't reach, you can then emphasize the shadows.

CREATING EMPHASIS

Similar to what I mentioned in the section about light and shadow, creating a sense of depth is vital in order to bring the building you're sketching to life.

As well as using light and shadow, you can use line weight to create depth and emphasis. It's visually appealing to create emphasis in certain parts of your sketch to help draw the eye around a sketch. Add more details, use thicker lines, stronger tones and/or colors for items or features that are in the foreground. Add fewer details, use thinner lines and fainter tones for anything in the background. This will give your sketch a real sense of depth as well as indicating to the viewer which parts of the sketch are the most important.

In this example, I wanted it to feel like you could reach out and touch the metal fencing. I was stuck behind it drawing this incredible church. Rather than ignore it, I emphasized the way it cut right across my view. I thought it was a fun effect and a slightly more unusual view of this iconic building.

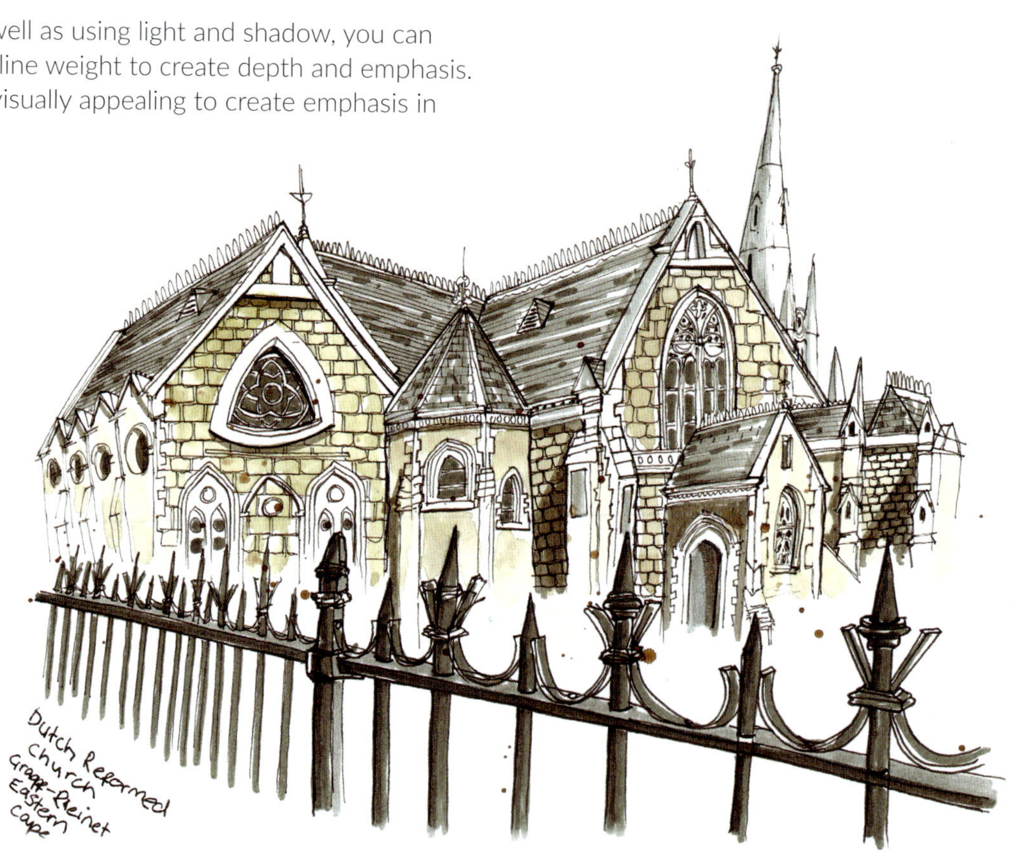

STORYTELLING

Take a step back, literally or figuratively, and just look at the building you're sketching.

1. What drew your attention to this particular building (or set of buildings)?

2. What are the distinguishing features and characteristics?

3. If you didn't have time to draw all of it, which bits would be the ones you would want to capture?

4. What story are you trying to tell?

This all may seem fairly tricky to discern at first, but once you get used to asking yourself these questions, you may find your sketching improves. If you can cut right to the heart of the building or scene and convey that in your sketch, you will nail the sketch every time.

STRATEGIES

FOCUS ON ONE PART OF THE BUILDING

This is a good way to avoid overwhelming your sketch, yet still practice your on-location sketching skills. It's also great if you don't have much time. I was on a sketchcrawl of some churches with Urban Sketchers Johannesburg, and we only had one hour to sketch at each church. This sounds like a lot but really isn't. At the first church, I tried to sketch the entire thing, but I ran out of time and left the sketch unfinished. I learned from my mistake, and at the second church, I focused on a particular element, which in this case, was one particular part of the entrance gate.

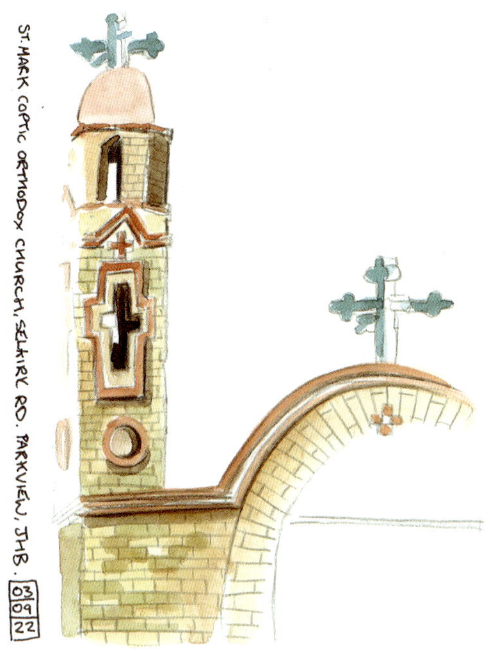

In the sketch below, back in January 2017, I didn't feel confident enough to sketch the entirety of St Paul's Cathedral in London. I decided to focus on the iconic dome instead, playing with warm and cool colors. It's not an elaborate sketch, but I had fun and I got to play with color.

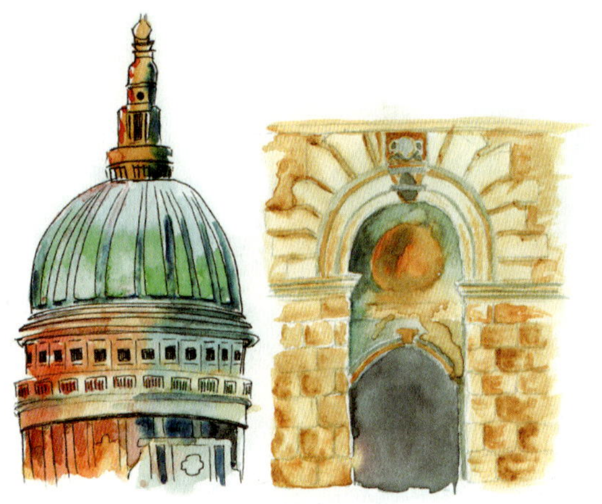

Sometimes treating sketches as an exercise can take the pressure off and allow you to be a little more playful. If I had spent one to two hours drawing the cathedral, I don't think it's likely I would have been so playful with my colors, because I would have been afraid to "ruin" something I had taken so long to draw. These are distinct feelings I remember having when starting my urban sketching journey. To the side of the dome, I decided to paint one of the window areas as it looked graphic, and I wanted to try a different way of sketching. I drew the window in pencil and painted in watercolor, without using any ink. I really liked the result, and it allowed me to try the style, again, without worrying about the end result too much. Side by side, these sketches show some of the details of St Paul's Cathedral without having to sketch the entire building.

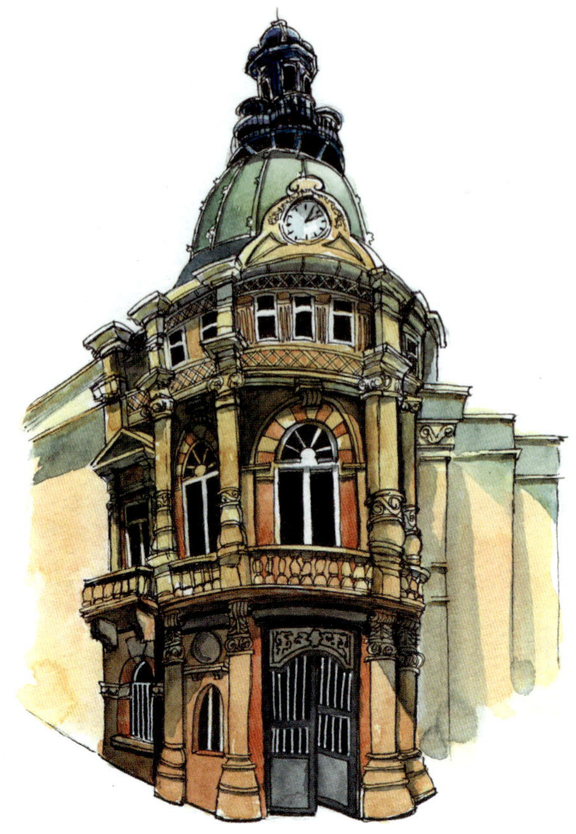

EDIT WHAT YOU SEE

You don't have to draw everything you see. It is perfectly acceptable to trail a sketch off. You can do this quite dramatically, such as in this sketch of a building in Cartagena, Spain.

I drew the front part of the building and actually really didn't feel like drawing the rest of the building on either side, so I just put some blank walls there to show the building continued, but I did not draw any details at all. There are no rules to say you must draw something in its entirety, so if there is one part of your subject matter you really want to draw, just do that part. I can't emphasize enough that your sketchbook is your own. It is your space to play and create and record. Of course, it's fun to share your work with others, but your own fulfilment is the priority when sketching.

HOUSE, RESTAURANT & SHOP FRONTS

A satisfying way to start sketching architecture, such as houses, shops or restaurants, is from a straight-on view of the front, especially if the outside of the building is quirky and decorative.

Many of the buildings in the places I have visited in Mexico are brightly colored and adorned with interesting objects.

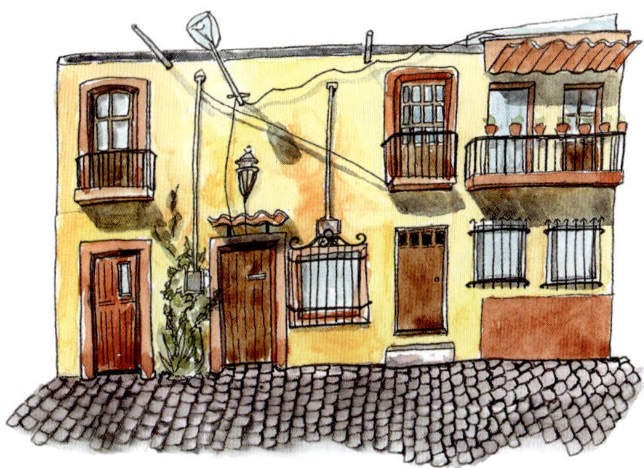

MAY 2019

This house caught my eye as it seemed to have an interesting arrangement of windows and doors, along with potted plants along the balcony and the bright yellow color of the walls. I couldn't stop thinking that it would make a fantastic sketch. I am glad I sketched it when I did, as a week later I walked past the same house, and the walls had been painted white! Somehow, it just didn't have the same character (to me). This is a great example of capturing something in a moment in time—everything inevitably changes. Urban sketching captures a snapshot of a place and time that will never be again.

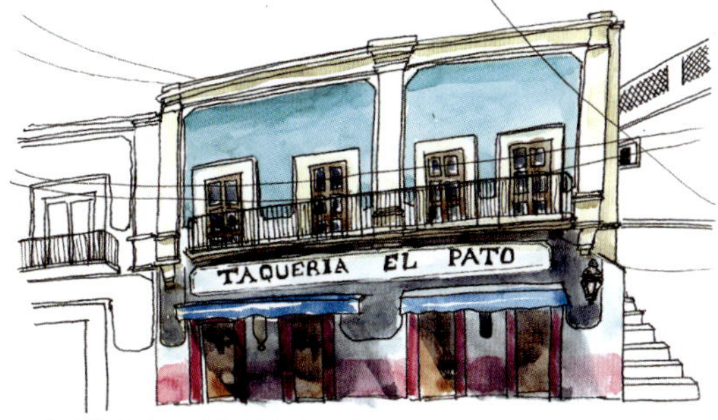

TAQUERÍA PATO, CALLE TEPETAPA. GUANAJUATO, MÉXICO

This was a restaurant front in Guanajuato. I really liked the colors of the building and the strong shadows cast by the canopies. I drew this quickly and kept the details very simple. I only painted the restaurant and left the elements on either side unpainted.

As you can see from this sketch, we can draw building fronts with nothing but simple geometric shapes.

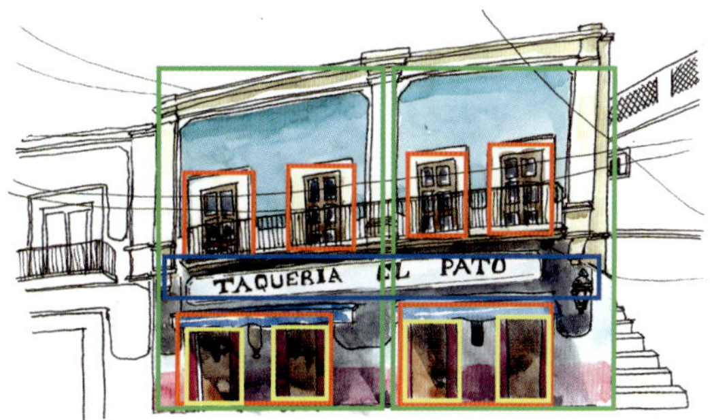

TAQUERÍA PATO, CALLE TEPETAPA. GUANAJUATO, MÉXICO

PERSPECTIVE

The easiest viewpoint to sketch a building from is front-on. Even though it may not make for the most dynamic of compositions, you don't have to deal with any tricky perspective. If you find an interesting house, cafe, restaurant or shop front, the sketch will still be interesting. It is one of my favorite subject matters to draw, and you will find many video demonstrations of how to approach it on my YouTube and Patreon channels.

PROPORTIONS

The most important thing when drawing houses or shop fronts is proportion. Follow the process on page 14 and assess how tall versus how wide your chosen building is. Draw the largest shapes on the page in pencil to make sure everything will fit. Then move inside the big shapes and divide it down into smaller shapes. Even if you can't see physical dividing lines on the building, you will still see where certain architectural elements are placed to provide natural divisions.

There are four distinct horizontal sections of this building and three vertical sections. Assessing these large shapes is always my first step. What size are they in relation to each other? Are they roughly the same? The three horizontal sections from the ground up look roughly the same to my eye. The top roof section is definitely narrower. The central vertical column looks smaller than the sections that flank it, which both look identical.

I make this kind of analysis every time I start a sketch. It could happen in a matter of seconds by just looking at the building. Once these large sections have been established, break them into smaller sections and then smaller sections again until you reach the finer details.

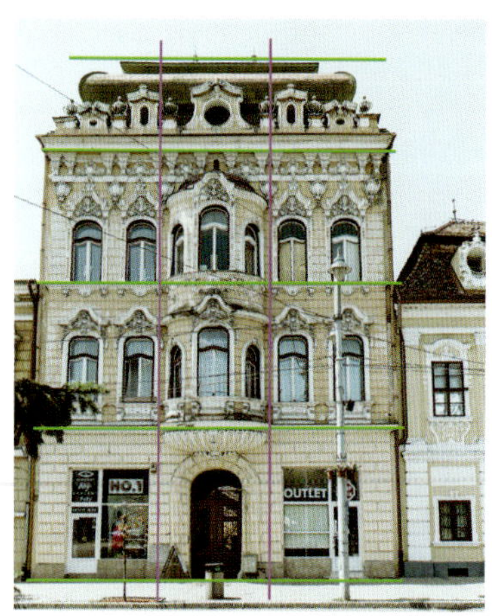

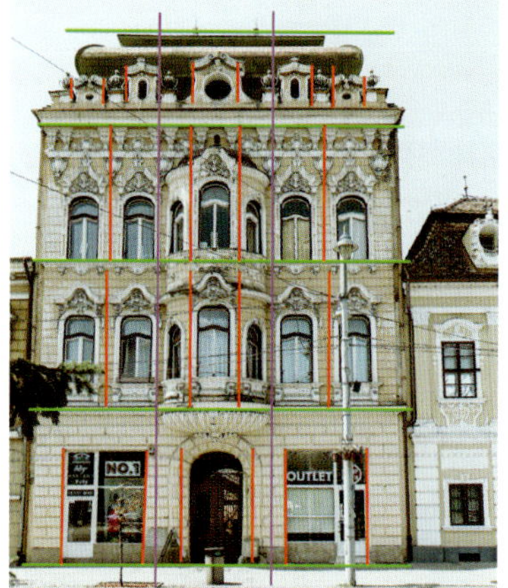

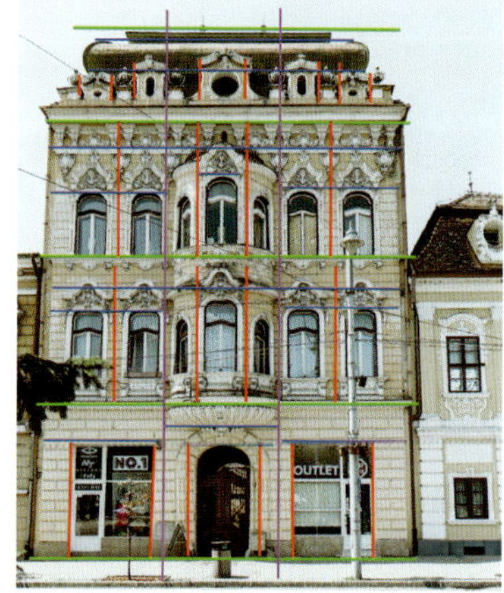

FOCUS

What are the most important elements of your scene? What made you stop and want to sketch that particular building? Whatever the answer is to those questions, make sure it's the focus of your sketch.

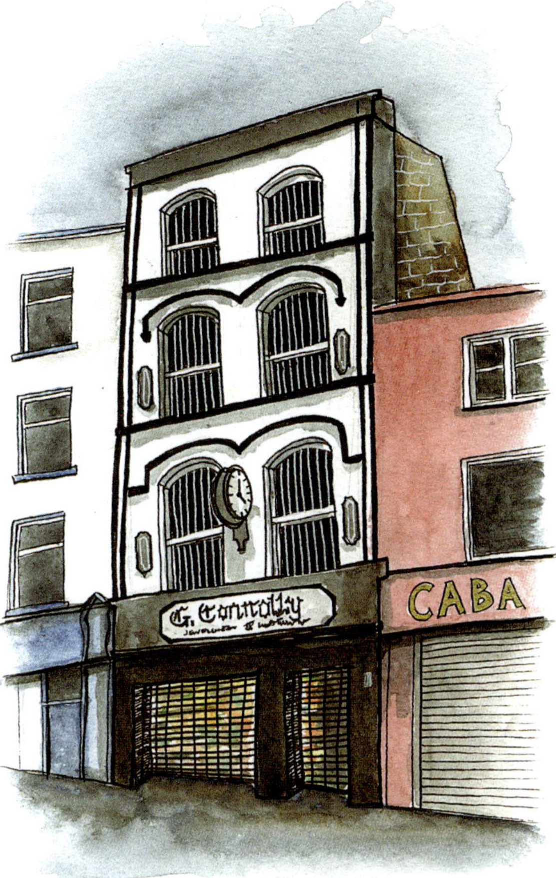

05·11·18 TRALEE, CO. KERRY, IRELAND

While this is not completely straight on, the focus of my sketch was the watchmaker's building. It doesn't even have that many details or flourishes, but I just really liked the graphic quality of the building, as well as the metal security poles across the windows.

Sometimes your interest can be piqued by something as simple as that. Other people may walk past this building without a second glance, but as an urban sketcher, it grabbed my attention immediately. As you can see, I only drew a little bit of the buildings on either side of the watchmaker's store that my sketch focused on. I wanted to add a little context but not detract from the star of the show.

TIP: *Notice that I filled in the windows with black (using a black brush pen in this case). I did this to allow me to draw the white metal poles on top with a white gel pen.*

DEPTH

I want to highlight a little trick in this sketch. The frame of the window is only visible on the top left of each window. This emphasizes that I was standing on the ground and to the right of the building. I can't see the inside of the wall and frame on the right side of the window for that reason. Small details like this quite literally add depth to your sketch.

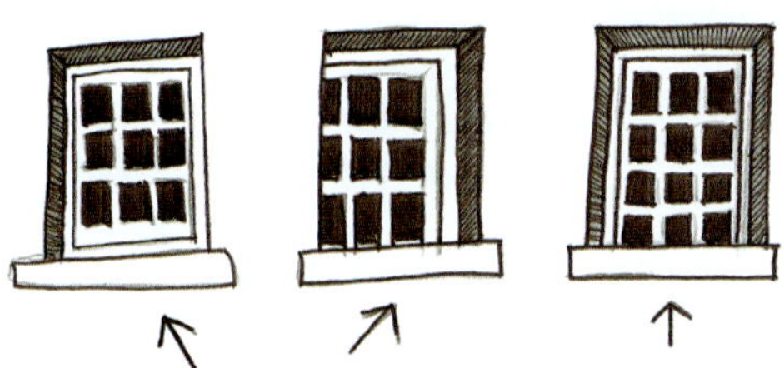

In this example, you can see that the direction you are viewing the window in will dictate which part of it you can see. If you are looking up and to the left, you will see the inside left edges of the window. Sometimes you may be at a more extreme angle and even some of the window frame will be hidden behind the wall. If you are looking up straight on, it's likely you will see a small sliver of both walls.

Take note of areas in your sketch where you can indicate depth or, more simply put, the thickness of the wall, such as where a part of the building may extrude from another, or parts of the building that are inset, such as windows and doors. Representing these areas will make your sketch more 3D and believable.

TIP: *I like adding subtle shadows underneath window ledges or roof ledges by using Faber-Castell Pitt Artist brush pens. I have the set of six grays: three warm and three cool in light, medium and dark tones.*

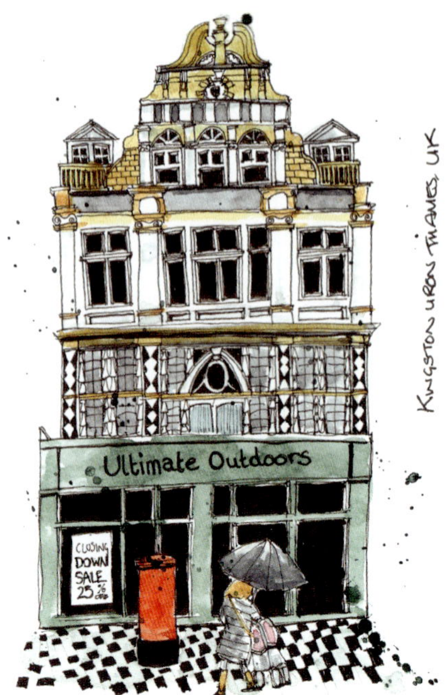

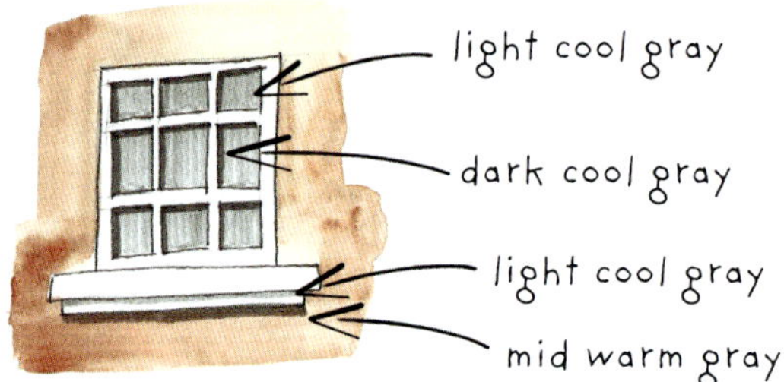

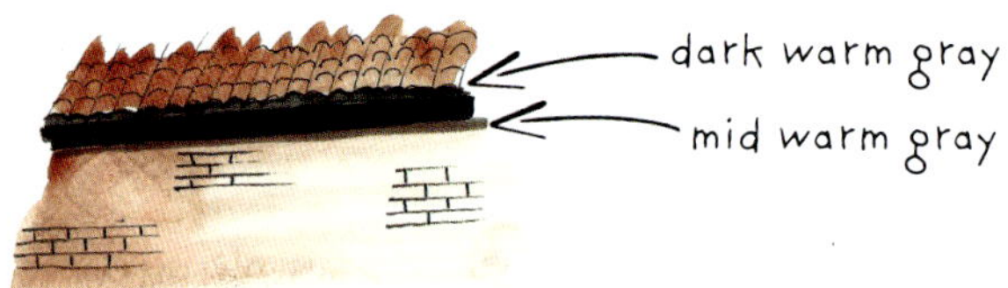

In this example, you can see how I apply these pens over watercolor to achieve a subtle yet defined shadow in tricky areas, such as under window or roof ledges. It's an easy way to apply a nice sharp shadow, as the pens are translucent so they layer over watercolor beautifully.

DETAILS

The super fun part of drawing shop or house fronts is adding all the details. This is when your sketch really starts to come to life.

This building is so much fun to look at and indicative of the beautiful old buildings that can be found around every corner in London. The shop at the bottom is an outdoor equipment shop, but if you just look up, there is a sublime building that houses it. Luckily this building was exactly opposite a coffee shop with a good view of it, as it was cold and rainy on this particular day.

You may notice the details I added in this sketch aren't perfectly drawn, straight or accurate; however, when taken as a whole, the sketch has a sense of drama. It's very graphic, especially the checkerboard tiles on the ground (which wasn't actually what the ground looked like; it was a similar pattern but in dark and light gray). I thought it would look more interesting if I showed them as black and white. It would mirror the black and white used in the building. As you can see, I have filled the windows in with pure black in this sketch too. It's not something I always do, but I felt like it fitted with the overall style of this building.

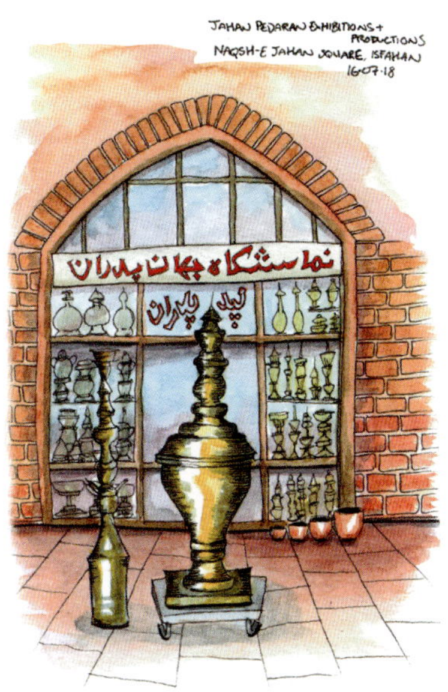

OTHER EXAMPLES

This is an example of simplifying a scene. There were many vases and pots in this shop window; however, I indicated just a few to fill each shelf, being careful to only somewhat indicate the unique shapes I was seeing. I painted a light wash of Cerulean Blue (light blue) and Quinacridone Rose (pinkish red) across the shop window and even over the top of the painted items on the shelf. This is an interesting yet simple way to show there's glass present. I drew the writing on the shop front the best I could, but I know it's incorrect (apologies to anyone who can read Farsi). The focus of the sketch was the two tall vases in front of the shop. I made them stand out by using thicker ink outlines and making the colors of them more vibrant than the ones in the shop window.

EXERCISE

1. **Find a building front that excites you, whether it's a house, restaurant, shop, pub or something else.**

Identify the main horizontal and vertical shapes and draw these on your page. You can use pencil or pen, whichever suits you. Now break each of those large shapes into smaller shapes using visual landmarks, such as windows or decorative features.

Do you just want to draw the building itself or do you want to add buildings next to it for context? Remember, you don't need to draw and paint the entirety of the scene. Refer to some of the sketches in this section for examples.

2. **Add details.**

Don't be afraid to fill windows in black if you like the style. You can then draw details, such as window frames, on top with a white gel pen. Indicate patterns of tiles or decorations in a simplified way. Don't forget to add thickness to windows and walls where you can.

3. **Add color and shadows.**

Paint the base colors of everything in your scene. The sketch will really start to come to life when you add shadows. Even small shadows under a roof, window ledge or shop sign will make a dramatic difference.

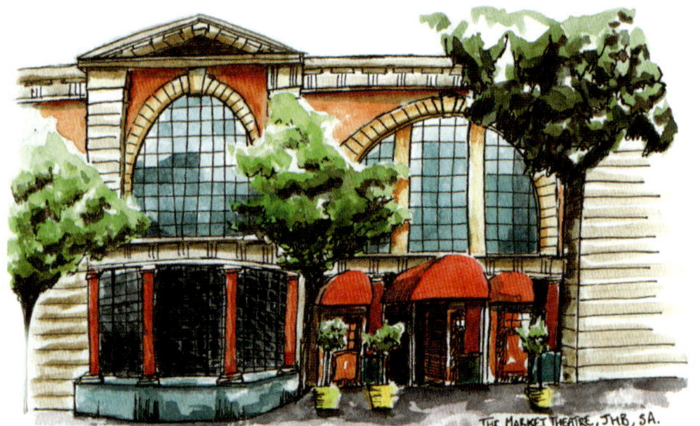

THE MARKET THEATRE, JHB, SA.

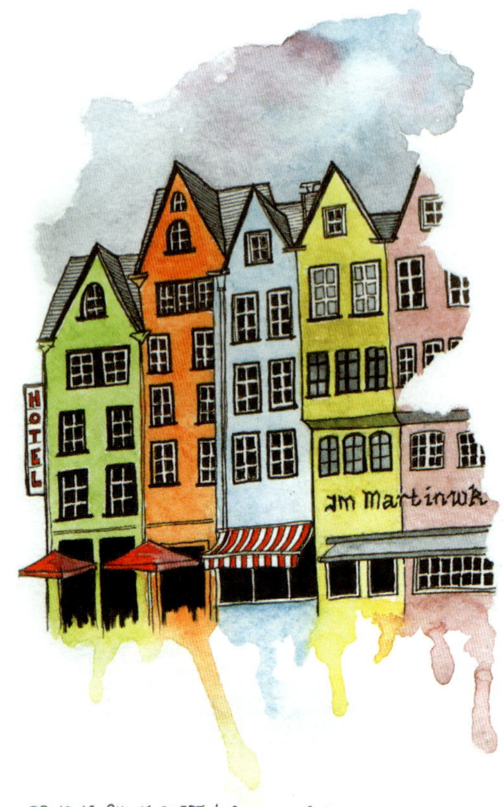

09·10·18 RHINE GARDEN, COLOGNE, GERMANY

Notice the lines of the paving slabs on the ground (previous page); they draw us in and make the scene more believable as they adhere to perspective. Don't ignore small details like this. Even though my lines are wobbly, they still make sense.

My favorite thing about this sketch of the Market Theatre (above) is the windows on the second level. It's a very simple sketch, but by varying the color of blue in the windows to indicate reflections, it makes it far more interesting. The window at the bottom was very dark and not reflecting the sky, so I painted it dark. The way I drew the bottom window is not quite right, but as you can see, you don't notice it too much as there are other interesting details to look at.

In this sketch of the Rhine Garden in Germany (right), I once more simplified the scene in front of me. I also added some stylistic elements in the vein of Danny Hawk (page 184). I decided to make the sky a shape, so I let the buildings trail off into drips and I kept a negative cutout area on the right side of the page where there was some foliage. Once you get past the basics of urban sketching, there's a whole world of techniques and stylistic choices to explore. This is something I very much delve further into week by week on my Patreon channel.

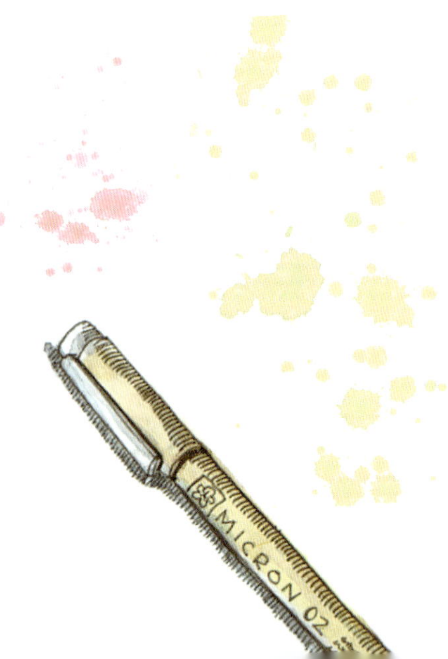

CITY SKYLINES

City skylines can be super intimidating. There is so much going on that it's hard to know where to start. The key is you don't have to draw every single detail you see. You can edit your scene and draw key parts, indicating the rest.

It's almost a game: How little can you get away with drawing in a busy scene while still retaining that sense of a lot going on?

When attempting a city skyline, composition is very important. Make sure you have some distinct foreground, mid-ground and background elements. Generally, the skyline lends itself to being in the background, if not the sole focus of the sketch.

In the mid-ground of this particular scene, there's the top of the rugby stadium, and in the foreground, there's some street art, a street sign and some posts. As we know from the Street Furniture section, these are equally as important and interesting details to sketch. The background is the city skyline. Identifying the three layers makes the sketch more dynamic than simply sketching a flat skyline on the page.

COMPOSITION

Look for the most iconic part of the skyline. In Johannesburg, and indeed this particular scene, it's the tall, thin structure called the Telkom Tower and the wider cylindrical building with the Vodacom sign on top, called "Ponte."

When I drew this scene, I started with these two buildings as I wanted to make sure they were placed deliberately on the page. In the photo, Ponte is in the center; however, in my sketch, I wanted it to be just off-center so the

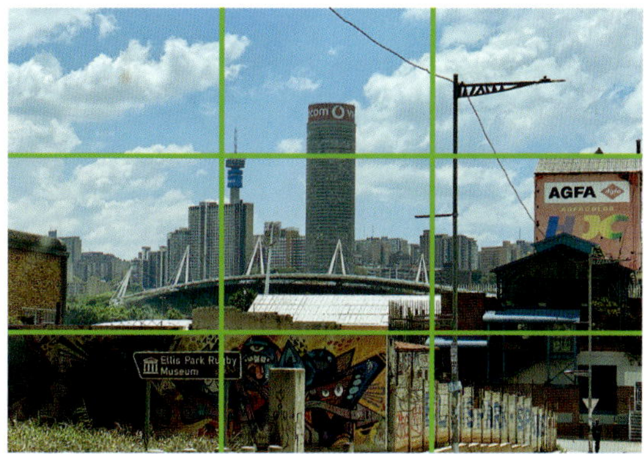

composition is a little more interesting. The Telkom Tower is almost on the left line of our imaginary rule-of-thirds grid, so I pushed it to the left so it's on the line. The other buildings are indistinct, so I played with them a little to make sure the two iconic buildings sit nicely in terms of composition.

I drew the rugby stadium roof a little lower than in the photo, so it's more toward the bottom horizontal line of the rule-of-thirds grid. I like that the signpost for the rugby stadium falls on the bottom intersection of the grid lines. The tall post on the right is almost on the right vertical grid line too. These are not hard-and-fast rules, as we already discussed on page 18, but when possible, I like to manipulate and compose a scene with the rule of thirds in mind, at least for the elements of focus.

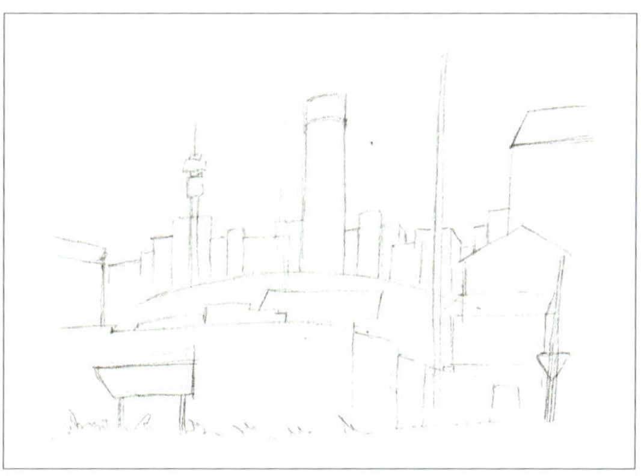

I drew the basic shapes in pencil of where I wanted the various elements of the skyline to go, and then I moved on to refining and adding details with a waterproof fineliner. I used a 0.1 as I prefer the lines to be fine to start with as I can thicken certain key lines later on if needed.

I drew the foreground elements first, followed by the mid-ground elements.

I decided to keep the skyline in pencil to emphasize the fact that it's in the distance. I can always add ink lines later if I feel I want to define the shapes a little more.

I finish off by adding additional details, like a rough idea of the street art on the wall and the writing on the signs.

I then moved on to adding watercolor. I wanted to keep the colors in the foreground nice and vibrant, while the buildings in the background are kept fainter to further emphasize the sense of distance and depth in the scene.

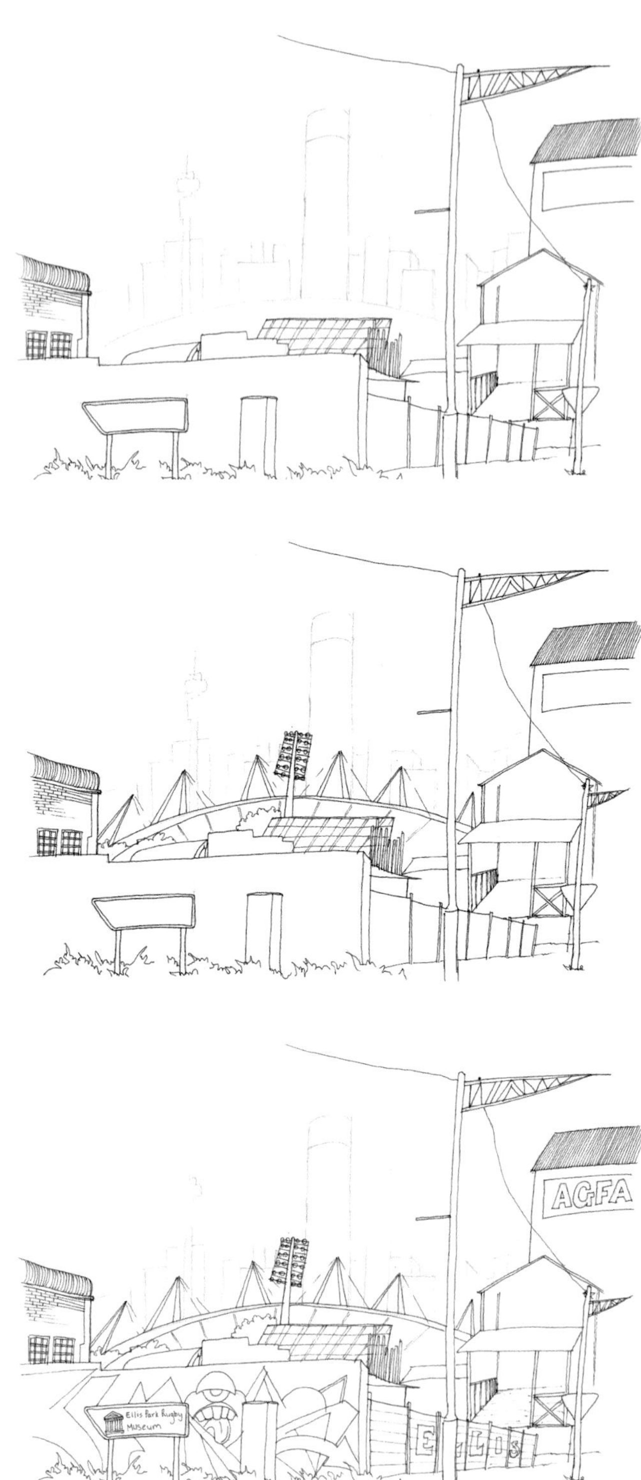

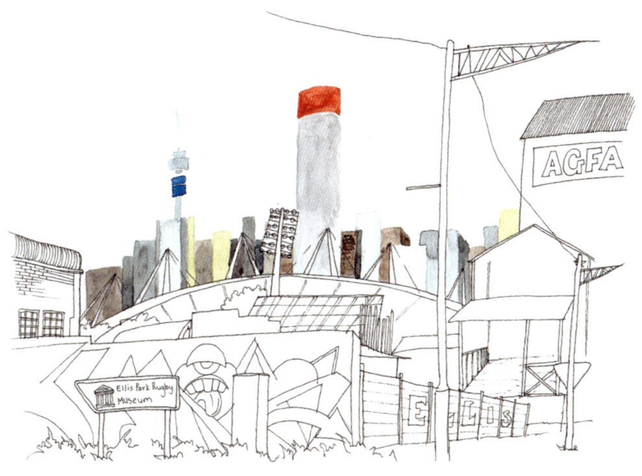

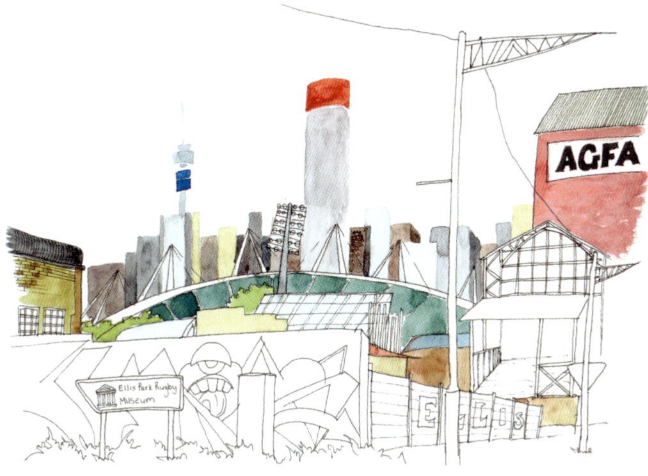

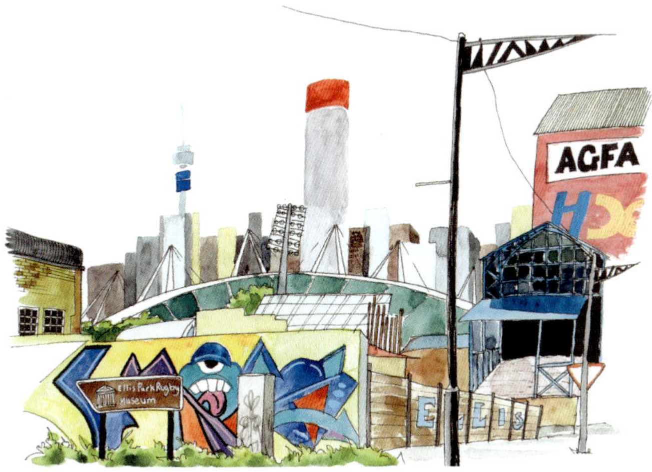

Unlike the drawing stage, I started painting the background of my scene first. This is where my palest colors are. I didn't stay true to the photo when painting the colors of the buildings. I find it more fun to interpret them how I choose. I used a combination of pale blues, browns and yellow ochres to vary the colors a little. Notice I have painted the blocks very simply with little to no detail.

As I painted the mid-ground, I realized I had forgotten to draw the details of the building on the right. Sometimes that happens. If I feel like I can't see what's going on or just don't feel like drawing something at that specific moment, I leave it and come back to it later. Perhaps that's just a particular foible of my personal sketching process!

Finally, I moved on to painting the most vibrant colors in the foreground. Thanks to the street art on the wall in front, I really went to town with my bright colors.

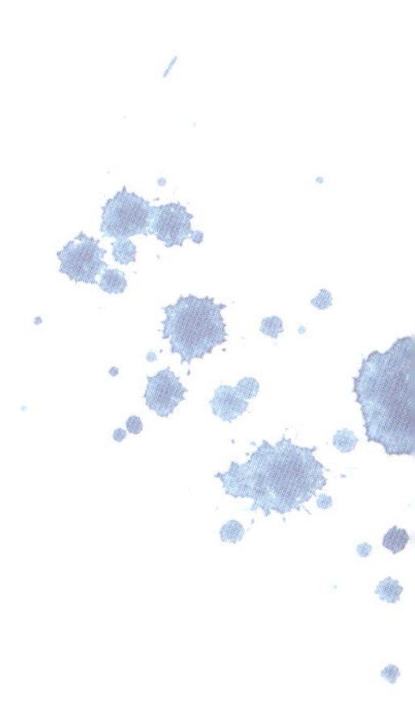

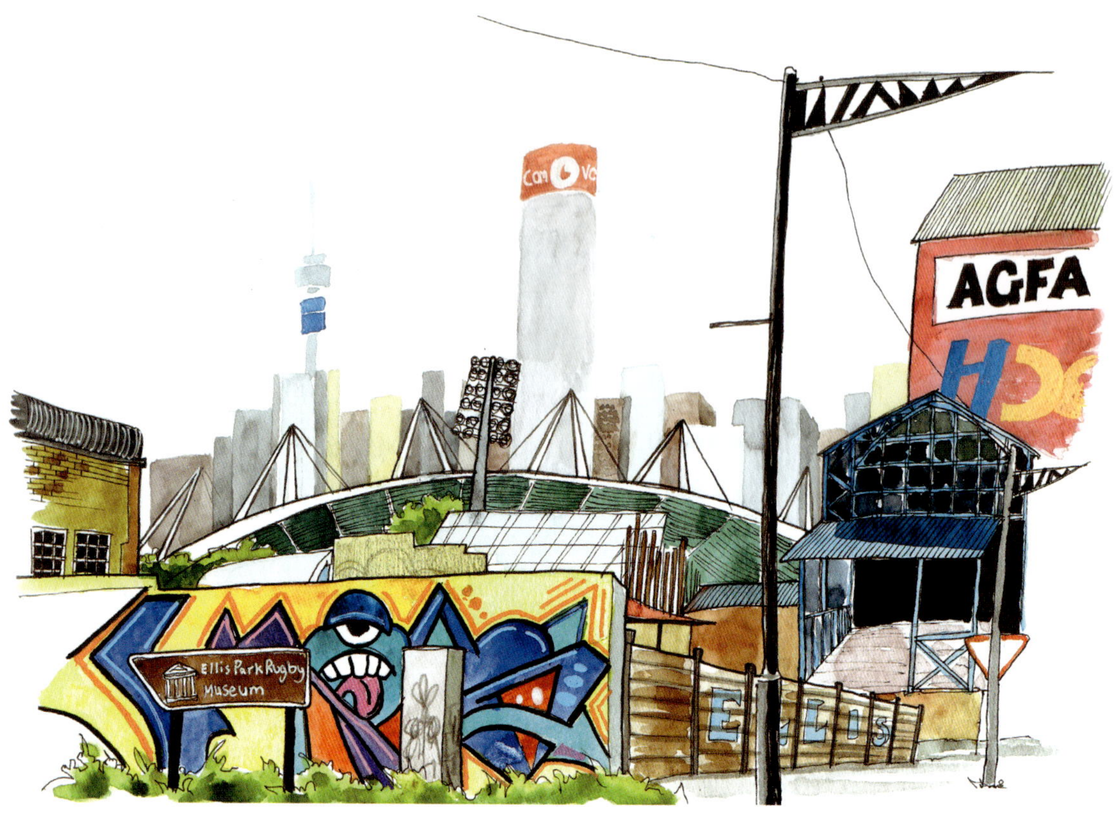

I'm a big fan of evaluating my work as I go and when I'm finished. I try to be constructive and look for things I would do differently if I sketched the scene again. In this scene, I think the skyline is too dark; it should have been much fainter. But let's see if we can fix it.

The first thing I did was thicken the lines of the outside edges of objects in the foreground with a 0.5 fineliner. I did the same for the mid-ground but with a slightly thinner line, a 0.3. This gives some more separation from the background.

The second thing I did was to add lots more detail to the foreground elements. Lines in the roofs, bricks in the walls, additional shadow areas. The more detailed you make the foreground elements, the more depth it will add to the sketch, like we spoke about on page 132.

TIP: *Feel free to use mixed media. In this scene, I used some acrylic paint markers to add some of the details of the street art and some of the painted elements on the pink building on the right-hand side. They layer over the top of watercolor easily and are opaque. They are also available in bright colors, which is perfect for a scene like this.*

EXERCISE

1. Identify the foreground, mid-ground and background elements.

I appreciate not everyone has a skyline scene in their backyard but when you get an opportunity to sketch a skyline, make sure to identify the layers in your scene. If you focus purely on the buildings of the skyline with no foreground or mid-ground elements, the scene will appear very flat and lifeless.

Not every scene translates well into a sketch. Therefore, purposefully choosing a favorable vantage point, as well as composing the scene deliberately, will set you up for maximum success.

2. Draw the big shapes in pencil.

Start with the most iconic buildings of the skyline. If it's not a famous or iconic skyline, which are the tallest buildings and which fall on the rule-of-thirds grid lines? Draw those first so you can compose them on your page and also to make sure everything will fit on your page.

3. Ink the details.

Work from front to back. You may like to keep the very background in pencil and not use any ink. The choice is yours.

4. Paint the background first.

Keep your colors as pale as possible. You can always come and make them slightly darker later if you feel they are too light. Exaggeration is the key to fun and quirky sketches.

5. Paint the foreground.

Make everything in the foreground bold and vibrant, including your watercolor as well as your lines. This will really make the foreground pop versus the distant skyline.

ANOTHER EXAMPLE

Another approach to sketching a skyline, depending on the view you have, is to choose a section to sketch.

In this example, there is no clear foreground and background, but I knew I wanted to focus on the Diamond building. I didn't even know this building existed until I had this vantage over Johannesburg from the roof of a hotel. The building is literally shaped like a diamond. It's quite beautiful as shiny skyscrapers go. As I knew the building was my focal point, I made sure to place it on the right vertical line of my imaginary rule-of-thirds grid.

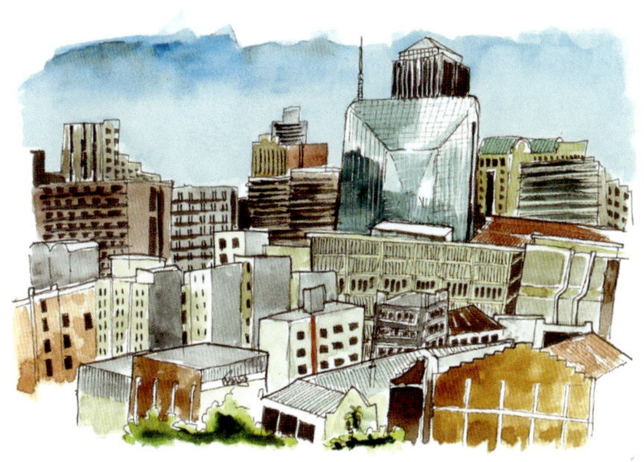

SKETCH A SCENE

STORYTELLING

Storytelling is a key component to urban sketching. We are showing the world one sketch at a time (as per the Urban Sketchers Manifesto). The city is an ever-evolving landscape, and it's our job as urban sketchers to record it. Our story in this demonstration is the juxtaposition of new architecture versus old architecture. In cities all over the world, you can find historical buildings surrounded by newer designs: An old church dwarfed by tall, shiny skyscrapers, such as in this example.

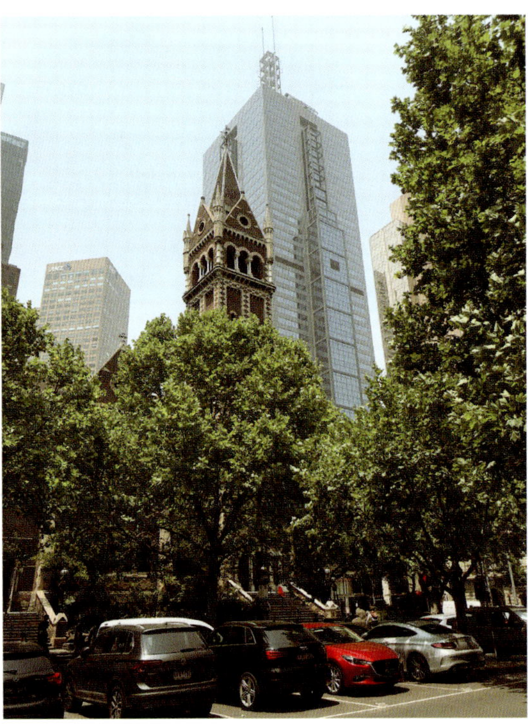

Urban sketching is an enjoyable way of documenting the development of cities. Your sketches could capture buildings prior to them being ripped down, as well as what now stands in their place.

COMPOSITION

1. Find a location that helps you tell the story of new versus old architecture and plan your composition.

Remember, you don't need to draw everything you see—just the bits that tell the story and that you personally will find fun to draw. I found an old church next to a skyrise and really wanted to show how they stand side by side within the landscape of the city, so I focused my attention on the tops of the two buildings with a bit of tree line at the bottom for interest.

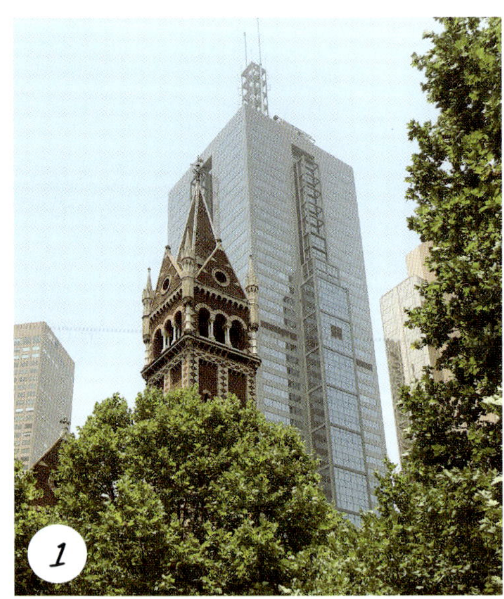

2. Keep the "rule of thirds" (page 18) in mind.

In order to communicate a clear theme or story through your sketch, consider the composition before you draw anything. I placed the old church tower on the vertical line with the focal point roughly falling on one of the crosshairs.

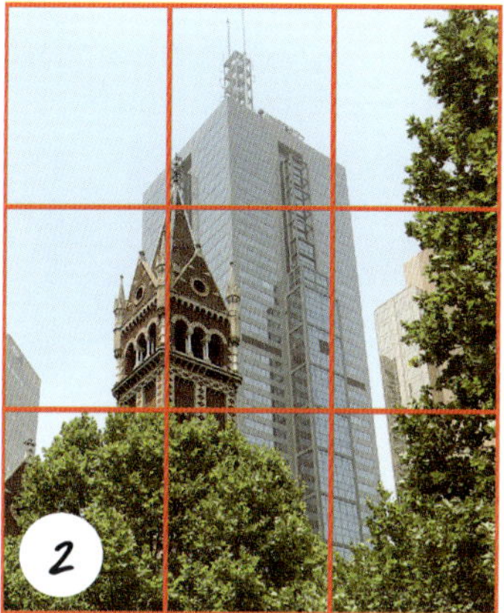

I did this because I wanted the church tower to be the focus of the sketch, with the skyscraper as a supporting actor. As discussed on page 14, placing your focus point on a key vertical as well as on an intersecting horizontal line makes for a more pleasing composition.

PENCIL SKETCH

Where you choose to sit and how you frame your scene will inform the perspective of the architecture you want to draw. At this stage, I urge you not to worry about the technicalities. Rely on your observation skills. Assess the angles of the top edges of your buildings using the concept of a clock face for reference as we discussed in the Perspective section (page 19).

3. Decide which building to start with and break it down into its most basic shapes, then draw those shapes lightly in pencil.

I started with the old church tower as it is the focus of my sketch. It is the most interesting building in the scene and the skyscraper next to it only serves to tell the story of new versus old architecture side by side in the modern cityscape.

The tower, in its most basic form, is a long box. I drew the box as per the red lines.

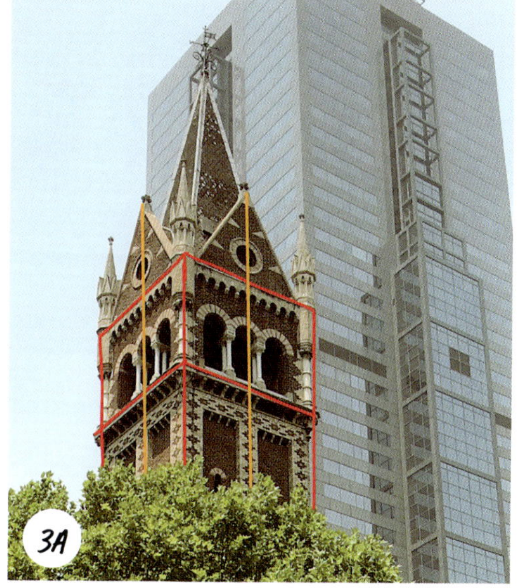

I lightly penciled in the center line of each side of the box and extended it past the top of the box, like the yellow line (3A). Having this center line in place helped me draw the triangles on top with a better sense of perspective and accuracy. Remember, we are not architects or technical illustrators. Things can be slightly wonky. It only enhances a sense of personality in the sketch.

I drew the triangles at the top of the box, like the purple lines.

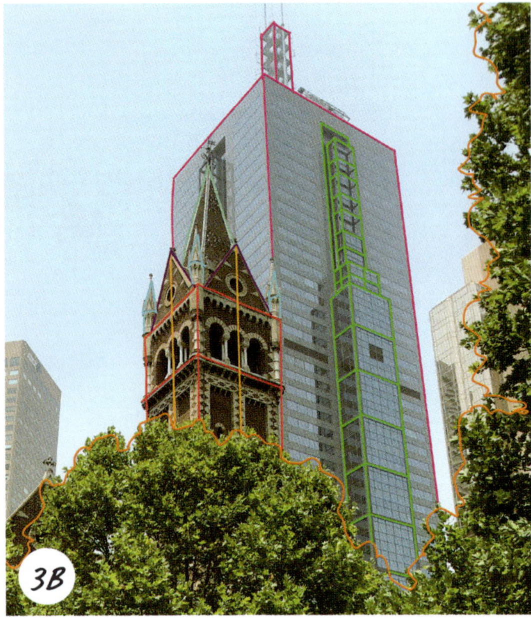

Then I drew basic shapes for the pointy towers on the corners of the box and the steeple.

4. Use your starting shapes as a reference to finish the sketch.

I used the triangles (drawn in purple) as a reference as to where to start and finish the steeple. When drawing triangles, it can help to draw dots where each point of the triangle shape should be and then join them with lines. I also drew the center line of the steeple to help with this too.

After this, I drew the simple box shape of the skyscraper behind the tower. Notice how the leftmost edge of the skyscraper is in line with the left purple triangle of the church. And the center line of the skyscraper is in line with the small, pointy tower on the right-hand corner of the church (drawn in image 3B in light blue). Look for references in your own scene as these will help you keep your sketch in proportion.

Then I drew the box on top of the skyscraper. There's a second series of box structures on the right face of the building, which were slightly trickier; if you come across difficult areas in your sketch, just remember to break everything down into simple shapes similar to how I did in image 3B, drawn in green. I was not worried about details at this point. I was just building the skeleton.

I finished the pencil sketch with a rough wiggly line of where the trees go. This was deliberately loose—there's no precision required. There are some other brown towers in the background of the photograph. I didn't want to include them, and that's the artist's prerogative!

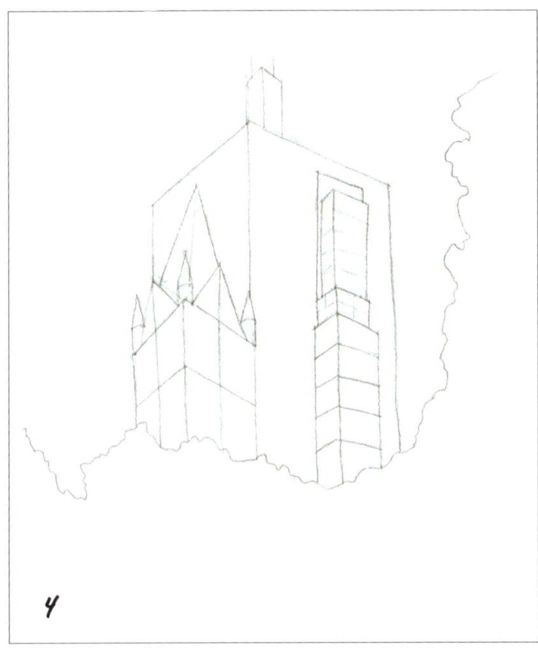

INK DETAILS

5. Add details to your architecture scene with a waterproof pen, simplifying ornate details as you go.

I used a 0.2 fineliner and started inking the things in the foreground and worked toward the background. This means I won't accidentally draw through something that should be in front of something else.

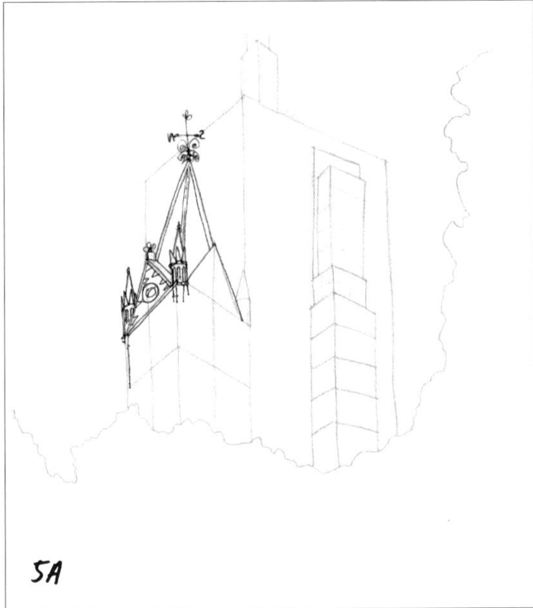

5A

Notice that I haven't drawn everything perfectly accurately on the church tower—I have just indicated what I'm seeing (5A). Also, from a distance, I can't make out too much detail on the tower, even with my glasses on! The arches are wonky and not evenly spaced but again, it's not a big deal.

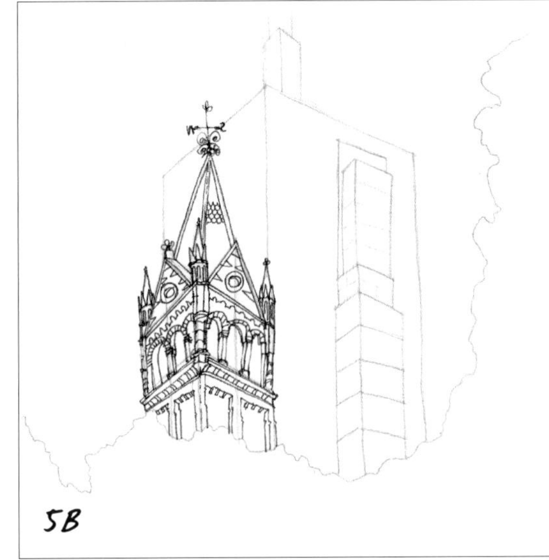

5B

I added some basic window details to the skyscraper—the block on the right and the little tower on the top (5B)—but I have left the main body of the skyscraper blank (5C) (there's a reason for that, which we shall cover in our final step).

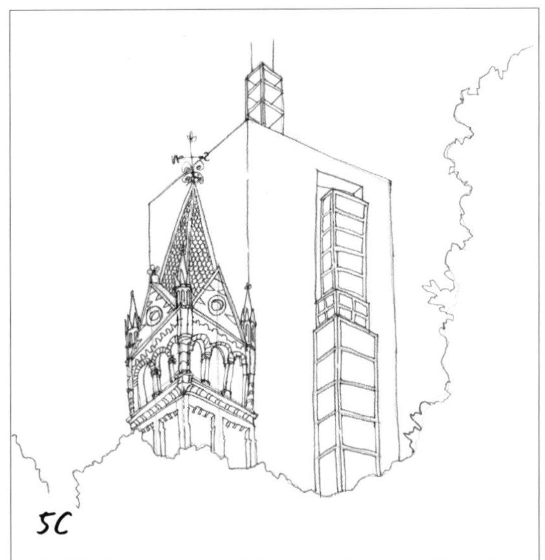

5C

Please do not worry about exact numbers of windows. I've heard urban sketcher Ian Fennelly say, "Life's too short to count windows." I couldn't agree more.

6. Once you have finished and made sure your ink is dry, gently erase the pencil lines.

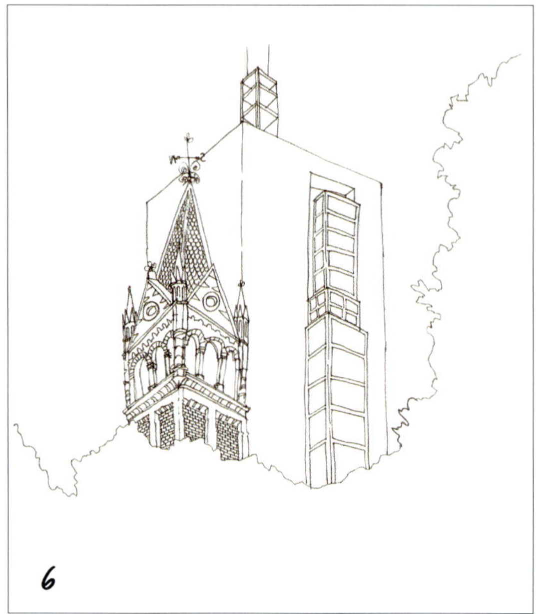
6

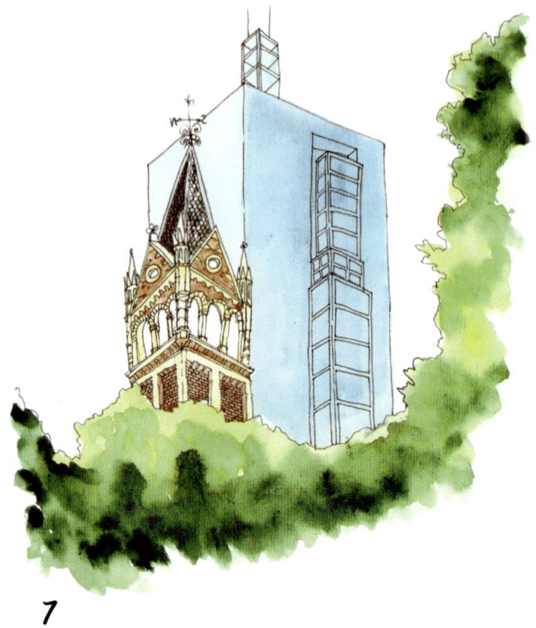
7

FIRST WATERCOLOR WASH

7. Start with the lightest, largest areas of color first.

In contrast to the ink stage, we need to start painting the background colors first, building the scene in layers and working from large light shapes to darker defined details.

I painted the skyscraper behind the tower first as it's a light blue color. It's a large area, so I used a large brush as it will make it easier to cover the area quickly. A ½-inch flat brush is ideal due to the straight-edge shape of the building but a round brush (size #10 or thereabouts) is also fine. I painted the whole building, including the structure on the right and on the top.

Some of the areas of my sketch that I needed to paint are quite small, at least on the church tower, so I used a ¼-inch dagger brush. A size #2 or #4 round brush would also work. Assess the areas you need to paint and decide which size of brush will be appropriate for your needs.

I started with the lightest color of the church tower, which is a sandy color on the edges and pointy towers, etc. I didn't worry about getting the exact color. After this, I used a dark brown color for the bricks and other areas on the church tower.

There are some areas of white on steeple roof tiles in the photo. This was a good opportunity to practice leaving some small white (i.e. unpainted) areas, which can give some visual interest to the sketch. See if there are areas of white you can leave in your own sketch.

There are many stylistic choices you can make with your sketch. I decided not to paint the sky for this particular sketch. I wanted the buildings to be the focus of attention, and I felt the skyscraper may have blended in with the sky too much. Every sketch is an experiment. I encourage you to explore and play with choices such as these.

I painted the tree line using the wet-on-wet technique as discussed on page 23. I used a yellow-green (in this particular case, Indian Yellow) to paint around the edge of the tree line that surrounds the buildings. I wanted this part to be lighter and yellower as it's where the sunlight hits the trees. While the Indian Yellow was still wet, I painted some green slightly on top and also expanded the painted area. I wanted some of the green to mix in with the wet yellow on the page. I then painted an even darker green, expanding the painted section even farther but allowing the dark green to mix with the previous green I put down.

The page was quite wet, so I needed to wait a few minutes for it to dry before continuing. The speed at which your paint dries will vary depending on your paper, your climate and how much water you used.

SHADOWS

8. When the initial layer of watercolor is dry, add a second layer of watercolor to build up depth.

I added a darker shade of brown under the window arches, under the ledge and in the brick areas to show they are receded. As mentioned on page 21, squinting your eyes is an effective method of identifying where the shadows are in the scene.

I painted the panes of glass on the extruding structure on the right-hand side of the skyscraper with a darker blue than the main body of the building. Notice how the left window panes are slightly darker than the panes on the right side. I also painted the shape of the shadow cast by this structure onto the skyscraper itself.

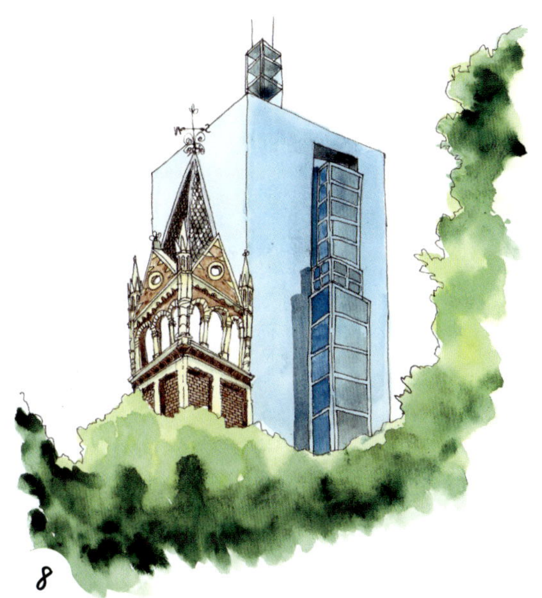

I was not too concerned with the very dark areas, as I addressed these in the next step with a black brush pen.

FINISHING TOUCHES

9. Look for areas to add strong contrast to your sketch.

I used a black brush pen to fill in the arch windows on the church tower and the round windows toward the top of the tower (9A). Adding black like this is a stylistic choice and one that works well for windows and doorways. I don't do it in every sketch, but it adds a lovely sense of drama and contrast.

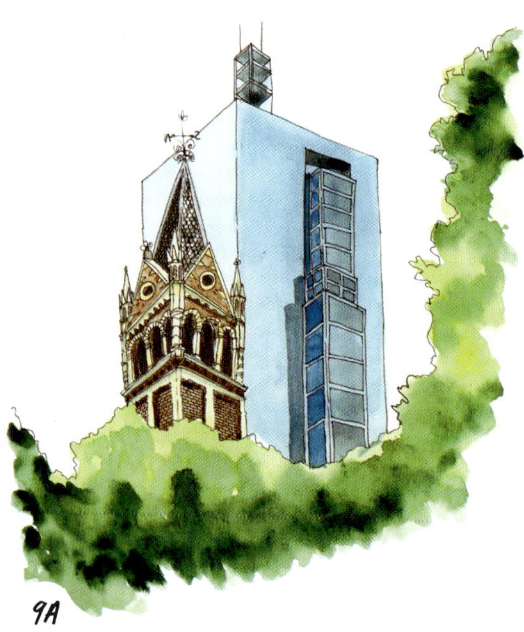

9A

You can certainly use watercolor to add very dark areas too. Experiment and see what you prefer.

Next I finished the skyscraper off by using a gray marker pen (9B). I recommend a watercolor marker or one filled with India ink (such as the Faber-Castell Pitt Artist Pens mentioned on page 113). Make sure to test your marker on a separate page in your sketchbook. Alcohol markers, for example, will probably bleed through the page, so if you have a sketch on the other side, it may ruin it. This is why I recommend a watercolor or Indian ink marker.

With the marker, I drew across the top of the painted skyscraper to indicate the darker gray frames you can see in the photo.

Finally, I added a slightly thicker line around the edge of the church tower to bring it forward. Again, this is a stylistic choice but adding a thicker line can be very effective in showing that one object is closer than another.

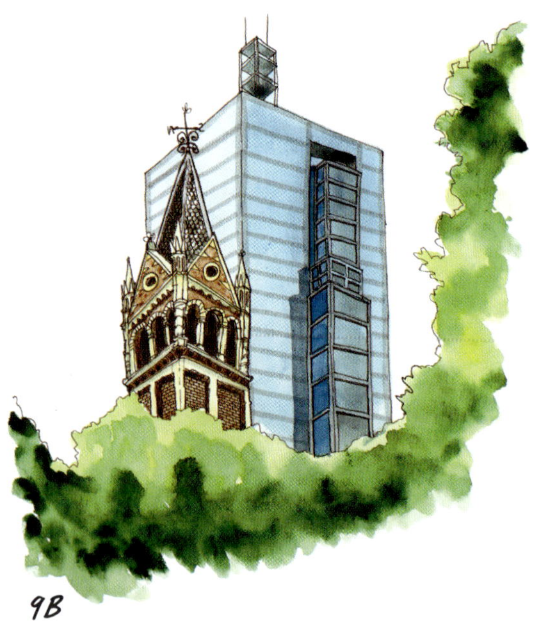

9B

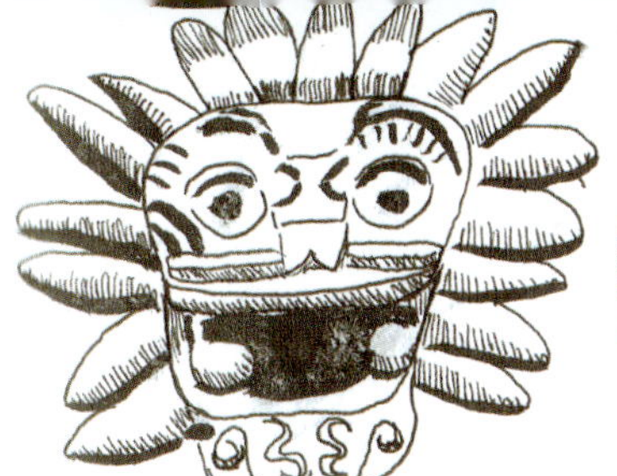

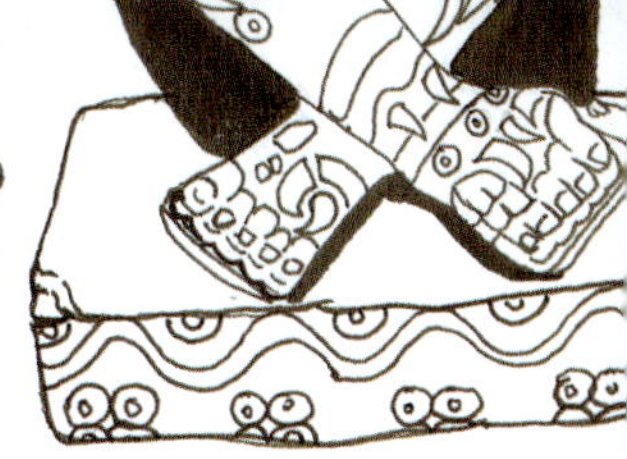

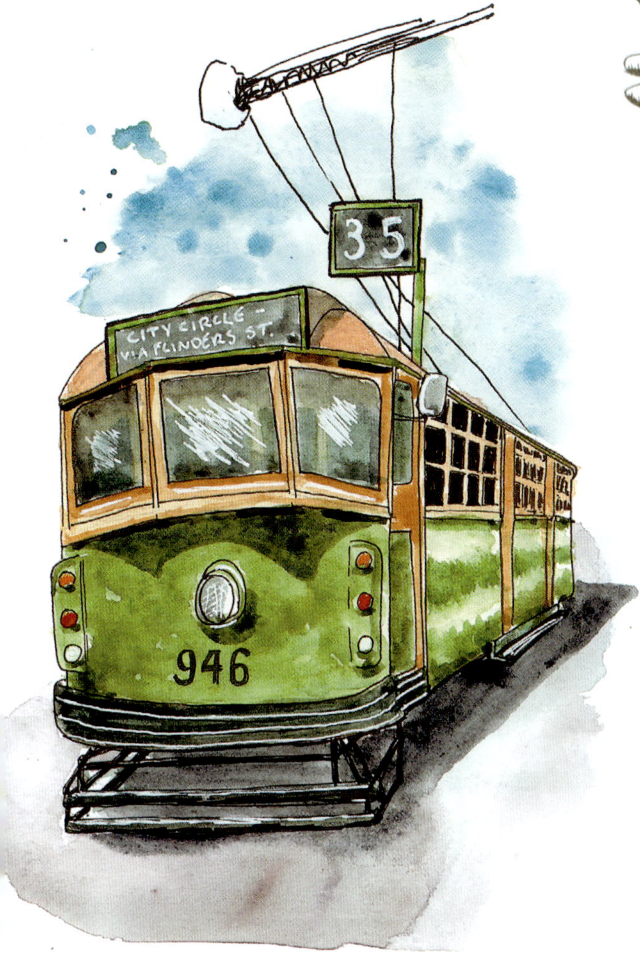

TRAVELING THE WORLD

Travel is what got me hooked on sketching in the first place. Or was it the other way around? Either way, the two go hand in hand. I can't imagine traveling anywhere without my sketchbook, and I'm sure you will develop the same habit if you haven't already.

A sketchbook is the perfect travel companion. It keeps you occupied in any situation, especially dull ones that involve waiting. It's a great conversation starter if you want it to be and don't mind people asking what you're up to. It can record your most special memories to your most mundane of trips. You will find that everything you sketch you will remember in great detail: the sights, sounds, smells, tastes and feel of a place, as well as all the people you encounter along the way.

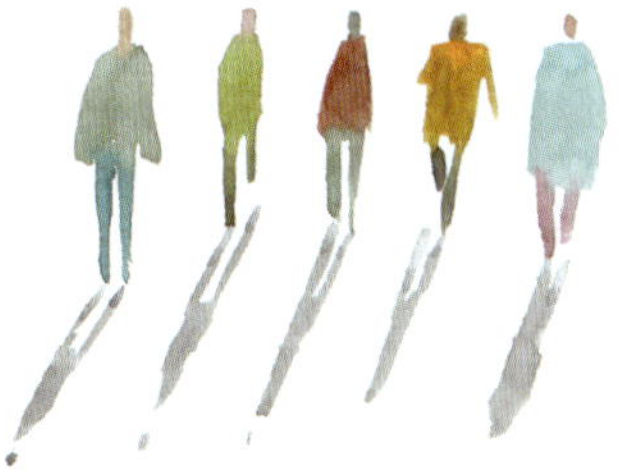

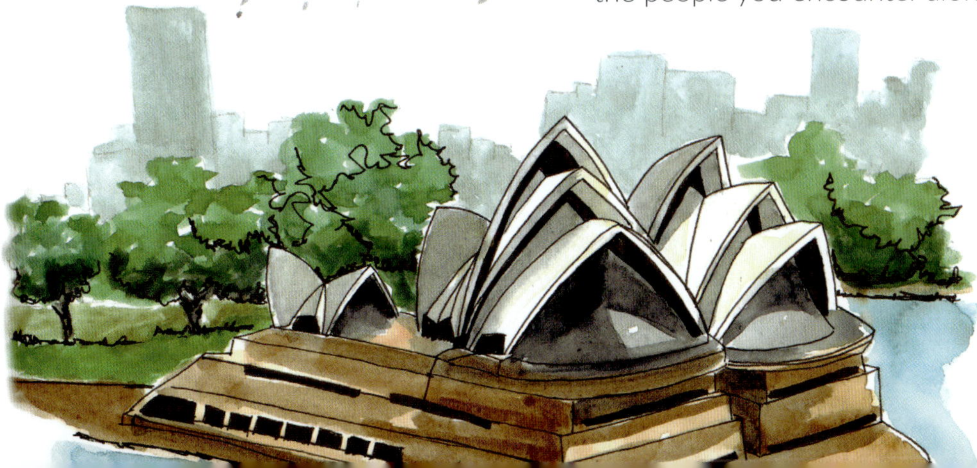

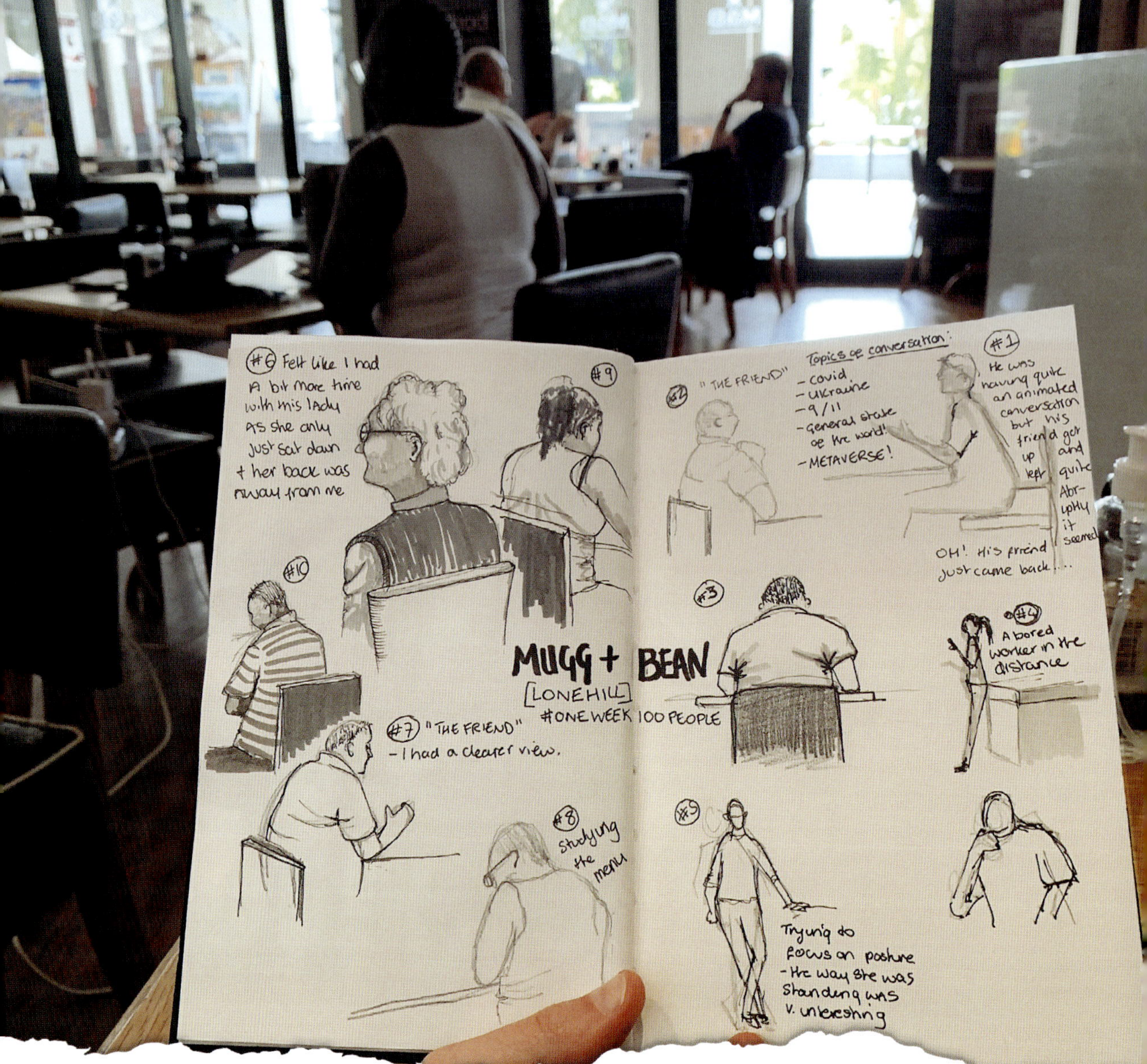

PEOPLE SKETCHING

Not all urban sketchers like to sketch architecture and not all urban sketchers like to sketch people. Some actively avoid it, deleting people from their sketches, such as Ian Fennelly. Some urban sketchers draw around people, leaving a negative shape where people were, such as Danny Hawk.

Some urban sketchers, such as Lynne Chapman, Adebanji Alade and Róisín Curé, prefer to draw nothing but people—although they can and will draw whatever is front of them.

As your sketching habit progresses, you may find you develop a strong preference for one or more particular subject matters. At the beginning of your journey, I recommend sketching anything and everything to maximize your practice.

STRATEGIES

If sketching people intimidates you, you are not alone. It's an area I am still actively trying to improve on. Sketch by sketch, I am seeing some improvement. There are strategies you can use to get more comfortable with sketching people.

1. **Sketch people from behind.**

This is a great way to start people sketching. Half the battle is getting your sketchbook and pen out. The other half is drawing what's in front of you. Drawing someone from behind is less intimidating because (a) they can't see what you're doing and (b) you don't have to draw a face!

2. **Sketch people's hands or shoes, zooming in on details.**

Again, this is a great strategy to get used to getting your sketchbook out in public and drawing from life. People are less likely to notice you drawing them if you are looking in the direction of their shoes. Also, sketching smaller details, such as hands or shoes, will give you more time and allow you to draw more details, which can also be fun. You can draw many different hands and/or shoes and collage them across your sketchbook page.

3. **Look for people with hats, glasses or beards.**

Accessories such as these help to draw the overall shape of the person and help with drawing tricky bits, like the shape of the head and facial features. The Covid-19 outbreak proved useful for my people-sketching attempts as face masks took most of the tricky bits of the face away.

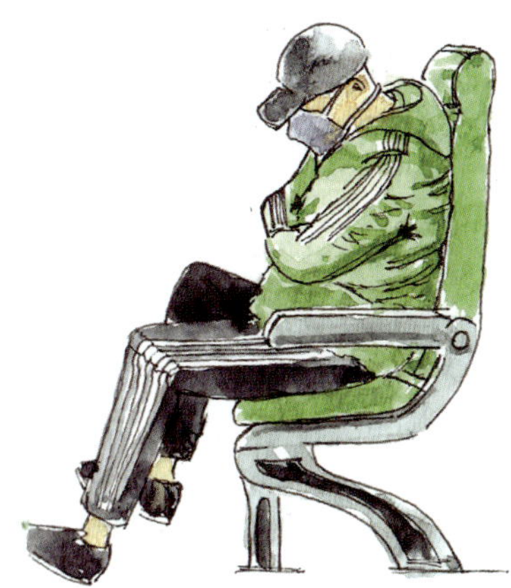

In this sketch, the man is wearing a baseball hat and a face mask, making him the perfect subject to draw.

4. **Look for distracted people.**

People who have their noses buried in a book or newspaper or smartphone are unlikely to notice you. Likewise, people in deep conversation or those on transport who have dozed off make excellent sketching subjects. They are more likely to stay in a similar position for several minutes or more, allowing you time to put down your initial lines or shapes before they move.

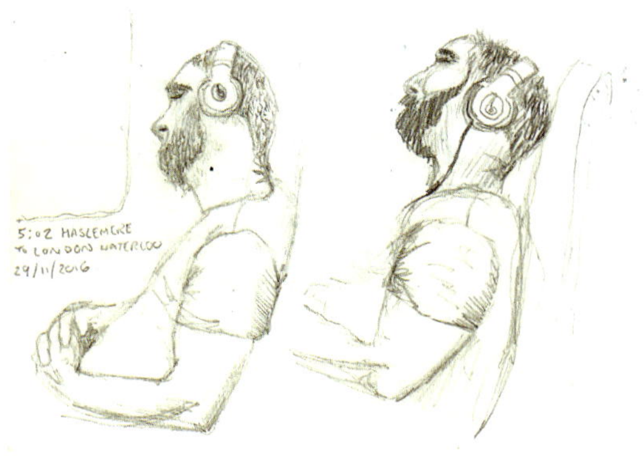

I sketched this man who had fallen asleep on the train with his headphones on. I don't think there was any way he was going to notice me sketching him. This made a perfect subject for my early people-sketching attempts. I also drew in pencil as this was the medium I was most comfortable with at the time. I talk about ink and watercolor a lot throughout the book, but don't forget, you can urban sketch just as much with a humble pencil.

LOCATIONS

The great thing about people sketching is that there are people everywhere, so it's easy to find somewhere to practice when you are out and about.

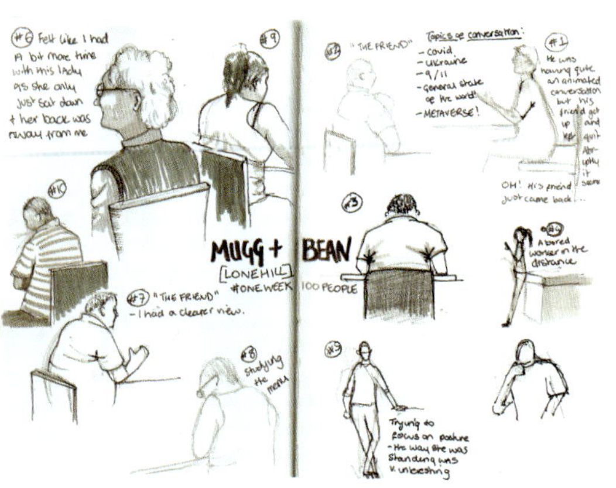

- Cafes (along with pubs and restaurants) are fantastic places to sketch. Find a busy one and try to sit at a table in the corner or with a wall behind you. I personally prefer this so people can't really see what I'm doing. Most people don't care of course, but I just prefer to remain low-key. With an A5 sketchbook that looks like a notebook along with a pencil or pen, people will assume you're taking notes. That's if anyone even registers what you are doing at all.
- Waiting rooms or traveling on public transport are other great situations for the practicing people sketcher. People are most definitely distracted in these areas as they are bored and therefore entertaining themselves. They won't notice you scribbling away in the corner.
- Meetings, talks or conferences are also great places to sketch people, especially from behind. Most are listening to the speaker or probably falling into a snooze (depending on the subject matter and entertainment value of the speaker). In addition to drawing the back of audience members, you can draw the speaker.
- The beach tends to be a place where people sunbathe for hours on end or play beach games, so you could get some good practice with capturing people in motion.

It can feel intimidating drawing people from life as you may feel they know exactly what you're doing. The key is to not look up and down from your page as much as you normally would as that will attract their attention.

PERMISSION

A common question that's asked: "Do you ask permission to sketch someone?" My answer is always no. I don't think there are many urban sketchers who ask permission. You are not trying to draw a portrait of someone specific. Most of the time they are one of many people in a scene and essentially could be anyone. Or if they are the only person in the drawing, like my sketches, nine times out of ten, it would be hard to recognize the person as a specific individual. If the man saw my sketch, he would recognize himself by his clothing but that's all, even if I had drawn his face.

An example of a situation in which I would ask for permission is if I attended an event, class or workshop with the intention of drawing people. For example, we attended a dog-training class in the park and asked permission to sketch the participants. We asked the instructor rather than every individual participant. She announced to the class what we were doing and asked if anyone had any issues or concerns. No one had an issue with us sitting on the sidelines drawing.

HOW TO START

Much like with the ducks, it's useful to warm up when sketching people. I recommend doing some quick blind contour drawings, followed by looking at your page a little bit while trying to draw some figures (as discussed on page 96). This a great warm-up to strengthen your hand-eye coordination, as well as loosen you up (mentally and physically).

A fast way to sketch people is to paint directly in watercolor. Keep the colors light and focus on the shapes of the body. This is a great strategy to force you to focus on shape rather than lines. By keeping the colors light, you can come back and darken certain areas or refine them later if you want to.

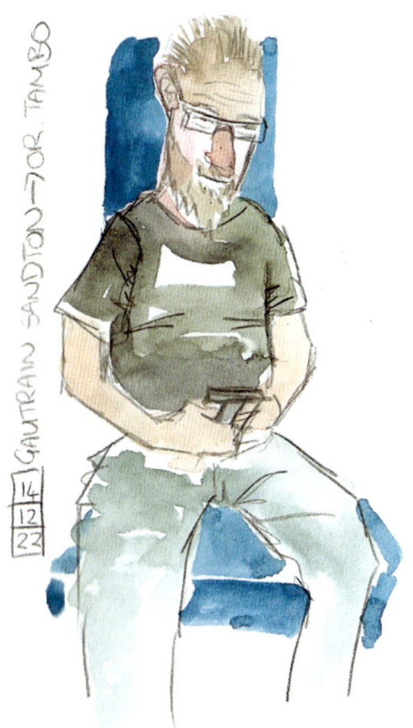

In this sketch, I quickly put shapes down with somewhat realistic colors I could see in the scene. Once dry (which didn't take long), I drew over the top with a Pitt oil base pencil. I prefer this over a graphite pencil, as it has a matte black finish rather than a shiny gray finish. That's as complicated as it needs to be. The sketch took 10 minutes maximum. Doing little sketches like this when you are in an environment with many distracted people is the perfect way to practice people sketching.

Don't worry about facial details at this stage. Getting the posture of the body and the story of what the person is doing is far more interesting, at least when it comes to urban sketching. Whether you capture the likeness of a stranger is unimportant. Also, when you are sketching the person quite small to begin with, it's incredibly difficult to capture the fine details of a face.

Another way to start sketching someone is with a line drawing first and adding watercolor on top afterward (if you want to—you don't have to).

If you are drawing with line first, remember your blind contour drawing exercise and try to stay loose. Another exercise to help with this is continuous line drawing.

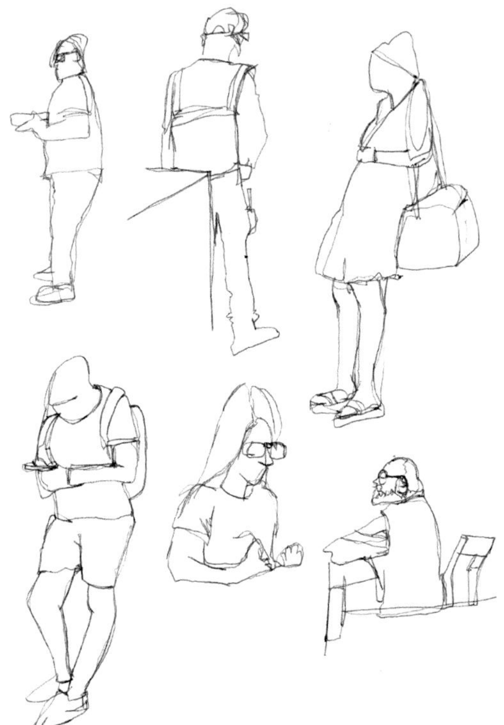

You can look at your page as well as your subject while drawing, but you cannot lift the pen or pencil from the page. This technique forces you to stay loose. It also makes you focus on the relationship of each line to one another. You can't lift your pen off the page, so you must look closely at where one line meets another so you can plan your journey to where you need to go. Forget the details and just focus on the different lines that make up the overall shape of the body. This is another moment where you need to forget what you're drawing and just draw what you see.

You will end up with restated lines and squiggles here and there, but the overall essence of the person you are sketching will be there. You can use this technique with any subject you draw, not just people. Remember, this is an exercise first and foremost, and don't worry about the end results.

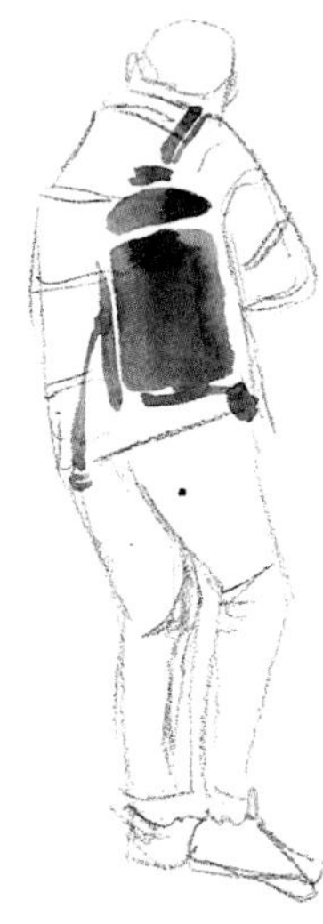

Remember, you don't have to draw or paint everything. In this sketch, I just painted the backpack and decided to draw the rest of the man with a black pencil. Just painting the shape and size of the bag helped me to draw the rest of the figure as I used the bag as a visual landmark, and I could judge where and what size the arm and head should be in relation to the bag.

The path to success with people sketching is to not strive for a literal sketch with realistic details. Given the timeframe that you have to sketch someone, it would be difficult to do.

GROUPS OF PEOPLE

It's tricky to sketch one person quickly before they move, let alone a group of people. Be strategic when deciding who and when to sketch. If there is a group who has just sat down at a table in a cafe, for example, then you can be assured that while they may move their bodies within their seats, they won't be getting up and leaving entirely for a while. Most people return to a similar pose after some time, so don't get disheartened. Patience is key. Also, as mentioned earlier, you can use other people's bodies to finish off a sketch. If someone else is holding a similar pose elsewhere, you can use them as your model.

In this sketch, I started by quickly painting the areas of skin I could see. I find this a very useful way to place the faces and hands of the group in relation to each other. If I don't quite get it right, it's no problem, but it gives me a starting point. I have heard over the years that heads and hands are key to a successful sketch of a person.

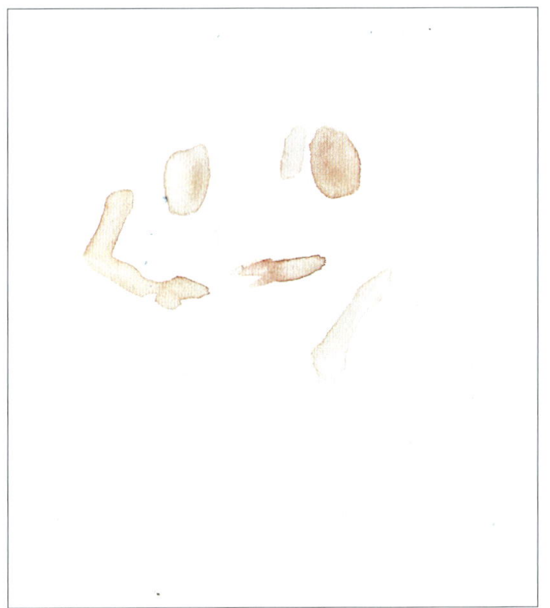

This group was standing, so they could have moved off at any time, but they seemed to be fairly engrossed in looking at something together. It is better to take the risk and have an incomplete sketch than not try at all. I remind myself, more so with people sketching than any other subject, that it is the practice that matters and not the outcome so much.

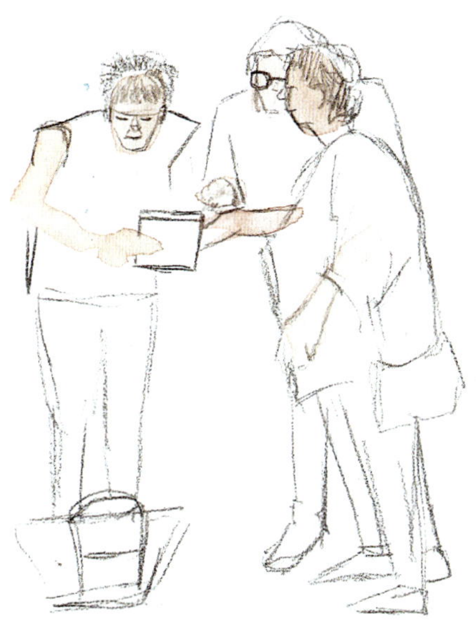

The second stage of the sketch was to add line with a black pencil to define their body shapes. I used very simple geometric shapes and focused on where their bodies met each other. I drew the lady on the left first, followed by the lady on the right, and using her body as a reference guide, I added the male figure behind her.

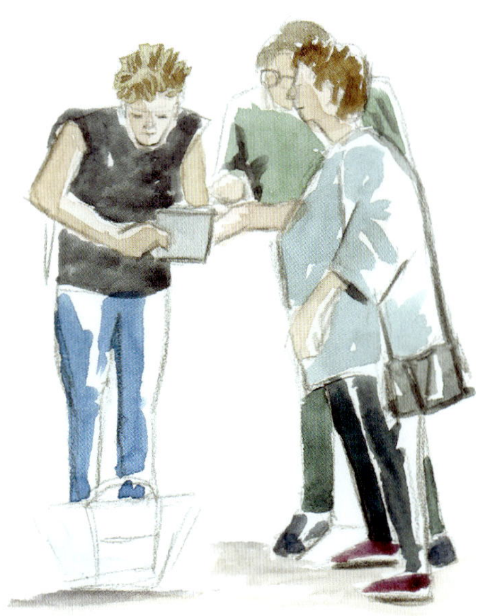

QUICK FIGURES

Don't be afraid to get scribbly. Some of the most dynamic, beautiful people sketches are those that are free and loose. They appear scribbly and hurried, so they can portray the sense of motion and the overall feeling of the person they are sketching far more than a neat line drawing.

Don't worry if the arm or the bag are in the wrong place—just draw it again, right over the top. This is where something like a graphite or color pencil comes in nicely, as you can draw softly and loosely at first and then draw hard and more deliberately over the top to refine any areas you want to correct. Sketches with restated lines like these look super dynamic and interesting.

In the final stage, I added some color with watercolor paint. I tried my best to exaggerate the highlights and preserve the white of the page. This makes for a dynamic effect and can offset the fact that there weren't many exciting colors in the scene. I also painted some subtle shadows on the skin of each person. Otherwise, I kept it very simple and tried not to overwork the sketch. There's no time to get too picky when you are sketching people on location. Try to capture the scene with minimal detail and in as little time as possible.

While the faces and hands have very little detail, you still get a sense of their body language, and you can sense the overall story. They are all looking at the information, deciphering what it means in the confines of their little huddle. In this way, as an urban sketcher, we captured a particular story at a particular time and place, recording life one drawing at a time.

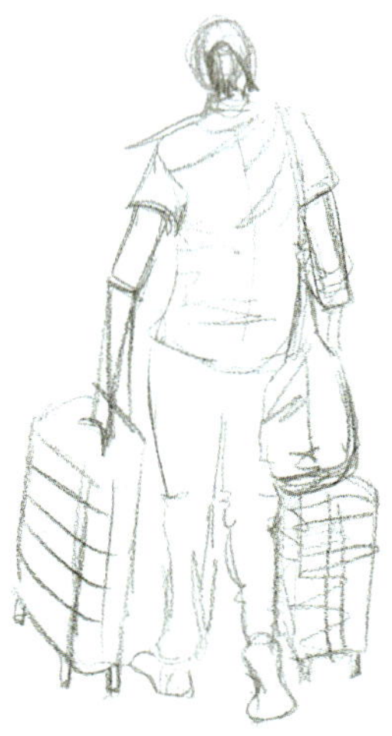

You won't always get parts of the body in proportion or at the right angle and that's okay. People sketching, more so than anything, is all about practice. Over time, you will get to understand the general proportions of the head and body, certain postures, how body weight is distributed when someone stands, walks or runs and how the shoulders hunch when someone is sitting.

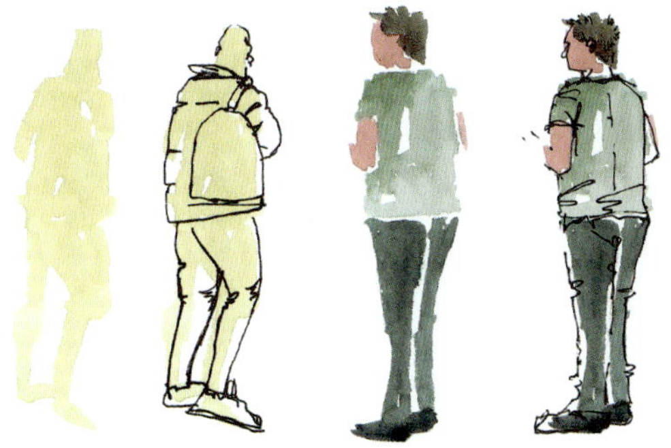

Sketching directly in watercolor is a quick way to get the basic silhouette of a person on the page very quickly, which is useful when someone is in motion. You can then decide if you want to refine the figure further with watercolor or to draw over the top with line. Your subject may be waiting, walking or busy doing something, but often they will eventually return to the same sort of position, so you can get the quick, loose marks you need to complete your sketch.

PEOPLE IN A SCENE

You may want to add people into a scene as context rather than sketching them as the main focus. There a few shorthand ways to add generic people into a sketch, along with a few tips to bear in mind.

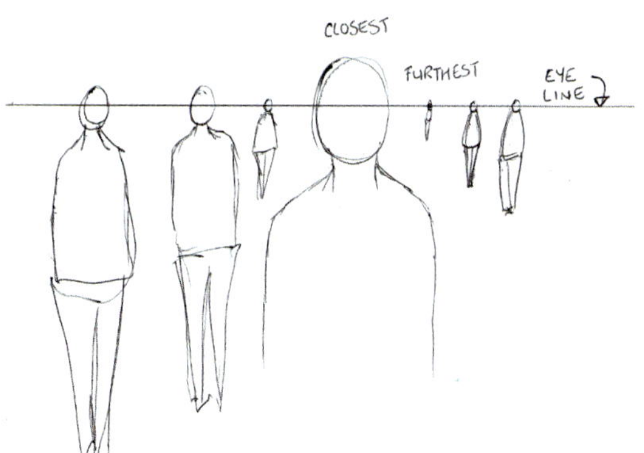

First, most of the heads of the people will fall on the eye line of your scene, no matter if they are close to you or farther away. The distance the person is from the viewer is indicated by the size of the head and body in relation to each other. This rule depends on your vantage point, as this will not be true if you are looking up or down a hill, for example. If you are seated, your eye line is lower than if you are standing up. However, if you are drawing other people who are seated too, then their head heights will more or less fall on a flat horizontal line too.

Remember, people are there just for context, so you do not need to draw any detail. The more people there are, the less detail. The people are not the focus of the scene. You just need to get the general shape so that it is recognizable that there are people present. As such, you can use a shorthand to do so. You can do this either in ink, directly with watercolor or both. It depends on what the overall style of your sketch is.

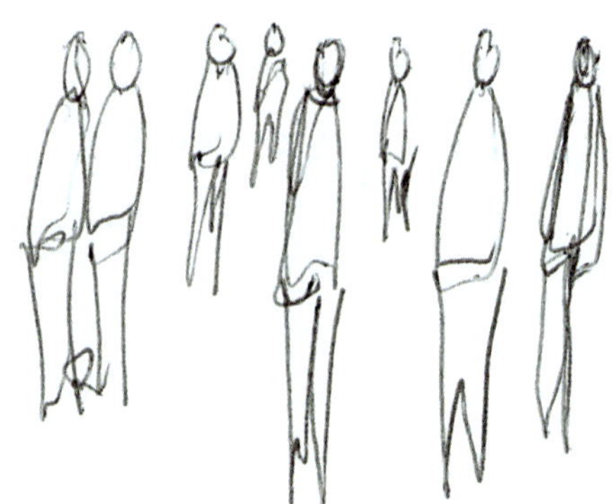

You can use line or shape when drawing people with ink, watercolor or both. You can have a lot of fun with this. I suggest taking some printer paper and just filling a page or two with small drawings of figures like these and see what you can come up with.

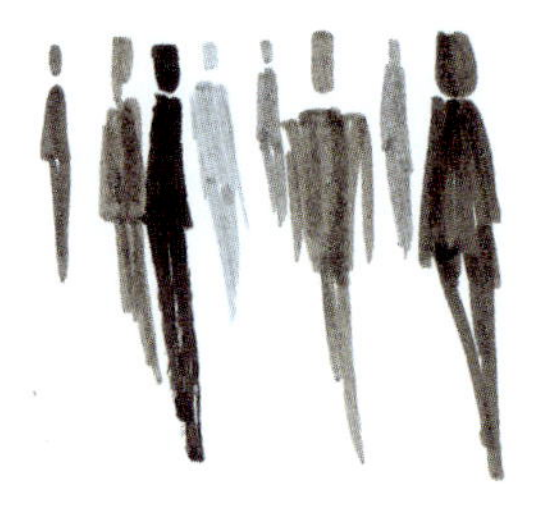

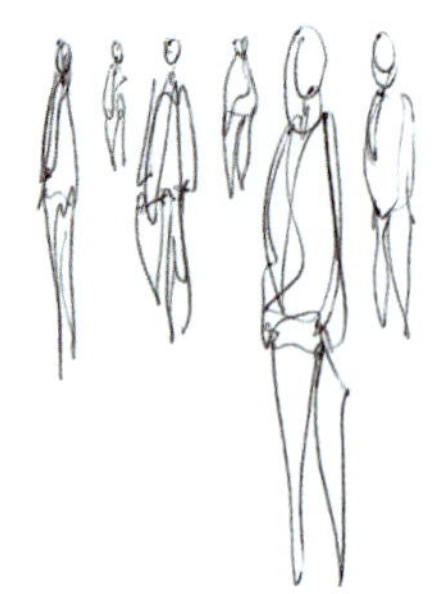

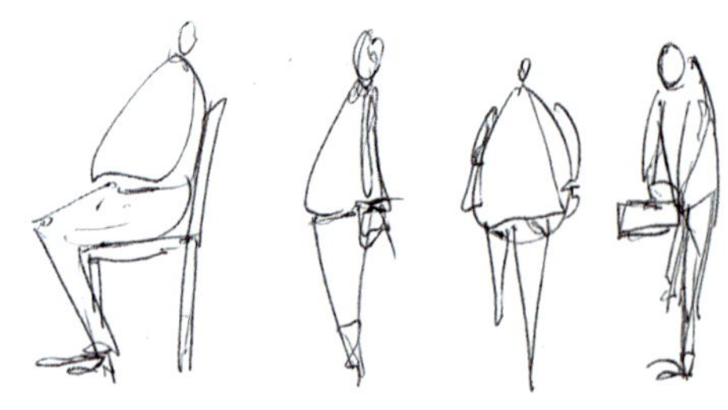

A small dot for the head, a rectangle body and two lines extending down for legs works very well. You don't even need to add arms if you don't want to.

If you want to make it look like someone is walking, one of their legs will be shorter and the other longer.

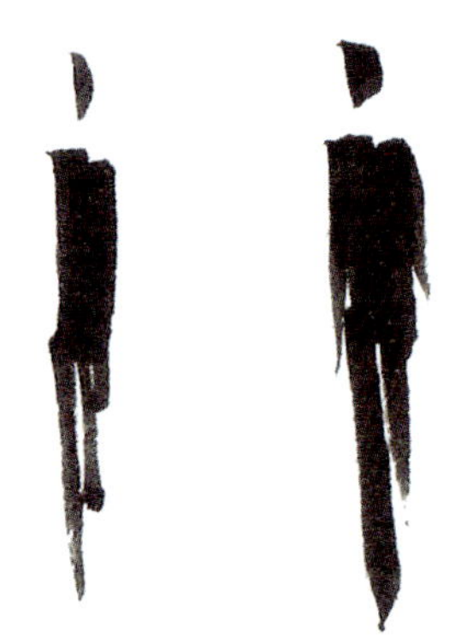

Notice there are no feet, arms or hands in these little sketches. There's no need. The human brain fills in the details.

You can also have fun exaggerating body shapes by making them shorter and fatter, elongating them, giving someone a very tiny head and a huge body—the options are endless. It depends on how much you wish to stylize the figures in your scene. As long as you keep in mind that the heads will generally all be at the same level (taking into account the exceptions mentioned previously), then you can get away with a lot!

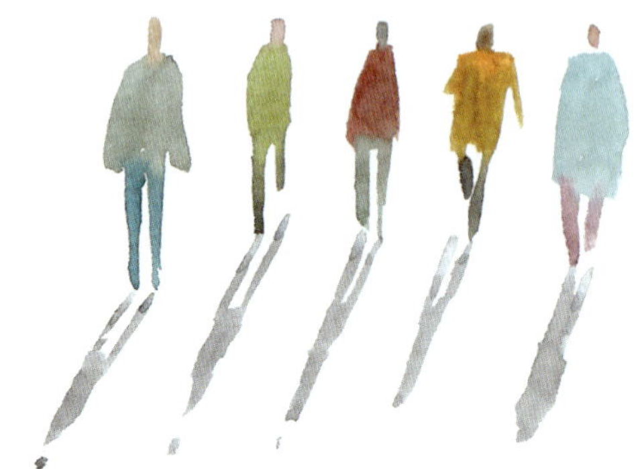

Don't forget to add shadow shapes underneath your figures as that really brings them to life.

Do not feel you absolutely must include people in a scene. Do what you feel is right for your particular sketch at that particular moment. I encourage you to practice people sketching in general though. It's super fun and accessible to all. You may not have Notre Dame in your backyard, but I'm sure there are plenty of places you can find people to draw.

I set up a website, https://peoplesketching.com, which offers video references of people going about their business to sketch from. It's a great substitute if you don't have time for or are a bit fearful of sketching in public just yet.

TRANSPORT

When I was starting to sketch on location, one of my favorite ways to practice was to sit in my car on my lunch break from work and sketch "car portraits" of the cars in the parking lot. I had a landscape A6 Moleskine, a fountain pen, a small set of Winsor & Newton Cotman watercolors and a water brush.

Here are some of my early attempts:

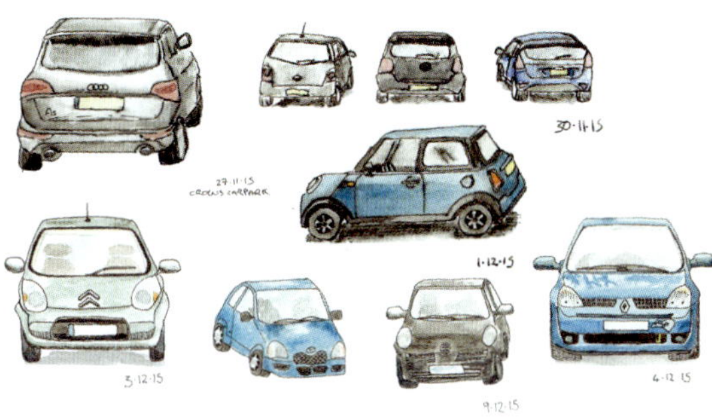

This is a great way to approach sketching cars. Reduce the likelihood of overwhelming yourself and just sketch them straight on, either from the front or back. Once you are comfortable with that, you can try sketching the car from a different angle.

Lapin, one of my favorite urban sketchers, has a fantastic knack for caricaturing cars. He draws them from extreme angles and just knows how and where to exaggerate certain things. He wasn't born with this ability. He has drawn for many years and developed his eye so he can now draw a car directly in ink.

Vehicles can tell a lot about the location you are in. Think about the iconic red buses and black taxis of London and the yellow cabs of New York and the streetcars in San Francisco. In Mexico, the streets are loaded with old Volkswagen Beetles and campervans (heaven!) or how about those 1950s cars in Cuba?

PERSPECTIVE

When drawing cars or any other vehicles, it's useful to simplify them to their most basic geometric shapes. An easy way to get started sketching transport is to sketch your subject from the front. Viewed from the front, a car, bus or train can be reduced to a simple box shape. From there, it's a case of dividing the box into further basic shapes in proportion to each other, such as the windscreen and the body and adding details, such as lights, signs, wing mirrors, etc.

I like to sketch everything quickly and loosely in pencil first in case the subject moves. This was not a problem with the VW campervan sketch on the following page (because the van belonged to me) but was a risk with the tram. As long as I have the shapes and details in, if it moves, then I still have enough to finish my sketch. You can also add color notes too, in case there are very specific colors you need to use. Just paint some swatches of colors matching your subject to the side of your page. You can even write the name of the color underneath. This also lends an authentic sketchbook vibe to your page. Sketchbooks were traditionally used as visual notebooks. In modern times, sketchbooks are a work of art in their own right. It's up to you how you wish to treat yours—crisp and perfectly presented or loose and messy. You may change your mind page by page!

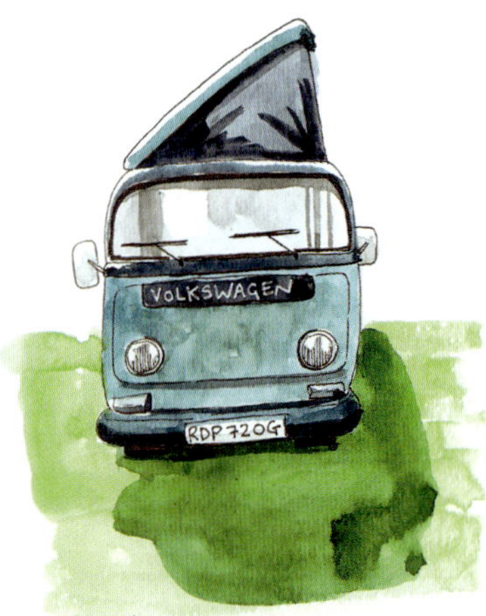

"PUFF" 1969 VW CAMPER VAN

The first example is actually my campervan. I sketched it from the front while at a VW festival. I kept the shapes very simple, but the overall sketch was made more interesting by the elevated roof and the shape of the shadow on the ground. It's a basic sketch but reminds me of the place and time and of the 1969 campervan I no longer own.

TIP: *Classic car shows are a great place to sketch stationary vehicles from any angle you choose. It's probably a little safer than plonking yourself in the middle of the street to sketch a car! Older cars tend to be far more interesting to sketch. Some have unusual body shapes and strange "doo-dads" on them (that's technical speak FYI). I recommend sketching the vehicle you are interested in, but if you have more time, then sketch the surroundings too, so you are recording the context, as well as the car.*

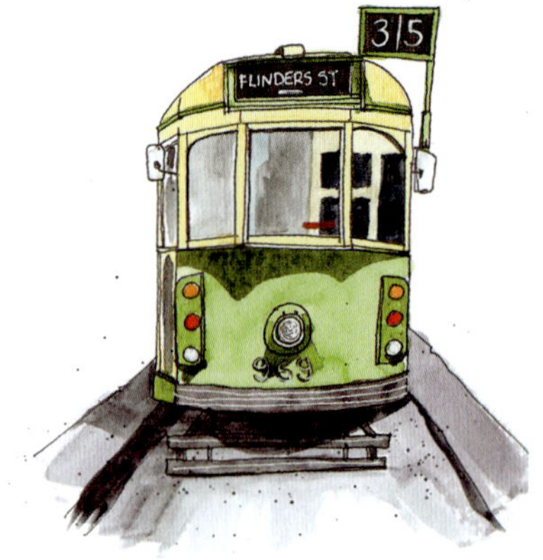

In this second example, I sketched the historic free tram in Melbourne. Even though its overall shape is just a box, it has interesting details that really bring it to life, such as the distinctive shadow shape under the window, the sign poking out on the right side and the lights on the front.

Things get a bit more interesting when you draw a vehicle from an angle. Do you notice how static the sketches above feel? The subject becomes more dynamic when there's a sense of perspective and depth.

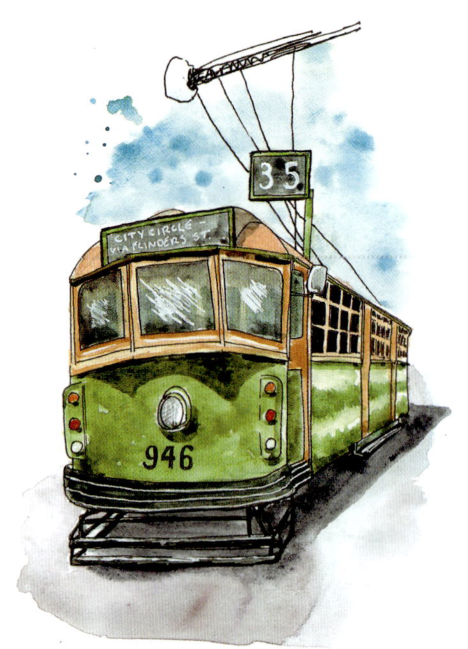

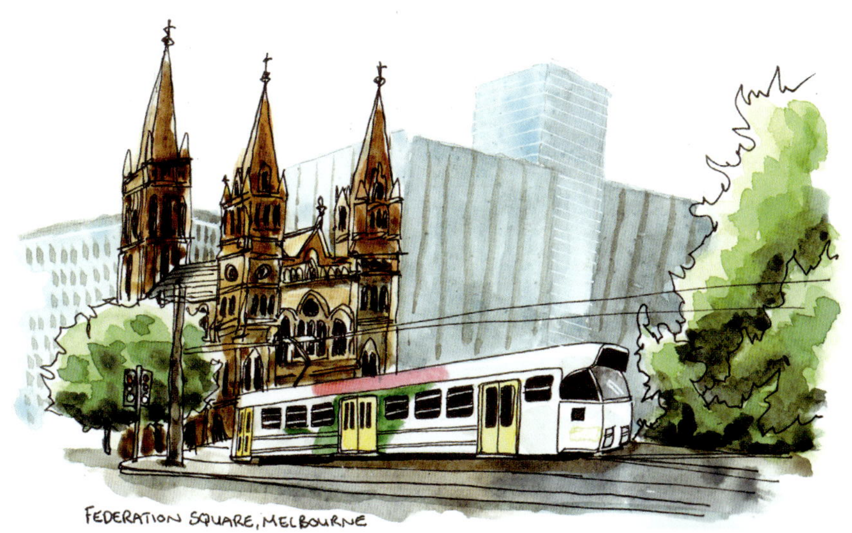

STORYTELLING

As urban sketchers, we would ideally sketch some of the background or surroundings too, so we fulfill the storytelling aspect of the Urban Sketchers Manifesto (page 7). As you can see from some of the examples in this book, I don't always do this. It depends on how much time I have and what I feel like. Don't feel constrained by the "rules."

In this sketch of Federation Square in Melbourne, I added a basic background. I wanted the tram and the church behind it to be the main focus of the sketch. If you look closely, you can see all the elements are very basically drawn. The tram is a long cuboid, but the particular colors and placement makes it recognizable as a Melbourne tram. I also simplified the church. I focused on the number and shapes of the towers and windows, but there are no further details and I filled in the windows with black. There are a couple of other elements in the foreground that add to the story: the telephone pole, the traffic lights and a tree. In the background were multiple glass office buildings. I decided to paint them gray without any detail at all in ink. This serves to push both the church and the tram into the foreground, making them the focus of our attention.

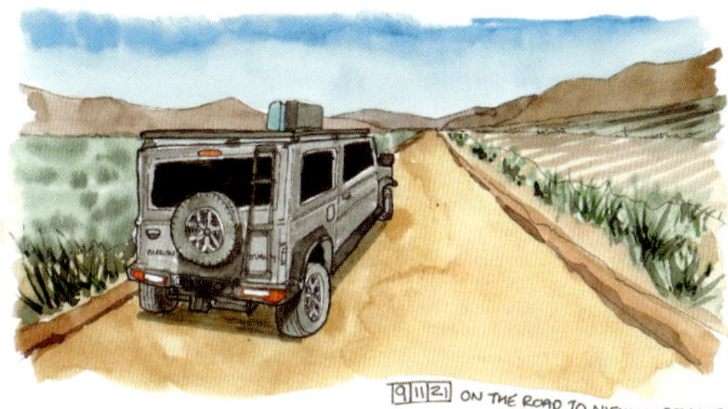

In this sketch, the vehicle was still the focus but I added some of the scenery to show we were in the absolute middle of nowhere, driving through the Karoo desert, having not seen another car for a few hours and with no phone reception to be had. Luckily we didn't break down! I drew the car first. As you may be able to tell, I didn't quite get the proportion right; it's a bit too stretched in my sketch. It felt easy and quick enough to add some of the landscape around the car. You can see there is a one-point perspective where the road disappears off into the distance. Again, I kept the background elements purely in watercolor, as I did not want to detract from the sketch of the car.

This is an example of a non-urban scene; however, as discussed earlier, your scenes do not always have to have an urban setting. This is especially true when travel sketching.

So far we have looked at how to sketch transport as the main focus, either by itself or with some background details. Now let's look at how we can include transport in a scene when the vehicle itself is not the focus but is an "accessory."

SIMPLIFYING

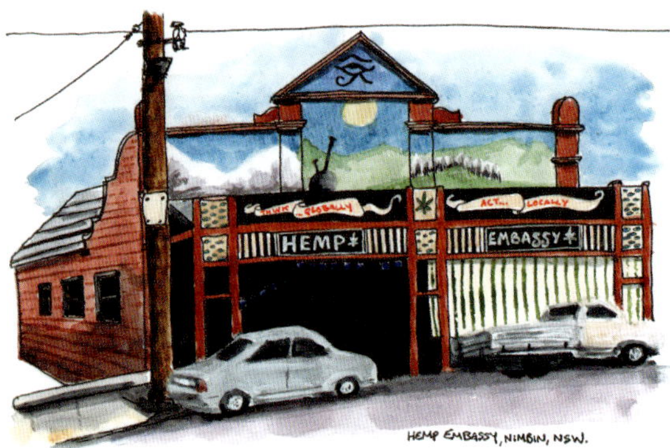

In this scene, the building was the focus. However, I wanted to include the cars parked outside. Although I didn't draw them accurately, it is still clear what they are and it adds to the overall scene.

Including vehicles in an overall scene is challenging, but I cannot emphasize enough that the key is to keep it simple. The vehicle is not the sketch's focus, therefore a rough or vague indication of the object is good enough. You do not have to draw all the details.

Urban sketcher Danny Hawk draws around cars and leaves them as blank shapes in his sketch. It's super stylistic and gets around the issue of including them but not drawing them! I encourage you to look at his work on Instagram for some inspiration.

When sketching a scene with cars parked, keep thinking of them as boxes. You can even sketch them in pencil as boxes when you start your sketch. As you keep working, you can eventually refine them to look a little more like cars. Remember, cars also follow the rules of perspective. So, if you have a street filled with parked cars, they will follow the perspective line of the road.

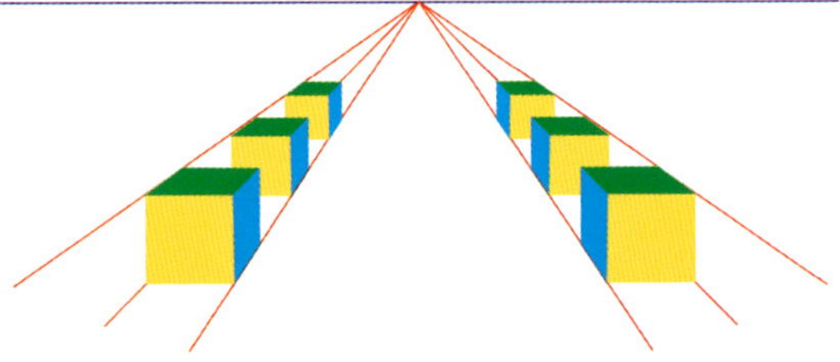

I enjoy sketching transport as the main focus of my sketches. I am less inclined to sketch them as incidental objects that just happen to be in the scene. Many urban sketchers also omit cars, for example, in their street sketches. It's entirely up to whether you like to include them or not.

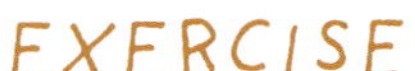

1. Draw a car, bus, train or tram from the front.

I would recommend a parked car for this. Please don't get run over in the name of urban sketching. You need something that's going to stay still for a while. Draw the overall box shape, divide it into the smaller shapes inside and then add some of the details. You can do all this very quickly in pencil if you like and then refine with your ink pen on top. Paint the vehicle and then finish off with some shadows and thickening lines in places.

2. Draw the same vehicle from an angle.

Keep imagining the box and sculpt the vehicle out of it. This is harder for a car than a bus, train or tram, as they are pretty boxy anyway. The most important thing is to do your best to get the sense of perspective as closely as possible to make the sketch believable.

3. Add context to your sketches by adding some background elements.

You can make this as simple or complicated as you like. Perhaps just some grass and the sky or the road and some rail tracks or if you're feeling bold, some buildings, people, foliage—whatever you can see in front of you. Remember, don't put too much detail in the background. The vehicle should remain the focus of your sketch.

ANOTHER EXAMPLE

AIRPLANES

Airplanes can be a little trickier to sketch due to the nose shape and the foreshortening of the wings. Because of that, they are also fun. Many urban sketchers also travel and enjoy sketching the plane they will be flying in at the beginning and end of their trip.

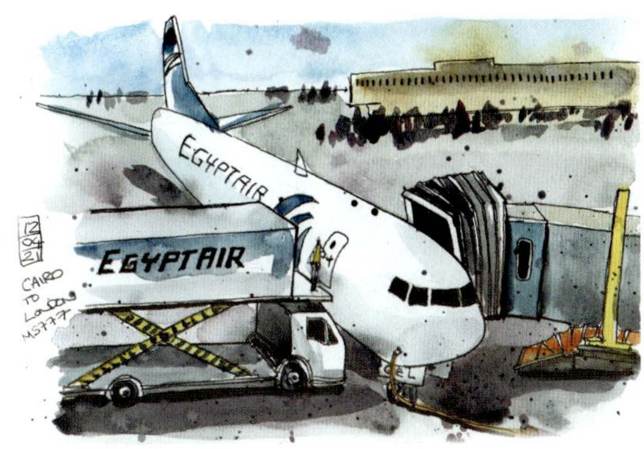

MUSEUMS & TOURIST ATTRACTIONS

This section ties together what we have covered so far: architecture, statues, transport and people.

Museums are amazing places to draw for a variety of reasons. First, some museums are housed in beautiful old buildings, and they have grandiose surroundings. They can be a great spot to practice sketching both architecture and foliage. Second, the interiors can be extremely interesting (yet often challenging) to draw. And third, the subject matter they display may not be objects you would otherwise get to draw (or even see) in everyday life. Dinosaur or whale skeletons that you would find inside a natural history museum, an ornate sarcophagus in the Egyptian Museum or even famous paintings in many of the world's art galleries are but a few examples.

Museums are peaceful places where you may find other people drawing too. Therefore, it's a great place to start sketching on location, as it is a natural activity to do and won't attract much attention. In some museums, you can even borrow a free stool so that you can sit and draw. Do note that while most museums are happy for people to draw, they will not allow any wet media so as not to risk any of their exhibits. However, when sketching the outside of the museum, you can use whatever you would like.

EXTERIORS

In this example, there was a statue of a sphinx outside the Egyptian Museum in Cairo. I wanted to draw both the sphinx and the building, so I tried to position myself accordingly.

TIP: *You can't always sit in the exact vantage point you would like when urban sketching. There may be nowhere to sit (although, if you are able, sitting on the ground is perfectly adequate, or you can use a camping stool), so you may be in the way of foot traffic or, even worse, vehicle traffic. For whatever reason, you may have to compromise your ideal view, but that is one of the challenges and therefore fun parts of urban sketching.*

I chose to sketch on toned paper as I thought it would add an extra element of antiquity to the sketch, which seemed appropriate to the subject matter.

TIP: *When you're ready, experiment sketching on top of different tones of paper. It unlocks another way of sketching and painting.*

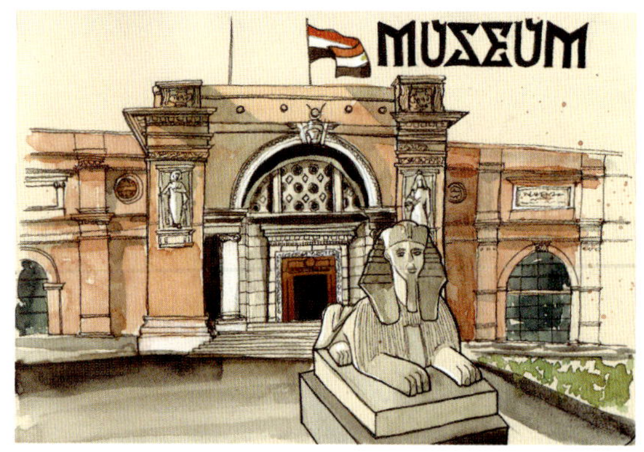

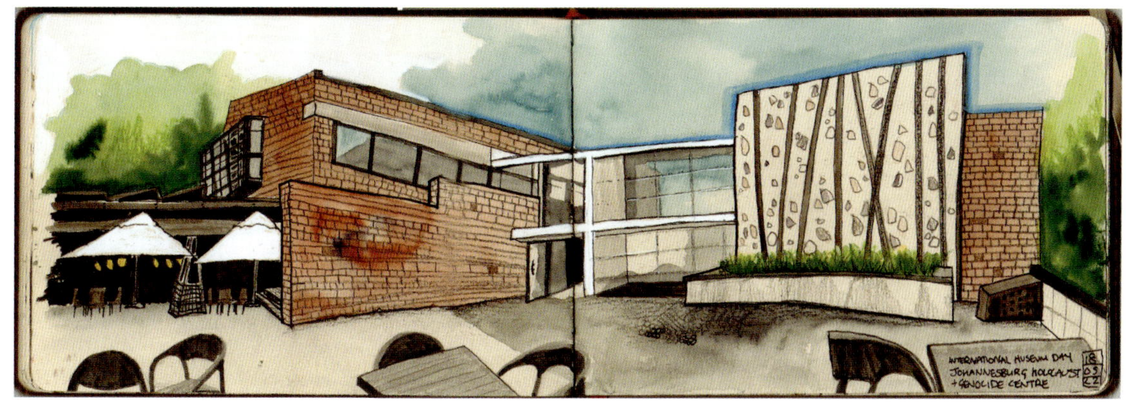

Admittedly, some museum settings are more stark than others (sometimes deliberately so) but still interesting to sketch. Finding the best way to approach tricky scenes is another quirk of urban sketching. When sketching from photos, the photographer (whether you or someone else) has already composed the scene, and it has definitive edges. When you are sketching on location, you have to visualize where the edges of your scene are and how you are going to put the 3D environment that surrounds you on a small 2D surface.

I enjoy sketching a wide scene across a double page of a landscape sketchbook. It's extremely satisfying. From the tour we were given of the Holocaust & Genocide Centre, I learned a lot about the symbolism of the architecture of the museum building. Having this information prior to drawing the building helped me understand what the architect's decisions were on how to design the museum. I was contemplating this as I drew, and it gave the entire experience a deeper level of meaning.

ITEMS ON DISPLAY

Sketching many exhibits across a double page of a sketchbook is an excellent way to collect potentially disparate items in one place and create an overall impression of the items you found while in the museum. We cover more about designing sketchbook spreads on page 175. This is an early example from my travels in Mexico. I captured a few of my favorite objects on display at the Museo Nacional de Antropología in Mexico City. I decided to draw in ink and use a black brush pen for the shadow areas. I really like this method because it's a great way to keep your sketching kit down to a minimum.

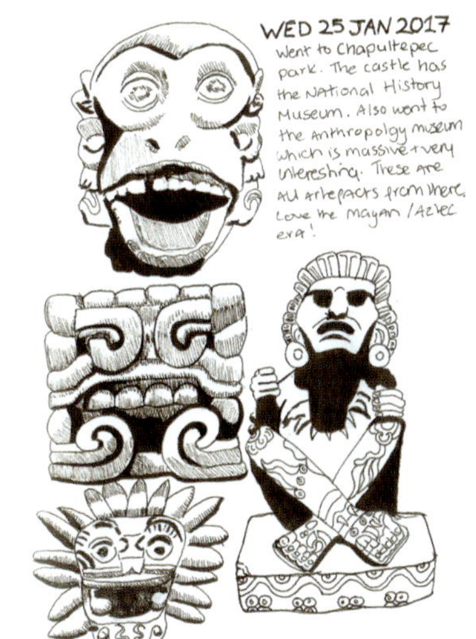

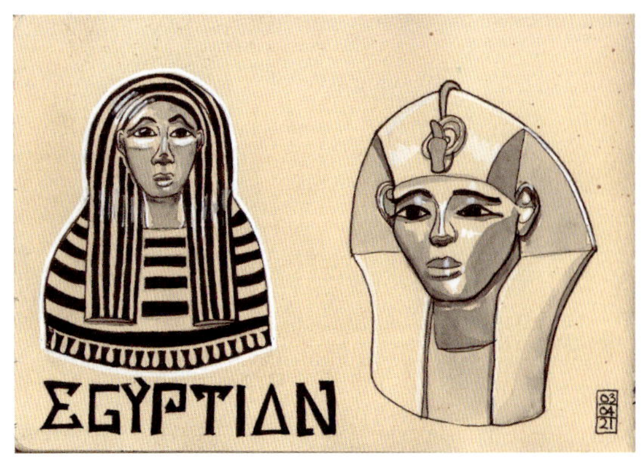

In this second example, I sketched a couple of statues in the Egyptian Museum in Cairo. I used toned paper and drew with black ink, adding exaggerated highlights with a white gel pen. In this case, I did add some pale gray shadows with my small set of watercolors and a water brush. But you can see how the toned paper does the heavy lifting in providing the mid-tones for my sketch. The drawings are a little cartoon-y, but I enjoyed that aspect of them.

TOURIST ATTRACTIONS

Some tourist attractions are living museums. I remember visiting the Mayan Pyramids in Guatemala, walking around by myself without another soul in sight, following my map in search of each set of pyramids, hearing the dinosaur-like growls of howler monkeys. I felt like I was in an *Indiana Jones* movie! I only managed a few small sketches at the time, as I was relatively new to travel sketching and had a time restriction. But it demonstrates you don't have to spend hours capturing the scene—quick small sketches are just as valid.

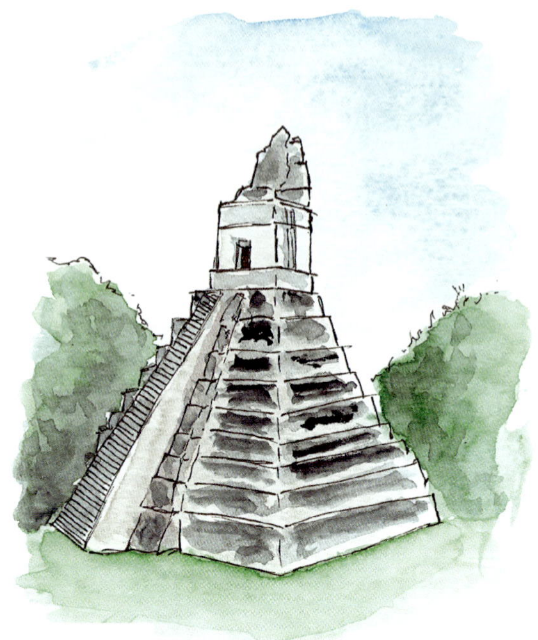

You don't always have to go for the stereotypical postcard-style shot of a tourist attraction. We have all seen that picture before. Think about what interests you about the scene.

In the example on the following page, I drew what interested me—the two ladies on their chairs sitting a distance apart. This was during Covid when social distancing was still enforced. After drawing the two ladies, I just decided to fill in the background around them. Is this a particularly well-composed sketch? Not really. Is it a stereotypical scene of the V&A Museum? Certainly not. Is it a pretty picture? Not really. Does it make you ask questions, wonder what it's all about and show a snapshot or slice of life? Yes, I think so.

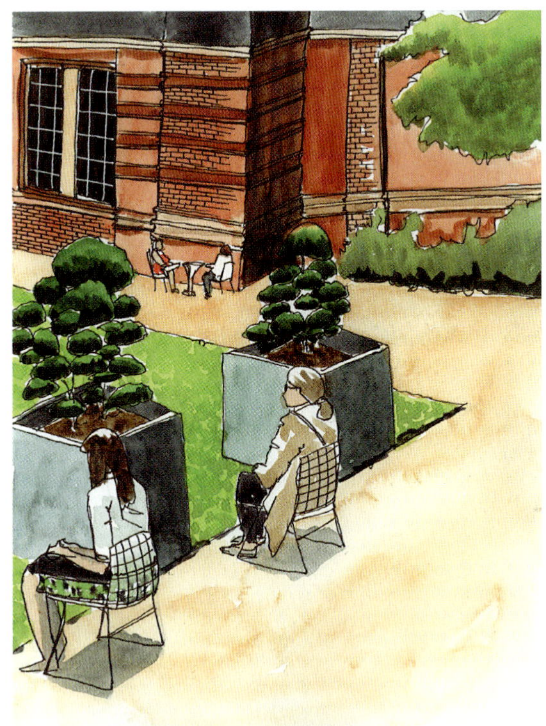

VICTORIA + ALBERT MUSEUM, LONDON

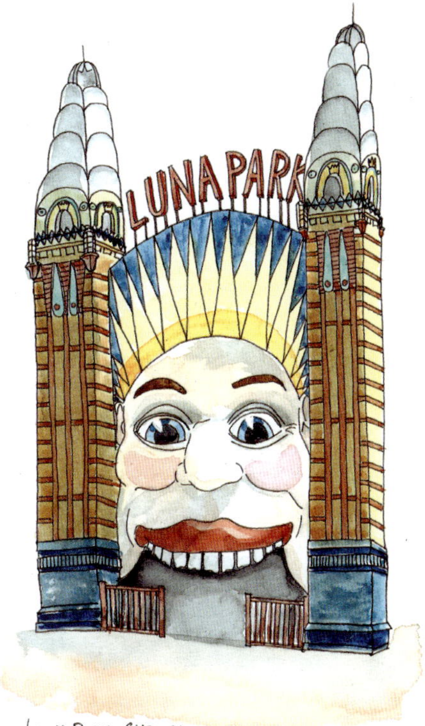

LUNA PARK, SYDNEY

Remember the essence of urban sketching and its roots in visual journalism. You don't always have to go for the "pretty picture" option (which I am certainly guilty of). Draw what grabs you in the moment. Tell a story. Break some rules. This may seem like an overwhelming instruction right at the start of your urban sketching journey, but I say it to take the pressure off and encourage you that whatever you choose to draw, it's important, because you chose it.

Conversely, you may want to capture the essence of the attraction you're sketching and leave it at that. I really enjoyed sketching the facade of Luna Park in Sydney. I liked the minimal nature of the sketch with the white space around it. I decided I did not want to sketch the entire scene. It may take a little while, but when you're in the moment, you will decide what is best for you. The sketch you decided on may also be determined by external factors, such as the amount of time you have, the weather and the people around you.

Saying that, this drawing is also a bit "stiff" and almost more of a careful illustration than an urban sketch. It doesn't really represent the busy, excited atmosphere of a theme park. Does it tell a story? Not really.

Consider this sketch of the Sydney Opera House on the right. Again, it's stiff and, well, a bit boring. The angle is cliché, the colors are flat and it doesn't tell much of a story.

But from another angle entirely, as depicted in the image below, it is so much more interesting even though it's still a basic sketch.

The building is so iconic that we still know it's the Opera House, but now there are some people milling about, the Harbour Bridge is visible in the distant background, and I left a huge white space on the right where another one of the buildings should be. It makes us feel like we are peering through the scene. I also used very bold colors, as I knew I wanted to keep the scene as simple as possible. This is a great example of how to take a potentially overwhelming location and simplify it into a clean, graphic sketch.

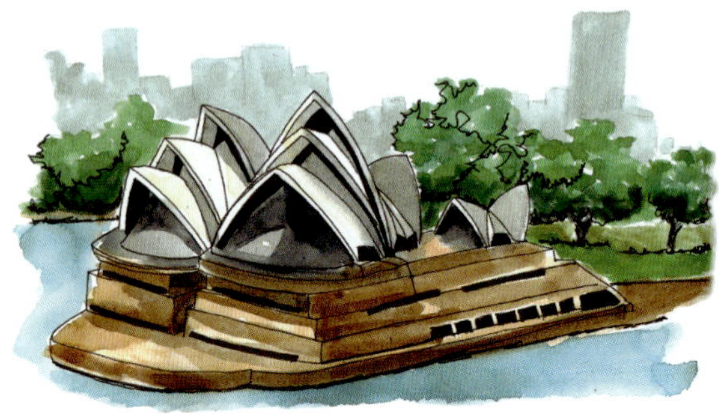

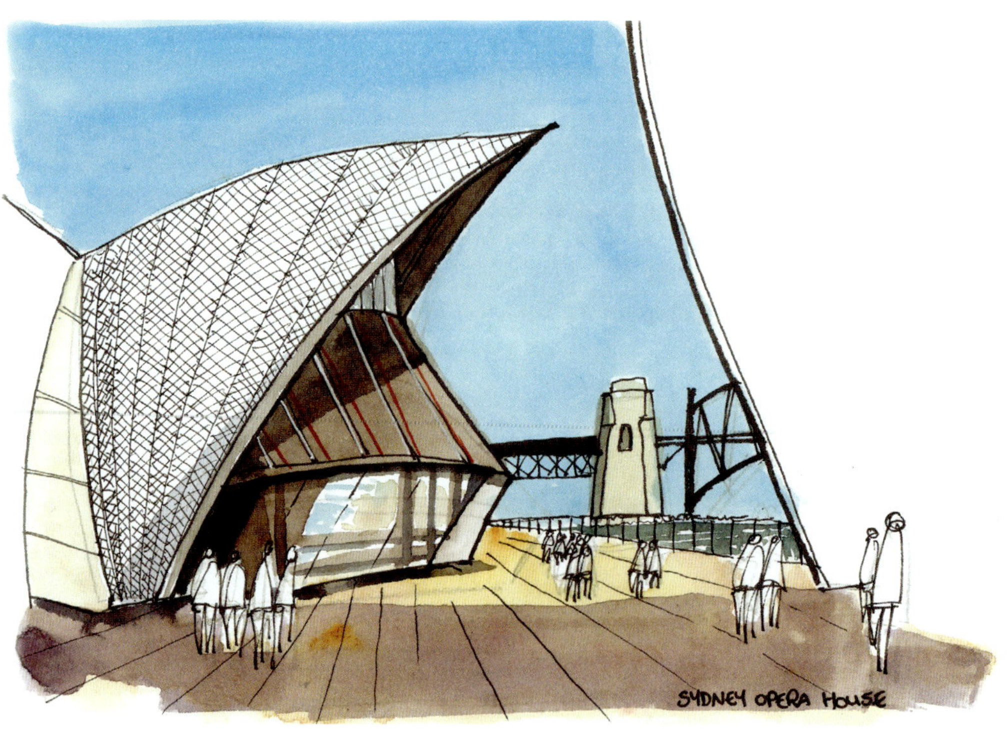

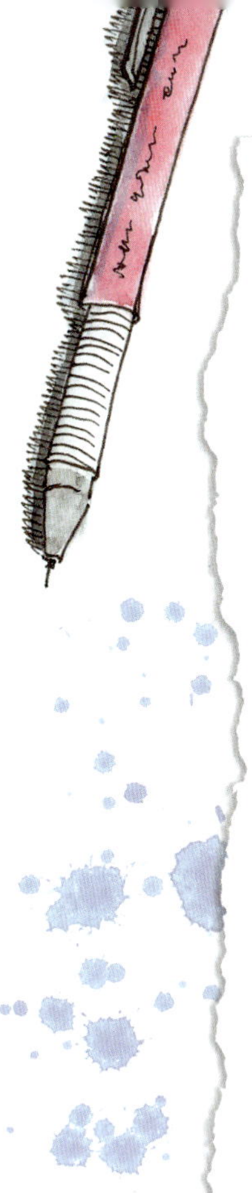

EXERCISE

1. Visit the museums close to your home.

Start with sketching singular objects on display. Draw them across the pages of your sketchbook (see page 175 for more on sketchbook spreads).

2. Think about some of the "attractions" in your local area.

You may not be from a typical tourist destination, but everywhere has some points of interest that locals and visitors alike go and see.

Think about the usual photographs you see of the landmarks in your local area. Visit some of them over time and think about how you would capture a different angle and how you may tell a different visual story to the mainstream versions. Drawing the same subject matter again and again is something a lot of urban sketchers do. In some cases, it may be to document the evolution of the subject (for example, a building being constructed, renovated or demolished). In other cases, it could be to try different angles, media and styles. Liz Steel, for example, has sketched the Sydney Opera House hundreds of times over the years. No two sketches are the same. There's always something new to try.

TRAVEL JOURNAL & SKETCHBOOK SPREADS

A natural extension of urban sketching is to sketch wherever you travel. It doesn't matter if your subject matter is not "urban," as we discussed on page 166. In fact, sketching while traveling allows you to draw a wider variety of things that you wouldn't otherwise find in your local area. Don't be afraid to sketch at the beach, while out on a hike or a drive or even in the local bar.

A great way to explore a new place in your sketchbook is by creating a sketchbook spread. This is a fantastic way to capture a few small vignettes of a place that build up to make an overall impression. It's also a great strategy if you are short on time. You may be traveling with friends or family, or in a tour group, and as such, you may not have total control over your schedule.

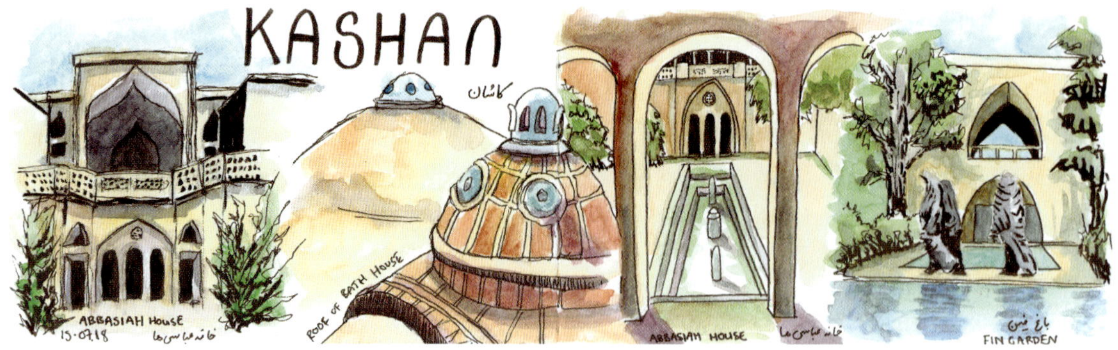

When I visited Iran and South Sudan, I was with a group of people each time. I wanted to see and experience everything with the group, but I also wanted some time to sketch. I found the best way to achieve both things was to make smaller sketches and montage them together to make an overall impression of the place I was visiting.

In the spread above, you may notice I drew four sketches next to each other across the sketchbook spread. This worked well as I had a wide landscape-oriented sketchbook. One sketch merges into the next. Some are of details and others are bigger scenes, but I kept each one simple, and I was happy with the overall effect. I asked the guide to write the names of places in Farsi on the page too. This made the experience interactive. The guide enjoyed adding to my sketches (and as such, my memories) in this way.

In the spread below, the divide between the sketches is less obvious, as much of the scenery and color palette is similar. Rather than drawing a sweeping vista, I decided to sketch individual statues or small scenes and merge them together. This was wise as it was approximately 116°F (47°C) with little to no shade. Trying to sketch something solidly for one to two hours in the sun would have been impossible.

HOW TO START A TRAVEL JOURNAL

A great way to start a travel journal is by drawing a map of the country or region you are visiting, as well as marking some of the places you are visiting (you can add to this as you go), as well as things like a flag or the route you are taking.

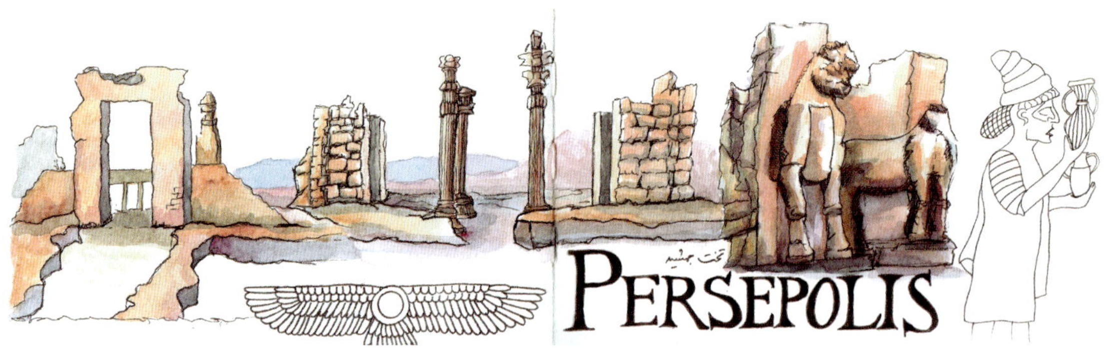

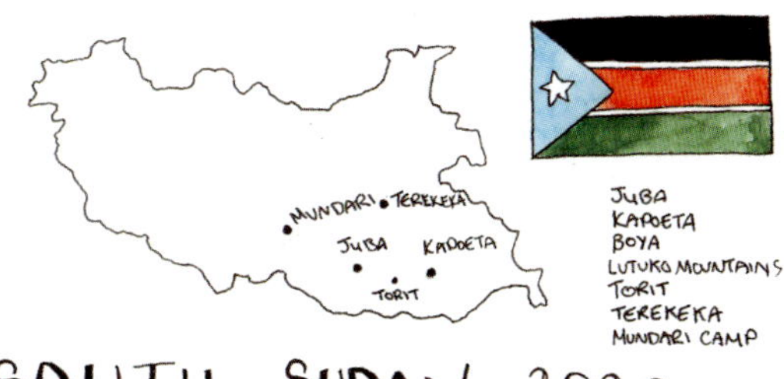

SOUTH SUDAN 2020

You can take this idea further and stick ephemera such as tickets, leaflets or stickers on your sketchbook page too, making them part of the spread. Urban sketcher Tom Pajdlhauser (a.k.a. Captain Tom) takes Instamatic photographs and includes them on his page as part of the overall sketch. I met an American architecture student in Mexico while traveling who was doing a similar thing. He sketched the beautiful architecture he came across and included photos of the people he was with to keep a travel journal of his sketches, as well as friendships he forged. Some urban sketchers, like Teoh Yi Chie, like to start off with sketches of the items they are taking on a trip and some, like Liz Steel, sketch their art materials, such as the palette of watercolors they are taking, pens, brushes and so on.

COMPOSING A SKETCHBOOK SPREAD LAYOUT

A sketchbook spread contains a series of sketches that can communicate a narrative. Experimenting with spreads can also help build your compositional and layout skills. Learning how to connect disparate sketches and place them in a visually pleasing way across a page is an important design skill that's worthy of practice in its own right.

There are some well-established design principles when it comes to layout. These elements are universal across the visual arts and as such can be useful things to think about when creating your sketchbook spread, especially if you are trying to make it dynamic.

When designing a sketchbook spread, it is always important to keep composition in mind. There are certain rules you can follow to help with this, such as the rule of thirds (page 18), scale, repetition, symmetry and color, that create visual harmony in your layout.

RULE OF THIRDS

When dividing your sketchbook spread or deciding where to place things, using a well-established compositional tool, such as the rule of thirds, will make your layout feel more harmonious. It also helps to prevent you from plonking things right in the center of the page. A central composition can work but more often than not, placing elements according to the rule of thirds is going to look far more interesting.

SCALE

Visual artists use the concept of scale to help create dynamic work. The size and proportions of one item next to another, especially if unexpected, can create visual tension. You can also play with zooming in to certain details versus a wide-angle or zoomed-out view. Scale can also help build a sense of hierarchy. Elements that are larger on the page have more emphasis and lead us to feel they are more important or significant.

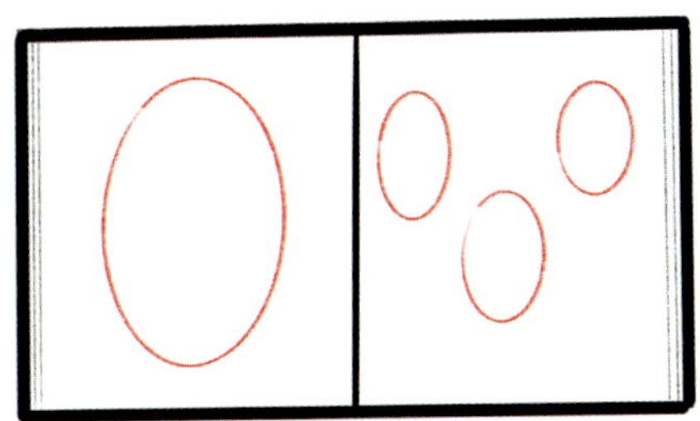

REPETITION & RHYTHM

Repetition can be used to connect elements throughout a layout and help to create an overall harmony. You could use the repetition of a certain color or technique or theme.

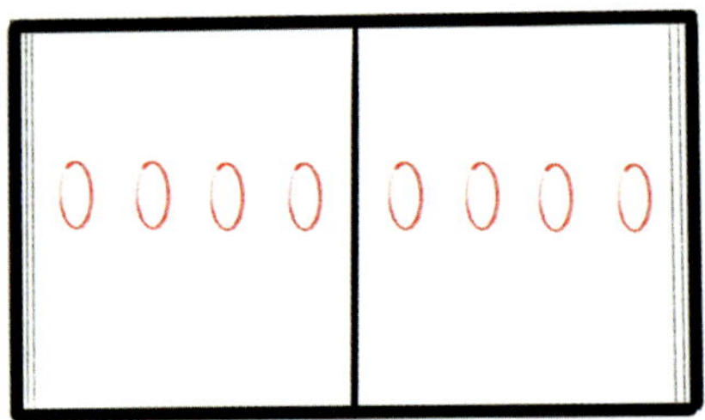

The concept of rhythm (in design) takes the idea of repetition a step further and refers to the repositioning of design elements to create a flow. Elements are not repeated in the same way as their first iteration or in the same sequence. You can repeat elements playing with scale, placement and color, just as examples. The idea is to create a flow throughout the spread.

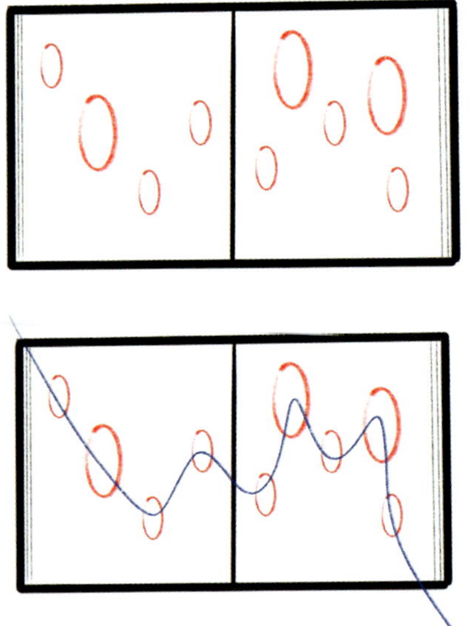

SYMMETRY & ASYMMETRY

Symmetry is everywhere when it comes to design, especially architecture. Symmetry helps to create a sense of balance.

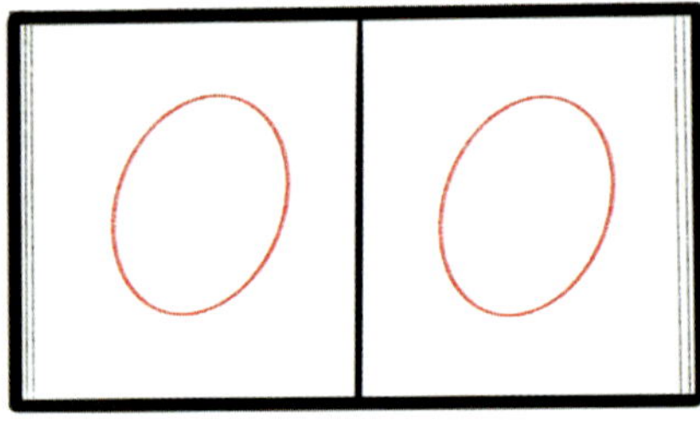

Asymmetry is the absence of symmetry. In design, asymmetry can be used to create tension and drama. Asymmetry is when elements on either side of an axis are unbalanced; for example, they differ in number or size. Even though the elements on either side differ, it is still possible to create a sense of balance. Using asymmetry effectively is a bit more complex to master but can lead to more creative freedom. Likewise, using symmetry can also appear boring and uninspired as it is an easy and expected way to lay out elements. It's a fine line to tread but something worth experimenting with.

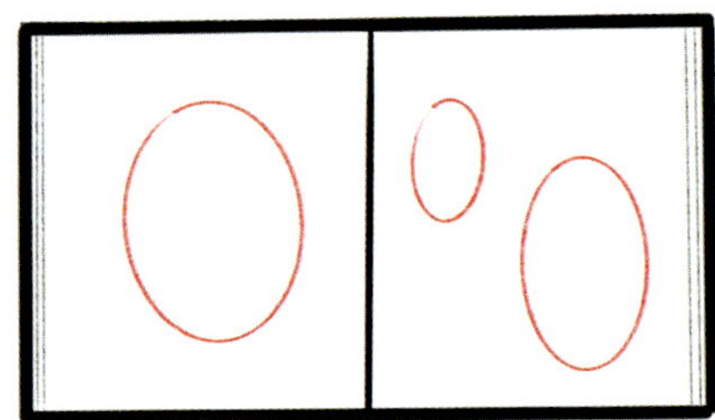

WHITE SPACE / NEGATIVE SPACE

Keep in mind that the space you don't fill is just as important as the space you do fill. You can create beautiful minimal spreads with lots of white space, giving your elements breathing room. You could deliberately do the reverse though. I love seeing super busy sketchbook spreads with things overlapping and a cacophony of color. I don't know where to look first but trying to figure things out keeps me drawn to the spread. It's more of an advanced concept, but if you would like to delve further into using white space as a compositional tool, download the free PDF workbook from:

learn.sketchyouradventures.com/workbook

COLOR

Color is such a powerful tool to tell a story with. An urban sketcher who springs to mind is Inma Serrano (page 187). She uses fluorescents, singularly or as accent colors, to tell stories with her sketches. Think about how you can use color in your sketchbook spread as a layout tool. Perhaps you could create monochromatic sketches and use one additional accent color throughout? Or you could use a limited palette of colors for each of the sketches? Or take a leaf out of Inma's (sketch)book—sorry, I had to—and use some fluorescent yellows or pinks to tie everything together.

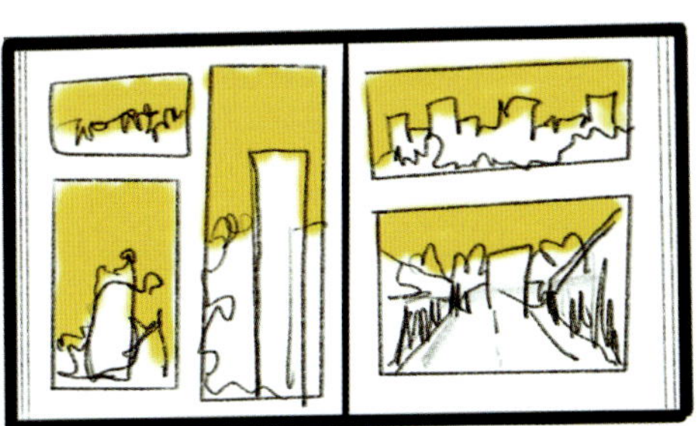

STORYTELLING

There are many ways to tell a story with your sketches; here are a few ideas that you can try for yourself.

CREATE A COLLECTION OF ITEMS

You may find pleasure in sketching certain things and over time you could build a collection of these items. It looks great to have this collection on one sketchbook spread. You can start the spread and come back to it over time as you come across new items to add to your collection. It doesn't always have to be the same item many times over; it could also be a collection of items that fit a certain theme. For example, urban sketcher Pete Scully collects sketches of fire hydrants as he comes across them. In this example, I collected a variety of sketches on one page of our cat over the course of a few days.

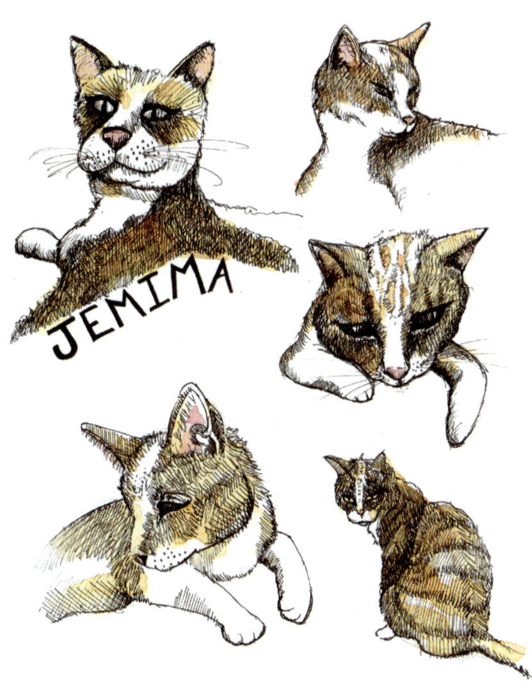

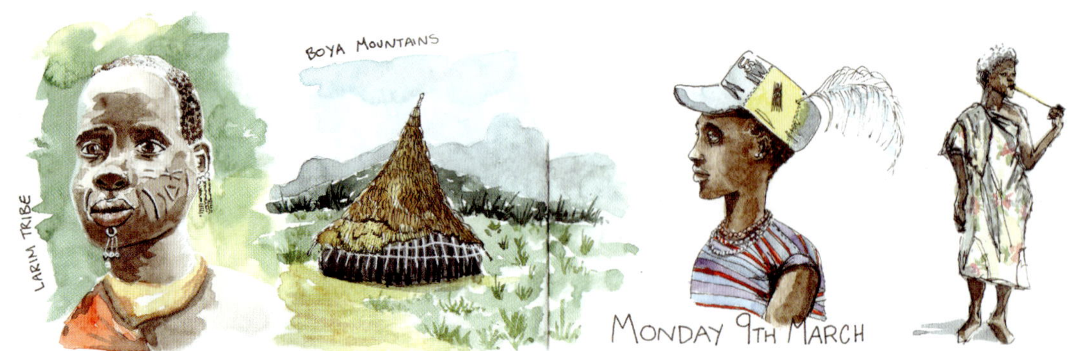

TRAVELOGUE / TRAVEL JOURNAL

This is very much the type of spread I am used to creating. Sometimes, I will make a collage of scenes or angles of one place, such as the spread above of a day in South Sudan, that runs across a double page of a landscape-format Moleskine watercolor album.

GRAPHIC NOVEL / COMIC BOOK

Split your sketchbook spread into boxes and fill each box with a different element of the scene you're sketching. I love this idea because it really helps to make a scene less overwhelming, capturing just the parts that interest you, such as the way a roof slants, a decorative streetlamp or some curious pigeons.

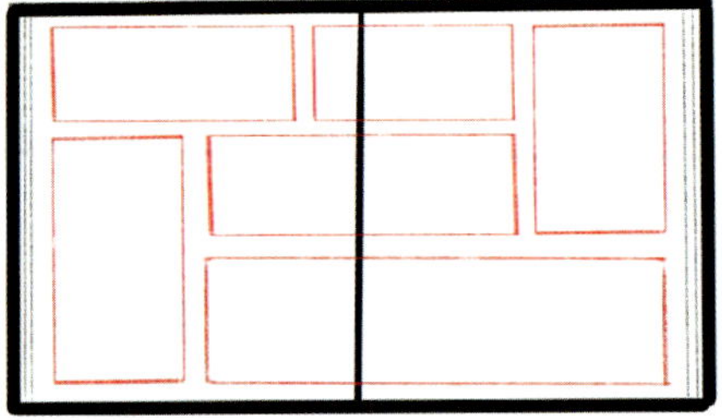

This is a basic version with just three wide boxes drawn very wobbly on the page (I was in a moving vehicle at the time)! I managed to capture some scenes as we drove to Cape Town.

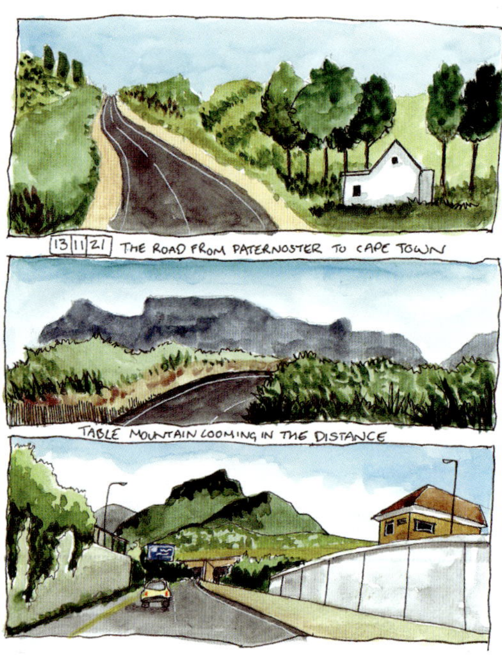

You could take this a step further than just using the layout device of a comic book and include snippets of conversations you hear or thoughts you're having while sketching or about your sketch. I love sketches that include annotations or notes within them.

DECONSTRUCTION

You could draw a deconstruction of an item, such as close-up sketches of certain angles, or sketch the various parts, like how something works or fits together, almost like a manual or scientific illustration.

TIMELINE

Another way to create a spread is by documenting a certain building, location or project over time. Perhaps you live in a city where the skyline is ever-changing, and things are constantly being built and torn down. You could keep a record of this evolution by keeping the spread available to go back and add to over a period of time. Or you could just sketch the course of a day or week, such as my example in the exercise section (page 180).

LETTERING

Some urban sketchers enjoy adding lettering to their sketchbook spreads, even incorporating them as part of the art itself. Some sketchers are a little messier and just use their own rough handwriting, even scribbling out when making a mistake! It's up to you if you want to include any written notes or titles and whether those are in your everyday handwriting or if they are designed beautifully.

Liz Steel uses rubber stamps to record the day of the week and date. She also draws lines with a blue pen and then handwrites some notes. Pat Southern-Pearce adds beautiful and highly distinctive lettering to her sketches—I immediately recognize her lettering. Lapin sometimes includes little speech bubbles within his sketches for things he overhears while sketching. This is such a great idea and adds even more fun to his drawings.

There are many books, YouTube videos and courses on hand lettering. It's a distinct rabbit hole one can wander down. I tend to just write locations, dates and any notes I want to include in my own natural handwriting. I am quite a fan of the hurried, messy notes that urban sketchers such as Santi Sallés and Inma Serrano add to their sketches. It feels a little more in keeping with the spirit of urban sketching. For a special travel journal though, I understand the desire to include some well-presented hand lettering. You can find lots of inspiration online. I have included a list of some of my favorite resources and examples of hand lettering for sketchbook spreads in the free PDF workbook that you download from:

learn.sketchyouradventures.com/workbook

For any sketch, I recommend making a note of the date and location at a minimum.

EXERCISE

Think about how you would design a sketchbook spread. Do you like the idea of sketches flowing seamlessly from one to another? Or would you prefer a comic book–style layout with boxes of different sizes to fill? Experiment with both compositions.

You don't need to take a trip to make a travel journal. How about designing something for your local area? You could make a small map of a few points of interest and go for a walk (or drive) and sketch a collection of things and collage them across the page. You don't need to do this in a single day; you could spread it out over several weeks if you like.

I did the spread below as part of the seven-day Urban Sketching at Home challenge that I run (if you'd like to join, visit urbansketchingworld.com to sign up for free). The final day of the challenge was to put together everything we had covered previously in one sketchbook spread and to sketch your day. We were in the Covid-19 lockdown at the time, so my sketches consisted of various things around the house: the cat, my mother-in-law and so on. You don't need to be going on a three-month adventure across the continent to use the concepts discussed in this chapter. In fact, the more you experiment with these ideas now, the more ready you'll be for when that big, exciting trip does come along.

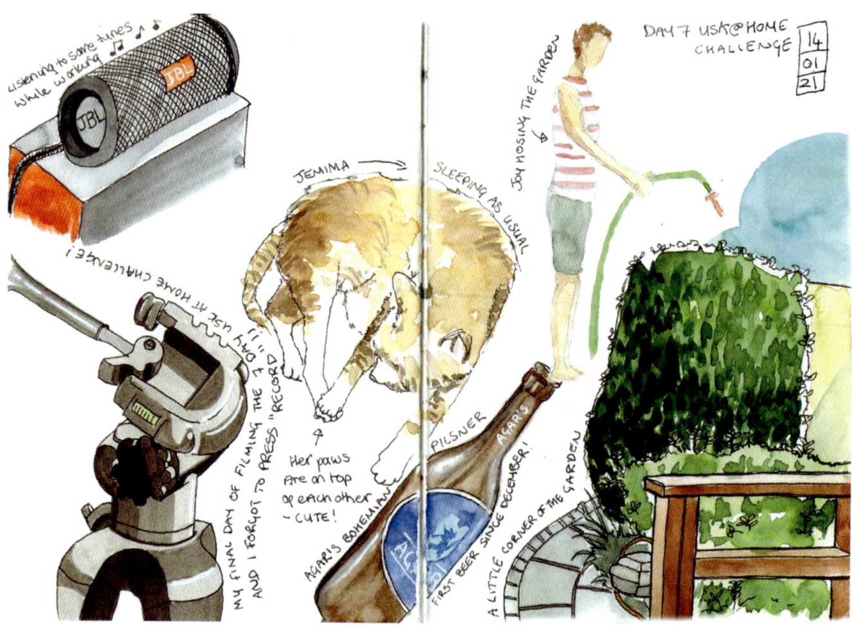

WHAT NEXT?

KEEP A REGULAR SKETCHBOOK HABIT

I hope you are super excited and enthused about urban sketching. Don't put too much pressure on yourself. I know what it's like to promise yourself that you're going to sketch everywhere, every day. I can assure you this won't happen (at least at first) and that's okay. The worst thing you could do at this beginning stage of urban sketching is put yourself off. Just try your best to sketch on location when you can. Sometimes obvious opportunities will present themselves and sometimes you may go weeks without sketching. Remember, urban sketching at home is just as valid. In fact, it became quite a movement during the height of the Covid-19 lockdown when we weren't allowed out of our homes. If you want some inspiration on how to go about urban sketching at home, you can always head over to my website and join my seven-day challenge. I send you prompts each day, along with a video of me doing my sketch at home too.

https://learn.sketchyouradventures.com/7-day-usk-at-home-challenge

For some, getting out a sketchbook and drawing in public is quite nerve-wracking. It will take time and practice to start getting comfortable to do this. Please do not feel bad if you are too shy at this stage. There are ways and means to combat this issue, such as only sketching with a pen or pencil (no paint) and using a sketchbook that looks notebook-sized. People will assume you are just writing in your notebook.

Another tip is to situate yourself with a wall behind you; this way people cannot walk behind you and see what you're doing. Some sketchers wear headphones or sunglasses to dissuade people from talking to them or approaching them while sketching.

Another great way to overcome the fear of sketching in public is to join with other people who sketch. This greatly increased my own confidence and leads me seamlessly to my next point.

JOIN AN URBAN SKETCHING GROUP

As a grade-A introvert, I resisted this advice for a long time. However, since moving to Johannesburg, I now have an urban sketching chapter that's more accessible to me (in terms of location). I've lived in various parts of the world in the past and never seemed to be close enough to a chapter to make it possible to join. Of course, you don't need to join an official Urban Sketchers chapter to go out sketching with people, but it does help as the people in the group are aware of urban sketching and the general ethos behind it.

I have found urban sketching groups to be very inclusive and welcoming. As a shy introverted person, it took a few meetings to start to get to know people. Everyone is kind, nonjudgemental and keen to chat about all things to do with sketching . . . especially art supplies!

I am now proud to state I am one of the "admins" of the USk Johannesburg group, and I absolutely love meeting the group at a different location each month to sketch. We don't even necessarily sit side by side, but just knowing there are other people in the same location doing what you're doing gives a sense of community.

GO ON A SKETCHCRAWL

The next stage in one's urban sketching career should certainly involve joining a sketchcrawl. It's like a pubcrawl but with more sketching and less alcohol . . . well, generally.

If you join an urban sketchers chapter, I am sure you will find your way to one of these. The idea is that you move from location to location as a group throughout the day (or during a few hours) sketching as you go. Generally, there is a "throwdown" (where people display their sketchbooks as a collection on a table or on the ground for everyone to look at). Sometimes, we have other artists join in too, such as photographers. All are welcome. Again, you do not need to be in an official group to do this. You can gather your local art group or a couple of friends or whoever you sketch with and organize one for yourself.

EXPERIMENT WITH DIFFERENT MEDIA

A natural offshoot to your progression as both an urban sketcher and an artist (yes, that *is* what you are) is trying different media. Generally speaking, most urban sketchers lean toward ink and watercolor due to the portability and ease of use on location. But there are some who use gouache (opaque watercolor), markers or even crayons. You can also mix different media together. I love to use Faber-Castell Pitt Artist pens over the top of watercolor for shadows and contrast. I also use watercolor pencils on top of watercolor, as well as acrylic paint markers. Once you've got the basics, don't be afraid to experiment and use different supplies to make your marks on the page.

I also encourage you to experiment with toned paper. Toned watercolor sketchbooks are widely available from brands such as Stillman & Birn, Hahnemühle and Strathmore® to name but a few. Just remember, not all toned paper accepts watercolor, so take care to check the weight of the paper (200 gsm or higher is advisable) and the product information.

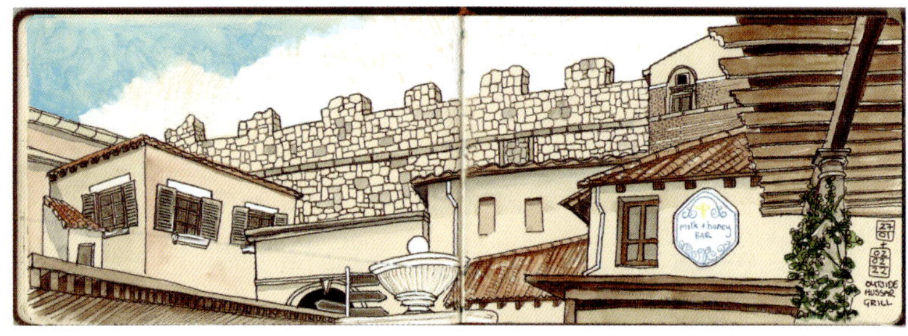

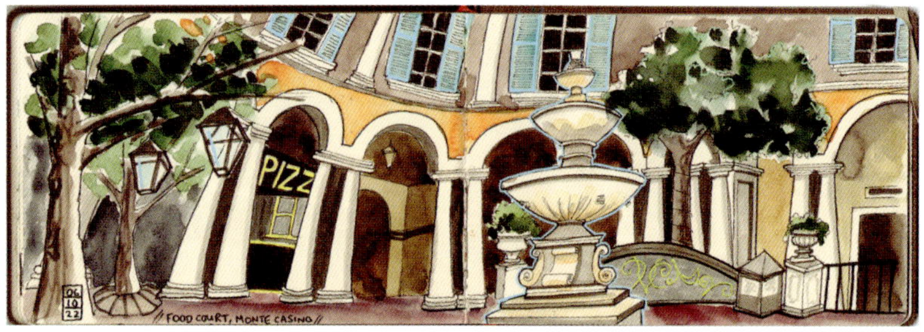

EXPLORE OTHER STYLES OF URBAN SKETCHING

One of the most fascinating things about urban sketching is that every sketcher has their own style. No one style is regarded as better or worse—just different. Some urban sketchers favor a more realistic approach, some favor a more illustrative or cartoon-y approach and some really bend the boundaries of color and perspective.

I have done my best to classify some popular styles below so you can understand what I am discussing, but these are by no means official labels, or what the artists themselves would even label their work. This is my opinion and interpretation. By looking at different styles, you will be able to assess which style you see.

REALISTIC / TRADITIONAL

Shari Blaukopf is an urban sketcher from Montreal, Canada. She cofounded the Urban Sketchers Montreal chapter and has a love for painting en plein air (painting outdoors). Shari has more of a traditional approach to watercolor, as well as "line and wash" (using pen and watercolor together in the same piece). She both sketches and creates larger paintings of her urban surroundings, even in the depths of the Canadian winter!

What I love most about Shari's style is the way she captures both light and color in her work: reflections in puddles and the colors she finds in snow and the beauty she creates from the seemingly mundane.

I highly recommend both of Shari's courses on the platform Craftsy as well as her online workshops found on her website:

learn.shariblaukopf.com

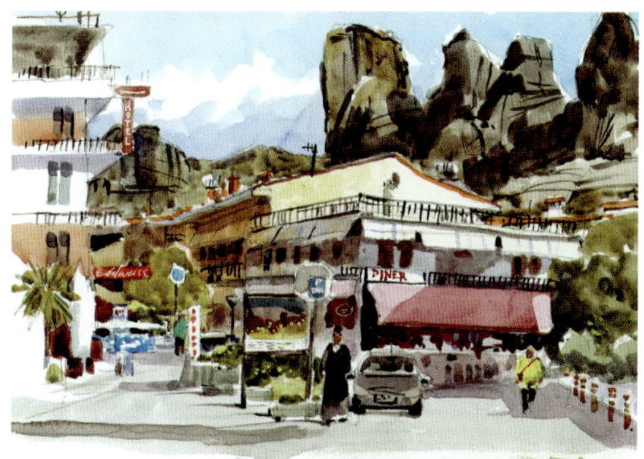

Shari Blaukopf

MINIMALIST

Simone Ridyard is an artist and architect based in Manchester, UK. She is also a senior lecturer at Manchester School of Art. Although Simone's work may look loose or sketchy on the surface, you can sense the architectural structure in her ink lines behind it. She seems to blend organic and structural in the same sketch and all while embodying a minimalistic vibe with her use of white space, accented with tiny splashes of accent colors. It is an incredibly unique style, and I think it perfectly represents both sides of her: the artist and the architect.

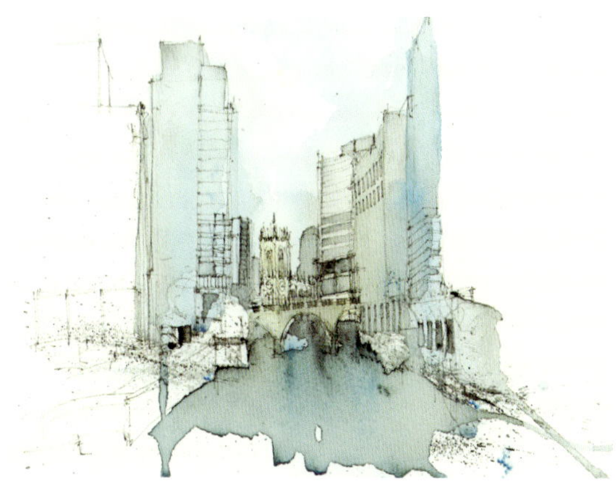

Simone Ridyard

BOLD

James Hobbs is an urban sketcher based in London. In fact, he is one of the founders of the Urban Sketchers London chapter. His style is extremely distinctive due to his almost exclusive use of thick black markers to record the world around him. His style is bold and immediate. Every time I look at his work it makes me want to grab a marker and head out into the world. James proves that you don't need anything more than a pen and a sketchbook—just a love for sketching on location. James is also the author of the book *Sketch Your World*, which I highly recommend checking out.

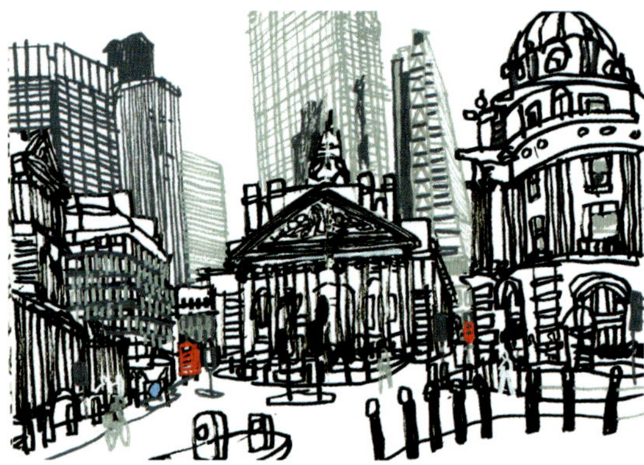

James Hobbs

ILLUSTRATIVE

Danny Hawk is an American living in Germany. I adore his crisp, illustrative style. He uses composition very cleverly, framing his sketches in such a beautiful way. He uses negative space to outline elements such as people or vehicles. In this way, he is adding those notes to his sketches while not actually drawing them.

Danny's style is so clean and well presented. A distinctive element of his style is the way he paints the sky as a deliberate, hard-edged shape. To fill in excessive white space, he uses dots of watercolor to give some visual interest before moving on to add some lettering to indicate where the scene is.

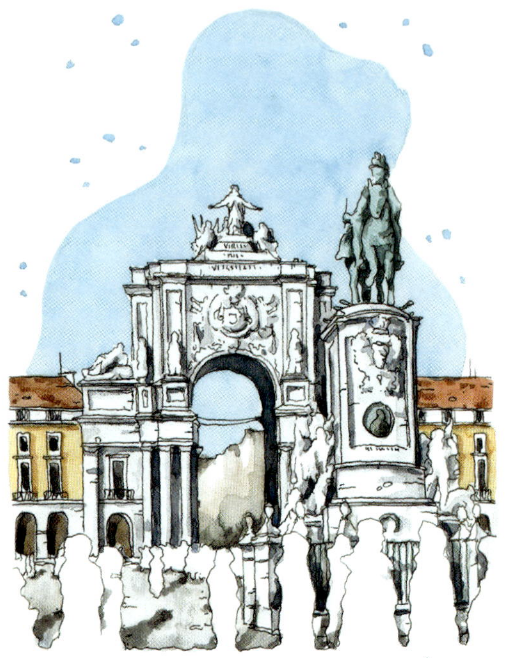

Danny Hawk

GRAPHIC

Lis Watkins is also a member of Urban Sketchers London. She is a master of working in shapes rather than line. Her shapes are strong and graphic. I think the most striking element of her style is the way she uses white space. The white of the paper is perfectly utilized, adding a sense of drama to the overall sketch. Lis adds smaller details with line to include some context but loosely and without too much detail. Sometimes Lis paints first and then draws on top, which is a particular sketching process I am a big fan of.

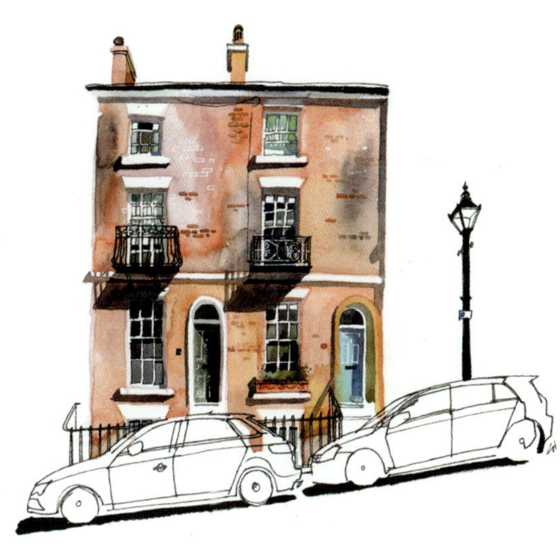

Lis Watkins

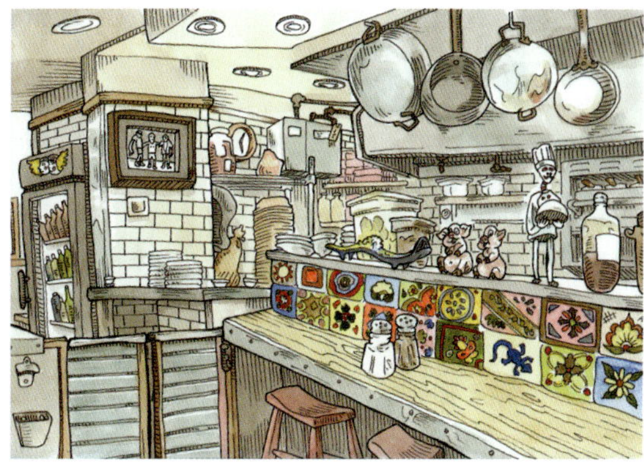

Steven B. Reddy

CARTOON / CARICATURE

Steven B. Reddy is an urban sketcher and teacher based in Seattle, USA. His style is very cartoon-like. In fact, I think I heard it described as "chubby" in an interview with him. I think that's a good descriptor. However, it still has a sense of realism to it. His drawings are not distorted; they very much depict real-life scenes, just in a rounder, lovelier way. Steven has an interesting process when it comes to creating his sketches. Once he has drawn everything in line, he shades his scene using various strengths of black India ink. Sometimes he leaves his sketch in grayscale and sometimes he will add color with watercolor over the top. I believe the process is based on the technique of grisaille, a painting technique used as far back as the fourteenth century. It basically refers to a painting done in shades of gray. Steven has made this process his own, and combined with his chubby drawing style and overlays of watercolor, it makes for an incredibly engaging modern style of sketching.

Lapin (page 186) is an urban sketcher I discovered almost immediately when I became interested in the activity. He is from France but based in Barcelona, Spain. I absolutely adore his style. His uniform of floral shirts and hats is as distinctive as his sketching style! Lapin uses old accounting books from the 1970s as sketchbooks. Apparently, the paper is very high quality. You can see the vertical red and blue lines run through his drawings, becoming yet another of his trademarks.

One of my favorite subjects Lapin draws is cars. He utilizes an interesting perspective and then exaggerates it, making the object so much more dynamic. Lapin also uses perspective in interesting ways to capture architecture, sometimes distorting the tops of buildings to make them fit on his sketchbook page. Another element of his distinctive style is his use of outlining certain parts of his sketch with a white gel pen.

QUICK & LOOSE

Liz Steel (page 186) is an extremely well-known urban sketcher from Sydney, Australia. She was an architect (are you sensing a theme here?) but now she is a full-time sketcher and teacher.

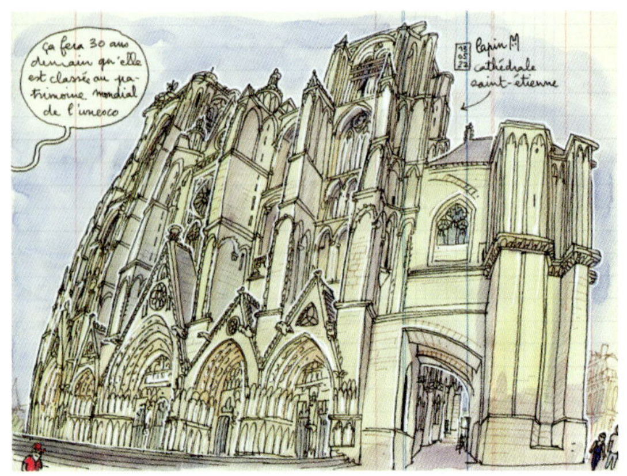

Lapin

She is particularly well-known for her daily teacup sketches on Instagram. She is a prolific sketcher and is always experimenting with different mediums and writing about them on her blog (lizsteel.com). Liz is a speedy sketcher and, despite her background as an architect, has a loose, seemingly effortless style. Liz tends to focus on architecture but is a cofounder of the 30-day challenge hosted each year called "Oneweek100people." By her own admission, she does not sketch people that often, so it's a way to force her to do so, at least for 30 days!

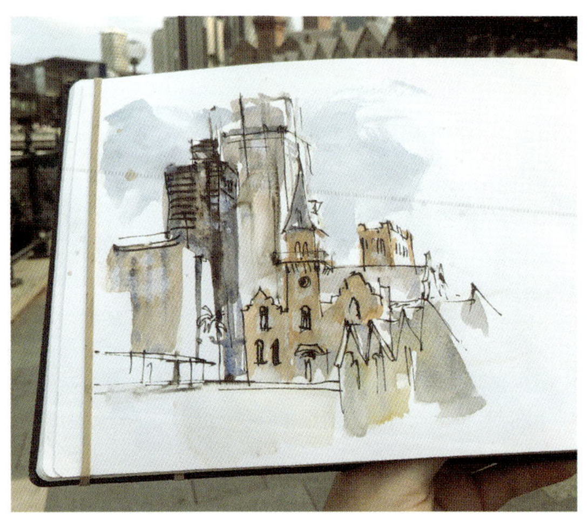

Liz Steel

EXPRESSIONISTIC & PLAYFUL

Ian Fennelly is a charismatic artist and urban sketcher from Liverpool, UK. He is well-known for his incredible translations of the world around him using ink, watercolor and markers. The specific elements of his style that make his work so recognizable are his playful exaggeration of perspective along with his dramatic use of color. Ian somehow manages to put his personality on the page: playful and fun. An interesting thing to note is that he does not include people or vehicles (unless they are the sole focus) in his sketches.

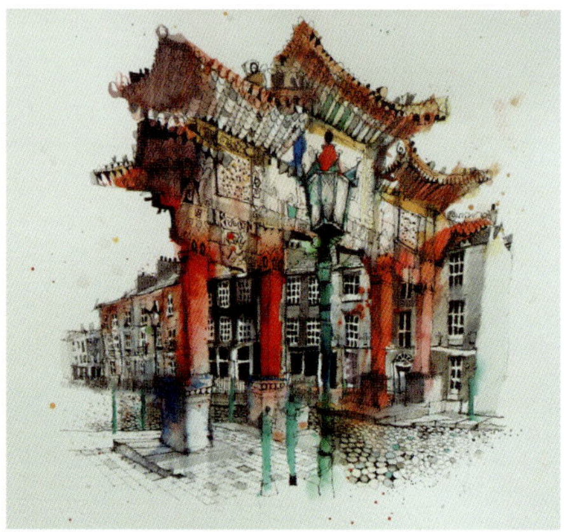

Ian Fennelly

Whenever I look at Inma Serrano's work, and more specifically her sketchbooks, all I can think of is the word *freedom*. Her drawings echo the free expressive lines of a child, as she uses vivid yellows and pinks to highlight certain areas. Her use of bold, raw colors—along with her quick lines and disregard for any sort of realism—just blows my mind because you still get such a sense of the scene, where she was and what she was experiencing. Inma really inspires me to just sketch whenever and whatever and not to agonize over the marks I make or whether I'm capturing the details correctly and to use whichever colors I *feel* like the scene needs.

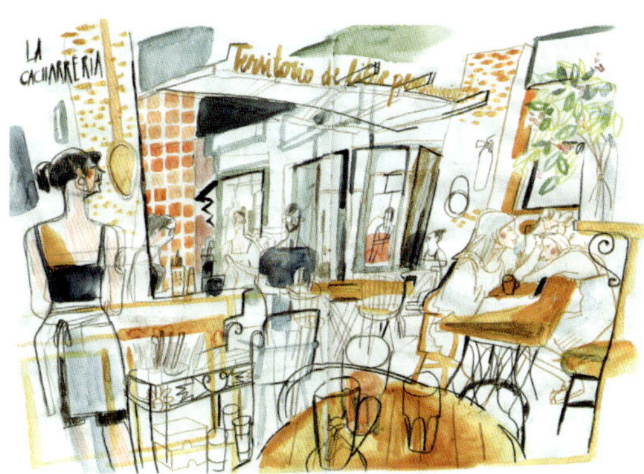

Inma Serrano

Felix Scheinberger is an illustrator and professor based in Berlin, Germany. I am completely enamoured by his urban sketching style. It's a style I love so much, yet I cannot even fathom how he does what he does. It's so loose, colorful and messy but depicts the subject matter so well. He also manages to inject such a strong sense of character into whatever he sketches whether it's people, a tree or a car. There is an intense feeling of freedom and confidence in his work. Felix is a great example of an artist with a distinctive style who is not beholden to one type of media; he uses all sorts of things. The elements that make his style distinctive have nothing to do with the way he uses a particular medium. I find this very interesting.

If you're anything like me, you don't like doing the same thing over and over again. I love seeking out fresh styles and new ways of doing things, which lead to unexpected results. In fact, if you feel the same way, I am sure you will enjoy some of the content of my YouTube channel where I share some of my experiments. Search for "Taria's Sketchy Adventures" and you will find me!

Many urban sketchers have online courses and in-person workshops. I encourage you to find an urban sketching style you like and take a

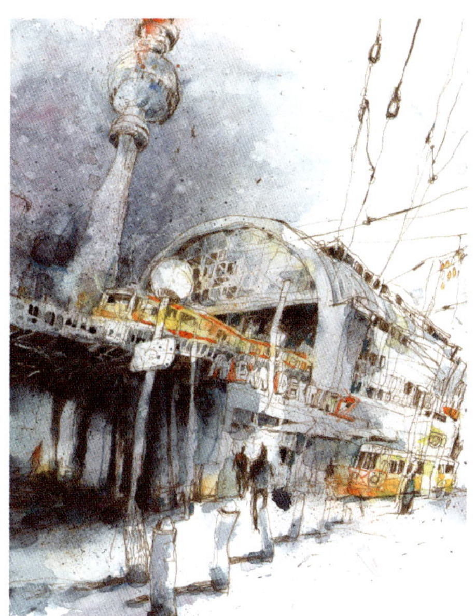

Felix Scheinberger

class with that sketcher. It may open your mind to different ways of doing things. Some of my favorite urban sketchers have courses on the platform Domestika (domestika.org) and many have their very own courses, such as Liz Steel (sketchingnow.com) and Ian Fennelly (urban sketchcourse.com/taria). Download the free workbook that accompanies this book for the link to all my favorite courses:

learn.sketchyouradventures.com/workbook

I also encourage you to create Pinterest boards and/or albums on Instagram of different styles you like that you can refer back to. My favorite styles of sketching seem to rotate on a monthly basis!

You can come and join me for experimental sketching demonstrations on my website:

learn.sketchyouradventures.com

I am so honored to help you get started along your sketchy adventure. I can't wait to see what you do.

ACKNOWLEDGMENTS

First, thank you Mum and Dad. I think you always knew I was an odd duck, but you trusted my decisions and let me forge my own path. Thanks to my twin brother, Tim, my sister, Lynsey, and my brother-in-law, Andy, for your ongoing support. Tim, I look forward to Jason seeing this book, and I hope it inspires him to follow his own path too.

Thanks to my "other" family for all your enthusiasm and support as well; there are too many of you to name individually but the Bells, Schnippenkoetters, Griffins and Bergmans, I am so lucky to have you. Also, thanks to my other, other family: Sarah, Kay, Ally, Kate, Jim, Pauric, Steph, Mel and Leah. You guys are the best.

I would really like to thank all the members of Urban Sketchers Johannesburg. You made me feel so welcome when I made "Joburg" my home, and it's been amazing to be part of such a friendly and inspiring group of artists. Special thanks to "The Monties"; our weekly sketch meetings made me realize quite how wonderful it is to meet and sketch with other people. You have all been so encouraging and enthusiastic about this book project.

I would like to thank all my students, my Patrons, everyone who watches my YouTube channel and all of you who receive my newsletter. I love receiving emails from you asking questions and sharing your sketches with me. It makes me smile knowing I can have a little impact along your sketchy adventure.

A massive thank you to Page Street Publishing and in particular, Alexandra Murphy and Sarah Monroe. Thanks for taking a chance on me and thank you for your happy, positive vibes throughout.

Finally, the biggest thanks has to go to my husband Duncan. He is the most disgustingly positive person I know, and he never lets me wallow. He picks me up, dusts me off, gives me a motivational chat and gets me back to work. He also makes me coffee every day and supports every single thing I do. That's true love, right? Oh, and thanks to the cats, Jem and Tex, for being cute.

ABOUT THE AUTHOR

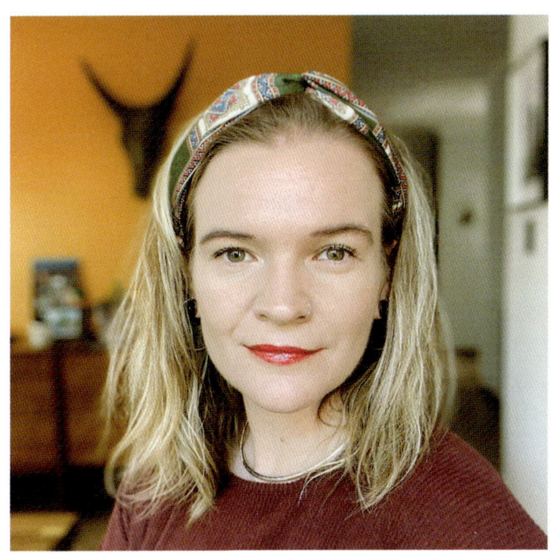

Taria Dawson lives in Johannesburg with her husband Duncan and their two cats. Originally from the UK, Taria traveled for several years before making South Africa her home. In her spare time, she enjoys overlanding in her 4x4 and exploring the African bush.

She started the popular blog urbansketchingworld.com in March 2020 and a few months later, her YouTube channel Taria's Sketchy Adventures. She has helped hundreds of students start sketching the world around them. Taria is one of the administrators for the Urban Sketchers Johannesburg chapter, helping to organize monthly meetups. One of her sketches was published in the Urban Sketchers London chapter's tenth anniversary book, *London*. She also conducted a workshop at Africa's first official urban sketching event.

Taria runs online courses and workshops at learn.sketchyouradventures.com.

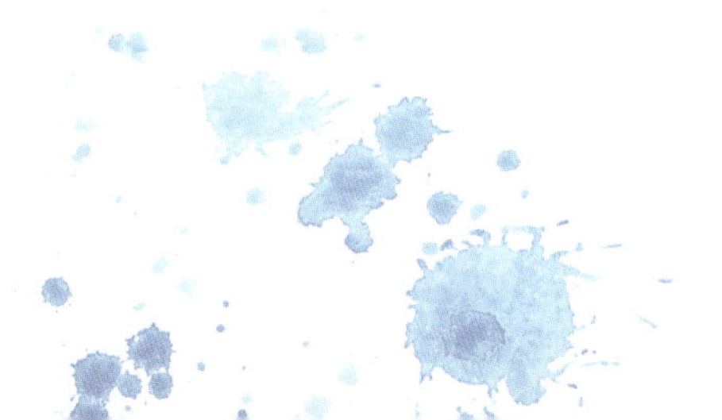

INDEX

F

G

H

I

L

M

N

O

P

Q

R